Inquiry Into the Origin and (

by Martin Van Buren

INTRODUCTION.

The following pages originally formed part of a much larger work, from the general course and design of which they constituted a digression. It seems therefore proper to preface them by a few words of explanation, relating chiefly to the work from which they are now separated.

Mr. Van Buren, eighth President of the United States, on the expiration of his term of office, in the year 1841, retired to a country residence near Kinderhook, (the place of his birth,) in the State of New York, which he had then recently purchased, and to which he gave the name of Lindenwald. Here, with infrequent and brief interruptions, he continued to reside for some twenty years, or until his death, which occurred in July, 1862. Although numbering nearly sixty years of age,--two-thirds of which had been years of almost incessant activity and excitement, professional, political, and social,--at the period of his withdrawal to the tranquil scenes and occupations of rural life, he embraced the latter with an ardor and a relish that surprised not a little the friends who had known him only as prominent in, and apparently engrossed by, the public service, but which were happy results of early predilections, an even and cheerful temper, fitting him for and constantly inclining him to the enjoyment of domestic intercourse, a hearty love of Nature, and a sound constitution of mind and body. After twelve years of the period of his retirement had passed, happily and contentedly, he began to apply a portion of his "large leisure" to a written review of his previous life, and to recording his recollections of his contemporaries and of his times. To this work, as he intimates in its opening paragraphs, he was mainly induced by the solicitations of life-long friends, who, (it may be here added,) knowing the importance and interest of the scenes and incidents of his extended public career, and the extraordinary influence he had exerted upon public men and questions of his time, and perceiving the tenaciousness of his memory and the charm of his conversation unimpaired by the lapse of seventy years, confidently anticipated a work of much interest in such a record as they urged upon him to make.

But although Mr. Van Buren so far complied with these suggestions as to set about writing his memoirs, he was not inclined to pursue the employment as a task, or to devote more of his time to it than could be easily spared from other occupations in which he was interested, and in order to keep himself from every temptation to exceed this limitation, he resolved, at the start, that no part of what he might write should be published in his lifetime. The work which he had commenced, was thus exposed to frequent interruption, even by unimportant accidents, and at length was altogether arrested by the serious illness of a member of his family, and by the failure of his own health, which rapidly supervened. It resulted that the recorded memoirs of his life and times closed abruptly when he had brought them down to the date of 1833-34, and that he never revised for publication what he had written. There is evidence that he contemplated such a revision when he should reach a convenient stage of his progress, but from the circumstances under which he wrote (which have been alluded to) as well as from his comparatively small interest in the mere graces of composition, the labor limae was continually postponed, and the "flighty purpose" was never o'ertaken. When, after his death, the subject of the disposition of these memoirs was presented to his sons, to whom his papers had been intrusted, they were embarrassed by questions as to the manner and form in which it was their duty to give them the publicity intended by their author. Should they, notwithstanding unaffected distrust of their qualifications, and a deep sense of special unfitness arising from natural partiality, undertake to continue the history of their father's life from the point at which his own account had ceased, to supply, as far as they could, the gaps in the previous narrative which had been left by him for further examination or after-construction, and to give to the work the extensive revision which, in the state in which it came to their hands, it seemed to require? Or should they publish the unfinished and unrevised memoirs, as they were left, as a fragment and a contribution, so far as they might go, to the history of the country? Would one or the other of these be such a history of the life of a statesman who had filled a large space in the observation of his countrymen, and who had exerted a controlling influence in the Government during interesting and critical periods, as would answer a natural and just public expectation, or satisfy the many warm friends who survived him? While occupied with the consideration of these questions, they received a note from Charles H. Hunt, Esq., informing them that he felt strongly inclined to write a Biography of Mr. Van Buren, and requesting the use for that purpose of any materials within their power to furnish. An additional paragraph of Mr. Hunt's note, referring to the rumor of writings left by Mr. Van Buren, showed that he had been entirely misinformed as to the nature and extent of those writings; he, in effect, supposing them to consist solely of disquisitions on various political questions.

The communication of Mr. Hunt not only superseded the necessity of deciding between the alternative propositions mentioned, but afforded them in all respects great satisfaction. His ripe and graceful scholarship, sound judgment, and pure taste were widely known, and especially to all who, like themselves, enjoyed familiar acquaintance with him. He had, moreover, recently advanced by a single step to the first rank among American biographers--a position readily accorded by recognized authority in the republic of letters, at home and abroad, to the author of the "Life of Edward Livingston." To such hands they could not hesitate to commit the work proposed, so far as they were able to control it, feeling assured that, while Mr. Hunt would bring to its performance the disinterestedness and impartiality indispensable to give it value as a history, and which are with difficulty maintained in family memorials, his inclination to undertake it was evidence of a general sympathy with, or at least respect for, Mr. Van Buren's character and public career sufficient to authorize the relinquishment to him of the materials in their possession. Accordingly the fragmentary memoirs, with all the correspondence and other manuscripts applicable to his purpose, and within their reach, were committed to Mr. Hunt, by Mr. Van Buren's representatives, with entire satisfaction and confidence that they will be used with fidelity and skill in the construction of the work he has undertaken,--a confidence that will be shared by Mr. Van Buren's surviving friends and by the public.

The main body of manuscripts left by Mr. Van Buren having been thus applied, some question remained in regard to that portion now published. Begun as an episode, the subject grew on the author's hands (as he explains in a note) to such proportions as to seem to stand more properly as a distinct production, and although, like the principal work, incomplete, it had been nevertheless carried forward to the point, chronologically speaking, that had been proposed, and that was in fact its natural termination. For this reason, and because it had no such connection with the memoirs as required that they should be printed together, it has been thought best to publish it without further delay in the form in which it was left by the writer. The subject is of peculiar interest at this time when our country, having suffered the rude shock and disorder of civil war, and our free and popular institutions having sustained with admirable firmness and substantial triumph a more fearful trial than any to which they had before been subjected, the sacred and momentous duty is devolved on patriots and good citizens throughout our borders to reconstruct whatever valuable parts have been thrown down, to restore what may have been injured or defaced in our political system and in the principles on which it rests; and the occasion seems auspicious for recalling the attention of our people to the study of the lives and doctrines--the grounds and motives of action--of the great men by whom the foundations of their government were laid.

The work of editing this volume has been inconsiderable, the sum of it having been to correct a few manifest inadvertencies, to divide it into chapters, with indexical heads, to furnish the whole with a title, and to add one or two foot-notes that appeared to be proper. Otherwise the aim has been to preserve the form and substance of the original. The citation from Cicero on the title-page was found on Mr. Van Buren's table, in his library, extracted in his own handwriting; whether only as a terse declaration of the law by the spirit of which his pen was guided, or as a possible motto for his complete work, is not known. The letter from Mr. Jefferson, forming an Appendix, was intended by Mr. Van Buren to be printed with whatever of his own might reach publication, and is spoken of in the present volume as "accompanying this work." It is now printed for the first time from the original manuscript letter, and a few errors in the edition published (probably from the draft) by the Library Committees of Congress are corrected.

The portrait fronting this book is engraved from Brady's imperial photograph, by Ritchie, and must be pronounced a very favorable specimen of his art. It represents Mr. Van Buren in the seventy-fifth year of his age.

EDGEHILL, FISHKILL-ON-HUDSON, N. Y., February, 1867.

POLITICAL PARTIES

IN THE

UNITED STATES.

CHAPTER I.

Gratifying Period in our History embraced by Administrations of Jefferson and Madison--The Caucus System and its Abandonment--The System useful to the Republican or Democratic Party, but not so to the Federalists--Questions proposed--Difficulties of the Subject--Two great Parties, under changing Names, have always divided the Country--Few and imperfect Attempts heretofore made to trace the Origin and Principles of those Parties--This the first Attempt with that object on the Republican or Democratic Side--The Sources of Differences in Opinion and Feeling which gave rise to our Political Divisions, and punctum temporis of their Rise--Principles established by the English Revolution of 1688--Application of those Principles to the Colonies--Grounds of the American Revolution--Abstract Opinions regain their Influence after the Settlement of the practical Questions involved in the Revolution--Diverse Character and Feelings of Emigrants to the different Colonies--Effect of that Diversity on Principles of Government and Administration in the New Governments--Repugnance of the People to any Revival of the System overthrown by the Revolution--Popular Reluctance to create an Executive Branch of the Government--Confederacy of the United Colonies of New England in 1643--Dr. Franklin's Plan of Union in 1755--The Sentiments of the Colonists those of the Whigs of the Revolution--Exceptions--Discordant Materials, in certain Respects, of which the Revolutionary Brotherhood was composed--Effects of that Discordance upon the subsequent Organization of Political Parties--The Confederation, and Parties for and against it--Perversion of Party Names--Conflicts and Questions in Controversy between Federalists and Anti-Federalists--The Constitutional Convention of 1787--Different Plans proposed before it--Motives and Views of the Authors of those Plans--The Views which determined Congress and the People to acquiesce in the Results of the Convention--Adoption of the Constitution and Extinction of the Anti-Federal Party as such.

There has been no period in our history, since the establishment of our

Independence, to which the sincere friend of free institutions can turn with more unalloyed satisfaction, than to that embraced by the administrations of Jefferson and Madison, moved as they were by a common impulse. Mr. Jefferson commenced the discharge of his official duties by an act which, though one of form, involved matter of the highest moment. I allude to the decision and facility with which, in his intercourse with the other branches of the Government, he suppressed the observance of empty ceremonies which had been borrowed from foreign courts by officers who took an interest in such matters, and were reluctantly tolerated by Washington, who was himself above them. Instead of proceeding in state to the capitol to deliver a speech to the legislature, according to the custom of monarchs, he performed his constitutional duty by means of a message in writing, sent to each House by the hands of his private secretary, and they performed theirs by a reference of its contents to appropriate committees. The Executive procession, instead of marking the intercourse between the different branches of the Government, was reserved for the Inauguration, when the President appeared before the people themselves, and in their presence took the oath of office.

A step so appropriate and so much in harmony with our institutions, was naturally followed by efforts for the abolition of offices and official establishments not necessary to the public service, the reduction of the public expenses, and the repeal of odious internal taxes. To these he added the influence of his individual example to keep the organization and action of the Federal Government upon that simple and economical footing which is consistent with the Republican system. In this branch of his official conduct he established precedents of great value, from some of which his successors have not ventured to depart.

With the single exception of his approval of the Bank of the United States, the administration of Mr. Madison was one of great merit, and was made especially illustrious by conducting the country through a war imperishably honorable for its military achievements and the consequent elevation of our national character.

Jefferson and Madison were brought forward by caucus nominations; they, throughout, recognized and adhered to the political party that elected them; and they left it united and powerful, when, at the close of public life, they carried into their retirement, and always enjoyed, the respect, esteem, and confidence of all their countrymen.

Mr. Monroe's administration did not introduce any very disturbing public questions. The protective policy was, toward its close, generally acquiesced in at the North and West, and no part of the South as yet even contemplated the resistance which was subsequently attempted. The agitation in regard to internal improvements was yet for the most part speculative and too far in advance of any contemplated action to stir the public mind. The Bank of the United States was having its own way without question on the part of the Government, and with but little if any suspicion on the part of the people. No very embarrassing questions had arisen in our foreign relations; yet the first year of Mr. Monroe's second term had scarcely passed away before the political atmosphere became inflamed to an unprecedented extent. The Republican party, so long in the ascendant, and apparently so omnipotent, was literally shattered into fragments, and we had no fewer than five Republican Presidential candidates in the field.

In the place of two great parties arrayed against each other in a fair and open contest for the establishment of principles in the administration of Government which they respectively believed most conducive to the public interest, the country was overrun with personal factions. These having few higher motives for the selection of their candidates or stronger incentives to action than individual preferences or antipathies, moved the bitter waters of political agitation to their lowest depths.

The occurrence of scenes discreditable to all had for a long time been prevented by a steady adherence on the part of the Republican party to the caucus system; and if Mr. Monroe's views and feelings upon the subject had been the same as were those of Jefferson and Madison, the results to which I have alluded, and which were soon sincerely deprecated, might have been prevented by the same means. There was no difference in the political condition of the country between 1816--when Mr. Monroe received a caucus nomination, on a close vote between Mr. Crawford and himself, and was elected--and 1824, when the caucus system was appealed to by the supporters of Mr. Crawford, which called for its abandonment. The Federal party were on both occasions incapable of successfully resisting a candidate in whose favor the Republicans were united, and they were on each sufficiently strong to control the election when the support of their opponents was divided amongst several. Mr. Monroe and a majority of his cabinet were unfortunately influenced by different views, and pursued a course well designed to weaken the influence of the caucus system, and to cause its abandonment. Mr. Crawford was the only candidate who, it was believed, could be benefited by adhering to it, and the friends of all the others sustained the policy of the administration. Those of Jackson, Adams, Clay, and Calhoun, united in an address to the people condemning the practice of caucus nominations, and announcing their determination to disregard them. Already weakened through the adverse influence of the administration, the agency which had so long preserved the unity of the Republican party did not retain sufficient strength to resist the combined assault that was made upon it, and was overthrown. Mr. Crawford and his friends adhered to it to the last, and fell with it.

It is a striking fact in our political history that the sagacious leaders of the Federal party, as well under that name as under others by which it has at different times been known, have always been desirous to bring every usage or plan designed to secure party unity into disrepute with the people, and in proportion to their success in that has been their success in the elections. When they have found such usage too strong to be overthrown for the time being, they have adopted it themselves, but only to return to their denunciations of it after every defeat. It would, on first impression, seem that a practice which is good for one political party must be good for another; but when the matter is more closely looked into, it will be discovered that the policy of the Federal leaders referred to, like most of the acts of those far-seeing men, rested upon substantial foundations. It originated, beyond doubt, in the conviction, on the part of the early Federalists, that a political organization in support of the particular principles which they advocated, and to which they intended to adhere, did not stand as much in need of extraneous means to secure harmony in its ranks as did that of their opponents.

The results of general elections for more than half a century have served to confirm this opinion. With the exception of a single instance, susceptible of easy explanation, the Republican, now Democratic party, whenever it has been wise enough to employ the caucus or convention system, and to use in good faith the influence it is capable of imparting to the popular cause, has been successful, and it has been defeated whenever that system has been laid aside or employed unfairly. With the Federal party and its successors the results have been widely different; with or without the caucus system they have generally found no difficulty in uniting whenever union promised success.

Why is it that a system or practice open to both parties, occasionally used by both, and apparently equally useful to both, is in fact so much less necessary to one than to the other? If this consequence springs from a corresponding difference in the principles for the defense and spread of which they have respectively been formed, what are those principles, whence are they derived, and what is their history?

These are grave questions, which have often presented themselves to the minds of our public men, and to answer which satisfactorily is neither an easy nor a short task.

Histories of struggles for power between individual men or families, long involved in obscurity, are becoming more frequent than they were, and far more satisfactory. Aided by a comparatively free access to public and private papers,--a privilege formerly sturdily refused, but which the liberal spirit of the age has now made common,--the literary men of most countries, with improved capacities to weigh conflicting statements as well as to narrate the results of their researches with simplicity and perspicuity, are probing the most hidden recesses of the past, and describing with reliable accuracy transactions of great interest, the causes and particular circumstances of which have been hitherto little or not at all understood. But to define the origin and trace the history of national parties is an undertaking of extraordinary difficulty; one from which, in view of the embarrassments that surround it in the case of our own political divisions, I have more than once retired in despair, and on which I now enter with only slight hopes of success. Yet it is due as well to the memories of the past as to actual interests, that a subject which has exerted so great an influence and which may be made so instructive, should be made plain, if that be practicable, to the understandings of the present and succeeding generations; and if my imperfect effort shall have a tendency to turn stronger minds and abler pens in that direction it will not have been made in vain.

The two great parties of this country, with occasional changes in their names only, have, for the principal part of a century, occupied antagonistic positions upon all important political questions. They have maintained an unbroken succession, and have, throughout, been composed respectively of men agreeing in their party passions and preferences, and entertaining, with rare exceptions, similar general views on the subjects of government and its administration. Sons have generally followed in the footsteps of their fathers, and families originally differing have in regular succession received, maintained, and transmitted this opposition. Neither the influences of marriage connections, nor of sectarian prejudices, nor any of the strong motives which often determine the ordinary actions of men, have, with limited exceptions, been sufficient to override the bias of party organization and sympathy, devotion to which has, on both sides, as a rule, been a master-passion of their members.

The names of these parties, like those of their predecessors in older countries, have from time to time been changed, from suggestions of policy or from accidental causes. Men of similar and substantially unchanged views and principles have, at different periods of English history, been distinguished as Cavaliers or Roundheads, as Jacobites or Puritans and Presbyterians, as Whigs or Tories. Here, with corresponding consistency in principle, the same men have at different periods been known as Federalists, Federal Republicans, and Whigs, or as Anti-Federalists, Republicans, and Democrats. But no changes of name have indicated--certainly not until very recently, and the depth and duration of the exception remain to be seen--a change or material modification of the true character and principles of the parties themselves. The difference between the old Republican and the Anti-Federal parties, arising out of the questions in regard to the new Constitution, was by far the greatest variation that has occurred.

Several hasty and but slightly considered attempts have been made to define the origin, and to mark the progress, of our national parties. But, with a single exception,--namely, that made by ex-President John Quincy Adams, in his Jubilee Discourse before the New York Historical Society, on the 30th of April, 1839, being the Fiftieth Anniversary of the Inauguration of George Washington as President of the United States,--they have not professed, so far as they have fallen under my notice, to do more than glance at the subject.

To say that this discourse of one hundred and twenty pages was written with Mr. Adams's accustomed ability, would be a commendation short of its merits. It was more. The political condition of the country, and the near approach of the memorable struggle of 1840, superadded to the stirring considerations connected with the occasion, seem to have persuaded that distinguished man that he was called upon to make an extraordinary effort. A severe philippic against his and his father's political enemies, this discourse, judged in the sense in which such performances are naturally estimated by contemporaries imbued with similar feelings, could not fail to be regarded as an eloquent and able production; but I deceive myself if it can be deemed by a single ingenuous mind either a dispassionate or an impartial review of the origin and course of parties in the United States. Such minds will be more likely to receive a paper, written so long after the transactions of which it speaks, with feelings of regret at the strong evidence it affords that the rage of party spirit, upon the assumed extinguishment of which its author had, years before, exultingly congratulated the people from the Presidential chair, was yet so active in his own breast. I say this more in sorrow than in anger. Other portions of this work[1] will, I am sure, exonerate me from the suspicion of cherishing the slightest sentiment of unkindness toward the memory of John Quincy Adams. When my personal acquaintance with him was but slight, and when our political relations were unfavorable to the cultivation of friendly feelings, my dispositions toward him were to an unusual extent free from the prejudices commonly engendered by party differences. In the later periods of our acquaintance, continuing to the end of his life, I regarded him with entire personal respect and kindness; and notwithstanding the occasional fierceness of our political collisions, I have never heard of any unfriendly expression by him in respect to myself personally.

[1] This refers to the Memoirs of the writer, to which the present essay was intended to be an episode. See Introduction to this volume. Eds.

It is not a little remarkable, though in harmony with other striking features in the relations of our parties, that no serious attempt has ever been made to trace their origin except by members of the same political school with Mr. Adams. If I am right in this, mine will at least have the weight, whatever that may be, due to the narration of one who, from the beginning to the end of an extended political career, has been an invariable and ardent member of the opposite school.

The author of the life of Hamilton confidently pronounces what occurred on the appointment of Washington as Commander-in-chief of the Revolutionary army, to be the true source of the party divisions that have so long and so extensively prevailed in this country. President John Quincy Adams, in his Inaugural Address, attributes them to the conflicting prejudices and preferences of the people for and against Great Britain and France at the commencement of the present government, and the discontinuance of them to the effects produced by the excesses of the French Revolution. Matthew L. Davis,--a man of much note and cleverness, who commenced his career an active member of the old Republican party, became the especial champion of Colonel Burr, and, soon seceding from the party to which he was at first attached, spent the remainder of his life in opposition to it,--in his life of Aaron Burr, attributes the origin of our two great political parties to the proceedings of the Federal Constitutional Convention and of the State Conventions which passed upon the question of ratification.

These various versions of the matter I shall hereafter notice, contenting myself, for the present, with the remark that party divisions which have extended to every corner of a country as large as our own, and have endured so long, could not spring from slight or even limited causes. No differences in the views of men on isolated questions temporary in their nature, could, it seems to me, have produced such results. Questions of such a character are either finally settled, with more or less satisfaction, or in time lose their interest, notwithstanding momentary excitement, and the temporary organizations springing from them give place in turn to others equally short-lived.

But when men are brought under one government who differ radically in opinion as to its proper form, as to the uses for which governments should be established, as to the spirit in which they should be administered, as to the best way in which the happiness of those who are subject to them can be promoted, no less than in regard to the capacity of the people for self-government, we may well look for party divisions and political organizations of a deeper foundation and a more enduring existence.

Ours arose at the close of the Revolution, and the leading parties to them were the Whigs, through whose instrumentality, under favor of Providence, our Independence had been established. They and the Tories constituted our entire population, and the latter had at first, for obvious reasons, but little to do in the formation of parties, save to throw themselves in a body into the ranks of one of them. It became at once evident that great differences of opinion existed among the Whigs in respect to the character of the government that should be substituted for that which had been overthrown, and also in respect to the spirit and principles which should control the administration of that which might be established. These spread through the country with great rapidity, and were respectively maintained with a zeal and determination which proved that they were not produced by the feelings or impulses of the moment. To ascertain the origin of those differences, and to trace their effects, we can adopt no safer course than to look to the antecedents of the actors in the stirring political scenes that followed the close of the war, to the characters and opinions of their ancestors, from whom they had naturally imbibed their first ideas of government either directly or traditionally, and to the incidents of the memorable struggle from which the country had just emerged.

The great principle first formally avowed by Rousseau, "that the right to exercise sovereignty belongs inalienably to the people," sprung up spontaneously in the hearts of the colonists, and silently influenced all their acts from the beginning. The condition of the country in which they settled,--a wilderness occupied besides themselves only by savage tribes,--to which many of them were driven by the fiercest persecutions ever known to the civilized world, and the stern self-reliance and independent spirit which most of them had acquired in contests with iron fortune that preceded their exile, combined to induce the cultivation and to secure the permanent growth of such a sentiment. Not being, however, for several generations, in a suitable condition, and from counteracting inducements not even disposed to dispute the pretensions of the Crown to their allegiance, they were content to look principally to its patents and other concessions for the measure of their rights. But their views were greatly changed, and their advance on the road to freedom materially accelerated, by the English Revolution of 1688. The final overthrow of James II., from whose tyrannical acts, as well in the character of Duke of York as in that of King, they had severely suffered, was not the greatest advantage the colonists derived from that Revolution. The principles upon which that most important of European movements was founded, and the doctrines it consecrated, paved the way to a result which, though not upon their tongues, or perhaps to any great extent the subject of their meditations as immediately practicable, was, doubtless, from that time, within their contemplation.

That Revolution, which shattered, "past all surgery," the blasphemous and absurd dogma of the divine right of kings; which replaced the slavish doctrine of passive obedience and non-resistance with the principle that the authority of the monarch was no other than a trust founded on an assumed agreement between him and his subjects that the power conferred upon him should be used for their advantage, for the faithful execution of which he was individually responsible, and for a breach of which resistance to his authority, as a last resort, was a constitutional remedy; which for the supremacy of the Crown substituted the supremacy of Parliament; which made the King as well as his subjects responsible to its authority, and which abrogated the right of the Crown to govern the colonies in virtue of its prerogative, and vested that power in Parliament, placed the colonists upon a footing widely different from that they had theretofore occupied.

The general principle that they were, by the laws and statutes of England, entitled to the political rights that appertained to British subjects, could not be denied, but commercial rivalry and political jealousies acting upon their excited feelings, soon generated questions of the gravest import, both as to the extent of the power of Parliament to legislate for them, and as to the participation in representation essential to authorize the exercise of that power.

The subjects of taxation and the regulation of trade by Parliamentary authority, excited the greatest interest on both sides of the Atlantic. In respect to the latter, the question was not a little embarrassed by an alleged acquiescence on the part of the colonists, and the consequent force of precedents. This circumstance, in connection with the consideration that, if the right to regulate the trade of the colonies was denied to the mother country, the allegiance conceded to be due would be paid to a barren sceptre, was calculated to deprive the cause of the colonists of the favorable opinion of those just men in England whose countenance and support were of so much service to them in the sequel. Duly appreciating the obstacles to success which there was reason to apprehend from this source, with the prudence and good sense that belonged to their character, and without waiving any of their rights, they placed their cause principally upon a ground that lay at the foundation of the Revolution, and was thoroughly immovable, viz., that by the fundamental laws of property no taxes could be levied upon the people but by their own consent or that of their authorized agents, and that by consequence the connection was indissoluble between taxation and representation.

In the justice and constitutionality of this position they were openly sustained by Lord Chatham, Lord Camden, Burke, Fox, and others,--men who were in their day and have since been regarded as leading minds of England. With but little of public sentiment against them beyond what was influenced by the inveterate hatred and the insane obstinacy of the King, wielding at will the majority of a notoriously corrupt Parliament and the brute force of the kingdom, the colonists appealed to the God of Battles in defense of a sacred principle of freedom, and in resistance to tyrannical acts of the most odious and oppressive character, and they were victorious. It is now, and will be in all time, a source of satisfaction to the people of these States, that the decision of the sword is not their only nor their highest title to the liberty they enjoy. The colonists were right in the contest. Of this no serious doubt is now entertained in any honest and well-informed quarter. The idea of virtual representation, and the attempt to justify one wrong by the practice of another, namely, the taxing other British subjects without giving them an adequate representation in Parliament,--the only replies that were made to the claim of constitutional rights,--are now well understood, and, it gives me pleasure to say, generally disavowed in England. Lord Derby, the manly and highly gifted leader of what is left of the old Tory party, not long since, in a speech delivered in the presence of an American minister, unreservedly admitted that we were right in the Revolutionary contest; and, if that question were now submitted to the free judgment of the people of England, such would be found to be the public sense of that great nation.

The only way in which the right in respect to taxation set up by the English Parliament could have been sustained consistently with the English Constitution, would have been by a joint government, securing to the colonies the representation in that body to which they were entitled as British subjects,--a plan to which both the mother country and the colonies were equally decided in their dislike, but for very different reasons. If a similar question were presented at this day it would, according to the present state of public opinion in both countries, be at once settled by an alliance of peace and friendship, substituting fraternal relations for those of parent and children.

Well would it have been for the interests of both and of humanity if the matter had been thus adjusted.

The immediate question upon which the Revolution turned was, of course, forever extinguished by its results. But it has been far otherwise with the his own motives, and confiding fully in those of his military associates, he allowed his name to be placed at the head of the list of members and consented to be its president.

The principle of hereditary distinctions could not well have been placed before the people in a less exceptionable form, and yet there were but few occurrences during the war by which the public mind was so deeply excited as that by which the officers intended to grace the closing scenes of their meritorious career. The measure was assailed in all the forms in which an offended public opinion usually finds vent. In addition to able and eloquent attacks from American pens, the movement was severely criticised in a pamphlet published in France and written by Mirabeau, entitled, "Thoughts on the Order of Cincinnatus."

General Washington informed himself of the extent to which the subject was agitating the public mind, and, justly alarmed at the consequences it might produce, determined to do all in his power to arrest its progress. He wrote to Mr. Jefferson in April, 1784, asking his opinion and the probable views of Congress (of which Mr. Jefferson was a member) upon the subject, and his advice in respect to the most eligible measures to be adopted by the society at their next meeting, which was to be held in the ensuing month of May. This letter does not appear in the published writings of Washington, but an extract from it is given by Mr. Sparks, from which and from Jefferson's reply its contents as stated are gathered. Mr. Jefferson's answer, containing an unreserved communication of his opinions in the matter, may be found in Vol. I. of his Correspondence. He stated at length the objections that were made to the society, the unfriendliness of Congress to it, and added, in conclusion, that if, rather than decide themselves upon the best course to be pursued, the members should, at their approaching meeting, refer the question to Congress, such a reference would "infallibly produce a recommendation of total discontinuance."

General Washington attended the meeting in May, and proposed several changes in the constitution, and among them, in his own words, taken by Mr. Sparks from memoranda in his own handwriting, "to discontinue the hereditary part in all its connections, absolutely, without any substitution which can be construed into concealment or a change of ground only, for this would, in my opinion, increase rather than allay suspicion." This amendment, and others having a similar bearing, were adopted.

In Mr. Jefferson's letter to myself, accompanying this volume,[2] to which, as it was prepared with great care, and avowedly designed "to throw light on history and to recall that into the path of truth," I shall have frequent occasion to refer, will be found a highly interesting account of what took place between himself and General Washington, on his way to the meeting in Philadelphia, and on his return, in May, 1784.

[2] See Appendix.

Some of the State societies rejected these modifications in toto, and others only agreed to them partially. The agitation of the subject was thus continued for several years, and as late as 1787 no State had yet so far yielded its prejudices as to grant the charter for which the constitution of the society made it the duty of the State meetings to apply. Whatever opinion may at this day be formed in regard to the sufficiency of the reasons for the alarm which this transaction produced, it cannot be doubted that the proceedings in regard to it afford strong proof that there was, down to the spring of 1787, a settled aversion in the minds of a majority of the people to any measure or course of measures which were indicative of the slightest desire to return in any degree to the system which they had overthrown; and that as early as 1783 strong suspicion existed that such desires were concealed in the minds of many who had previously stood faithfully by the country in all its perils.

The intense hostility of the colonists and their successors to monarchical institutions, and the recollection of the cruelties inflicted upon them and upon their predecessors under the authority of kings, had produced a determined repugnance on their part to the concentration of power in the hands of single magistrates. Their minds had become thoroughly impressed with a conviction that the disposition to abuse power by those who were intrusted with it was not only inherent and invariable, but incurable, and that it was therefore unwise to grant more than was actually indispensable to the management of public affairs. At no period anterior to the adoption of the present Constitution, could a majority be obtained in Congress for the creation of an executive branch of the Government, or an impression be made upon the public mind favorable to such a measure. The inconveniences experienced from a want of it during a protracted war, and which were again encountered in the public service after the recognition of our independence, were not sufficient to overcome this repugnance. The tenacity with which they adhered to an equal representation and influence for the colonies before, and for the States after, the Declaration of Independence, in the confederacies and governments they formed, sprang from like considerations. They could not be brought to believe that a State, to which was allowed a greater power than was reserved to its confederates, could be restrained from the ultimate exercise of her superior power to depress her smaller confederates and to elevate herself.

Proofs of the existence and force of these opinions are spread through every portion of our early history.

In 1643 the New England Colonies, with the exception of those "who ran a different course" from the Puritans, entered into a Confederacy. Its avowed design was the better advancement of their general interests, but its real object was to provide greater security against the savages by whom they were menaced. It was called the "United Colonies of New England." The plan was for a season defeated, because Massachusetts claimed more power than she was willing to concede to the other colonies; but it was finally established upon principles of perfect equality, no more power or influence being conceded to Massachusetts, by far the largest, than to New Haven, the smallest colony. The management of affairs was intrusted to commissioners, of which each colony had two, but no executive power was conferred upon them. They might deliberate and recommend, but the colonies alone could carry their recommendations into effect. This Confederacy endured for nearly half a century, and worked well.

In 1755 a convention of delegates from the colonies was held at Albany, under the stimulus of French encroachments, and a plan of union, drawn up by Dr. Franklin, was agreed upon and submitted to the colonies for their approval. The plan, as was to be expected from the character of its author, distributed the powers of the government between the people and the prerogatives of the Crown, much more favorably to the popular side than it would seem the latter might, in the then condition of things, have reasonably hoped for. Still the attachments of the colonists to their local governments, and, above all, their distrust and dread of a central government, which was provided for, were sufficient to deprive the plan of their favor, and to cause its ultimate abandonment.

The privilege of "Government within themselves," as "their undoubted right in the sight of God and man," and "to be governed by rulers of their own choosing and laws of their own making," were from the beginning objects of absorbing solicitude with the colonists and their Revolutionary successors.

The principles and sentiments I have attempted to define, which had sprung up at the earliest period in the colonies, and had grown with their growth and strengthened with their strength, and in explanation of which I have referred to a few of the many illustrations with which their history abounds, were doubtless those also of a great majority of the Whigs of the Revolution, in whose breasts was not wanting the feeling which rarely fails to be seen in those political divisions that lead to civil war,--a thorough antagonism to the general opinions, as well as to the particular policy of the power or party opposed; but it is equally true that those were far from being the principles or feelings of all by whose efforts the Revolution was achieved. A numerous portion of the Whigs of the Revolution, many of them greatly distinguished for their talents, high characters, and great public services, neither concurred in the principles nor sympathized with the feelings I have described, but were in a great measure driven by other considerations to take active parts in the struggle. The number thus influenced was, fortunately for the result of the contest, increased by specific tyrannical acts, which a prudent government would have avoided, but which were forced on the ministry and Parliament of the mother country by the obstinacy and bigotry of the king. Within a year after his accession to the throne he wound up a series of unnecessary interferences with the administration of justice in the colonies, by changing the tenure of office, which had till that period prevailed in relation to the colonial judges, from that of good behavior to that of the will and pleasure of the Crown. By thus using his prerogative to create a distinction in different parts of the realm degrading to the colonies, he left the colonial lawyers no other course consistent with self-respect, to say nothing of patriotism, than to unite with those engaged in other pursuits in an effort to overthrow a government capable of such practices. While subjecting the legal profession to such humiliating proofs of the royal displeasure, his government commenced its assaults upon that portion of his subjects engaged in commerce. His indignation against those who scouted the doctrine of the British Constitution, "that the king can do no wrong," was intense and unappeasable in proportion to their presumed intelligence. It was in this spirit that he appears to have selected judges, professional men, and merchants, as special objects of his wrath, and having exerted his power against the first two classes, he turned his attention toward the latter.

The Navigation Acts, as they stood at the period of his accession, had been framed in the illiberal and selfish spirit which characterized the legislation of the age. But though they had proved injurious to the trade of the colonies, and humiliating to the colonial merchants, in consequence of the extent to which they made their interests subservient to those of the mother country, yet their prejudicial effects had in neither respect been fully developed, in consequence of the remissness which had prevailed in their execution. This had in a great degree been occasioned by illicit contrivances between the colonists engaged in trade and navigation and the officers of government stationed in the colonies. A vigorous execution of the existing laws not only was determined upon, but new acts were passed imposing additional restrictions, and superadding cumulative penalties upon those who disregarded them. To enforce this vindictive policy the Government resorted to a measure at once the most arbitrary and odious of any that had ever been known to the public service,--that of "Writs of Assistance,"--and converted the army and navy into a police establishment to aid in the detection and punishment of the colonial offenders.

By thus giving vent to his persecuting spirit--a spirit always blind to its own interests--this infatuated Prince drove into the front rank of the Revolution two classes of the colonists who were, from the nature of their pursuits, least likely to embark in popular outbreaks, and most inclined to favor a strong government,--classes which are usually caressed by more sagacious rulers, and which had been so here before the reign of George III. All orders of the colonists, save a few favorites, were by these and similar means united, as a band of brothers, in a movement such as the world had never before, and has never since seen, for the overthrow of a government by which they were so sorely oppressed.

This union was in other respects composed of very discordant materials. It consisted, on the one hand, of men and the descendants of men on whose hearts the fires of persecution had burned a hatred of royalty too deep to be erased and too zealous to be trifled with; of men who were at the same time too conversant with human nature to allow themselves to believe that the love of power and the proneness to its abuse were confined to its hereditary possessors, and who were therefore anxious to restrict grants of authority to their public functionaries to the lowest point consistent with good government, and to subject what they did grant to the most stringent responsibilities. They continued, also, to cherish the same preference for their local organizations, and to entertain the same distrust of an overshadowing central government, for which the great body of the people had long been distinguished. They were men whose highest ambition and desire for themselves and the country was that it should have a plain, simple, and cheap government for the management of the affairs of the Confederacy, republican in its construction and democratic in its spirit,--a government that should, as far as practicable, be deprived of the power of creating artificial distinctions in society, and of corrupting and thus subverting the independence of the people by the possession of a redundant patronage. Such a government had long been the subject of their meditations, and they braved the hazards and encountered the hardships of the Revolutionary contest for the opportunity of establishing it.

The Revolutionary brotherhood by which the recognition of our Independence was enforced, contained, on the other hand, men respectable in numbers, and distinguished by talent, public service, and high social position, who dissented from many (I may say from most) of these views, and who regarded them as Utopian in themselves, or as too contracted for the exigencies of the public service.

This difference in the opinions of men who had been engaged in such a contest was all but unavoidable, and was never absent from any political struggle of sufficient importance to be compared with it. It results, besides those which have been indicated as peculiar to our own condition and history, from simple but potent causes of universal operation, such as diversities in social condition, in education, in the influence and tendencies of previous pursuits, and in individual character and temperament, producing diversities of views on such occasions.

Although an aversion to royalty and opposition to hereditary government in any form, were sentiments that pervaded the masses and exercised a controlling influence in the Revolution, there were not a few, of the character I have described, who, though they doubtless did not at the moment design the reintegration of those institutions after the overthrow of the actual Government, could yet contemplate, without great revulsion of feeling, their ultimate establishment in this country. Prompt to resist tyranny in any shape, and stung by the oppressions practiced upon the colonies by the British Government, they hesitated not to peril their lives for its subversion here, whilst theoretically they not only tolerated its form and constitution, but regarded them as the best that could be devised to promote the welfare and to secure the happiness of mankind. Of the existence of this opinion on the part of many sincere friends and able advocates of the Revolutionary cause, in every stage of the contest and for years after its close, we have indubitable evidence. I will notice a few cases of this description, on account of the influence exerted on the formation of political parties by the knowledge of the existence of such opinions, and by the suspicions, perhaps unjust, and in some respects certainly so, as to the extent to which those who held them were willing to carry them out. In so doing, it is by no means my design to cast reproach upon the memories of the great men who entertained them, and who stood by their country in her severest extremity, and established the highest claims to her gratitude and favor.

No ingenuous mind can doubt that a large majority of the Whigs were opposed to the substitution of a government similar either in form or spirit to that from which they had emancipated themselves. Our Revolutionary creed was, "That all men are created equal; that they are endowed by their Creator with certain inalienable rights; that among these are life, liberty, and the pursuit of happiness; that to secure these rights, governments are instituted among men, deriving their just powers from the consent of the governed; that whenever any form of government becomes destructive of these ends, it is the right of the people to alter and abolish it, and to institute a new government, laying its foundations on such principles, and organizing its powers in such form, as to them shall seem most likely to effect their safety and happiness."

Under such a creed all were entitled as of right to a perfect freedom of choice in regard to the character of the new government. Neither for the formation of their opinions, however erroneous these may have been, nor for the maintenance of them by lawful means, did any subject themselves to just reproach, or to other forfeiture than perhaps a loss of the confidence of those who thought differently.

James Otis, Stephen Hopkins, John Adams, Gouverneur Morris, and

Alexander Hamilton, may be selected from many others as representatives of the principles of that class to which I have referred as dissenting from the popular or preponderating ideas of the time.

I select them the more readily from a desire to avoid mistakes, as they were possessed of temperaments too sanguine and too fearless to be deterred from advancing openly opinions they honestly entertained, by their unpopularity.

There were certainly not many individuals, if there was one, who did more to set the ball of the Revolution in motion than James Otis; and if his career had not been cut short by the hand of violence he would have taken high rank among the great and good men who survived the struggle. His speech against the issuing of the Writs of Assistance had an effect corresponding to those of Patrick Henry. Yet this highly gifted man, whose patriotic spirit was sufficiently aroused by the oppressions of the mother country, while yet in their incipiency, to induce him to peril his life in acts of resistance, was an enthusiastic admirer of the principles of the English system, and honestly believed, as he said, "that the British Constitution came nearest the idea of perfection of any that had been reduced to practice."

The patriotic Hopkins, one of the Rhode Island Representatives in the General Congress, and a signer of the Declaration of Independence, wrote-- and that colony authoritatively published its concurrence in the declaration-- that "The glorious Constitution of Great Britain is the best that ever existed among men."

Gouverneur Morris's unyielding hostility to democratic principles, and his preference for aristocratic and monarchical institutions, were often exhibited and unreservedly avowed, as well on the floor of the Federal Convention as elsewhere, and have become familiar among his countrymen as household words. There were not many, if indeed there was a single one of his contemporaries, who went beyond him in hostility to the State governments. "State attachments and State importance," said he in the Federal Convention, "have been the bane of this country! We cannot annihilate them, but we may, perhaps, take out the teeth of the serpents." Such as were his principles at the commencement of his career they remained to the close of his life.

But the opinions of John Adams and Alexander Hamilton, from their larger agency in the politics of the country, in the administration of its government, and in the actual formation of parties, are of still greater importance. A full exposition of these, beyond the single point upon which there existed the greatest jealousy at the period at which we have now arrived,--that of their preference for the English system,--will be best postponed until we come to consider the times and occasions which were presented for an ampler display of them. I will, therefore, only refer at this place to the contents of a statement prepared and signed by Thomas Jefferson, in February, 1818, and designed to explain a portion of his writings. In this he says, among other things: "But Hamilton was not only a monarchist, but for a monarchy bottomed on corruption. In proof of this I will relate an anecdote for the truth of which I attest the God who made me. Before the President set out upon his Southern tour, in April, 1791, he addressed a letter of the 4th of that month, from Mount Vernon, to the Secretaries of State, Treasury, and War, desiring that if any serious and important cases should arise during his absence they would consult and act on them, and he requested that the Vice-President should also be consulted. This was the only occasion on which that officer was ever requested to take part in a Cabinet question. Some occasion for consultation arising, I invited those gentlemen (and the Attorney-General, as well as I remember) to dine with me, in order to confer on the subject. After the cloth was removed, and our question argued and dismissed, conversation began on other matters, and by some circumstance was led to the British Constitution, on which Mr. Adams observed,--'Purge that Constitution of its corruption and give to its popular branch equality of representation, and it would become the most perfect Constitution ever devised by the wit of man.' Hamilton paused and said,--'Purge it of its corruptions and give to its popular branch equality of representation, and it would become an impracticable government: as it stands at present, with all its supposed defects, it is the most perfect which ever existed.'"

The solemn responsibility under which this statement was made, the high character of its author, the time when it was recorded,--after one of the principal parties had passed from earth, and the two remaining were on the brink of the grave; when the passions excited by personal and political rivalry had died away, and friendly relations had been restored between the survivors,--would of themselves be sufficient to establish its accuracy, even if its description of the opinions of Adams and Hamilton had not been, as it will be seen that they were, abundantly confirmed as well by the speeches and writings of the parties themselves as by the recorded declarations of associates and friends who possessed the best opportunities to become acquainted with their real sentiments.

The natural presumption is--and there are many facts to prove its correctness--that opinions with which these most prominent leaders were so deeply imbued, had, to a very considerable extent at least, been diffused throughout the ranks of their followers.

The effects of this discordance on so many and such vital points in the political doctrines and feelings of those by whom the Revolution had been achieved, were postponed by the existence of the war; but when that restraint was removed by the recognition of our Independence they broke forth unavoidably, and were soon developed in the formation of political parties.

The Congress of the Confederation, and--from the dependence of the Federal Government upon the cooperation of the States for the performance of its most important duties--the State legislatures, as well as the public press, became the theatres for the display of these conflicting opinions.

The so-called Government of the Confederation was little else than an alliance between the States--a federal league and compact, the terms of which were set forth in the Articles of Confederation. Besides a control over questions of Peace and War, its powers and duties were chiefly advisory, and dependent for their execution upon the cooperation of the States. A federal system so defective was justly held responsible for a large share of the public and private embarrassments that existed at, or arose after, the termination of the Revolutionary contest. It was also, as was natural, charged in some degree with those which were, in truth, unavoidable consequences of a seven years' war, and which would have existed under any system. It is not surprising, therefore, that a party bent upon its overthrow should have arisen as soon as the public mind was by the course of events brought to a proper state to consider the subject. Of this party Alexander Hamilton became the leader, and its immediate objects were, of course, very soon frankly developed. These were in the first instance to divest the State governments of certain powers, and to confer them upon Congress, the possession of which by the Federal head they deemed indispensable to the exigencies of the public service, with the intention of following up this step by an attempt to abrogate the Articles of

Confederation, and to substitute for that system an independent and effective Federal Government, composed of executive, legislative, and judicial departments. In respect to the powers to be given to the new Government, and to its construction otherwise, there doubtless existed some differences of opinion among the members of this party; but all agreed that it should be what in the language of the day was called a "strong government." There may not have been entire harmony among them in regard to the expediency and practicability of attempting it, but I do not think there is reasonable ground to doubt that most of them desired a virtual consolidation of the two systems-- Federal and State. A few were, from an early period, suspected by those who differed from them, and who became their opponents, of desiring to return to the English system, and this suspicion, doubtless, contributed to make the latter more impracticable than they might otherwise have been.

The political feelings which lay nearest to the hearts of the great body of the people, as well during our colonial condition as in the States after the declaration and establishment of Independence, and of the strength of which I have referred to such striking and oft-repeated illustrations, were those of veneration and affection for their local governments as safeguards of their liberties and adequate to most of their wants; endeared to them as their refuge from the persecutions of arbitrary power, and hallowed by the perils and triumphs of the Revolution. Allied to these feelings, and nearly co-extensive with them in point of duration, was a distrust, at both periods, on the part of the masses, of what they called an overshadowing general government.

When to these sources of opposition to the views of the party which had arrayed itself against the government of the Confederation is added the natural and deeply seated hostility of those who dissented from its views in respect to hereditary government in any form, and the suspicion of a reserved preference for such, or at least for kindred institutions, we cannot be at a loss in accounting for the origin of the first two great parties which sprang up and divided the country so soon after the establishment of our Independence.

But the names by which these parties were distinguished are, it must be admitted, not so intelligible. The name of Anti-Federalists was strangely enough given by their opponents to those who advocated the continuance of the Union upon the principles which prevailed in its establishment, and according to which it was regarded as a Federal League or Alliance of Free

States, upon equal terms, founded upon a compact (the Articles of Confederation) by which its conditions were regulated,--to be represented by a general Congress, authorized to consider and decide all questions appertaining to the interests of the alliance and committed to its charge, without power either to act upon the people directly or to apply force to the States, or otherwise to compel a compliance with its decrees, and without any guarantee for their execution other than the good faith of the parties to the compact. On the other hand the name of Federalists was assumed, and, what is still more extraordinary, retained by those who desired to reduce the State governments, by the conjunction of which the Federal Union had been formed, to the condition of corporations to be intrusted with the performance of those offices only for the discharge of which a new general government might think them the appropriate functionaries; to convert the States, not perhaps in name, but practically and substantially, into one consolidated body politic, and to establish over it a government which should, at the least, be rendered independent and effective by the possession of ample powers to devise, adopt, and execute such measures as it might deem best adapted to common defense and general welfare.

That this was a signal perversion of the true relation between party names and party objects can scarcely be denied. Yet we who have, in later days, witnessed the caprices in respect to party names to which the public mind has been occasionally subjected, and the facility with which one party has, through its superior address or its greater activity, succeeded in attaching to its adversary an unsuitable and unwelcome name, have not as much reason to be surprised at that perversion as had the men of that day who were subjected to it.

The motive which operated in thus denying to men whose principles were federal the name which indicated them, and in giving it to their opponents, must be looked for in the fact that federal principles were at that time favored by the mass of the people. This was well understood at the time, and was made still more apparent by the circumstance that those who really adhered to them, though compelled by the superior address of their adversaries to act under the name of Anti-Federalists, maintained their ascendancy in the government of the Confederation to its close.

Those who require further proof of the truth of this position beyond what results from a mere statement of the principles contended for by the respective parties, will find it fully sustained by definitions of Gouverneur Morris and James Madison. (2 Madison Papers, pp. 747-8, and 893.) Mr. Morris explained the distinction between a federal and a national supreme government,--the former being a mere compact resting on the good faith of the parties, the latter having a complete and compulsive operation. Mr. Madison, in the debate on the propositions of Mr. Patterson, which constituted the plan of the Anti-Federalists, and which were rejected by a vote of seven States to three,--one (Maryland) divided,--said: "Much stress has been laid by some gentlemen on the want of power in the Convention to propose any other than a federal plan.... Neither of the characteristics of a federal plan would support this objection. One characteristic was that in a federal government the power was exercised, not on the people individually, but on the people collectively, on the States. The other characteristic was that a federal government derived its appointments, not immediately from the people, but from the States which they respectively composed."

It cannot be difficult to decide which of these parties was, in truth, federal, and which anti-federal, according to these authentic definitions of a federal government.[3]

[3] This contradiction between names and principles was obvious even to intelligent foreigners. The French minister Fauchet, in his famous despatch to his government (the publication of which worked the downfall of Edmund Randolph, Washington's Secretary of State) alluding to political parties in America, speaks of the whimsical contrast between their names, Federal and Anti-Federal, and their real opinions;--the former aiming with all their power to annihilate federalism, while the latter were striving to preserve it.

Between these parties, thenceforth distinguished by the misnomers of Federalists and Anti-Federalists, there was, from the close of the war to the establishment of the present government, an uninterrupted succession of partisan conflicts, in which the whole country participated. They grew, for the most part, out of propositions to take from the State governments the rights of regulating commerce and of levying and collecting impost duties, and for the call of a Convention to revise the Articles of Confederation. The first two of these propositions were introduced by the Federalists, and for six years vigorously supported by their party, with Hamilton at its head; and, although advocated by Madison whilst he was in Congress, such was the strength of the

Anti-Federal party in that body and in the States that they were not able to carry either. Advances were occasionally made in respect to imposts, but these were so restricted as to the officers by whom the duties should be collected, whether State or Federal, and in regard to the application of the money when collected, that the movers of the principal measure considered its value so much impaired that they declined to push it further under the existing circumstances.

A distrust of the motives of the Federal leaders, and an apprehension that they designed to employ the powers asked for in the establishment of a strong and absorbing general government, capable of becoming, and which the Anti-Federalists feared would, in the progress of time, become, disposed to practice a tyranny upon the people, as oppressive as that from which the Revolution had relieved them, with the suspicion already referred to, that many would not be willing to stop at that point, were doubtless the true causes of these otherwise unaccountable failures. The accounts which have been brought down to us of the proceedings of public bodies, and of appeals to the people, through different channels, abundantly sustain this assumption. These, in a work like this, can only be glanced at.

The grounds taken by the opponents of these measures, and which, backed by popular suspicions, made them so powerful, were that the views of the Federalists were rather political than financial,--that they were at least as solicitous to gratify their well-understood passion for power, through the adoption of these propositions, as they were to maintain public credit. Beyond all doubt the belief that the government which the Federalists wished to create would, whatever it might be called, provide for the greatest practical extent of irresponsible power, led the Anti-Federalists not unfrequently to oppose measures which they would otherwise have supported.

General Hamilton's speech, most able as it was, went far to strengthen these impressions. The debate commenced on the 28th, and was continued to the 30th January, 1783, and was throughout one of great power. It resulted in the adoption, with slight amendments, of a proposition, submitted and vigorously supported by Mr. Madison, "That it is the opinion of Congress that the establishment of permanent and adequate funds to operate generally throughout the United States, is indispensably necessary for doing complete justice to the creditors of the United States, for restoring public credit, and for providing for the future exigencies of the war." Although this proposition finally passed without a dissenting vote, yet when an attempt was made to carry it into effect by an impost--the only way in which it was attempted--the measure was defeated, as has been before remarked, by restrictions in regard to the officers by whom it should be collected, and to the application of the money. In the course of his speech General Hamilton signified, as an additional reason why the impost ought to be collected by officers under the appointment of Congress, "that as the energy of the Federal Government was evidently short of the degree necessary for pervading and uniting the States, it was expedient to introduce the influence of officers deriving their emoluments from, and consequently interested in supporting the power of Congress."

Upon this Mr. Madison, in a note, observes: "This remark was imprudent and injudicious to the cause which it was meant to serve. This influence was the very source of jealousy which rendered the States averse to a revenue under the collection as well as appropriation of Congress. All the members of Congress who concurred in any degree with the States in this jealousy, smiled at the disclosure. Mr. Bland, and still more Mr. Lee, who were of this number, took notice in private conversation that Mr. Hamilton had let out the secret."[4]

[4] 1 Madison Papers, 291.

It is scarcely possible, at this distant day, to appreciate the terror of irresponsible and arbitrary power which had been impressed upon the minds of men who had themselves suffered from its excesses, or had witnessed the cruelties it had inflicted on others, or whose fathers had been victims of its crimes. Even Mr. Jefferson, who differed from the Anti-Federalists in respect to these questions, as I shall hereafter have occasion to show, though he sympathized with them in their general feelings, in a letter to Mr. Madison in December, 1787, from Paris, upon the subject of the Constitution, did not hesitate to say, "I own I am not a friend to a very energetic government. It is always oppressive."[5]

[5] 2 Jefferson's Correspondence, 276.

Similar feelings were exhibited by Massachusetts in 1785. That leading State in the confederacy was, during the whole of this period, strongly imbued with the feelings of the misnamed Anti-Federal party. This was in no small degree owing to the talents, zeal, and activity displayed in their behalf by Samuel Adams and John Hancock, two of the three persons (John Adams having been the third), who were excepted by the British Government from the offer of pardon to its rebellious subjects. Hancock was a leading merchant and a zealous Revolutionary patriot, who had the honor of placing his name first to the Declaration of Independence, and the higher honor of sustaining the contest which it provoked to its close with inflexible firmness and at unusual risks, growing out of his large interests in commerce. Samuel Adams was equal to any man of his day in intelligence, integrity, and patriotism. He was among the very first who embraced the Revolution in the sense which it finally assumed,--that of entire separation from the British Crown,--and he supported the principles upon which it was founded, as well during the conflict as for the residue of his long life, with great ability and unsurpassed devotion. Whilst many of his associates, not less sincere than himself in resistance to the despotic acts of the mother country, could yet express their admiration of the English system and were consequently inclined to limit their efforts to a redress of temporary grievances, he at the earliest period avowed his hostility to kingly government, and rallied around himself the advocates for an entire separation, most of whom became with him early and prominent members of the Anti-Federal party.

The legislature of Massachusetts, momentarily diverted from the Anti-Federal track by influences which will be noticed in another place, adopted a resolution urging Congress to recommend a convention of the States "to revise the Confederation, and to report how far it may be necessary in their opinion to alter and enlarge the same, in order to secure and perpetuate the primary objects of the Union." Governor Bowdoin, who had recommended the measure to the legislature in his message, addressed a letter to Congress including the resolution, and sent it to the delegates of the State to be presented by them. The delegates suspended its delivery, and assigned their reasons for doing so in a letter dated September 3, 1785, addressed to the Governor, with a request that it should be laid before the legislature. From this letter, which is ably written and occupies throughout Anti-Federal ground, I make the following extracts:--"The great object of the Revolution was the establishment of good government, and each of the States, in forming their own as well as the Federal Constitution, have adopted republican principles. Notwithstanding this, plans have been artfully laid and vigorously pursued, which, had they been successful, we think would have inevitably changed our republican governments into baleful aristocracies. These plans are frustrated, but the same spirit remains in their abettors; and the institution of Cincinnati, honorable and beneficent as the views may have been of the officers who composed it, we fear, if not totally abolished, will have the same tendency.... 'More power in Congress,' has been the cry from all quarters, but especially of those whose views, not being confined to a government that will best promote the happiness of the people, are extended to one that will afford lucrative employments, civil and military. Such a government is an aristocracy, which would require a standing army and a numerous train of pensioners and placemen to prop and support its exalted administration. To recommend one's self to such an administration would be to secure an establishment for life, and at the same time to provide for his posterity. These are pleasing prospects which republican governments do not afford, and it is not to be wondered at that many persons of elevated views and idle habits in these States are desirous of the change. We are for increasing the power of Congress as far as it will promote the happiness of the people; but at the same time, are clearly of opinion that every measure should be avoided which would strengthen the hands of the enemies to free government, and that an administration of the present Confederation, with all its inconveniences, is preferable to the risk of general dissensions and animosities, which may approach to anarchy and prepare the way to a ruinous system of government."

This letter of the delegates was laid before the legislature at their next session, and produced a vote annulling the resolution recommending a convention. The letter was signed by Elbridge Gerry, Samuel Holton, and Rufus King. Mr. King, in the course of the following year, married Miss Alsop, the only child of John Alsop, a wealthy merchant of New York, and after having represented his native State with credit in the Federal Convention of 1787, moved to that city; was appointed one of the first senators in Congress from the State of New York (General Schuyler being the other); was the friend and associate of Hamilton, Gouverneur Morris, and Jay, and became, and continued for many years, a prominent member of the Federal party.

Every step that was taken toward a convention was regarded with distrust,--a distrust founded on a prevalent apprehension that the talented and, as was believed, ambitious men who would get the control of it, would in some way defeat those republican principles for the right to establish which the country had made such great sacrifices.

The Commercial Convention, representing five States, which originated in Virginia and met at Annapolis, and by which the movement that resulted in the present Constitution was commenced, permitted Hamilton to draw up their Address to the other States, which was also to be laid before Congress; but insisted on giving a shape to their proposition which would confine the Federal Convention within narrow bounds. They did this in deference to the well understood sentiment of the country, and as the only course, in their opinion, by which a convention could be obtained; and accordingly they proposed "That a convention should be called to meet at Philadelphia in May next, to devise such further provisions as should appear to them necessary to render the Constitution of the Federal Government adequate to the exigencies of the Union, and to report such an act for that purpose to the United States in Congress assembled, as when agreed to by them, and afterwards confirmed by the legislatures of every State, will effectually provide for the same."[6]

[6] See Address; 2 Madison, 698. Not more than one, if one, of the five States was fully in favor of a Convention.

The final action of Congress upon the subject, a majority of which entertained similar views, consisted of a resolution, introduced by the delegates from Massachusetts, declaring it to be the opinion of Congress that a convention should be held at the time and place named by the Commissioners who met at Annapolis, "for the sole and express purpose of revising the Articles of Confederation, and reporting to Congress and the several legislatures such alterations and provisions therein as shall, when agreed to in Congress and confirmed by the States, render the Federal Constitution adequate to the exigencies of government and the preservation of the Union."[7]

[7] Journals of that Congress, Vol. IV. p. 724.

But for the sanction thus given to the measure by Congress no convention would have been held--at least none at that time. Washington, as appears from his Correspondence, would not have deemed a convention legal without it, and would not have attended;[8] and his example, added to the hesitation of most of the States, and the decided opposition of some of them, would have been sufficient to put a stop to the project.

It was under such circumstances that the Convention assembled. Its proceedings have become so familiar to the public mind, from the full publications that have been made of them, and the extent to which they have been reviewed, as to render it unnecessary to go very far into their details. The Anti-Federal plan was introduced by Mr. Patterson, of New Jersey, more in obedience to the ascertained wishes of his constituents, than in conformity with his particular views. It proposed an amendment of the Articles of Confederation for the construction of executive and judicial departments in the federal government; to make its laws and treaties the supreme law of the land; to increase the powers of Congress in several important particulars, among which were the right to levy and collect taxes and imposts, to regulate foreign commerce and commerce between the States, and to give to the federal government power to enforce its requisitions upon the States when it should become necessary,--and to leave the government in other respects as it stood.

The plan which Hamilton desired the Convention to propose to the people and the States, of which he left a copy with Mr. Madison as a permanent memorial of his opinions,--now published with Mr. Madison's "Papers," and in the "Life of Hamilton" by his son, and agreeing with each other in all respects,--consisted, in its most remarkable features, of the following provisions, viz:--

First: The President should hold his office during good behavior, removable only on conviction upon impeachment for some crime or misdemeanor; and he should have an absolute negative upon all bills, resolutions, and acts of Congress about to be passed into a law.

Secondly: The Senators should hold their offices by the same tenure, and should have the exclusive power of declaring war.

Thirdly: The General Government should have the right to appoint the future Governors of the States, who might hold their offices during good behavior, and who should have the power to negative all laws about to be passed by the respective State legislatures, subject to such regulations as Congress might prescribe, and also to appoint all the militia officers if Congress should so direct; and,

Fourthly: Congress should "have power to pass all laws which they shall judge necessary to the common defense and general welfare of the Union."

The first of these plans, which professed to represent the views of the Anti-Federalists, was rejected by the Convention, after full discussion, as has been already mentioned, by a vote of seven States to three, one being divided. Hamilton's scheme was not brought to a vote, nor, except by himself, made the subject of particular discussion. This course was obviously induced, in no small degree, by motives of respect for the feelings of its author. Every body praised his candor and independence, but the popular opinions in respect to its provisions were too well understood to allow of any vote, other than his own, being given in its favor, whatever private sympathy it may have enlisted.

Fortunately for the country at this, perhaps the most decisive period in its history, a majority of the Convention, composed of every shade of opinion, became thoroughly satisfied that a crisis had arrived which demanded a liberal sacrifice of extreme views. They were convinced that whilst, on the one hand, no system would stand the slightest chance to be acceptable to any thing like a majority either of the States or people, which was designed, or obnoxious to the suspicion of being designed, to degrade the State governments, or even to impair their capacities for the successful management of those portions of public affairs which, under a proper distribution of the powers of government, would be left under their control, or which was in the smallest degree calculated to do violence to the well-known feelings of the people upon the subjects of hereditary or irresponsible power; so, on the other, there was no room for two opinions in respect to the ruinous consequences that would, in the then condition of the country, inevitably result from the failure of a convention, brought together with so much difficulty, to remedy the manifest defects of the existing government by suitable and effectual additions and improvements, and to make a Constitution which would prove satisfactory both to the States and people. Kept together by this overruling conviction, they entered upon the construction of the present Constitution. The State governments had been until that period, in point of fact, the ruling power. The federal head, from the want of power to act directly upon the people, or, in a compulsory manner, upon the State authorities, was dependent on them for the execution of its most important decisions. Though much depressed by the adverse current of events, it was yet in the State governments that the pride of power stood relatively at the highest point. Any attempt, under such circumstances, to humiliate the State authorities, would inflame the passions of their supporters; but they might be, perhaps, to a sufficient extent conciliated, and the Convention prudently adopted this course. Irritating subjects were, with that view, as far as possible, avoided. Propositions to give to the new government a direct negative upon the legislation of the States, and to empower it to appoint their governors and militia officers, which had produced so much ill blood, were effectually discountenanced. The sovereignty of the States, to which State pride was so keenly alive, was not interfered with in respect to the powers of government which were left in their hands. An impartial and wise division of powers was made between them and the government proposed to be established. To remove apprehensions which had been long entertained, and which had sunk deep in the minds of many, the State authorities as such were allowed a liberal participation in the first formation, and their cooperation was made necessary to the subsequent continuance of the new government. The manner of choosing the electors of President and Vice-President was, with the same general view, left to the regulation of the State legislatures exclusively; and when a failure to choose by the electors should occur--a result then believed likely to happen frequently--the President was to be chosen by the House of Representatives of the United States, and, in the performance of that important duty, each State had reserved to it the right to appear and act in its federal character--that of a perfect equality with her sister States--whatever might be the difference in their respective population, territory, or wealth. The choice of the Senate of the United States was also left exclusively to the State legislatures. The result of all these arrangements was, that the Federal Constitution was so constructed as to put it in the power of a bare majority of the States to bring the government proposed by it to a peaceable end, without exposing their citizens to the necessity of resorting to force, by simply withholding the appointment of electors, or the choice of their Senators, or both.

No provisions could have been devised better calculated to remove apprehension and allay jealousy in respect to the new government. They hit the nail on the head. Although they might not avert the opposition of excited partisans, they answered the expectations of moderate men,--of that large class whose paramount object was the relief of the country as well as their own private affairs from the embarrassments under which they were suffering, and which were, as usual on such occasions, attributed altogether to the defects of the existing system. The question could with great propriety be put to Anti-Federal opponents (and doubtless was put),--Are you afraid to trust a numerical majority of the States? If not, they can at short intervals put an end to the new government if it proves to be as bad as you apprehend.

Having already, in a spirit of devotion to duty and a hazardous disregard of responsibility which was made necessary by the occasion, set aside the instructions of Congress by making a new Constitution, the Convention pursued a similar course to the end. Instead of reporting the result of their labors to Congress for its approval and submission to the States for their unanimous sanction, according to the Articles of Confederation, as was proposed at Annapolis and provided by Congress in the act of sanction to the holding of the Convention, that body sent the instrument it had framed to Congress, not for its approval, but to be by it submitted to the States and people in the first instance, under a provision, prescribed by the Convention, that if it was ratified by nine of the thirteen States it should be binding upon all,--an heroic though perhaps a lawless act.

The dangerous condition of the country, and the general opinion that some decided step was necessary to its safety, added to the imposing character of the instrument itself, which, though not satisfactory to Congress, was yet far less objectionable than had been anticipated, and a general expectation that important amendments rendering it still more acceptable to the people would follow its ratification, deterred the national legislature from refusing to comply with the request of the Convention, notwithstanding its flagrant disregard of congressional authority. The same considerations should have induced the Anti-Federal party to acquiesce in the ratification of the Constitution. They should have looked upon the marked effect of that instrument upon Congress as a prophetic warning of the danger to which they would expose themselves as a party by opposing it. But they did not see their duty, or, perhaps, their interests, in that light; honest in their intentions and obstinate in their opinions, they opposed the ratification, were defeated, and, as a party, finally overthrown.

The Anti-Federal party represented very fairly the ideas and feelings that prevailed with the masses during the Revolution. These, as we have described, having been deeply rooted by the persecutions suffered by Puritan, Huguenot,

Hussite, and Dutch ancestors, and, however crude and unsystematized at first, having been gradually stimulated into maturity and shape by the persevering injustice of the mother country, became political opinions of the most tenacious and enduring character. At the moment of which we are speaking, alarm in respect to the character of the General Government about to be established, with increased attachments to those of the States, were predominant feelings in the Anti-Federal mind, and closed it against a dispassionate consideration of the Constitution submitted to their choice. The local governments were entitled to all the regard which had been cherished for them by the Anti-Federalists and by their political predecessors under the colonial system; neither were the dangers which threatened them overrated. Hamilton could not tolerate the idea that they should be continued otherwise than as corporations, with very limited powers. Morris, in his usual rough and strong way, was for "drawing their teeth," as I have already quoted him; and even the temperate Madison was in favor of giving the General Government a direct negative upon all their laws,--a proposition which, though not so humiliating as Hamilton's, or so harshly expressed as that of Morris, would have been far more fatal to their future usefulness. Standing now on the vantage-ground of experience, no sensible man can fail to see that the State governments would have perished under the treatment thus proposed for them, nor can any such man doubt the immense advantage they have been and still are to our system. A short reflection upon what has been accomplished through their agency, and upon what our condition would probably have been if they had been blotted out of the system, as was virtually desired in most influential quarters, must satisfy candid and intelligent minds of the fatal unsoundness of the policy proposed. The States would under it have been governed as her numerous colonies were governed by Rome, and a comparison of our present condition with what it must have been under the satraps of a consolidated federal government, will cause every patriotic heart to rejoice at our escape from the latter. For that escape we are largely indebted to the old Anti-Federal party. They stood out longest and strongest in behalf of the State governments, after the establishment of our Independence; and although they failed in other respects, they made impressions upon the public mind which have never been effaced, and for which we owe them a debt of gratitude. Their motives, as is usual in political collisions, were misrepresented; they were spoken of as men of contracted views, of narrow prejudices; and their preference for the State governments was attributed to the preponderance they possessed in them, and to a consciousness that their greatness and power were derived from local prejudices and from their skill in fomenting them. Hence was inferred their hostility to an efficient federal government, whose extensive affairs they were incapable of managing, and in which, consequently, it was alleged that they would not retain the influence they possessed at home.

Although I unite fully in condemning the course pursued by the Anti-Federalists in respect as well to the Constitution as to their refusal to grant an adequate revenue to the federal head, and the right to regulate commerce, I regard those imputations which ascribed to them a readiness to sacrifice the great interests of the country to merely factious purposes, as the ebullitions of party spleen produced by party jealousies, as unjust and unfounded as was the charge brought forward by the old Republican party against Alexander Hamilton of a design to plunge the country into war with France to subserve the wishes and interests of England. I do not think there were ten in every hundred of that party who did not believe that imputation well founded, and most of them went to their graves without having yielded that conviction. I came upon the political stage when this matter was only viewed in the retrospect, and am free to say that I even believed that, if there was any thing true in the party criminations of the preceding era, this was so. Judge, then, of my surprise, on discovering from his papers, as well as from those of some of his contemporaries recently published, that there was probably no man in the country more sincerely anxious to prevent a war with France; that he applied his great mind incessantly to that object; that he was willing, indeed desirous, to send either Mr. Jefferson or Mr. Madison as one of the commissioners to negotiate with France, a proposition in respect to which he could not obtain the concurrence of either Mr. Adams or his cabinet, the latter of whom were sufficiently prompt to adopt his advice save when it conflicted with their party prejudices; and that so far from acting on that occasion at the instigation or to promote the policy of Great Britain, although entertaining strong--in my opinion too strong--preferences for England as between her and France, he was, in respect to every thing that affected the interests of his own country, purely and strictly American. Of this no man, whose mind is not debauched by prejudice, can entertain a doubt on reading the papers referred to.

The imputations upon the motives of the Anti-Federalists were of the same general stamp and origin. It was too soon for those who were yet fresh from the self-sacrificing and patriotic struggle on the field of the Revolution, where they had nobly done their duty, to fall under the influence of such petty motives as were attributed to them. Like their opponents, they might and did peril much of their own standing to further political views of great magnitude which they honestly, if erroneously, believed would promote the welfare of their country; but base incentives and merely factious calculations are not predicable of the times or of the men.

We should be slow to attribute narrow views to a political party to whose principal leaders, more than to any other portion of the Whigs, we owe the great change in the character of our Revolutionary struggle by which the assertion of Independence was substituted for the demand of a redress of grievances.

If the Anti-Federal party had been accused of cherishing morbid and impracticable ideas on the subject of a general government, the charge would have come nearer the truth. Many of them had so vivid a recollection of cruelties practiced upon their fathers, and had themselves seen and felt so much of the tyranny of the mother country, as to destroy all hope on their part that political power could be vested in remote hands, without the certainty of its being abused. Although they may have been right in respect to the monarchical preferences of many who were the most zealous for a convention, still they overrated the danger that such views would be encouraged by that body, and in their apprehensions of subsequent efforts to establish monarchical institutions here, they did not sufficiently appreciate an existing security against the accomplishment of such an object, the character and adequacy of which shall be hereafter noticed. We have every reason to believe that they regarded the project of a general convention as involving, if successful, the fate of republican principles in this country; and under the influence of feelings of so sombre a character, their course, as a party, was, it must be admitted, substantially adverse to any change, content rather to bear the ills they had than to encounter others of which they knew not the precise extent, but which they dreaded more. In this they fell behind the progress of events.

If our Revolutionary contest had terminated in a compromise with the mother country, as was for a long time expected, the existing system, with the amendments which would then have been generally favored, might have sufficed. It might have answered all the purposes contemplated by that which Franklin took so much pains to establish in 1755. But when our country had taken her position among the nations of the earth as a sovereign and independent power, she acquired rights and incurred obligations which could not be properly cared for by any agency short of a well-constructed and efficient general government, and the existing organization was neither. By an efficient government I do not mean one capable of absorbing or neutralizing the State authorities, or not fully responsible for the faithful exercise of the powers conferred upon it, or possessing more power than was necessary for the discharge of all the duties assigned to it, but one amply furnished with the ability to discharge them by its own means. To this end it was necessary that it should have competent and well organized executive, legislative, and judicial departments, and at least the power requisite to raise its necessary revenues from the people directly. To all this the Anti-Federal party was opposed, and therein it was wrong. The risk of having exceptionable principles incorporated into the Constitution was one that had to be encountered at some time, and there were cogent reasons for meeting it then. The condition of the country, in regard to its credit and other interests, presented an argument of great urgency for the necessity of a competent government. But above all other considerations stood the fact that the Convention had proposed for the approval of the people and the States a constitution which, when interpreted according to its plain and obvious meaning, conferred on the government proposed by it powers fully adequate to the public service, but none from which danger could be apprehended to any interest. That this was so is no longer an open question. Time and experience have demonstrated the error of the Anti-Federalists, who, under the influence of strong prejudices, although doubtless honestly, thought differently. No one will now question the devotion of the people, for whose benefit it was framed, and who are the best judges in the matter, to the existing system. With full power to alter or abolish it, they have lived under it for the greater part of a century, without making or desiring to make any essential alterations in its structure. By the exercise of those powers only which were plainly given by the Constitution to the government established by its authority and expressed on its face, in regard to which there has been no dispute, and which were at the times of its adoption well understood by those who made and those who adopted it, our country has prospered and grown to its present greatness. I say by those powers only, because the spurious interpolations which have from time to time been attempted have in no instance been productive of good.

The Convention was held with closed doors, and the result of its labors was not known to the public before it was communicated to Congress, nor the particulars of its proceedings, the votes, resolutions, and speeches, till many years afterwards. The public mind, and especially the Anti-Federal portion of it, was impressed by those circumstances, operating upon long entertained suspicions, with the most unfavorable anticipations in respect to the character of the instrument that had been agreed upon. All found it so different from what it was feared by many that it would be, and so many received it according to its real merits, that it carried a large preponderance of the public sentiment, drawn from both parties, to the conclusion that it ought not to be, and could not with safety be rejected. The reflection of this sentiment was distinctly seen in the action of Congress. It had given its assent to the holding of a Convention, without which that body would not have met; but it had, as we have seen, restricted its action in two most important points: 1st, that the Convention should limit its action to a revision of the Articles of Confederation and to suggestions for their improvement; and, 2d, that its doings should be reported to Congress, to be submitted to the States, under those Articles which required the assent of every State to any alteration. The Convention disregarded both; it sent to Congress a new constitution, regulated its submission to the States, and decided that the assent of nine of the thirteen should make it binding upon all. Congress, with its resolutions and limitations thus set at nought, and without even a protest, did what was asked of it. Yet the leaders of the Anti-Federal party in the States determined upon opposition. The course and character of that opposition indicate that those who embarked in it were conscious of their approaching defeat.

In the three largest and most strongly Anti-Federal States, in which the power of that party, when cordially united, was irresistible, the Constitution was ratified. It was adopted by the required number of States, and the fate of the Anti-Federal party, as such, was forever sealed by the result of the contest in which it had unwisely engaged.

CHAPTER II.

The Federal Party in Power under the New Constitution--Agency of Individuals in the Formation and Ratification of the latter--Prospects of the Opening Administration of the Government--Unwise Course of the Federal Party--President Washington--His Peculiar Relations with the People and with Parties--His first Cabinet--Character of the Differences between Jefferson and Hamilton--The latter sustained--Hamilton's Position, Power, and Influence upon the subsequent Course of Parties--His Monarchical Views--Various Authorities in Relation to the latter--Fidelity of Washington to the Republican Form of Government--Importance of correctly Understanding the Extent of Hamilton's Influence during the Administrations of Washington and John Adams--Personal and Official Relations between Washington and Members of his Cabinet--Evidences of the Spread of Monarchical Views among Officers and Public Men in Washington's Time--His Steadfast Adherence to the last to the Republican Form--His Permanent Hold upon the Affections of the People, even while they repudiated certain Leading Principles of his Administration.

The period in our political history to which our inquiry has conducted us, was one of the greatest interest. The successful effort that had been made to compel Great Britain to acknowledge our Independence; the government of the Confederation, and the causes that led to its abandonment; the grave step taken in a better direction by the formation and ratification of the new Constitution, with the hopes and fears excited by the last great movement, were well calculated to impress profoundly the minds of those who had been actors in such important scenes. The success of the Federal party in the first election held under the new Constitution was complete. For the first time since its organization, that party possessed the unrestricted control of the national legislature. If any thing could have been thought wanting to insure its permanent success, that was believed to be secured by the consent of General Washington to be the first President of the new government about to be organized under a constitution, to the paternity of which they had established so fair a claim. Neither the formation nor the ratification of that instrument were altogether the work of avowed members of that party; but as between the two parties they had clearly the best title to be regarded as its authors. The merits of individuals in that great work were various. Alexander Hamilton, the able and undisputed leader of the Federal party, from its origin to his death, did comparatively nothing either toward its formation or adoption by the Federal Convention. His most useful services were rendered in the New York State Convention, by which it was ratified, and in his contributions to the numbers of "The Federalist." These were formally declared as the measure of his services in that regard, in reply to a direct inquiry long after Hamilton's death, by his best informed and always devoted friend, Gouverneur Morris, as will be seen hereafter. It was, beyond all doubt, from Madison that the Constitution derived its greatest aid in respect as well to its construction as to its passage through the Convention, and its ratification by the States.

The character and political career of James Madison were sui generis--as much so as though far different from those of John Randolph. Possessed of intellectual powers inferior to none, and taking an unsurpassed interest in the course of public affairs, he seemed invariably to bring to the discussion of public questions a thoroughly unprejudiced mind. Whilst in the speeches of his contemporaries we seldom fail to perceive that the argument submitted was framed to support a foregone conclusion,--to recommend a measure for which the speaker cherished a personal preference,--it is rare indeed, if ever, that any such indications are to be found in those of Mr. Madison. Whilst the former present themselves as advocates, the latter appears in the attitude of an umpire between rival opinions, who has made it his business to search for the truth, and is determined to abide the result of his investigations, uninfluenced in the formation of his decision by preferences or prejudices of any description. The most acute observer in reviewing the writings, speeches, and votes of Mr. Madison during the exciting periods of which we are speaking, when governments as well as individuals were to an unusual extent in a state of transition, would find it difficult to place his finger upon any of them in respect to which the justice of this description would not be manifest.

Mr. John Quincy Adams, in his Jubilee Address, heretofore alluded to, describes Mr. Madison and General Hamilton as being, at this period, "spurred to the rowels by ambition."[9] Both of these gentlemen were, doubtless, ambitious of the fame which is acquired by serving one's country honestly and efficiently, and we have no sufficient reason for assuming that Mr. Adams meant more than that. It is, nevertheless, but justice to those truly great men to add that so far as high-reaching ambition is indicated by abjuring unpopular opinions and assuming those which are believed to be otherwise; by professing attachment to principles not really cherished for their own sake, or by personal intrigues of any description to acquire or increase popular favor, I sincerely believe that there were no two men of their day less liable to the imputation. Mr. Madison's course at the period of which we are speaking and during his antecedent public life, was, to a remarkable extent, divested of a partisan character. He supported, ably and perseveringly, many, if not most of the propositions for the adoption of which the Federal party was particularly solicitous, whilst representing one of the most decided Anti-Federal States in the Confederacy, without losing the confidence of his constituents, or even hazarding its loss. He was, throughout, in favor of giving to the federal head an independent right to levy and collect its necessary revenue and to regulate commerce, and was from the beginning in favor of a convention to revise the Constitution. In that body he was one of the majority in favor of the course I have described, and which resulted in the present Constitution. His successful and brilliant efforts in favor of the new system of government placed him at the head of its friends; but there was no time when Mr. Madison can, with truth and fairness, be said to have belonged to the Federal party; he all the time represented a State which took the lead in opposition to that school, his political affinities and associations were in general adverse to that organization, and, as I have said, he never forfeited the good opinion of his State. She seems always to have confided in his sincerity and in the integrity of his motives, and to have been willing to allow him to follow the dictates of his own judgment in regard to particular measures.

[9] Mr. Van Buren, in making the above quotation from the Jubilee Address, doubtless relied upon his memory. "Both spurred to the rowels by rival and antagonist ambition," are the words used by Mr. Adams; but they, in fact, refer distinctly to Jefferson and Hamilton, though Mr. Madison's name is incidentally coupled with that of the latter in the same sentence. Eds.

The most auspicious prospects beamed upon the opening administration of the new government, and it is fair to presume that the anticipations thus inspired would have been triumphantly realized if those who had been selected to conduct it, and their successors for the ensuing twelve years, had accepted the Constitution in the sense in which it was known to have been understood by those who framed it, and by the people when they adopted it. A course thus right in itself, and thus acquiescent in the popular will by men, some of whom had been long suspected by many of their Revolutionary associates of not holding that will in very high respect, would not have failed to conciliate large portions of the Anti-Federal party. Their dread of the exercise of unauthorized power by a general government, of which the responsibility was, in their estimation, too remote to be safely trusted, and their apprehensions for the safety of State institutions, always an object of their greatest solicitude, might have been allayed, if not substantially subdued. These valuable objects accomplished, the great improvements in the condition as well of public as of individual affairs, unavoidably flowing from the reasonably harmonious action of a government which the Federal party had done so much to establish, and the crowning fact that these gratifying results were brought about in the name, and with the active cooperation of Washington, the object of universal respect and affection, would have secured to that party through the long lapse of time that has since intervened, at least as large a share in the control of the government as has been possessed by a party which became its successful rival, but which can scarcely be said to have then existed.

But the Federal party rashly turned its back upon the only course by which these advantages might have been secured, and in doing so, showed itself regardless of considerations which would not have escaped the attention of more discreet, if not wiser bodies. Its influential and leading men forgot that the administration did not, in point of fact, represent the political opinions in respect to the proper uses and spirit of governments in general of a majority of the people; that their party had acquired power solely by its wise course in regard to a single, though doubtless most important measure; and that even in respect to that large portions of the people felt, as expressed by John Quincy Adams, "that the Constitution itself had been extorted from the grinding necessity of a reluctant nation." The Federal party took its course also in momentary forgetfulness of the characters of those whose opinions it was about to violate, whose feelings were to be offended, and whose resentments it must incur. It overlooked what it had the fullest reason to know, that those whom it was about to drive into opposition were men, and the descendants of men, who had from the beginning, and at all times, and under all circumstances, been enthusiasts in devotion to liberty, and stern and uncompromising in demanding stringent restrictions upon delegated authority,--as inflexible in their opinions, and as incapable of being driven from their support by the hand of power, or seduced by corruption, as human nature could be made in the schools of fiery trial in which they had been trained. The Federalists in power, or rather he who, through the great confidence of his chief, wielded that power, did nothing, if we except the personal efforts of Washington in favor of conciliation, absolutely nothing to soothe the feelings of their defeated opponents, or to allay their apprehensions, but much to exacerbate the former and to confirm the latter.

The justice of these allegations is fully proved by the acts of the public men of that day. From the official position of the first President, and the part he consequently took in the management of public affairs, a faithful survey of these cannot be made without embracing him in the review. This is treading upon privileged ground. No American, no good man, can approach it without feeling that it is such, or without being embarrassed by the apprehension that, however pure his intention, he may undesignedly outrage the sentiments of admiration and reverence by which it is naturally and properly intrenched. General Washington retired gracefully from his military command, with more true glory than ever fell to the lot of man. There have, doubtless, at times, appeared military leaders of more professional genius and science, but never one better adapted to the high duties to which he was called; never one of whom it could with more truth be said, to use a modern and comprehensive expression, that he was "the right man in the right place." Certainly without his seeking it, and doubtless against his wishes, he was transferred to the civil service of his country by his election to the office of President under the new Constitution. The administration, of which he thus became the constitutional head, adopted certain measures, proposed others, and set up claims to power under that instrument, of which many of his countrymen and personal friends could not approve, and which they felt themselves obliged to oppose; these, in the progress of time and events, became organized as a political party by which those objectionable measures and claims of power were perseveringly resisted, but without any diminution of respect for his character, position, and feelings. They overthrew the administration of his successor, which claimed to act upon his principles, succeeded to the control of the Federal Government, and have kept it ever since, with rare and limited exceptions, attributable to special causes.

There is, notwithstanding, in this great country, no hamlet, town, city, or place in which American citizens congregate, where the name of Washington is ever pronounced without the profoundest reverence, or in which there does not prevail an undying sense of gratitude for his public services. The history of the world will be searched in vain for a tribute of love and gratitude at all comparable to that which the people of the United States have rendered to him who was the commander of their armies in the war of the Revolution, and their first republican chief magistrate--a tribute, in paying which the only contest between political parties is as to which shall manifest the most zeal, and which shall attain the highest success.

Was ever before so great and so gratifying reward bestowed, including in its wide extent the noble, exalted, and well-won title of Pater Patriae! This, the highest honor that man can receive on earth, was not, as of old, a title given to an adored chief by victorious soldiers who, however renowned for their valor, were always open to the influence of personal and temporary feelings; nor was it obtained through the instrumentality of a venal senate; neither did it originate in state-craft or priest-craft, which have in every age paid homage to the great men of the world for selfish and sinister purposes. The high honors paid to Washington proceeded from no such sources, nor were they exposed to the suspicions from which such bestowments are rarely free. They sprang from the disinterested and deliberate judgment of an intelligent, virtuous, and free people, who felt that he had, in his military capacity alone, done incomparably more than any other man for the establishment of their Independence, and that in all his civil service he had been actuated by the same upright motives which had governed his whole previous career, and that in that sphere also, as in every act of his life, he had placed the performance of public duties and the advancement of public interests before all other earthly considerations. Although many of them had differed from him in respect to some measures which had received his sanction, they were not on that account the less satisfied that he had, in the exercise of a rightful discretion, been influenced only by an earnest desire to promote the welfare of his country. So regarding his whole career, they with one accord gave him the highest place on the roll of fame and the first in their hearts.

This spontaneous and ample recognition of a debt of imperishable gratitude to a public benefactor, whose modesty was equal to his unsurpassed merit, was the act of a people often misrepresented, and as often misunderstood, but who have never been found wanting, in the end, in what was due to faithful public servants, to themselves, or to their political institutions.

We are, perhaps, yet too near the period of these great transactions to pronounce safely upon the general justice of their dealings with the contemporaries of Washington. But when time shall have relieved the subject more thoroughly from the adverse influences of family connections and partisan feelings, I have not a doubt that some American historian, loving his country and admiring the character of his countrymen, will take pleasure in holding up to the world a picture of the distribution of popular confidence and popular favors in their case also, which may safely be compared with that drawn from the history of any people.

Unbelievers may gainsay, and disappointed aspirants may rail at these deductions, but they nevertheless do no more than justice to the character of our people, before whom every public question and the acts and opinions of every public man, be he whom he may, may be freely canvassed. All that can be asked of him who seeks to vindicate and perpetuate the truth of history, is that he shall deal justly and candidly with his subject. From a scrutiny so conducted, no citizen will ask or expect that any public transaction, or the course of any public man shall be exempted.

No man could have accepted office with fewer temptations to depart from the line of duty than offered themselves to President Washington. His claims to the admiration of his countrymen and of the world were complete; reasonable in all his desires and happy in his domestic relations, he was possessed of property beyond either his wants or his desires, and was without children to inherit his estate or to succeed to the glories already attached to his name. The advantages to be derived by a republican magistrate from the consciousness of occupying such a position and of its being also appreciated by his constituents, are very great. The confidence inspired by these considerations was also strengthened by the fact that in the high and responsible stations in which he had been placed he had never failed to increase the good-will and respect of those by whom he had been appointed. But these circumstances of encouragement did not blind his cautious mind to a proper sense of the difficulties incident to the new duties he had assumed and to his want of experience in regard to them. In addition to the command of all the military force in the country in a more plenary form than that in which he had before possessed it, he was now intrusted with the superintendence and direction of large portions of the domestic and of all the foreign concerns of a great people just taking their position in the family of nations. First on the list of his responsible duties stood that of organizing a government constructed upon new and to a great extent untried principles, at a moment when the tendency of the French Revolution had been sufficiently developed to threaten political convulsions more portentous and more difficult to be dealt with than any that the world had ever witnessed; and he was called to the performance of this delicate task amidst party dissensions at home of the most violent nature, which many people apprehended might extend to a revolution in the character of the government itself. Firm in all his purposes Washington did not shrink from the application of his well-balanced mind to a survey of the difficulties that stood in his way, in making which no exaggerated estimate of his own capacities prevented him from foreseeing the embarrassments that might arise, and to some extent must arise, from the difference in the nature of many of the duties he was now called upon to discharge from those with which his past public life had made him familiar; and I have always thought that, among the great transactions of his career, there was scarcely one in which were exhibited more strikingly the strength of his judgment and the nobleness of his disposition, than in the formation of his first Cabinet.

It is difficult for one not particularly conversant with such matters to realize the obstructions which not unfrequently present themselves in the work of forming a good cabinet. These are sometimes the consequence of an overestimate of his own qualifications on the part of the chief magistrate elect, and a resulting disinclination to bring into the government men whose prominence before the country and whose great accomplishments as statesmen may depress his own importance in the action of the administration. This feeling, when it exists in only a moderate degree, is certain to be encouraged by the flatteries of friends, or more often by selfish men for the purpose of promoting their designs upon the patronage at the disposal of the incumbent. Against the dangerous influences of these classes President Washington was effectually guarded by elements in his own character decidedly unpropitious to both. But he was not so free from embarrassments arising from another source. He was at the commencement of his government surrounded by his fellow-soldiers, the officers of the army of the Revolution,--veterans who had acquired high consideration by their meritorious services, and were endeared to him by their personal characters and their past and present sufferings. They were generally men whose judgments he could not but respect, and who, like their class in all countries, were not disposed to consider the aid of civilians in the administration of public affairs as imperatively necessary. The actual state of the country also, in regard to its party divisions and dissensions, was, as I have already said, perhaps the greatest source of perplexity and trouble.

Not discouraged by these difficulties, he proceeded to the formation of his cabinet in a spirit of patriotism and good sense, manifesting an anxious desire to allay, if he could not neutralize, the violence of party spirit, and to enlist in the administration of the new government and secure to the public service those of highest character and talents who belonged to, or were disposed to sympathize with, the party which had opposed the Constitution. With these noble views, he divided his cabinet equally between gentlemen of that school and members of the Federal party, and equally also between civilians and military men. For the two most responsible, as well as most difficult offices, to which were assigned duties least familiar to himself, he selected two gentlemen, who from their active patriotism and distinguished talents occupied high, if not the highest positions in the country, had already been placed at the head of the rival and conflicting opinions which divided it, and of whose personal uprightness and political independence he was well assured.

Down to the period which we have now reached, President Washington had, to a remarkable extent, kept himself aloof from partisan strife. This was partly owing to his great self-command and to his perception of the incompatibility of a participation in that field of action with the positions he occupied in the public service; and possibly, to some extent, to anticipations, not unnatural, that the future held in store for him a fame which would soar above parties. He had seen and known too much of men to allow himself to hope that the cabinet he had selected would be entirely free from disunion, or from those distractions likely to arise from the conflicting materials of which it was composed; but he did not at first appreciate fully the extent and bearing of the differences that existed between the opinions and public views of Jefferson and Hamilton. Hoping that these would be confined to particular points in the administration of affairs, he doubtless relied upon his personal influence to soothe the asperities they might produce, and at least to limit their adverse effect to the measures to which they might be from time to time applied. His confidence in this regard was well warranted by his past good fortune in removing obstacles that threatened injury to the country, by means of the general respect that was paid to his opinions and wishes by all classes of his countrymen. His success in allaying the spirit of insubordination that manifested itself among the officers of the army at Newburgh and for a season menaced seriously the character of the army and the peace of the country; in arresting a design which was supposed to be on foot in Congress, to make the sufferings and consequent indignation of the troops subservient to the promotion of the financial schemes of civilians; and in dispersing the storm which threatened to follow the establishment of the Cincinnati, with its hereditary honors, strikingly justified his confidence in the efficacy of any future efforts in the same direction.

More could not have been done, or in a better spirit, than Washington did to preserve harmony between the two leading members of his cabinet, and to secure their cooperation in the public service. No steps, consistent with a proper self-respect, as it now appears, were omitted on his part. If the differences in their views had been less radical these friendly efforts and applications must have succeeded, received as they were by both in the most becoming and grateful spirit.

But these commendable exertions were doomed to an unavoidable and final disappointment. The President might as well have attempted to combine the elements of fire and water as to secure a harmonious action in the administration of the Government between Jefferson and Hamilton. The antagonistic opinions of these great men upon the subjects of government and its proper administration were too profoundly planted in their breasts, and they were both too honest to depart from them without a corresponding change in their convictions, which there was no reason to anticipate, to admit of a hope for a different result.

Of the nature and extent of their differences of opinion it is my purpose to attempt some explanation in another place; but here I will only say, as I desire to say in advance, that I do not now believe, whatever my impression may have been, that they originated in any difference as to the objects at which they aimed, or that those objects, in either case, were other than the welfare and happiness of those for whom they were selected to act. They may have differed in opinion in respect to the condition, social and political, in which the mass of the people would be most likely to be prosperous and happy; they certainly did so, and that very widely, in regard to the public measures by which that prosperity and happiness would be promoted or diminished; and that diversity in their opinions arose mainly from their conflicting estimates of the capacity of the people for self-government. Upon that point they were opposed diametrically, and that opposition produced an unavoidable antagonism in their views of almost every public question.

In a conversation between these gentlemen in 1791, to which a more particular reference will be made hereafter, General Hamilton thus expressed himself:--"For that mind must be really depraved which would not prefer the equality of political rights, which is the foundation of pure republicanism, if it can be obtained consistently with order." This was, I do not in the least doubt, his real sentiment; but unhappily circumstances, to which we may hereafter recur, had impressed his mind with a conviction, which was never removed, that the great desideratum which he mentioned--the preservation of order-- could not be secured where the control of public affairs was largely in the hands of the people. He very correctly regarded the security of the rights of persons and of property as an indispensable ingredient in good government; and distrusting the respect of the people, when acting in masses, for both, he was adverse to that equality of rights which he truly said was "the foundation of pure republicanism." These great objects he thought could in no other way be secured than by a strong government, in which there would be what he called a "stable will," independent of popular control. This he endeavored openly, and with a candor that belonged to his character, to obtain in the Convention, and failing there, he hoped to realize its advantages, in some degree, by strengthening what he described as the "organs" of the Government, through the action of a popular President and a good administration. The most important of the measures by which he designed to accomplish these objects Mr. Jefferson regarded as so many violations of the Constitution, and he looked upon the spirit in which they had their origin as evidence of disaffection to republican government, the differences in opinion between these master spirits of the cabinet, who engrossed a share of the attention of the people inferior only to that paid to the President, were therefore, not limited as Washington hoped they would be, to particular measures but presented contradictory and irreconcilable theories for the administration of the Government, which could not even be discussed in the cabinet without producing interminable distractions. As was to be expected from minds like their respective systems left no middle ground, and required the adoption of the one or the other as a rule of action for the Government. The unavoidable obligation to make a selection between them devolved therefore on Washington, and he discharged it, as he did all his duties, courteously and firmly. He gave the preference to Hamilton, and sustained him in the measures he proposed to carry out the policy he recommended.

Mr. Jefferson, sensible that the necessity of his retirement from the cabinet had thus become absolute, determined to take that step in a way as little annoying to the President and as little injurious to the public service as possible. To this end he gave early notice that he would resign at the expiration of the President's first term of office; and when that time arrived he retired. This left General Hamilton without any check from his associates in the administration, save what might proceed from the Attorney General, Edmund Randolph, who became Secretary of State on Jefferson's retirement, and of whom the latter said that his habit was to give his opinions to his friends and his votes to his opponents.

Thus, next to Washington, Alexander Hamilton became the most powerful man in the nation, abundantly able to give to party divisions their form and pressure, and in effect to shape the action of the Government according to his judgment by the authority with which he was invested, and which he exerted with less restraint than had ever before or has ever since been encountered by any minister in this country or in Europe.

To no quarter, therefore, could our attention be more profitably directed for instruction in the history and course of parties during his political career than to the opinions and acts of that remarkable man. The time has been, I am sensible, when, with vision distorted by partisan prejudices, which seldom allow both sides of any question to be seen, I could not have reviewed his course with the impartiality due to truth and justice; but I am happy to believe that those feelings have sufficiently lost their force to permit me, while dissenting more thoroughly than ever from his principles, to do justice to his motives, and to admit his sincerity and his desire to serve his country in the very acts which I unreservedly condemn. The most obnoxious of his opinions have here, thank God, become obsolete and exploded theories, not at all dangerous as examples, and mainly referred to as historical marks of our progress. Believing, as I think all liberal minds now do, that they were honestly formed, we can speak of them without reproach to their author, and censure them without being suspected of a design to cast obloquy on his memory. The history of our partisan warfare has presented, since his time, the anomalous feature of a persevering denial in his name, by some of his followers, of the political opinions which he not only did not affect to disclaim, but which he made it his business on all fitting occasions to publish and advocate, believing them to be right, and to the last moment of his life confidently expecting that they would become, at no distant day, the general sentiment of the country.

I have already referred to contemporaneous declarations, made in April, 1791, by John Adams and Alexander Hamilton, at an informal meeting of General Washington's Cabinet, to which the Vice-President had been invited, in favor of monarchical institutions according to the English model. The terms in which those gentlemen expressed their admiration of, and preference for, the English system of government, though differing in particulars, were in no sense equivocal, nor can there be, at this day, the slightest doubt of their authenticity. On the 13th of August, in the same year, General Hamilton held another conversation with Mr. Jefferson, of which the latter leaves the following notes:--

"I own," said Hamilton, "it is my own opinion, though I do not publish it in Dan or Beersheba, that the present government is not that which will answer the ends of society by giving stability and protection to its rights, and that it will probably be found to be expedient to go into the British form. However, since we have undertaken the experiment, I am for giving it a fair course, whatever my expectations may be. The success, indeed, is so far greater than I had expected, and therefore success seems more possible than it had done heretofore, and there are still other and other stages of improvement which, if the present does not succeed, may be tried and ought to be tried before we give up the republican form altogether; for that mind must be really depraved which would not prefer the equality of political rights, which is the foundation of pure republicanism, if it can be obtained consistently with order. Therefore whoever by his writings disturbs the present order of things is really blamable, however pure his intentions may be, and he was sure Mr. Adams's were pure."

"This," Mr. Jefferson adds in his memorandum, "is the substance of a declaration made in much more lengthy terms, and which seemed to be more formal than usual for a private conversation between two, and as if intended to qualify some less guarded expressions which had been dropped on former occasions. Thomas Jefferson has committed it to writing the moment of Alexander Hamilton's leaving the room."

The measures described by Hamilton as the stages of improvement already adopted were doubtless the bank and funding system, and those still in reserve were such as are recommended in his report on manufactures, subsequently made.

In the Federal Convention which framed our present Constitution General Hamilton submitted a series of propositions to be adopted as a basis for the new government, which he supported in an elaborate and very able speech. The debates of the Convention were reported by Mr. Madison, who submitted the notes he had taken of his speech to General Hamilton, which the latter admitted to be correct, contenting himself with a few formal and verbal amendments. In the year 1810, before the proceedings of the Convention were ordered to be published, the Rev. Dr. Mason, intending to write the life of Hamilton, applied to Mr. Madison, then President of the United States, for a copy of that speech, which was furnished to him accompanied by the following note:--

"James Madison presents his respects to Dr. Mason with the promised copy of Mr. Hamilton's observations in the General Convention on the subject of a Federal Constitution, as noted at the time."

"WASHINGTON, January 12th, 1810."

Dr. Mason abandoned the idea of preparing the life, and a descendant of his, a few years since, placed in my hands two of the documents collected by his grandfather, one of which was the above note with a copy of the speech. The following are extracts from the latter:--

"This view of the subject almost led him to despair that a republican government could be established over a country of so great an extent. He was sensible at the same time that it would be unwise to propose one of any other form. In his private opinion he had no scruple in declaring, supported as he was in the opinion of so many of the wise and the good, that the British government was the best in the world; and he doubted very much whether any thing short of it would do in America."

Speaking of the executive, he said: "As to the executive it seemed to be admitted that no good one could be established on republican principles. Was not this giving up the merits of the question, for can there be a good government without a good executive? The English model was the only good one on this subject. The hereditary interest of the king was so interwoven with those of the nation, and his personal emolument so great, that he was placed above the danger of being corrupted from abroad," &c. Also, "their House of Lords is a most noble institution. Having nothing to hope for by a change and a sufficient interest by means of their property in being faithful to the national interest, they form a permanent barrier against any pernicious innovation, whether attempted on the part of the Crown or of the Commons."

On comparing these extracts with the speech, as published in the "Madison Papers," I find them to accord in all respects. In the life of Hamilton, by his son, the author indulges in harsh imputation upon the conduct of Mr. Madison, in this connection, in the justice of which I am deceived in the general sentiment of the country if he finds many to agree with him; and through a fatality which often attends similar demonstrations, he publishes in the same volume Hamilton's plan of government, the original draft of which Dr. Mason informed Mr. Madison was yet among the General's papers, and which is, word for word, the same as the copy published in the "Madison Papers;" and also Hamilton's own notes for his great speech in the Convention, which indicate the character of the speech upon the point in question as fully as notes ever prefigured a speech, and both of which confirm all that Mr. Madison has said in regard to it.

The following are extracts from the notes:--

"Here I shall give my sentiments of the best form of government--not as a thing attainable by us, but as a model which we ought to approach as near as possible." "British Constitution best form." "There ought to be a principle in the government capable of resisting the popular current." "No periodical duration will come up to this." "The principle chiefly intended to be established is this, that there must be a permanent will." "A democratic assembly is to be checked by a democratic senate, and both these by a democratic chief magistrate: the end will not be answered; the means will not be equal to the object." "The monarch must have proportional strength. He ought to be hereditary, and to have so much power that it will not be his interest to risk much to acquire more." "The advantage of a monarch is this, he is above corruption,--he must always intend in respect to foreign nations the true interests and glory of the people." "Republics liable to foreign corruption and intrigue. Holland--Athens." "Effect of the British government." "A vigorous execution of the laws, and a vigorous defense of the people will result." "Better chance for a good government." "It is said a republican government will not admit of a vigorous execution." "It is therefore bad; for the goodness of a government consists in a vigorous execution."

It thus appears that the opinions avowed to Mr. Jefferson on different occasions, one of which seems to have been sought for the purpose, were no more than repetitions of those he had avowed on the floor of the Convention, and of which he knew that Mr. Madison possessed an authentic record that would some day see the light; indeed, if such had not been the fact he would have just as frankly repeated them, for they were the settled convictions of his mind during his life--as fresh when they were announced to Mr. Jefferson as when promulgated in the Convention. Nor had he any motives for concealment of his views, if concealment had been, as it was not, characteristic of the man, for he was equally convinced that the government which had been established would prove a failure, and that the wisdom of his plans and the propriety of adopting them would thus become apparent to all.

We have here the words of General Hamilton himself--in his declarations deliberately made and attested in the most solemn and responsible form by Thomas Jefferson, and in his speech as reported by James Madison, under still more specific responsibility, confirmed by his own notes for that speech now published by his son and biographer--all going to the same end, viz: to show that he was in principle a monarchist, and that he preferred a monarchical to a republican form of government.

But Jefferson and Madison were politically his opponents. Let us now see what his oldest and best friend says upon this point. Gouverneur Morris, his coadjutor in the Convention and in politics through life, and his eulogist at the grave, gave in 1811 an unreserved expose of Hamilton's opinions on this very question, in a letter to Robert Walsh, then editor of the "National Gazette," written, doubtless, in answer to inquiries. The reader should procure this letter, and will find in it much matter of interest. I omit, among other things, what it says in respect to Hamilton's purity, and his frank and honorable character and bearing in political matters, having said as much myself, and with no less sincerity.

"General Hamilton," says Morris, "had little share in forming the Constitution. He disliked it, believing all republican government to be radically defective. He admired, nevertheless, the British Constitution, which I consider an aristocracy in fact though a monarchy in name.... General Hamilton hated republican government because he confounded it with democratical government, and he detested the latter because he believed it must end in despotism, and be, in the mean time, destructive to public morality.... But although General Hamilton knew these things from the study of history, and perceived them by the intuition of genius, he never failed on every occasion to advocate the excellence of, and avow his attachment to monarchical government."

In another part of the letter, "one marked trait in the General's character was the pertinacious adherence to opinions he had once formed."[10]

[10] Sparks's Life of Gouverneur Morris, Vol. III. p. 260.

In a previous letter, written shortly after Hamilton's death, (December, 1804,) to Governor Aaron Ogden, Morris says: "Our poor friend Hamilton bestrode his hobby to the great annoyance of his friends and not without injury to himself. More a theoretic than a practical man, he was not sufficiently convinced that a system may be good in itself and bad in relation to particular circumstances. He well knew that his favorite form was inadmissible unless as the result of civil war; and I suspect that his belief in what he called an approaching crisis[11] arose from a conviction that the kind of government most suitable, in his, opinion, to this extensive country, could be established in no other way."

[11] The italics are mine.

Hamilton not only cherished his preference for monarchical institutions to the very close of his life, but we have good reason to believe that the expectation that some crisis in the affairs of the country, encouraged by the weakness of our political system, would yet arise and would lead to their introduction, was equally abiding. His letters and writings will be found to contain many intimations to that effect. I will notice two instances. His letter to Timothy Pickering in 1803, is the only attempt that I have ever seen, coming from himself, to explain his course in the Convention. There may have been others, but I would be surprised indeed by the production of any thing from his pen denying his preference for the monarchical form of government, although such was the standing charge of his political opponents. None such, I feel very confident, ever existed. That letter concludes with the following very significant remark:--

"I sincerely hope that it may not hereafter be discovered that, through want of sufficient attention to the last idea," (that of giving adequate energy to the Government,) "the experiment of Republican Government, even in this country, has not been as complete, as satisfactory, and as decisive as could be wished."

The explanation of "his conduct, motives, and views" in accepting the challenge of Colonel Burr--probably the last paper containing any allusion to public affairs that he ever wrote--closes with expressions, italicized by myself, remarkably in harmony with the intimations of Gouverneur Morris to Aaron Ogden:--

"To those who, with me, abhorring the practice of dueling, may think that I ought on no account to add to the number of bad examples, I answer that my relative situation, as well in public as private, enforcing all the considerations which men of the world designate honor, imposed on me, as I thought, a peculiar necessity not to decline the call. *The ability to be in future useful, whether in resisting mischief or effecting good, in those crises of our public affairs which seem likely to happen, would probably be inseparable from a conformity with prejudice in this particular.*"

Although not so pointed in expressing it, his disposition toward the State governments was scarcely more favorable than toward the plan of the general government. In his letter to Pickering, at a period when their usefulness and importance to the system were better appreciated, he says: "Though I would have enlarged the legislative power of the General Government, yet I never contemplated the abolition of the State governments, but, on the contrary, they were in some particulars a part,--constituent parts,--of my plan." But let us see what part it was that he would have them perform. He said in the Convention: "If they (the State governments) are extinguished, he was persuaded that great economy might be obtained by substituting a general government. He did not mean, however, to shock the public opinion by proposing such a measure. On the other hand, he saw no other necessity for declining it. They are not necessary for any of the great purposes of commerce, revenue, or agriculture. Subordinate authorities, he was aware, would be necessary. There must be district tribunals, corporations for local purposes. But cui bono the vast and expensive apparatus now appertaining to the States?"

These were Hamilton's views in respect to the State governments, as expressed in the Convention, according to Mr. Madison's report. In this case it is also fortunate for the cause of truth that, from a paper written by Hamilton just as the General Convention adjourned, and published by his son, it appears very plainly that his views upon the subject cannot have been greatly misreported by Mr. Madison. In this paper he speculates upon the probable fate of the Constitution; after saying, in confirmation of my suggestion that he doubted the dispositions of the people in other respects than their intelligence and capacity, that the Constitution would have in its favor "the good will of men of property in the several States who wish a government of the Union able to protect them against domestic violence, and the depredations which the democratic spirit is apt to make on property," he adds: "If the Government be adopted, it is probable General Washington will be the President of the United States. This will insure a wise choice of men to administer the Government, and a good administration. A good administration will conciliate the confidence and affection of the people, and perhaps enable the Government to acquire more consistency than the proposed Constitution seems to promise for so great a country. It may then triumph over the State governments and reduce them to entire subordination, dividing the larger States into smaller districts. The organs of the General Government may also acquire additional strength." The italics in the above extracts are all my own except as to the word organs. He would not "shock the public opinion" by proposing to extinguish the State governments, but there was no other reason for omitting to do so. It would be well if it were done, but it was not wise to shock the public mind upon a point in respect to which it was known to be sensitive. But he would reduce them to entire subordination, triumph over and consequently humiliate them. It would be a poor compliment to Hamilton's knowledge of men and of the effect of public measures, to assume that he did not know that such would be the surest as well as the safest way to extinguish them in the end.

In a letter to Gouverneur Morris, so late as in 1802, a little more than two years before his death, and which will be found in "The Works of Hamilton," edited by his son, (Vol. VI. p. 529,) he thus unbosoms himself to his friend: "Mine is an odd destiny. Perhaps no man in the United States has sacrificed or done more for the present Constitution than myself; and contrary to all my anticipations of its fate, as you know from the very beginning, I am still laboring to prop the frail and worthless fabric. Yet I have the murmurs of its friends no less than the curses of its foes for my reward. What can I do better than withdraw from the scene? Every day proves to me more and more that this American world was not made for me."

There would seem to be no force in evidence, however appropriate its source or credible its character, if that we have produced is not conclusive in regard to the opinions of General Hamilton upon certain points. It proves, first, that he regarded monarchical institutions, according to the English model, as being the most perfect government that ever existed; secondly, that he would have preferred the establishment of such a government here, and was only prevented from advocating it by a conviction that it was made impracticable by the adverse public opinion of the time; thirdly, that he thought it was our duty, nevertheless, to approach that model with our Government as nearly as the prejudices of the people would permit, and that he introduced into the Convention a plan by which that object might be reached; fourthly, that he regarded the present Federal Constitution, which, as lately as two years before his death, in a free communication to his trusted friend, he called "a frail and worthless fabric," as inadequate to the purposes of a good government; that he had accepted it at the time as a temporary bond of union, but believed from the beginning that it would prove a failure and fall into contempt; that he believed that this result would open the way to popular tumults forcing intervention, and to convulsions through the evils of which the people would, at no distant day, become convinced of their error, and consent to institutions substantially similar to those he favored; and, fifthly, that his preference for monarchical institutions was a fixed and cherished sentiment; that although at times encouraged by his success in measures he had no right to hope for under the Constitution as he knew that instrument was intended to be, he yet invariably returned to his first opinion adverse to the sufficiency of the Constitution, and descended to the grave not only without a change in his opinions, but with increased convictions of their perfect soundness.

It has been a question often mooted whether the idea of using the power with which he was or might be clothed to overthrow the actual government, and to introduce the system he so earnestly preferred, was ever seriously entertained by Hamilton. Such designs were freely charged upon him by many of the old Republicans, who, under the full influence of partisan prejudices, doubtless believed that he waited only for a fit opportunity to attempt them. His repeated and undisguised expressions of a preference for monarchical institutions, to friends and foes, when the people of the United States, whose officer he was, had established a government which they intended should be so widely different from such institutions, were well calculated to engender the suspicion. Plain men naturally imagined that a man like Hamilton would do much and incur high responsibilities for the accomplishment of an object so near his heart. Mr. Jefferson, who was not a man of a suspicious temperament, through the fiery and protracted contests of parties, at the head of which they respectively stood, was evidently at times alarmed by similar apprehensions. But toward the close of his life, when partisan asperities had been long since forgotten, in a letter to myself he virtually exonerated Hamilton from the charge in these expressions:--"For Hamilton frankly avowed that he considered the British Constitution, with all the corruptions of its administration, as the most perfect model of government that had ever been devised by the wit of man,--professing, however, at the same time, that the spirit of this country was so fundamentally republican that it would be visionary to think of introducing monarchy here, and that therefore it was the duty of its administrators to conduct it upon the principles their constituents had elected."[12]

[12] See Appendix.

Mr. Charles Francis Adams has placed before us, in his life of his grandfather, John Adams, a series of facts bearing upon this point with no ordinary significance. They are not brought forward in support of any such charge, but as raising a question for the consideration of his readers, whether it is not possible that in the pains he took to increase greatly the provisional forces authorized to meet our difficulties with France, and to convert the whole into a permanent military establishment; in the readiness with which he fell in with the scheme of Miranda, to conquer, through the joint operations of Great Britain and the United States, the Floridas, Louisiana, and the South American possessions of Spain, in case of a rupture between us and France; and in his prompt consent to take command of the troops to be so employed, General Hamilton was influenced by a desire to bring about the crisis to which he had always looked as one that would present a fit opportunity for the establishment here of the political institutions he preferred.

These are grave matters, and of a nature calculated to challenge a new and stricter examination of one of those critical periods which have often occurred in our history, and from which we have had so many providential deliverances. The subject is treated with becoming delicacy and great caution by the author, whose conclusion, of which we have only a hint, may possibly have been influenced by family traditions, tinctured unavoidably with strong personal prejudices but never wanting in intelligence. I will not undertake to speculate even as to what General Hamilton might have done or have left undone if he had found himself at the head of a large and permanent military force, and the country convulsed by those popular outbreaks, the expectation of which seems to have been never absent from his mind or from the minds of his disciples. He might have mounted his "hobby"--as Morris termed his passion for monarchical institutions--and have struck a blow in their behalf, acting in the spirit of other "strong minds" who, as Mr. C. F. Adams well and truly says, "seldom fail to associate with dreams of their own glory the modes of exercising power for the good of their fellow-men. Considering their happiness as mainly dependent upon a sense of security from domestic convulsions, his first aim would have been to gain that end at any rate, even if it should be done at some expense of their liberties." But looking at the subject with no other feeling than a sincere desire to arrive at a correct solution of the circumstances narrated by Mr. Adams, I cannot bring my mind to the conclusion referred to.

I can well conceive that Hamilton might have been led to avail himself of such a state of things for a coup de main of some decided character if its existence had been brought about by others, or had been the result of fortuitous circumstances--a contingency which his mind had doubtless often contemplated. But I do not think that he would have planned or contributed to bring about such a state of things involving to so grave an extent the public order and the peace of the country. Such a course would have been at variance with some of his most cherished principles and inconsistent with his personal character. The preservation of order, and a respect for the individual rights of persons and of property, appeared always to be the objects of his greatest solicitude. It was only because he did not think that these could be effectually secured under any other form of government that he preferred monarchical institutions, acknowledging at the same time that they were at war with the principles of natural justice, and only allowable upon that of their absolute necessity to secure society against the occasional waywardness of a majority of its members. It was mainly because of the very erroneous opinions he had formed of the dispositions in this respect of a majority of his adopted countrymen that he was induced to devote his splendid talents to hopeless efforts to sustain principles so irreconcilable with those for which he had periled his life in the war of the Revolution. I say erroneous, not only because I think them such, but because experience, the only unerring test, has so proved them. We are, at the moment when I write, a half century from the transactions which form the subject of our consideration, and I venture nothing in saying that there is no country in Europe in which order has, in the interim, been better preserved, or the rights of persons and property been more secure, than in the United States; none in which the power of government has been more stable or more adequate to the purposes of its institution.

But this is a wide field, for which I have neither space nor time. It becomes me to remember, whilst occupied not without pleasure with these retrospective investigations and meditations, that I have already passed by several cheerful years, the allotted threescore-and-ten,--that period of such solemn import which the undeserved favor of an always kind Providence has permitted me to pass, not only with life but with the means and the faculties to enjoy life,--and that if I hope to complete the work before me I must confine myself more to the highway of my subject, and leave its by-paths to the explorations of younger men.

I cannot, nevertheless, refrain from a brief reference to transactions which have more than once occurred in this country, have made a greater impression on my mind than they seem to have made on others, and which I think have a strong bearing upon the question of the American love of order and respect for property and its rights. Although it is not probable that the facts of these can ever be sufficiently understood abroad to be correctly appreciated, it is otherwise here, and they are well worthy of our profoundest meditations. I allude to scenes which have been presented at San Francisco, which were at the moment of such thrilling interest, but appear already to have sunk into oblivion amid the ceaseless bustle and never-halting progress of American life.

Look at that young but already large and flourishing city! Regard her as she stood at the commencement of the extraordinary steps that were taken for her relief! Think of the scenes through which she was made to pass, and the condition to which she has been restored! An active and artful portion of her population thoroughly steeped in corruption, vice, and crime; her municipal authorities, the direct offspring of that corruption, not only regardless of duty but fraternizing with criminals, deriding the complaints of the injured, and scoffing at their prayers for official interference; despair succeeding hope, and the opinion that protection is at an end, and that nature may soon reassert her empire at length ripening into conviction in the breasts of the good of all classes; the general meeting of the citizens, and the appointment of the Committee of Vigilance with unlimited powers and subject to responsibility to no other tribunal than to the congregated mass of the people from whom they derive their authority and their power; the regular military organization adopted by the Committee and forthwith called into the field of duty, sufficient in men, arms, and equipments to crush resistance to the authority of the Committee in the city, and to deter the exercise of any other authority at that remote distance that might have a right to claim cognizance of the crimes they seek to suppress; all legal rule superseded by that of the Committee of Vigilance and put down on the instant of its assertion; criminals who had been set at large by the former authorities re-arrested on charges of capital offences, tried before the Committee, informally but honestly and intelligently, found guilty and executed; the functionaries who had connived at those offences arraigned at the bar of the same tribunal and dealt with according to their deserts; crimes detected and felons dragged from their hiding-places to meet a just punishment; men to whom no specific offence could be traced, but who were notorious enemies of order and abettors of crime, banished not to return under penalty of death, and every effort made to resist or defeat the action of the Committee crushed by an all-sufficient military force. The power of the Committee continues in active and constant exercise for nearly three months, when the purification of the city from crime and from criminals being accomplished, the authority of the laws is restored, also the use of the ballot-box which had been desecrated; this restoration is by the order and in pursuance of the authority and power of the Committee which are voluntarily laid down with the approbation and consent of a community consisting of from 25,000 to 30,000 persons.

There is no good reason for saying that during the whole of that period and in the midst of such stirring scenes the power of the Committee was in a single instance exercised to divest any innocent man of his property, or to oppress him in any way, or to interfere with his legal rights further than to compel submission to the temporary supremacy of that body, or to punish the innocent, or to enable the guilty to escape, or to aggrandize the Committee, or to benefit its members, their friends, or its employees, or to do an act of intentional injustice to any human being. During the government of the Committee the business concerns of the city and the vocations of its citizens were carried on with at least as much regularity and success as ever. Since its resignation and the consequent dispersion of its power not a banished man has returned contrary to the terms of his expulsion, and no member of the Committee, nor any one who acted by and within its authority, has been called to account for his acts within the bounds either of the city or of the State to which it belongs.

Is it probable that there is any city in Europe of equal size in which its legally established authorities could have been suspended by the irregular action of its own people with similar results,--in which the substituted power could be exercised with equal wisdom and forbearance, and laid down with so few causes for individual complaint? My opportunities for observation, although considerable, have been less than those of some others, and I may be wrong in thinking as I do that such things could not be done by any other people in the world.

The remedy for the social and political crimes which called the Committee of Vigilance into existence was a fearful one, and must be so regarded by all thinking and virtuous minds, and it would seem paradoxical to set up such a crowning act of disorder--that of the subversion of all legal authority, for even the shortest period--as an exhibition of a love of order and respect for the rights of persons and of property on the part of the actors; but I cannot resist the belief that the transaction afforded the strongest proof of the existence of those great principles in their minds, and that a proper sense of them and a determination to maintain them will seldom be wanting on the part of those who can act as did the Committee of San Francisco and its supporters.

But I ask pardon for this digression, and return to my subject. Many considerations besides those suggested by Hamilton's invariable solicitude for the preservation of order and by his constant respect for the individual rights of persons and of property, press themselves upon my mind against the conclusion intimated by Mr. C. F. Adams, and against the probability that General Hamilton ever contemplated the creation of a state of things that would justify or facilitate the employment of force to establish institutions more congenial with his taste and judgment than those we possessed. But I forbear to urge them, partly because I have devoted as much time and space to the subject as I can afford, and also because I am well satisfied that his knowledge of the certain opposition of General Washington to any such scheme or design would have been sufficient to deter him from undertaking either during the lifetime of the General, even if his own disposition had pointed in that direction.

It was at no time the intention of President Washington to give his sanction to the opinions so generally, and as it now appears so justly, attributed to General Hamilton. Never was man more strongly pledged to the support of republican government, or more unchangeably determined to maintain the responsibilities he had incurred in that regard. Embracing with all his heart the Declaration of Independence, in which its principles were delineated with the pencil of truth, he did more than any other man to overthrow the government against which it was hurled, and to open the way for the establishment of a republic in its place. None knew better than he that such was the object of the Revolution, and his resolution was immovable that the sufferings and sacrifices which had been incurred in support of that object should not fail to accomplish it through any act of omission or commission on his part. Every important act in his eventful career shows that he regarded himself on that point as invested by his country with a sacred trust. When the bright prospect which he had largely contributed to open to his countrymen for the realization of their wishes in this respect was in danger of being obscured, if not forever blasted, by means similar to those which have so often prevented or subverted free government, by the violence of an exasperated soldiery, he threw himself into the breach, and saved at the same time by his heroic and patriotic effort their interests and the honor of his brothers-in-arms. When the minds of the earnest and jealous friends of liberty were frenzied by an ill-advised attempt in the same quarter to introduce hereditary distinctions amongst us, he was again found at the post of duty; and, though feelingly indulgent to his military companions, as well as satisfied of the perfect purity of their intentions, he nevertheless promptly and successfully employed the great influence he derived from their respect for his character and their confidence in his friendship to induce them to abandon their project.

In the full possession of such claims to the esteem, gratitude, and trust of his countrymen, superadded to those which were due for his military services, he closed the first great period of his splendid life by presiding over the Federal Convention, and by assenting to, and recommending to the favor of the people, a Constitution eminently republican in its form, and in the principles upon which it was founded. So far was he from encouraging the spread of opposite sentiments that there is, on the contrary, much reason to believe that it was by making his views of the subject known to those about him that the anti-republican tone which Jefferson found, on his arrival from France, so prevalent in social and political circles at the seat of government, was kept in check until public opinion became strong enough to extinguish it altogether. Speaking to this point, Mr. Jefferson says, "The truth is that the Federalists, pretending to be the exclusive friends of General Washington, have ever done what they could to sink his character by hanging theirs on it, and by representing as the enemy of Republicans, him who of all men is best entitled to the appellation of the father of that Republic which they were endeavoring to subvert, and the Republicans to maintain. They cannot deny, because the elections proclaimed the truth, that the great body of the nation approved the republican measures. General Washington was himself sincerely a friend to the republican principles of the Constitution. His faith perhaps in its duration might not have been as confident as mine; but he repeatedly declared to me that he was determined it should have a fair chance of success, and that he would lose the last drop of his blood in its support against any attempt which might be made to change it from its republican form. He made these declarations the oftener because he knew my suspicions that Hamilton had other views, and he wished to quiet my jealousies upon the subject."[13]

[13] See Appendix.

Independently of his principles, which were the main source, doubtless, of the personal solicitude he often manifested upon this point, General Washington was a man of too much sense and reflection not to know that the world would in all future time hold him responsible for the overthrow of the republican principle here, if its extinguishment occurred in his day, and he was too careful of his well-earned fame, and anticipated too correctly the elevation it was destined to reach in connection with the history of his country, not to do all in his power to guard it from detriment upon a point at once so delicate and so momentous. Hamilton was the first man to whom he would make his sentiments known, and I can find nothing in the positions which they occupied toward each other which would induce me to entertain the opinion that Hamilton would have ventured on an attempt to shake his patriotic resolutions on that point through the influence he was supposed to possess over the actions of Washington in other respects.

There is, I am quite sure, nothing more essential to a right appreciation of many of the most important incidents in our political history, than a correct understanding of the relations that existed between those distinguished men. It cannot fail to shed considerable light on much that occurred during the government of the Confederation, and is perhaps the only touchstone by which the measures of government and many other public transactions between 1789 and 1799--between the organization of the new government and the death of Washington--can be safely tested.

I will give my interpretation of the character of those relations, fully aware of the misrepresentations and misunderstandings to which they have been subjected, and from which no subject connected with partisan conflicts can, it appears, be entirely free, but conscious of a single desire to state things truly, and of an inability to do intentional injustice to either. It will be for others to judge of my success.

Mr. Charles F. Adams, in the work to which I have referred,[14] says, "Without much hold upon the judgment or affections of the people at large, he (Hamilton) had yet by the effect of his undisputed abilities and his masculine will gained great sway over the minds of the intelligent merchants along the Atlantic border. His previous doctrines, in unison with the feelings and interests of the most conservative class, had drawn to him their particular confidence, whilst his position in the first administration had facilitated the establishment by him of a chain of influence resting for its main support on his power over the mind of Washington himself, but carried equally through all the ramifications of the executive department. Thus it happened that even after he ceased to be personally present his opinions continued to shape the policy of Washington's second administration, and even that of his successor." This declaration extending so far would have been deemed quite credible at the period to which it relates, and, coming from the grandson of that "successor"-- himself the undisguised enemy of Hamilton--was probably called forth by the recent publication of the private papers of the latter.

[14] Life of John Adams. The italics are my own.

As far as Mr. Adams affirms that the policy of Washington's administration, and also, in many very important respects, that of his successor, were guided by the opinions of Hamilton, his declaration has my full concurrence. No candid and intelligent man can, I think, read the evidence which has recently appeared, in connection with facts previously known, without acknowledging the undeniable truth of these positions. But I do not by any means intend to concede the control of Hamilton over the mind of Washington which is implied by the terms employed by Mr. Adams without qualifications which limit and very materially change its character. The policy of both administrations was guided by the opinions of Hamilton, but those opinions received their influence through different channels, and were enforced in very different ways. Hamilton's opinions, when known as his, had very little weight with the successor of Washington, save, in many cases, to secure a bad reception for themselves; but that successor had little if any control over, or influence with, the members of his own cabinet, and not much with Congress or the Federal party, by whom the policy of his administration was shaped. With them Hamilton's opinions established the rule of action. In respect to the two latter, this arose mainly from the sway he was capable of exerting over them by the force of his great talents, and from a general concurrence in his views. In respect to the prominent members of Mr. Adams's cabinet his control arose from the power he had in part acquired over their minds whilst they were also members of General Washington's administration. Timothy Pickering, who, after the retirement of Mr. Jefferson and the brief term of Randolph, was Secretary of State under both Presidents, was a remarkable man, sincere and honest, I am willing to believe, in his political opinions, but savagely bitter in his feelings toward his opponents. It seemed pretty much a matter of course in him to hate those to whose political course he was opposed, and, as is usually the case with minds thus constituted, he was equally bigoted in his devotion to those with whom he agreed and acted.

General Hamilton was his beau ideal of a politician and statesman, and it would not have been an easy matter in him to have dissented from any opinion positively advanced by Hamilton, whatever his own first impressions on the subject might have been. Mr. McHenry, Secretary of War in both cabinets, was undoubtedly an honorable and well-disposed gentleman. He was, in the opinion of those who had the best opportunities for judging, including Washington and Hamilton, not entirely competent for the duties of his office, and that circumstance drove him the more to rely for support on Hamilton, for whom he cherished an early and ardent friendship. His personal devotion to Hamilton was such as to prevent Mr. Adams from longer overlooking his incompetency, as Washington had done, and precipitated his resignation. Oliver Wolcott, Secretary of the Treasury, the member of his cabinet most trusted by President Adams because the least suspected, was, notwithstanding, the one among his official advisers who went the greatest lengths to testify his entire allegiance to Hamilton, who had been the artificer of his political fortunes from the beginning and by whose influence he had been advanced to the high position he occupied. Throughout he advised with and was assisted by

Hamilton in the performance of his official duties. Such was Hamilton's "power over his mind" that he was applied to successfully by the former for evidence of facts to be derived from the treasury archives to sustain an attack that Hamilton contemplated making upon the President--an attack that he did make, although he acknowledged to Wolcott that it would not be regarded as proper that he should have received the evidence at his hands, and that that fact ought not therefore to be known.

No one can read the correspondence between General Hamilton and Mr. Wolcott, as recently published with Hamilton's Works, without regretting that the parties to it should have been so forgetful of the proprieties due to the occasions to which it relates, or without a disposition to excuse the strong expression of Mr. Charles F. Adams, in speaking of his grandfather's cabinet, applied to Mr. Wolcott "as the most venomous serpent of them all."

Mr. Charles F. Adams places Hamilton's sway over the mind of Washington upon the same footing with that which he exerted over the executive department, composed principally of the members of his second cabinet of whom we have been speaking. From this view I entirely dissent. If Hamilton possessed any power over the mind of Washington, it was of a very different character from that which he exercised over those members. Washington was to an unusual extent free from the weakness of overrating his own powers; with just conceptions of his capacities for public service he was always ready to place them at the public disposal, but he was very far from pretending to qualifications which he did not possess. No one was more sensible than he that the science of civil government--the construction of constitutions and the administration of the civil affairs of the State--were not best learned in the camp, where so large a portion of his life had been spent. He therefore, as we have seen, selected two of the ablest statesmen in the country, particularly versed in those portions of the public business which he devolved upon them. They differed irreconcilably in respect to the policy of the administration, and in the performance of his duty he decided between their conflicting opinions in favor of those of Hamilton. Preferring the policy of the latter he adopted the measures he recommended to carry it out, which happened also to appertain principally to Hamilton's department, and sustained him in their execution. In doing so he but sustained the measures of his administration and views which were either originally his own or made such upon conviction. Participating in the general opinion in favor of Hamilton's remarkable talents, having full opportunities to judge of his character, and confiding in his integrity, he extended to him, it is true, but with the purest motives, the degree of countenance and trust which established his extraordinary power and influence. Of the consequences, as well to his administration as to the country, we will have much to say hereafter. But it would be a great mistake to suppose that there ever was a period at which, or a transaction between them in which, their relative positions, rights, and duties were either forgotten or disregarded. It was well understood that the degree of weight to be attached to Hamilton's advice would depend upon the unbiased opinion which Washington himself should form of its soundness, influenced as he naturally would be, and always was, by a conviction of Hamilton's undoubted integrity, and his superior capacity for the decision of the question under consideration. There certainly never was a time when the slightest indication of a desire or design on the part of Hamilton to sway the mind of Washington in his official acts through his personal influence, or by any considerations which did not point distinctly and exclusively to the public good, would not have been peremptorily and indignantly repelled. It is evident from the whole tenor of Washington's life that no man ever lived who was more tenacious of self-respect, or more absolute in his reservation of the right to judge for himself of what belonged to his individual independence and personal dignity, or more prompt to resist every attempt to encroach upon either. No one understood his temperament in that respect better than General Hamilton, or would have been less likely to bring himself in conflict with it. Many indications of this understanding and of its effects are to be found in the accounts of their personal intercourse. The correspondence between them in regard to the discreditable use that Washington thought was being made in Congress of the sufferings and dissatisfaction of the army, already referred to, will be found to throw much light upon the sense of both as to the nature of their personal relations.

In June, 1793, Hamilton announced to President Washington, that considerations relative both to the public interest and his own dignity had brought his mind to the conclusion to resign his office at the termination of the close of the next session of Congress, and one of the reasons he assigned for delaying his final retirement to that period was to give Congress an opportunity to complete the investigation that had been instituted in regard to his official conduct. In March thereafter Hamilton informed the President that the committee charged to inquire, among other things, "into the authority of the President respecting the making and disbursement of the loans under certain acts of Congress," were about to meet. He sent to him at the same time, a copy of a paper he had presented to the committee, containing his opinion in relation to the proper limits of a legislative inquiry, but said that he deemed it expedient to fix in advance, with the President, on the true state of facts, of which he proceeded to make a statement, and requested the President to sanction it. General Washington soon thereafter made a declaration, in the form of a letter to Hamilton, of his recollections and opinions in respect to the matter. The latter, in reply, protested vehemently against the sufficiency of the declaration for the protection of his honor, and in a letter of considerable length, written with his usual ability, undertook to show that the character of the President's declaration would enable, his (Hamilton's) enemies to say that "the reserve of the President is a proof that he does not think that Hamilton's representations are true, else his justice would have led him to rescue the officer concerned even from suspicion upon the point."

The subject of loans and their frequency produced much excitement in Congress, and not a few calls upon the President and the Secretary of the Treasury for information in regard to them. It does not appear from the published works of Hamilton, that any answer was made by General Washington to his letter, or any other explanation of the subject; and no one, I think, can read the correspondence without feeling that the interpretation I give to its abrupt termination is the correct one, viz.: that Washington intended by his silence to reprove the freedom of Hamilton's letter. The resignation of the latter was deferred, with the approbation of the President, till January, 1795, when it was accepted in a letter from General Washington, containing an approval of Hamilton's official conduct as full as words could make it.[15]

[15] Hamilton's Works, Vol. IV. pp. 436, 510, 516, 562; Vol. V. pp. 74, 78.

The construction I have placed upon the character of their personal relations is also sustained by a correspondence between them in May, 1798, after Hamilton's retirement from office, which will be found in the sixth volume of Hamilton's "Works," at p. 289. Hamilton's object appears to have been to impress the mind of Washington with a proper sense of the dangerous crisis which had arrived in the condition of public affairs. His letter contains the following extraordinary paragraph: "I am sincere in declaring my full conviction, as the result of a long course of observation, that the faction which has for years opposed the government are ready to remodel our Constitution under the influence or coercion of France, to form with her a perpetual alliance, offensive and defensive, and to give her a monopoly of our trade, by peculiar and exclusive privileges. This would be in substance, whatever it might be in name, to make this country a province of France. Neither do I doubt that her standard displayed in this country would be directly or indirectly seconded by them in pursuance of the project I have mentioned."

In such a state of things it was impossible, he said, not to look up to him, (Washington,) and to wish that his influence might, in some proper way, be brought into direct action, and he added: "Among the ideas that have passed through my mind for this purpose, I have asked myself whether it might not be expedient for you to make a circuit through Virginia and North Carolina under some pretense of health, &c. This would call forth addresses, public dinners, &c., which would give an opportunity of expressing sentiments in answers, toasts, &c., which would throw the weight of your character into the scale of the government, and revive enthusiasm for your person which might be turned into the right channel."

Although Washington himself had been highly excited, by the course of events, against those to whom Hamilton attributed such treasonable designs, he was yet enabled by his good sense and by his knowledge of his countrymen to see at a glance the reckless extravagance of Hamilton's imputations, and he was doubtless dissatisfied with the uses, little creditable, which it was proposed to make of himself. His answer was a truly imposing production. It narrowed Hamilton's description of the portions of his countrymen whose course he deemed objectionable, virtually disapproved his charges by giving his own views of the extent of the danger which was to be apprehended from those whose patriotism Hamilton so grossly impeached, and placed the objectionable character of the course recommended to him in a striking light by showing that, his health never having been better, he would be obliged to commence his journey with the propagation of a falsehood.

Those who wish to read these letters will do well to look for them in Hamilton's "Works," as I am sorry to say that in Mr. Sparks's "Writings of Washington" the above extract from Hamilton's letter, containing his suggestion of an electioneering tour in the South by Washington, is omitted, and the whole paragraph in Washington's reply, in which he rejects and virtually rebukes it, suppressed. Neither is that part of Hamilton's letter given in which he denounces "the powerful faction which has for years opposed the government" with fanatical violence, (for his description of them deserves no other name,) whilst what Washington says upon that point is set forth with considerable aggravation. The results of those omissions and suppressions are not only to conceal the fact that such a proposition was made to Washington, and the grounds upon which he declined to adopt it, but his remarks, condemnatory of a portion of his fellow-citizens, are left to stand as voluntary denunciations of his own instead of, as they in truth were, modifications of the charges to which Hamilton had called his attention.

I have thus selected a few transactions between these great men, occurring at long intervals and embracing the entire period of their intercourse, to show that the influence which it must be conceded Hamilton exercised over Washington's conduct in the civil service of his country was not of the character which is commonly understood and intended by the imputation of it in the case of high official personages, and which necessarily involves the sacrifice of personal independence and, at least in some degree, of self-respect on the part of the person influenced.

Anecdotes of distinguished men are always interesting, although their accuracy is not so reliable, of course, as that of statements substantiated by their own writings. I was told of one, several years since, which struck me as throwing light upon this subject of the personal relations between Washington and his immediate associates and friends. So thinking, and especially as General Hamilton was in one sense a party concerned, I have recently obtained reliable testimony of its authenticity. Judge Fine, the writer of the following note, is well known in New York, and not a little in other States; he has been a State Senator, a Representative in Congress, a State Judge, &c., &c., and is regarded as a gentleman of the utmost probity and of superior intelligence. Judge Burnet, with whom I have served in the United States Senate, was also well known as a gentleman in whose statements entire confidence might be placed, and was, withal, a Hamiltonian Federalist, and never, politically, any thing else; in whose eyes, I am very sure, any statement disparaging to the memory of either Washington or Hamilton would have appeared a grave offense against morality and truth.

FROM JOHN FINE.

OGDENSBURG, N. Y., April 30, 1857.

Hon. M. VAN BUREN:

DEAR SIR,--During the session of the Presbyterian General Assembly in Cincinnati--May, 1852--I dined twice at the hospitable mansion of Hon. Jacob Burnet, now deceased. He was born in Newark, New Jersey, in 1770, and was the son of Dr. William Burnet, who was in the medical service of his country through the Revolution.

Judge Burnet was acquainted with our early distinguished statesmen, and his conversation was rich in the recollection of their manners and characters. He related an anecdote of Washington which he had from the lips of Alexander Hamilton.

When the Convention to form a Constitution was sitting in Philadelphia in 1787, of which General Washington was President, he had stated evenings to receive the calls of his friends. At an interview between Hamilton, the Morrises, and others, the former remarked that Washington was reserved and aristocratic even to his intimate friends, and allowed no one to be familiar with him. Gouverneur Morris said that was a mere fancy, and he could be as familiar with Washington as with any of his other friends. Hamilton replied, "If you will, at the next reception evening, gently slap him on the shoulder and say, 'My dear General, how happy I am to see you look so well!' a supper and wine shall be provided for you and a dozen of your friends."

The challenge was accepted. On the evening appointed a large number attended, and at an early hour Gouverneur Morris entered, bowed, shook hands, laid his left hand on Washington's shoulder, and said: "My dear General, I am very happy to see you look so well!" Washington withdrew his hand, stepped suddenly back, fixed his eye on Morris for several minutes with an angry frown, until the latter retreated abashed and sought refuge in the crowd. The company looked on in silence.

At the supper which was provided by Hamilton, Morris said: "I have won the bet but paid dearly for it, and nothing could induce me to repeat it."

Yours truly, JOHN FINE.

Better proof of the truth of this statement could not, at this day, be expected or desired, and assuming it to be substantially true, the transaction, in my estimation, illustrates the character of the personal relations that existed between Washington and the two distinguished men, Hamilton and Morris, who, in respect to the management of public affairs, enjoyed perhaps his fullest confidence.

It is without doubt true, that in his intercourse with public men Washington observed an extraordinary degree of dignified reserve, and there is every reason to believe that this invariable habit was natural to him, and in no degree assumed for effect. We indeed know nothing of his character if he was at all capable of practicing the low device of hiding mental deficiencies under a wise look and a mysterious manner, which is sometimes the resort of meaner minds; but some such foundation (or some degree of it) for his habit must have been presupposed by the very unusual proceeding of Morris and it is quite impossible to believe that a man was in danger of being unduly influenced by his personal friends who could thus, by the power of his eye and the solemnity of his countenance, abash and punish the presumption of a man of Morris's standing, confessedly the sauciest man in his society, without causing the slightest confusion or excitement in the surrounding company.

He had nothing to conceal; he never desired to pass for more than he was worth, and there have been few men who formed a juster estimate of their own qualifications and capacities. In respect to military affairs he was evidently self-reliant, but not more so than was justified by his large experience and by the success which had crowned his efforts; but neither in that nor in any other department was he above receiving advice. In the intricate and complex affairs of civil administration, and in grave questions of constitutional construction and of national law, he felt that his experience and study had been much less than those of some who were associated with him in the public service, and he did not hesitate to recognize the difference. The principal aid he could bring to the settlement of such questions consisted of a clear head, a sound judgment, and an honest heart. These he never failed to apply after such questions had been prepared for decision by the previous examination and discussions of those of his cabinet whose attention had been more directed to them than his own. To secure these prerequisites he had, as I have said before, availed himself of the highest talent which the country afforded, without reference to distinctions of party.

This was the way in which he dealt with the grave questions that arose during the early stages of his administration, touching the numerous and complicated difficulties between us and our old friend and ally France, the reception and treatment of her ministers, Genet and his successor Adet, our assumption of a neutral position between European belligerents, the claims of France under the treaty of alliance and guaranty, the powers of Congress under the Constitution in relation to a national bank, and other subjects. In respect to the first of these matters he went so far as to consult Hamilton by letter on the question of his own personal demeanor at a Presidential levee toward the French minister, by whose conduct he had been offended. Whatever may be our regret at finding the confidential note asking that advice preserved to so late a period and now recklessly published, we may yet be satisfied that the step itself only affords additional evidence of the prudence and manliness of Washington's character. Few men stood less in need of advice in respect to his treatment of those who had given him offense in a matter purely personal; but it was natural for him to assume that the usages of diplomacy had settled rules for the action of the heads of government in such cases, of which he was not informed and in respect to which he was not ashamed to ask advice and information from proper sources. The constancy with which he invoked the aid of his cabinet upon all questions of the general character to which I have alluded, the unreserved manner in which he submitted them to their consideration, the delicacy with which he withheld his opinions until theirs were pronounced, and the spirit in which these were received, whether agreeing with or differing from his own, were above all praise. The information we possess of the details of those interesting proceedings is principally derived from Mr. Jefferson, and in all that he has written or in all that we have understood him to have said upon the subject no word of complaint or allegation at variance with the description here given of them is to be found. The idea that Washington ever sought to advance his objects by indirect or exceptionable means, or that he was actuated in his public measures by any other motive than an honest desire to promote the good of his country, seems never to have presented itself to Mr. Jefferson's mind, however erroneous he considered some of those measures. I spent some days with him, as I have elsewhere described,[16] two years before his death, and in the course of our repeated conversations he dwelt long and particularly upon these early transactions. I attributed the circumstance at the time to a desire, consistent with his very genial disposition, to gratify my curiosity, which was strong and not concealed; and it did not occur to me that he might have had other views, until, after my return home, I received his long letter avowedly written for the purpose for which I now use it, "to throw light on history, and to recall that into the path of truth when he was no more, nor those whom it might offend." In all that he said--and he spoke with perfect freedom of men and things--there was nothing inconsistent with the inference I have here drawn from his writings, but much to confirm it. The President's decisions upon cabinet questions were generally in favor of Hamilton's views; but that circumstance, very much to his credit, was not permitted to influence Jefferson's estimate of motives, but was regarded as the natural result of Washington's general sympathy with Hamilton's political opinions, and his confidence in his ability and integrity,--a sympathy, however, that never even approached the subject of a change in the existing form of our Government. That was a question as to which we have the best reason to believe that Washington would have never taken counsel except from his God and his conscience. He more than once declared to Jefferson "that he was determined that the republican form of our Government should have a fair chance of success, and that he would, if necessary, spill the last drop of his blood in its defense,"--a resolution, and the likelihood of its being sustained, that no one understood better than Hamilton.

[16] See Note on page 9.

By these repeated declarations to Mr. Jefferson, Washington only renewed to a civilian, whose character and position made them the more significant and impressive, a pledge which he had given to the world at Newburgh in the presence of the companions of his glory, yet with arms in their hands--that his name should never be added to the list of those who, having done much to emancipate a people from thralldom, were the first to blast their hopes and sacrifice their dearest interests at the promptings of selfish and unhallowed passions. They only proved that the flattery of the world during the ten intervening years had not corrupted his heart nor endangered the observance of a pledge which had derived its value from the character of the man who gave it, and on whose continued fidelity to the principle it involved the future liberties and welfare of his country were in so large a degree dependent.

It has always been believed that if Washington had inclined a favorable ear to the suggestions of the Newburgh letters, and in due season had given his name and influence to the counter-revolution they were intended to promote, it might have been made successful, and the system which the Revolution had overthrown might have been in some modified form restored. The disparity between the means which were at his disposal when propositions looking to such a result were thrown before the army at Newburgh and those within his reach when the declarations to Mr. Jefferson were made was not as great as might be supposed. At the former period it is true that the army of the Revolution was yet in the field, mortified, irritated, and indeed highly inflamed by the assumed injustice and ingratitude of their country, and in all probability prepared to follow his lead in furtherance of any views he might disclose which did not exceed the proposed limits; and the government to be overthrown was feeble, distracted, destitute of the sinews of war, and with but a slight hold upon the confidence and affections of the people. But it must also be remembered that the fervor and spirit of the Revolution--that intense hatred of royalty and monarchical institutions in any shape--which had roused the country to the contest, had as yet in no sensible degree abated amongst the masses, neither had they surrendered those sanguine anticipations of the blessings and advantages of republican government by which their hearts had been fortified and their arms strengthened for the struggle. That any attempt to bring about a counter-revolution under such circumstances, however popular the name and character of him by whom it was sanctioned, or however imposing the means by which it was sustained, would meet with a formidable opposition from the great body of the people was certain; and it was not easy to estimate the nature and extent of the resistance that might spring from the sources to which I have referred to confront an army which had so lately been the object of their unalloyed admiration and affection.

In the lapse of time between that period and the one at which Mr. Jefferson received the assurances he describes great changes had taken place in respect to all these matters, but, as I have said, not so adverse as might on first impression be supposed to the practicability of an attempt such as Washington referred to. The army of the Revolution had indeed been dissolved, and, in regard to the elements of which it was principally composed, beyond recall; but its officers, who, next to Washington, were capable of giving a tone and direction to the spirit of the troops, were alive, several of them again under his command, not a few about his person, and all filled with unabated admiration and affection for their idolized chief. If the account given us by Mr. Jefferson of the feelings he found most prevalent in our principal cities and at the seat of government on his return from France and in his progress to Philadelphia, to take upon himself the office of Secretary of State, is to be relied upon,--and many important contemporaneous occurrences corroborate his statement,--sad changes had taken place in the public opinion and feeling, of absorbing interest in this connection. "The President," he says, "received me cordially, and my colleagues and the circle of principal citizens apparently with welcome. The courtesies of dinner-parties given me, as a stranger newly arrived among them, placed me at once in familiar society. But I cannot describe the wonder and mortification with which the table conversations filled me. Politics were the chief topic, and a preference of kingly over republican governments was evidently the favorite sentiment." In his description of what he heard and saw there can be no mistake; but it is more than probable that changes among the people at large, upon the point spoken of, had not occurred to any thing like the same extent as among those portions of society to which he more particularly refers. Still it is undeniably true that from the influence of examples set by men in high places, from the difficulties under which the late government had labored, and from other causes, there had been at that moment a falling off from the true faith respecting governments and the administration of them which could now be scarcely credited. Add to these favoring circumstances the fact that the man, without whose countenance or cooperation no reactionary attempt would have been thought of even by the rankest advocate for monarchical institutions, was at the head of the Government to be overthrown, and the unquestioned object of the national confidence and affection, and the scheme, with his cooperation, was not likely to be then regarded as so impracticable as it would now certainly be considered. If such a work were at this day thought of by any man or men, however elevated in position or loved by the people, they could reap no other harvest than contempt and derision; but the single fact that Washington, who always handled serious matters seriously, and who was not liable to be alarmed by "false fires," treated the subject as he did, is sufficient to mark the difference between the condition of the country and of the public mind then and now.

But happily for us he was the same man in 1793 that he was in 1783. The principle upon which he acted upon both occasions was maintained through life without spot or blemish. The world believed, and for the best reasons, that he had refused to become the master of a people, whose liberties he had, through the favor of God and the fortitude and bravery of his countrymen, been made instrumental to establish, because he deemed it a higher honor to be their servant. It compared his acts with those of the Caesars, of Cromwell, and of Napoleon, and glorified his name above that of any other mortal man. Such has been his reward for his faithfulness to the most sacred of human trusts--a reward and a fidelity unparalleled! Services have been rendered in every age which entitled the actors in them to the gratitude of their country, and to the thanks of mankind, but lacking the distinguishing feature of Washington's, their traces have become fainter with the lapse of time, whilst the remembrance of his unequaled merits grows more distinct and strong with each revolving year.

That he committed grave errors in giving his sanction, probably with considerable reluctance, to some of the measures of his administration, is certain. I say this not merely on the strength of my own poor opinion, but because such is the unreserved and irreversible judgment of the country, to which, under a republican government, the acts of all public men are subjected. But the assent which he gave to these measures was never, even by those most opposed to them, attributed to him as a fault, but was regarded only as an honest error of opinion; and hence the extraordinary political phenomenon of a party having its origin in the adoption by him of those measures expelling from power his immediate successor, who claimed to act upon his principles, placing those principles by protracted and diligent efforts under the ban of public opinion, and keeping them and their supporters there, in the main, for more than half a century--and yet being not a whit behind those who approved them in its respect for his name and character, because its members, in the eloquent language of Mr. Jefferson, "would not suffer the temporary aberration to weigh against the immeasurable merits of his life; and although they tumbled his seducers from their places, they preserved his memory embalmed in their hearts with undiminished love and devotion, and there it forever will remain embalmed in entire oblivion of every temporary thing which might cloud the glories of his splendid life."

CHAPTER III.

The Fact that Hamilton shaped and guided the Administrations of Washington and John Adams at the Time generally believed, now clearly established--Occasions when his Influence did not prevail--His Views and Purposes on entering the Cabinet--Some of his early Measures not authorized by the Constitution--True Character of that Instrument--Hamilton as Secretary of the Treasury--His extraordinary Ability--His exaggerated Ideas as to the Embarrassments of the Country--Unfounded Alarm at that Period on the Subjects of the Public Debt and Public Revenues--Device for surmounting Constitutional Obstacles to Hamilton's Plan--Source of the Doctrine of Implied Powers--Foundation of Hamilton's Policy under his Construction of the Constitution--His Measures and the Effects he anticipated from them--The Funding System--The Weakening of State Authority a leading Feature of Hamilton's Policy--Further Aims and other "Stages of Improvement"--Hamilton's Report on Manufactures; its Ability, Spirit, and Political Effects upon its Author and his Party--Hamilton's Desire to build up in this Country a "Money Power" similar to that of England--Such a Power antagonistic to the Democratic Spirit of our People--The Real Object of Hamilton in endeavoring to transplant the System here--His temporary Success, and the Influence thereof in forming a School that survived him--His Motives and the Convictions upon which they were Founded.

That the policy of every administration of the Federal Government for the first twelve years of its existence was shaped, and the action of the Federal party guided, by the opinions and advice of Hamilton, was the general impression of the opponents of that party, and of course known to the leading Federalists. I have in another place[17] referred to the fact that Mr. Jefferson, in all my conversations with him in 1824, when he spoke of the course pursued by the Federal party, invariably personified it by saying "Hamilton" did or insisted thus; and, on the other hand, "the Republicans" held or claimed so and so; and that upon my calling his attention to the peculiarity of his expression, he smiled and attributed his habit to the universal conviction of the Republicans that Hamilton directed every thing. But the evidence they possessed of the truth of that impression was slight indeed in comparison with that which is now before the country. They had only the opinions given in the cabinet upon the important public questions that arose during that period, with the decisions of the President upon them and other public documents relating to them, and the general conjectural impressions on the minds of politicians, which can seldom be traced to any specific authority, in respect to the influence which governs the action of parties. The additions now made by the publication of Hamilton's private papers alone, and more especially when they are read in connection with those of other distinguished public men, prove those impressions to have been well founded, and to an extent far beyond what was even imagined in those days. I had read these papers with care, and, I hope, weighed their contents with candor, before I gave my assent to the declaration of Mr. Charles F. Adams upon the subject, quoted on p. 96 above. Many of General Washington's letters to Hamilton are marked "private," and some "private and confidential." It is not for me to decide upon the propriety of their publication, however much I may regret that the friends of the latter should have deemed that course necessary in respect to many of them. I content myself with a general reference to those which have a bearing upon the point under consideration, without making extracts or adding remarks explanatory of their tendency and effect. The letters between Washington and Hamilton more particularly in point will be found in the fifth volume of Hamilton's "Works," p. 106, in answer to letter at p. 12; and in the sixth volume, at pp. 19, 34, 35, 36, 52, 63, 64, 73, 90, 143, 156, 179, 197; those between Hamilton and members of Washington's cabinet, in the sixth volume, at pp. 29, 41, 67, 129, 238.

[17] See note, p. 9.

The steps taken by General Hamilton to shape the policy and to prescribe the action of Mr. Adams's administration were designed to embrace its entire course, and were carried into effect with but little respect for the wishes or opinions of its constitutional head. Three weeks had not elapsed after Mr. Adams's inauguration before General Hamilton wrote a letter to Mr. Pickering, Secretary of State, in which he expressed "his extreme anxiety that an exactly proper course should be pursued in regard to France," and suggested for his consideration, under seven different heads, what he thought that course ought to be. The Secretary was not requested to submit these views to the President, nor was any desire indicated that he should do so, nor any notice taken of the President in the letter further than may be found in the closing paragraph,-- "The executive, before Congress meet, ought to have a well-digested plan and cooperate in getting it adopted."

If there was a single instance in which Hamilton, in his numerous letters of advice to the Secretaries, requested them to submit his views to the consideration of the President, it has escaped my observation. He was several times spoken of, but generally as to what he ought to do and what he might or might not be induced to do. The letters and papers bearing upon the subject will be found in the sixth volume of Hamilton's "Works," at pp. 213, 215, 218,

246, 250, 251, 252, 269, 278, 292, 294, 381, 444, 447, 471, 477, 484.

During the whole period Hamilton was regarded as the leader of the Federal party by most of the prominent members of that party,--Mr. Adams and a few of his friends excepted,--by those who represented the country abroad, by members of Congress, &c., &c. He was considered the fountain head of partisan authority, was freely applied to for advice, and gave it when it was asked, and quite as freely when it was not. He from time to time furnished members of Congress with specifications of steps proper to be taken, in one of which will be found suggested the passage of the celebrated sedition law. A few instances of his interference in this form will be found in Volume V. Hamilton's "Works," pp. 79, 86, and in Volume VI. at pp. 92, 94, 381, 383, 390.

The most important, if not the only occasions on which the influence of Hamilton over the action of the Federal party was exerted without success, were those of the formation of the Federal Constitution, and the support of Aaron Burr, by that party, for President, and for Governor of New York in 1801 and 1804. The first can scarcely be regarded, however, as such an occasion, because it was one in which party distinctions were merged in a compromise to which he himself ultimately assented. The others belong to the number of those occasions which, from time to time, present themselves in the history of all political parties, when the lust of power overrides the advice of their ablest and best friends. A party which has been long out of power, or which, having long held it, is threatened with imminent danger of losing it, can rarely resist the temptation when it is presented of securing success by dividing its opponents. Such a temptation is almost always strong enough to silence other objections, and Hamilton, on those occasions, shared the fate of party leaders who place their individual influence in opposition to the excited passions and short-sighted schemes of their party.

It was my fortune to hear Hamilton's great speech against the support of Burr for the office of Governor of New York by the Federalists of the State. I happened to visit Albany on the day appointed for the meeting, in company with William P. Van Ness, who was a few months afterwards Burr's second in his duel with Hamilton; and we lodged, as we were in the habit of doing, at Lewis's Tavern, the place where the meeting was to be held. Our room adjoined and communicated with the larger one in which the meeting took place; and after its organization, Mr. Van Ness threw open the door between the rooms, giving us a full view of the assemblage and exposing our presence to them. I mention these circumstances, which I recollect well, because it is my impression that it was very unusual at that day for politicians of one party to attend the meetings of the other. Mr. Van Ness and myself differed irreconcilably in respect to the support of Colonel Burr, but we were both members of the Republican party. The meeting consisted of about one hundred very respectable looking men, generally well advanced in life, and I remember many gray heads among them. Such was a gathering of the Federalists, in a city in which they had complete control, called together to hear the leader of their party, decidedly the most eloquent man of his day, a little more than fifty years ago. Quantum mutatus! My seat was so near to Hamilton that I could hear distinctly every word he said, and three impressions of the scene are still strong in my memory--his imposing manner and stirring eloquence, the obvious disinclination of the larger portion of his audience to be governed by his advice, notwithstanding the unbounded respect and love they bore him, and the marked indignation which often sparkled on the countenance of Van Ness whilst he was speaking.

Preferring monarchical institutions because he conscientiously believed that republican government could not be maintained "consistently with order," but satisfied that public opinion would not then admit of their establishment in this country, and indisposed for the reasons I have assigned to advocate the use of force for that purpose, yet expecting a crisis to arrive by which the opinions of the people would be changed, or the use of force be rendered justifiable, Hamilton entered the cabinet of President Washington determined to recommend a line of policy and the adoption of measures, which, whilst they would give the Government sufficient power to sustain itself against the democratic spirit of the country,--always the object of his dread,--would not be out of place when a resort to the English model, the object of his life-long choice, should have become necessary. If, in the execution of this policy, he had confined himself to the powers intended to be conferred upon the Federal Government by the Constitution, however much his conduct might have been censured on account of the anti-republican spirit it evinced, it would nevertheless have presented a very different aspect to posterity. But this was unhappily far from his intention. No one knew better than Hamilton that power to adopt some of the most important of the measures included in the chart he had devised for the action of the Federal Government was not designed to be granted to it either by those who framed, or by those who had adopted the Constitution, and that if there had been any reason to suspect that that instrument conferred such powers there would not have been the slightest chance for its ratification.

The Convention that framed the Constitution was well aware that the portion of its labors which related to the extent of the powers to be given to the new government was that upon which the public mind was most sensitive. It was not ignorant how far the apprehensions of the people upon that point had, through the entire period of our colonial history, prevented the establishment of any general government, and even the institution of one since the Declaration of Independence that was adequate to the necessities of the country. It knew that the powers given to Congress, particularly, would be the part of the Constitution to which the attention of the friends of the State governments would be directed, and upon which their opposition would be most likely to arise. Understanding these things, the Convention, with that good sense and prudence by which its entire course was so greatly distinguished, bestowed upon that branch of its business the utmost care and circumspection. Instead of describing the power given to Congress in general terms, as was done by Hamilton, in the plan submitted by him for its adoption,--viz.: "To pass all laws which they shall judge necessary to the common defense and general welfare of the Union,"--by which much would of necessity be left to the discretion of those who were to execute the power, the Convention specified the powers it intended to grant under seventeen heads, and described them in the simplest and plainest language, so that none should be at a loss to understand their import. So well was this design executed that no room for doubt or cavil remained to those who had no other desire than to arrive at the meaning of the framers of the Constitution.

Here the Convention might have stopped, for no implication could have been more unavoidable than that Congress should have the right to promulgate the rules they adopted by the enactment of laws. But as if aware of the uses which the able men from whom it apprehended opposition might make of the fact that a necessity of a resort to implication had been left by the instrument, it granted that power also in express terms. The principal part of that clause was moreover designed to constitute Congress the law-maker for the other great departments of the government, and to exclude the idea that they should also have the power of legislation.

Having thus, as it thought, guarded the work of its hands from misrepresentation or misinterpretation upon what it justly considered the most delicate and, if disregarded, the most vulnerable point, and having framed a Constitution with which all friends to republican principles ought to be satisfied, the Convention appealed with confidence to the ratifying conventions, and in doing so it did no more than justice to those bodies,--the instrument, thus guarded, was ultimately ratified by the votes of all the States.

If Hamilton, either in the articles of the "Federalist," to which he largely contributed, or on the floor of the Convention of Ratification, of which he was a member, had only countenanced that construction of the Constitution which he set up for it as Secretary of the Treasury, or if in any other way a suspicion had been produced that it was intended to give that instrument such a construction after its ratification, its rejection would have been inevitable. No one who has studied the state of the public mind at that period can for a moment doubt that this would have been the result. Such was the true character of the Constitution which the people of the United States intended to establish, and thought they had established, and such were the circumstances under which it was ratified.

Hamilton was placed by Washington virtually at the head of his administration; for, although the Secretary of State has, since that period, been regarded in that light, no such impression had then obtained, and in the government of Great Britain, to which attention had been most directed, it was otherwise. The Treasury Department wielded infinitely the most influence, and the superior confidence of the President in the incumbent decided the point of priority, at least for the time being. Perhaps the only question in respect to Hamilton upon which there has never been any diversity of sentiment was in regard to his talents. That they were of the highest order was the opinion of all who knew him. Jefferson scarcely ever spoke of him in his letters to Madison without admonishing him of the extraordinary powers of his mind, and in one of them he says,--"Hamilton is really a Colossus to the Anti-Republican party; without numbers he is a host in himself. In truth when he comes forward there is nobody but yourself (Madison) that can meet him." When I was Minister of the United States in England I saw much of Prince Talleyrand, then French Ambassador at the same Court, and enjoyed relations of marked kindness with him. In my informal visits to him we had long and frequent conversations, in which Hamilton, his acquaintance with him in this country, and incidents in their intercourse, were his favorite themes. He always spoke with great admiration of his talents, and during the last evening that I spent with him he said that he regarded Hamilton as the ablest man he became acquainted with in America,--he was not sure that he might not add without injustice, or that he had known in Europe.[18] With such advantages, greater at that time certainly than the public service of any country afforded to any other man, it is difficult to conceive of a more commanding position than that which he occupied. With a mind that dwelt habitually upon great ideas, the political career of such a man could not fail to produce important results for good or for evil. It must not, however, be forgotten, for it is a truth which exerted a powerful influence on his whole course, that he was at the same time, as his friend Morris described him, "more a theoretic than a practical man." It was natural that a mind so easily excited and an imagination so vivid as Hamilton's seem always to have been, should have formed exaggerated ideas as well of the extent and character of the embarrassments under which the country was laboring, as of the causes from which they sprang. These were undoubtedly very serious, very difficult to be dealt with; and it is equally true that they had been greatly aggravated by, if they were not, as he was very willing to consider them, mainly attributable to the defects of the former federal system. But there was some misapprehension, and no small degree of exaggeration upon these points. We are indeed an imaginative people, and the transfer of our fathers to a new country and climate doubtless accounts for the great difference in this respect between ours and the cool, deliberate, and unimpressible temperaments and character retained by those in Europe who have the same descent. It was not to have been expected that a country so young as our own, and as unprepared, could have passed through a seven years' war with a powerful nation without involving itself in grave embarrassments; but when the extent of those embarrassments, the difficulties of dealing with them, and the then resources of the country are now regarded, it seems impossible to avoid the conclusion that the grounds for the alarm then so prevalent upon the subjects of the public credit and the public revenues were greatly overrated.

[18] At the same interview Talleyrand told me an anecdote which, considering the depressed condition of Colonel Burr at the period to which it referred, I thought descriptive of a harsh act on the part of my informer, and I do not repeat it without hesitation. "Burr," he said, "called in pursuance of a previous communication from him, and, his card being brought up, he directed

the messenger to say that he could not receive a visit from Colonel Burr, and referred him, for an explanation of his refusal, to a painting hanging over the mantel-piece in the antechamber, which was a portrait of Hamilton."

The visit was probably one of courtesy, with a possible hope of being able to enlist Talleyrand in his (Burr's) Mexican schemes.

Our whole foreign debt amounted to but twelve millions of dollars, payable by installments, the last of which did not become due until seven years thereafter. The domestic debt amounted to forty-two millions, for the payment of which the Government was under no obligation to make immediate provision, amounting in all to fifty-four millions, and the annual expenses of the Government were estimated at less than six hundred thousand dollars. This was the full extent of federal responsibilities. Hamilton assumed some fifteen millions of the State debts, but that was an act entirely voluntary, neither asked nor desired by the States, unconstitutional and inexpedient, and caused as much unpopularity to his administration of the department as, perhaps more than, any act by which it was distinguished.

To meet these responsibilities the new Constitution had placed in the hands of the Federal Government the power of collecting a revenue from imposts and taxes, to borrow money on the credit of the United States to any amount which the public service might be deemed to require, and to regulate commerce, both foreign and domestic,--a power from the exercise of which great improvements in the trade of the country were justly anticipated. In aid of these resources we possessed a population of some three and a half millions, as active and enterprising as any on the face of the earth, just emerging from the discouragements of a defective government, and bounding with hope into all the varieties of business and labor, for which a fertile soil and a salubrious climate afforded the most ample facilities. The comparison may be, and doubtless by many will be, regarded as inappropriate; but with the views-- simple but practical--which experience has taught me, I cannot but think that if one were instituted between the liabilities of the United States in 1790 and those of the State of New York in 1842,--between the means at the disposal of each, and the extent to which the credit of each had been depressed,--it would be found that speedier and more substantial relief, and under less eligible circumstances, was obtained for the latter by the simple and direct efforts of those unpretending financiers, Michael Hoffman and Azariah C. Flagg, than was accomplished for the United States by the manifold schemes that were resorted to at the period of which we are speaking. Certain I am that if a similar comparison were made between the difficulties which the Treasury Department of the Federal Government had to contend with in 1790, and those which it encountered in 1837, combined with the powerful and active hostility of the United States Bank, the former would lose much of the apparent importance with which tradition, the influence of a great name, and the rhetorical applauses of modern political orators, of the Federal school, have invested them.[19]

[19] "He smote the rock of the national resources and abundant streams of revenue gushed forth. He touched the dead corpse of the public credit, and it sprang upon its feet. The fabled birth of Minerva from the brain of Jove was hardly more sudden or more perfect than the financial system of the United States, as it burst forth from the conceptions of Alexander Hamilton."--Daniel Webster.

The condition of things at the period we are considering was such as to promise the greatest advantages from the simplest, though persevering and well-considered, employment of the means then for the first time placed at the disposal of the General Government.

If it had fortunately so happened that General Washington had placed Hamilton at the head of the State Department, in which the theories which he appears to have studied from his earliest manhood--he having, though anonymously, at the age of twenty-three, sent to Robert Morris, then a member of Congress, the first plan for a bank of the United States, accompanied by an elaborate examination into monetary and financial affairs generally, and those of the United States in particular--would not have been called into action, and if he had appointed Madison to be Secretary of the Treasury, the fate of his administration and the effects of its measures in respect to parties would have been very different. The practical character of Madison's talents and disposition had been exemplified in the whole of his previous career, and was conspicuous in his course on the subject of revenue. On the second day after the votes for President and Vice-President under the new Constitution had been canvassed, and twenty days before the inauguration of President Washington, he commenced operations in the new House of Representatives, of which he was a member, to enable the new government to avail itself of the advantages secured to it by the Constitution in regard to revenue.

To this end he introduced a bill to impose impost and tonnage duties by which he believed all the objects of a national revenue could be secured without being oppressive to the country, and pursued his object day in and day out, until his bill became a law. A prompt application of the means thus acquired to the regular payment of the interest on the public debt, with a resort to others authorized in express terms by the Constitution if the impost had not proved adequate to all the objects of a national revenue, as he believed it would, and a discreet use of the power to borrow exerted in the ordinary way, accompanied by proper efforts to keep public expenditures at the lowest point consistent with an efficient public service, would in all probability have been the sum of the measures which Mr. Madison would have deemed necessary to place the public credit at the highest desirable point and to discharge all the existing obligations of the Government. They constitute all the means employed by the department now, and for several years past have proved abundantly sufficient to meet infinitely higher responsibilities, and there is in truth no conclusive reason to be found in the history of the period referred to why they would not have performed the same offices then.

But these simple and usually efficacious measures did not come up to Hamilton's standard. They fell short of what he thought necessary to the actual wants of the public service, and still more so in regard to what he deemed due to the efficiency, stability, and dignity of the Government. To secure all of these objects he desired to build up a financial system which would approach to an equality with the English model after which he designed to construct it; and he believed that it was in that way only that the public necessities could be amply provided for, the public credit placed at the point which he wished it to occupy, and the respectability of the Government be properly consulted. But this plan required the adoption of measures which, it is not too much to say, he knew that neither those who framed nor those who adopted the Constitution intended to authorize. This difficulty, which to ordinary minds would have appeared insurmountable, was overcome by a device either of his own creation or, as I have for many years believed, the suggestion of another.

The subject of internal improvements by the Federal Government, in regard as well to the power of the latter over the subject as to the expediency of its exercise, was repeatedly and very fully discussed in Congress, whilst Mr.

Rufus King and myself represented the State of New York in the Senate of the United States. Upon the question of power we concurred in opinion, he adhering to that of Hamilton--the construction of such works being one of the very few powers which the latter did not claim for the Federal Government. Notwithstanding this agreement the subject was often canvassed between us in respect to the arguments advanced, from time to time, in Congress, by others. On one of those occasions, he told me that on Gouverneur Morris's visit to the city of New York, soon after his return from the Federal Convention, he was congratulated by his friends on the circumstance that the Convention had succeeded in agreeing upon a Constitution which would realize the great object for which it had been convened, and that Morris promptly and, as Mr. King seemed to have understood it, significantly replied--"That will depend upon the construction that is given to it!" Mr. King did not state any inference he had drawn from the remark and seemed to me indisposed to prolong the conversation upon that point, and, knowing his habitual reserve in speaking of his old associates, I yielded to what I believed to be his wish not to be questioned, although I was at the moment strongly impressed by the observation. I referred to it afterwards in a speech I made in the Senate upon the powers of the Government, which was extensively published. At a subsequent period this ready answer of Morris would not have attracted notice; but spoken before even a single officer had been elected to carry the Constitution into effect, and of course before any question as to its construction had arisen, it was to my mind, and, as I believe, to the mind of Mr. King, evidence of a foregone conclusion to claim under that instrument powers not anticipated by the great body of those who framed it, or by those who had given it vitality by their approval. The facts that this reply had been so long remembered by Mr. King, a prominent and sagacious member of the Convention, and repeated under the circumstances I have detailed, were calculated to create such an impression. It gave, at least to my view, a decided direction in respect to the source from whence the doctrine of implied powers originated. I had found it difficult, with the opinions I had formed of Hamilton's character and dispositions, to reconcile the first suggestion of such a policy with them. I could believe that, in accordance with the principles which he avowed, he might be not unwilling to carry it into effect when it was suggested to him; but that, after advancing his opinions in a manner so frank and fearless, notwithstanding their well understood unpopularity, he should be found mousing over the words of the Constitution for equivocal expressions, containing a meaning intelligible only to the initiated, and by such methods preparing to spring a trap upon the people, was, it appeared to me, utterly foreign to his nature and habits. Neither was I disposed to believe that he would, at the very moment of signing, have denounced the Constitution as inadequate to the purposes of good government if he had then regarded it as possessing the very extensive powers he afterwards assisted in claiming for it, nor would he have subsequently declared it to be "a frail and worthless fabric." His complaint upon the latter occasion would have been against the construction that had been given to it, and not against the Constitution itself.

Morris, whose ability no one will question, was a constant attendant upon the Convention, took an active part in its proceedings throughout, was on most of its committees and the working-man of the last,--the duties of which were "to revise the style of, and arrange the articles which had been agreed to by the House,"--and the second and last draft of the Constitution was reported by him. But it is now comparatively unimportant with whom the latitudinarian construction of the Constitution, which has caused so much strife and contention and so little advantage to any person, party, or interest, originated. Hamilton, at least, adopted it as the corner-stone of his constitutional views, and, by his genius and the weight of his official influence, gave it a temporary success.

For reasons which will appear in the sequel, I will confine myself to a simple statement of the questions that were raised in respect to the construction of the Constitution, and a few illustrations of their character. That instrument, as has already been stated, contained a specific enumeration of the powers given to Congress, and the reasons have been also described for this particularity. The measures to which they referred were known by appropriate and distinct names, and applied to definite and well understood objects, and they have been ever since known and understood as they were then. This enumeration of the powers of Congress was followed, as we have seen, by a grant of authority to that body to "make all laws which shall be necessary and proper for carrying into execution the foregoing powers."

Under this winding-up clause of the Constitutional enumeration of the powers of Congress, the true sense and object of which was so easy to be understood, Hamilton claimed for that body the power of authorizing by law measures of a substantive character, described by well understood names, altogether different from those employed in the enumeration, such as the incorporation of banks, &c., &c., if Congress should declare itself of the opinion that the execution of the enumerated powers would be materially aided by any such measures, reserving to Congress the right of deciding whether the proposed measure would be sufficiently useful to create the "propriety and necessity" required by the Constitution, and placing in its breast alone the final decision of every such question.

The objects of the Constitution, as set forth in its preamble, were "to form a more perfect union, establish justice, insure domestic tranquillity, provide for the common defense, promote the general welfare, and secure the blessings of liberty to ourselves and our posterity." The first of the powers of Congress, contained in the enumeration of them in the Constitution, is in the following words:

"The Congress shall have power to lay and collect taxes, duties, imposts, and excises, to pay the debts and provide for the common defense and general welfare of the United States; but all duties, and imposts, and excises shall be uniform throughout the United States;"--and then follow all the other powers, to borrow money, &c.

The terms "common defense and general welfare," used in this enumeration, were taken from the Articles of Confederation, where they stood thus: "All charges of war, and all other expenses that shall be incurred for the common defense and general welfare, and allowed by the United States, in Congress assembled, shall be defrayed out of a common treasury, which shall be supplied by the several States in proportion," &c. Under those Articles they were never understood as a substantive grant of power to the Continental Congress, or as authorizing that body to ask from the States moneys, and to expend them for any purposes other than those which the Articles afterwards specified. By the new Constitution the manner of getting the money was happily changed from State requisitions to taxes, duties, imposts, and excises, to be expended, however, when so obtained, for the common defense and general welfare, as before, and the Constitution then, like the Articles of Confederation, says upon what objects it is to be expended. The Convention which framed and those which ratified the instrument, of course, understood the terms as used in the same sense. But after the Constitution was ratified, without an intimation of such a construction having been whispered before, it was contended by many that the manner in which the terms common defense and general welfare were used in it authorized Congress to adopt any measure which that body might deem calculated to subserve the common defense and general welfare of the country, whilst others, less reckless, limited the power they claimed for Congress to the application of money to any such measures. Among the former, as to the clause in the preamble, Hamilton placed himself, insisting that, under the grant of powers to make all laws which shall be necessary and proper for carrying its given powers into execution, Congress had the power to adopt every measure of government not expressly denied to it or exclusively granted to the States, which it should deem useful in the execution of its enumerated powers, however variant in its name, object, and general understanding; and under the clause quoted from the preamble an unlimited power of taxation, and an equally unlimited authority to expend the money so raised upon objects which it might think would promote the common defense and general welfare. He thus claimed for Congress substantially all legislative power, save such as was expressly prohibited to it, given exclusively to the States, or denied to both, falling but little if any thing short of the power he assigned to the national legislature in his propositions submitted to the Convention, which that body would not even consider, viz.: "to pass all laws which they shall judge necessary to the common defense and general welfare of the Union."

When the advocates of these doctrines were asked to remember the state of public opinion at the time when the Constitution was framed; the jealousy which then existed and had for so many years existed, of the power of the General Government; the fact that the apprehensions which had been entertained had so long prevented the calling of a Convention; the extreme improbability that the Convention, under such circumstances, could have intended to give to Congress the power to pass any law it might be pleased to regard as useful in the execution of an enumerated power, whatever might be its bearing upon the State governments; to add to the power to make peace and war and to raise armies and equip fleets; to make the power to raise money unlimited by authorizing its expenditure upon any measure Congress might assume to be conducive to the common defense and general welfare, and the absurdity of the supposition that the grant of such far-reaching and absorbing powers would have been conferred in so obscure a way, and that the Constitution would have passed the scrutiny of so many State Conventions without its ever having been intimated in any way that there lay concealed in its general terms grants of power which, if but suspected, would have set the country in a blaze, and would have produced instant refusals to ratify on the part of most of the States,--when such considerations were opposed to those bold pretensions, the only reply was, the Constitution must be construed by its letter, and we cannot look behind it or beside it for the means of doing so truly.

To the answer that extraneous matter has always been allowed by all laws, state and national, to be used in the interpretation of the highest acts of sovereignty, such as the construction of treaties between sovereign powers, of patents issued under the great seal, of acts of Parliament, of Congress, and of State legislatures, and in respect to the latter class the old law, the mischief and the proposed remedy to be taken into consideration in searching for the meaning of such acts, in the construction of wills, deeds, &c., &c., the only rejoinder was that a Constitution was an exception to those rules; in short that a Constitution was the sole exception to the application of the maxim which has grown out of the observation and experience of mankind,--qui haeret in litera haeret in cortice.

The nearness of the time when the Constitution was framed to the period of which we are speaking gave to this construction its most repulsive aspect. The members of the Federal Convention were yet on the stage of action, and many of them participators in the measures that were brought forward on the strength of it. The remonstrances of those who dissented on the ground of their own knowledge that the Convention did not contemplate such a construction were disregarded, not because they did not represent the truth but because the objection was inadmissible upon principle. This was emphatically the case in respect to the establishment of a national bank, the pioneer of constitutional infractions, the "wooden horse" from whose sides the most violent assaults have been made upon the Constitution. It was a fact well remembered by the members, and subsequently confirmed by the publication of the journal of the Convention, that a motion was made to give to Congress power to grant acts of incorporation, as facilities to public improvements. This fact was brought to the notice of President Washington by Mr. Jefferson, in his opinion upon the bank question: "It is known," said he, "that the very power now proposed as a means was rejected as an end by the Convention which formed the Constitution; a proposition was made to them to authorize Congress to open canals, and an amendatory one to empower them to incorporate, but the whole was rejected, and one of the reasons of rejection urged in the debate was that then they would have power to erect a bank, which would render the great cities, where there were prejudices or jealousies upon this subject, adverse to the reception of the Constitution."

This communication was made directly to General Washington, who had been President of the Convention, and made to defeat a measure of Hamilton's, who never failed to turn every proposition of his opponents against themselves when it was in his power to do so. It remained unnoticed, and its truth was therefore virtually admitted. Upon the very first question, then, which arose under the Constitution upon Hamilton's construction, and that one first also in importance, the well-known intentions of the Convention were directly and intentionally overruled.

President Washington gave no reasons for his decision in favor of the Bank Bill. I will hereafter state the principle upon which I think it fair to presume that he acted. Hamilton was influenced by views which governed his conduct in every constitutional question that arose in his day. He did not, because he could not with any show of propriety, deny that the Constitution ought in strictness to be construed according to the intentions of those who made it; but believing, doubtless sincerely, from the beginning, that, so construed, it was insufficient for the purposes of good government and must prove a failure, he designedly gave it construction, in cases where he deemed that course necessary to the public interest, in opposition to what he knew to have been the intentions of the Convention. The objection that this was setting at naught the declared will of the people had but little weight with him. He believed that a majority of the Convention would have been content to incorporate the powers he now claimed in the Constitution if they had not been deterred by the fear that it would not be ratified, and for the opinion of a majority of the people he made proverbial his want of respect. He held them incapable of judging in such questions. He was as anxious as any man to promote their happiness and welfare, but he thought it a political necessity that this could only be done in despite of themselves; no man could possibly be less prone than he was to the employment of sinister means in private life, and yet he held them excusable in dealing with the people; he thought nothing effectual and salutary could be done with them without appeals to their special interests, without exciting their passions and turning them to the side of the Government. This was the vicious feature of his political creed, and proofs of its existence could be multiplied almost without end; but, as the subject will unavoidably and often present itself, I will content myself here with an extract from a letter written by him to his friend Morris, after the great public transactions in which he had been engaged were principally ended. The last letter to Morris, from which I have quoted, spoke of the past; this looks to the future, and shows the lengths to which he was yet, as he had always been, willing to go. The letter is dated April 6, 1802, in which, after complimenting Morris upon his efforts "in resisting the follies of an infatuated administration," he thus points his friend to the work before them:--

"But, my dear sir, we must not content ourselves with a temporary effort to oppose the approach of evil. We must derive instruction from the experience before us, and learning to form a just estimate of things to which we have been attached, there must be a systematic and persevering endeavor to establish the fortune of a great empire on foundations much firmer than have yet been devised. What will signify a vibration of power if it cannot be used with confidence or energy, and must be again quickly restored to hands which will prostrate much faster than we shall be able to rear under so frail a system? Nothing will be done until the structure of our national edifice shall be such as naturally to control eccentric passions and views, and to keep in check demagogues and knaves in the disguise of patriots."[20]

[20] Hamilton's Works, Vol. VI. p. 536.

This speaks for itself, and certainly nothing could be more superfluous than an attempt to elucidate its import and extent. It deserves to be remembered that this was in the thirteenth year of the Constitution, now described as a "frail system," and which, in a previous letter to Morris, was called a "frail and worthless fabric." Hamilton enforced his construction, but upon that point we will say no more until we arrive at a period when it was exposed to a scrutiny by which it was forever exploded. Looking to the construction of the Constitution which I have described for his authority to adopt the measures he deemed necessary to establish his policy, he advanced in his work with his accustomed industry and perseverance. The outlines of that policy were substantially portrayed in his speeches in the Federal Convention, in his letter to General Washington from New York during the session of that body, and in a paper written by him after its adjournment, and now published by his son,-- all of which have already been referred to. It was founded on a conviction, doubtless sincere and at all events not liable to change, that great danger to the federal system was to be apprehended from the hostility of the State governments, and on a consequent desire to reduce their power and importance; on an immovable distrust of the capacities and dispositions of the masses; and on an unshaken belief that the success of the new government could only be secured by assimilating its action to that of the English system as nearly as that could be done without too gross, and therefore dangerous, violation of the well understood and most cherished sentiments of the people.

The power wielded by the English ministry, in Parliament and in the country, springs from influences derived from various sources, mainly from the funding system, from the Bank of England, from connection with the East India Company, and from ability to confer government favors on individuals and classes in the shape of offices and dignities in church and state, of titles, pensions, bounties, franchises, and other special privileges of great value. Its power in these respects is derived from the crown in virtue of its prerogatives, aided by acts of Parliament where these are required by the Constitution.

The measures which Hamilton deemed indispensable to the success of the new government, in addition to those authorized by the Constitution, consisted of

First. A funding system upon the English plan, with authority to assume the separate debts of the States;

Second. A national bank; and,

Third. An unrestricted exercise by Congress of the power to raise money, and the employment of the national revenue in patronizing individual, class, and corporate interests, according to the plan described in his report, nominally on manufactures, but embracing an infinite variety of other concerns.

The funding system, as presented to Congress by him, as well as the bank were not only on the English plan, but as far as that could consistently be effected were copies of the originals, and substantially the same reasons for their establishment here were assigned in his report as had been given for their first creation in England. The third measure, or rather the third in his system of measures, as set forth in the Secretary's report, partook largely of the general character of some of those alluded to above as sources of ministerial power in England, and, in connection with the means of securing legitimate influence allowed by our Constitution, would have clothed the administration here with equal power, even without authority to grant titles of nobility, ecclesiastical preferments and dignities, and other like privileges.

The advantages Hamilton anticipated from these measures consisted of the effect which the fact of their establishment would have upon every question of constitutional power, the popularity and political influence which the administration would acquire in and through their organization, and greater than all, of their inevitable influence upon the future character of the institutions of the country. He might well think that he would not thereafter have any serious difficulty in regard to constitutional power to do what he desired, if he could obtain the passage of acts, according to the forms of the Constitution, authorizing Congress to lend money to the States under a provision in that instrument giving it power to borrow money; to establish a national bank, when a possible ground for pretense to such a power had been expressly excluded from the Constitution, and when every body knew that both the Convention that made it and a vast majority of the States and people by whom it was adopted were at the time opposed to such an institution; and not only to raise money upon the principle of an unlimited power to do so, but also to expend it according to the pleasure of the Government, subject to no other limitation than that it should regard the purpose as conducive to the common defense and general welfare,--a principle he distinctly avowed in his report on manufactures. If he had succeeded in these points and secured his advances, he would have been fully warranted in regarding the enumeration of the powers of Congress contained in the Constitution as a sham, and the brief clause he proposed to the Convention, giving to the national legislature power to pass all laws which it should judge necessary to the common defense and general welfare of the Union, as inserted in its place. The increased power and influence derived by the administration in the course of the organization of some of these measures will be seen as we proceed, and my own views in respect to their combined effects upon our institutions and upon the character of the government, will be given hereafter.

In England the bank was first established, but Hamilton gave precedence here to the funding system and made it the first great measure of his administration of the Treasury Department, contenting himself in the first instance with a declaration, in his report in favor of the funding system, of his intention to connect a bank with it. The Secretary's annunciation of the principles upon which he proposed to found that system, and their resemblance to those by which the English system was regulated, were received with unmistakable signs of dissatisfaction by large portions of the people in all parts of the country. The Legislature of Virginia passed by decided majorities resolutions denouncing the Secretary's plan with great severity. These, with similar demonstrations in other States, show the depth of the excitement of the public mind upon the subject.

The public debt of England had its origin in an early practice of her government to anticipate her resources through loans effected upon pledges of portions of her revenues, to be re-imbursed, principal and interest, at specific periods. These were made to correspond with the time of the probable collection of the taxes out of which the loans were to be paid; and such, it may safely be assumed, was also the origin of public debt in all countries. For a time these anticipations were limited in their amounts to the actual value of the fund upon the credit of which they were obtained, the loans were discharged according to their terms, and the operation proved to be a great convenience to the government without prejudice to any interest. It was not long, however, before a practice, originally no other than a fair business transaction, was perverted to screen men in power from the odium of enforcing taxation to repay the principal sum borrowed. The disproportion between the revenues to be received and the anticipations successively charged upon them soon became too great to leave the government able to pay both principal and interest on the loans which its necessities required. Some device was therefore desirable by which it would be enabled to replenish the public coffers without a too great increase of taxation, which, for obvious reasons, is always the peculiar aversion of those intrusted with the management of public affairs. The plan adopted, in lieu of anticipations of the revenue of the character I have described, was to make loans upon the credit of the nation, re-imbursable at the pleasure of the government, with special and adequate provisions for the payment of the interest only, or to borrow money upon perpetual annuity equivalent to the interest of the sum borrowed, government being at liberty to redeem such annuity at any time by paying back the principal sum, with authority also to borrow on annuities for terms of years and for lives. These became thenceforth leading features in the English funding system.

These facilities proved amply sufficient for every exigency. The public debt increased with unheard of rapidity under the influence and the expenses of the wars in which England was successively engaged. In 1706, when its foundation was laid, it amounted to but little more than five millions sterling, and in 1777 it had increased to one hundred and thirty-six millions sterling. Near the latter period the subjects of public debt, the principles of the English funding system, and their effects in all countries where they had been adopted, were brought to a searching scrutiny by Adam Smith in his "Wealth of Nations," who demonstrated from reason and experience that they had invariably enfeebled every nation which had embraced them. He insisted that there was scarcely an instance in which a public debt contracted and established upon those principles had been fully paid, and that the revenues of the countries subject to such incumbrances had been relieved from the destructive effects of an irredeemable public debt, if relieved at all, either by avowed bankruptcy or by pretended payments through such artifices as adulterations of the coin, or raising its denomination, or by reductions of the rate of interest.

In 1786, four years before the introduction of Hamilton's funding system, the public debt of England had already increased to L276,000,000; and so rapid has been its subsequent growth that the strictures and predictions of Adam Smith are at this day receiving their confirmation in the existence of a national debt of more than L800,000,000. By no people were these facts and circumstances, so far as they had then transpired, better understood than by ours. They had watched the condition of England, in regard to her increasing debt, through the Revolutionary contest in the hope that she would be compelled by the very extent of her indebtedness to stay the hand she had uplifted to enslave them. It ought not therefore to have been a matter of surprise to Hamilton and his associates, and cannot be to us viewing these matters retrospectively, that his recommendation of a funding system, upon the English plan, with a national bank as its adjunct, as the first great measures of the new government, were received by large portions, probably a majority, of the people, with so much dissatisfaction and distrust of the motives in which the recommendation had its origin--a distrust naturally produced by the precipitate resort to the system of a nation against which the hostile feelings of the war had not yet subsided, and which under that system, in the estimation of many sober minded and sagacious men, was rapidly sinking into the gulf of hopeless indebtedness.

No necessity can now be perceived for the adoption at that moment of a scheme of such magnitude as that which Hamilton proposed--one so well calculated to excite jealousy, and against which the warning voice of experience had become so audible. The existing debt, sacred as the price of liberty and entitled to all solicitude for its satisfactory discharge, was not, in view of the increased resources of the Government, either very large or, in any other event than a failure in the payment of interest, ineligibly situated, or in any great danger of soon becoming impracticable or oppressive. The foreign debt then stood at eleven millions, the principal payable by moderate instalments, the last of which, not due till 1808, was never, save a small portion of the French debt, actually funded, and was paid off during the administration of Mr. Madison. The domestic debt of the United States amounted to forty millions, which Secretary Hamilton thought might fairly be regarded as payable at the pleasure of the Government. The interest and instalments as they fell due were therefore the principal subjects to be dealt with.

The change which had at last been effected in the Constitution, securing to the Federal head full power to levy and collect all necessary revenue, and the prospects of an improving trade and increasing prosperity in every branch of business gave of themselves to the Government a good right to anticipate an improvement in the public credit sufficient to enable it to make direct loans abroad upon fair terms, payable at specific and reasonable periods, as had been before done without these advantages. On the avails of these, with the surplus of an increasing revenue over and above the six hundred thousand dollars, which was all that was asked for the support of Government in other respects than the payment of debts, the Secretary might, it would seem, have safely relied to meet accruing demands on account of the public debt. It is well known that such favorable effects resulted from the change which had taken place in the Government and our credit abroad was so greatly improved that loans which had before been obtained with difficulty and in a considerable degree through favor, and in part by means of specific guaranties, were now sought after and taken with avidity in Amsterdam and Antwerp. The friends of the Secretary, and those who favored his policy, naturally claimed that this favorable change was due to his report, and to the acts that were passed in pursuance of his recommendation. A portion of the effects produced may have been attributable to this cause, but it was rendered quite clear that the improvement could not be thus explained as to Holland, where a large part of our foreign debt was held and to which country the whole was soon transferred, by the facts that her bankers not only continued to lend freely to our Government in the old way, upon direct loans, payable at specific periods,--principal and interest,--but expressly declined, as did also our creditors in Antwerp, to accept our proposal for converting the debts due upon loans of that character into a funded domestic stock.

The whole of our foreign debt in Holland, that which was due at the time of the passage of the act establishing the funding system as well as that which was subsequently contracted there and at Antwerp, and the principal part of that held elsewhere, was paid to the entire satisfaction of the creditors by the means I have described, and without being funded. The domestic debt, the least difficult or delicate to deal with, would doubtless have been seasonably and satisfactorily discharged in the same way, if General Hamilton had not, at an early age, imbibed an opinion, which he never changed, that a permanent national debt was an advantage to any country, and likely to be particularly useful in a confederacy like ours. That such was his sincere opinion there cannot be the slightest doubt, and that he contemplated a public debt here of a character as permanent as that was likely to be which then existed in England is fairly to be inferred from his acts.

Hamilton's mind was from a very early period turned to politics, and of political subjects that of finance was from the beginning the favorite theme of his meditations, among the most prominent results of which was a conviction that of the agencies necessary to good government, whatever might be its form, there were none more useful than a well funded public debt and a judiciously constructed national bank. At the early age of twenty-three, whilst filling a post of subordinate rank in the army, he addressed an anonymous communication (as I have before mentioned) to Robert Morris, whose mind was inclined in the same direction, and who was extensively employed in the management of fiscal affairs, enforcing with much ability his favorite ideas. Some of the contents of this communication are given in the "Life of Hamilton" by his son. In a subsequent letter to the same gentleman, he argues in support of kindred positions. In his report upon public credit he advances the same favorable opinion, and in substantially the same language, of the effects of the particular debt he proposed to fund upon terms which promised perpetuity. He did, it is true, accompany the latter declaration with a protest against the latitude, inviting to prodigality, which was sometimes given to the idea of the utility of a public debt, and with a recommendation in favor of the establishment of a sinking fund, and other reservations and qualifications, couched in the guarded terms usually employed by able men in state papers upon controverted public questions. But the report contained nothing inconsistent with the idea of keeping on foot a national debt as long as it did not become "too large,"--a condition that could scarcely fail to give way to the supposed exigencies of the moment,--and the farther condition of an indispensable necessity for its continuance never found a place in his reports or weight in his opinions. On the contrary, the advantages of a national debt in preparing the people for those periods of oppressive assessment to which all nations are occasionally exposed, by constantly levying a reasonable tax to discharge interest, a principal reason in favor of a public debt assigned in his letter to Morris; the utility and convenience of having always at hand a band whose special interest in the stability of the government would promptly rally them to its support,--an idea never long absent from Hamilton's mind; the benefits which the agricultural, manufacturing, and commercial interests would derive from the funding of seventy millions of debt in the form and upon the principles he proposed, giving to it the capacity of being "substituted for money" and increasing by that amount the floating capital, and to a great extent the circulating medium of the country; the beneficial influence of a funded debt in raising the value of land, in proof of which the experience of England is cited, besides supplying those important classes with means to improve and enlarge their respective pursuits, and increasing those facilities by reducing the rate of interest, constituted the arguments and persuasions set forth in glowing and captivating terms in his reports, and though not necessarily confined to a permanent national debt, indicate very clearly, to my mind at least, that it was such a debt that he had in view.

The uses to which the sinking fund had been applied in England and its inefficiency in the reduction of the national debt were well understood by the Secretary. The explanations of its greater efficacy here in after times will be given in another place. They had no connection with the views that were prevalent in the councils of the nation at the moment of which we are speaking. Every act of the Secretary was in keeping with the inference I have stated. In addition to the principle he proposed as the basis of his system, which, if not perpetual funding in express terms, postponed redemption to so remote and indefinite a period as to render it next to certain that it would never occur, there were other circumstances scarcely less confirmatory of the assumption that such was his intention.

The stand taken by Hamilton in the provision he proposed and which was adopted for a portion of the domestic debt had a great influence in creating the impression that his funding system had other than fiscal objects in view. His opponents not thinking either that system or the bank necessary for the public service--an opinion vindicated and sustained by subsequent experience--readily attributed the strong desire manifested for their establishment to political designs on the part of their author. Jefferson denounced the financial scheme as a "puzzle to exclude popular understanding and inquiry, and a machine for the corruption of the Legislature." In aid of the latter charge, besides going at least some length to sustain the imputation of Hamilton's desire for an unnecessary increase of the public debt, came these facts: A large proportion of the domestic debt consisted of certificates of indebtedness given by the United States to the soldiers who fought our battles, and to the farmers, manufacturers, and merchants who furnished supplies for their support. These had been given because the Government had no money, but under promises of speedy payment. The holders were frequently driven by their necessities, and by misrepresentations in respect to the chances of payment, to part with them for trifling amounts. Had the matter stopped there, however much regretted and condemned, it might not have attracted the notice which was taken of it. But when Hamilton proposed to put the original holders and the fraudulent purchasers of these certificates upon the same footing, and when it became known to the members of Congress, which sat with closed doors, that the bill would pass in that shape, every part of the country was overrun by speculators, sped by horse and packet expresses, buying up large portions of the certificates still held by those to whom they were originally given at the rate of five shillings and, in some instances, of two shillings and sixpence in the pound. It was never doubted that members of Congress and their particular friends participated in these speculations, and realized large sums by the certificates being funded at their nominal amounts. When the bill came up, several gentlemen, who afterwards became prominent members of the Republican party, earnestly supported a proposition to make a composition between the original holders and the assignees of these papers, allowing to the latter the highest prices they had ever brought in the market, and settling with the former for the residue. Such an arrangement might have been effected without embarrassment to the treasury by satisfactory grants of public lands, and the amount of debts might have been thus materially reduced. Mr. Madison in a sensible speech supported the justice of some such composition; but the friends of the Secretary in Congress, some of them interested in the result, carried the measure which had been elaborately argued in advance by Hamilton, in his report, and by which the whole was awarded to the speculators. The entire transaction caused deep disgust in the minds of many who felt solicitous for the purity of the Government, and not a few believed that the scramble which ensued was foreseen and counted upon as a source of influence to enlist Congress on the side of the administration. Their hostility to a system susceptible, as they thought, of such practices, was of course greatly inflamed.

The construction thus placed upon the Secretary's course received its strongest confirmation from his proposal and untiring efforts for the assumption of the State debts. The first object of a prudent financier would seem to be to keep the debt he has to deal with at the lowest practicable point. Hamilton, on the contrary, whilst struggling with embarrassments in respect to the debts for which the United States were legally bound, upon the largest portion of which many years of interest had been suffered to accumulate, proposed to increase the liability twenty-five millions by the voluntary assumption of debts which the Federal Government was under no obligations to pay; an assumption not only unsolicited on the part of the indebted States, but to which there was the best reason for believing that several among them would be opposed. The special representatives of the latter in the Senate, where the proposition originated, so earnestly contested it that the clause of the bill to carry it into effect could only be passed by a majority of two, was in the first instance rejected in the House of Representatives against the united influences of the administration, and could only be reconsidered and barely carried by means of a discreditable intrigue to which the Secretary and Mr. Jefferson, as the latter has acknowledged with shame and contrition, were parties.

The reasons assigned by Hamilton for this forced assumption of a debt which had never been audited, and the amount of which they were obliged to guess at, though framed with his usual ability, cannot, I should think, he now regarded as sufficient to justify the step. The weight which they might by any be supposed to possess was overbalanced by the obvious unconstitutionality of the measure. It adopted as well the debts of the States which, upon the final settlement between them and the United States, were found in debt to the latter, as of those which proved to have balances in their favor, and was therefore a loan by the Federal Government to the former class of States, made under the power in the Constitution authorizing Congress to borrow money.

This measure, like that which preceded it, was well calculated to strengthen the suspicion with which the minds of his opponents became thoroughly imbued, that Hamilton in all his measures had in view the advancement of partisan objects, from its peculiar adaptation to the promotion of a leading point in his whole policy,--that of weakening State authority and strengthening that of the General Government at their expense. The distinctness and strength of expression with which this policy was avowed by him, in papers published by his son, have already been seen. Among the means suggested was the adoption of measures by which the attention of the people might be diverted from the State governments, upon which it was thought to be too intensely fixed, and turned towards the Federal head, and by which their passions might be excited and turned in the same channel. What single measure could exert greater influence in giving effect to this policy or show more strikingly the hand of a master than that by which the intense and constant solicitude of the holders of twenty-five millions of debts, scattered, in comparatively small sums, through the different States, and embracing, it is fair to presume, the most active of their citizens, was turned from the local authorities to the Federal Government, first for the settlement of the amount, and next for the payment of their demands,--by which the States themselves became liable for the amounts so paid to a Government which, certainly in some of its departments, regarded them as rival not to say dangerous powers, and by which also the disreputable scramble for those debts, commenced in the case of the certificates of the United States, would be revived.

The conflicting views entertained upon these subjects by Hamilton and Jefferson soon assumed the form of a distinct and well defined issue between the friends and political followers of each,--the former composing the Federal party, and the latter constituting elements of which the Republican party, then in embryo, was formed. Hamilton's doctrine, and for a season the avowed creed of his party, was that there were advantages in the existence of a national debt which more than counter-balanced any evils that might arise from its unnecessary continuance, and this faith shaped the whole course of their action upon the subject. Its subjection to the operations of a sinking fund, and the qualification that the amount of the debt should be kept within proper limits, were of course features in their platform. Estimating the results of the former here by its efficiency in England, and instructed by the experience of all nations that restraints upon the accumulation of debt, however solemnly imposed, are of no account with applicants for grants from the public treasury, and unhappily little more respected by men in power when the importunities of friends and supporters are brought in competition with the interests of posterity, it was not difficult to foresee the futility of these conditions. Mr. Jefferson, on the contrary, from the beginning regarded a public debt as a "mortal canker" from which it was the duty of the Government to relieve the country at the earliest practicable moment, and in this spirit he and his friends acted throughout.

The subject of Finance had not at that early period been made as familiar to the American mind as it has since become, and the genius of Hamilton and the sanction of Washington, which his plans were supposed to receive, were well calculated to discourage opposition to them. But many of those who disapproved of his course were not to be moved from what they regarded as the line of duty by any considerations personal to themselves. They resisted Hamilton's financial schemes from the start, and it was in the discussions upon this issue that some, who subsequently became famous leaders in the old Republican party, fleshed their maiden swords. No two measures ever attracted a larger share of the attention of the American people, excited more deeply their feelings and their apprehensions, or exerted a greater influence upon the politics of this country than did the funding system and the first Bank of the United States. The peculiar results of the contest that was waged in respect to them will be noticed hereafter.

Hamilton had done much by their establishment and organization to strengthen the Federal arm, and proportionately to weaken the State governments, but the influence he derived from these measures was not sufficiently operative upon several classes whom he desired to conciliate. The wished for impression had been made upon the commercial class,--at all times a powerful body and by the nature of their pursuits inclined to favor strong governments, banks, and funding systems,--upon the domestic creditors of the General Government, upon the creditors of the several State governments, upon all who had a passion for gambling in stocks, to whose appetites he furnished so much aliment,--a numerous, crafty, and influential portion of almost every community,--and upon all who wanted to borrow or had money to lend, a class still more numerous. Besides these, whom Mr. Canning called the "train-bands of commerce," in general the most dangerous to encounter and the most efficient when at his service, there were still larger interests, and in the aggregate more powerful, upon whom the Secretary desired to make similar impressions and to secure their attachment to his system.

In August, 1791, whilst concocting the measures by which he hoped to secure the support of these, and flushed by the success which had hitherto crowned his efforts, he thus (as I have already quoted) addressed his great rival, Mr. Jefferson:--

"I own," said he, "it is my opinion, though I do not publish it in Dan or Beersheba, that the present Government is not that which will answer the ends of society, by giving stability and protection to its rights, and that it will probably be found expedient to go into the British form; however, since we have undertaken the experiment, I am for giving it a fair course, whatever my expectations may be. The success, indeed, so far, is greater than I had expected, and therefore at present success seems more possible than it had done heretofore, and there are still other and other stages of improvement, which, if the present does not succeed, may be tried and ought to be tried before we give up the republican form altogether."

First in the order of time among "the other and other stages of improvement" with which the prolific mind of the Secretary was busied, were doubtless those embraced in his "Report on Manufactures" which made its appearance four months afterwards, and was probably then in course of preparation. It contains more than a hundred folio pages, in print, and is perhaps the most thoroughly elaborated and artfully devised state paper to be found in the archives of any country. Manufactures were alone spoken of in the title, but it embraced every species of industry that offered the slightest chance of being successfully prosecuted in the United States, and contained a very full and carefully considered exposition of their respective conditions, and of the facilities by which their success might be increased, to extend which to those diversified interests it undertook to show was within the power and the duty of the Government. This report, on account of the striking illustration it affords of the progress of parties, and the powerful influence it exerted upon their fate, is well entitled to the fullest notice. But it is not possible within the limits I have prescribed to myself to go as fully into the review of such a paper as justice to the subject would require. I must therefore content myself with an abridged account of the various branches of industry the advancement of which was the design of its author, and of the manner in which he proposed to accomplish his object.

The manufactured articles which he specified as fit subjects for governmental aid were those made of skins, of iron, of wood, of flax and hemp, bricks, coarse tiles, and potters' wares, ardent spirits and malt liquors, writing and printing paper, hats, refined sugars, oils of animals and seeds, soap and candles, copper and brass wares, tin wares, carriages of all kinds, snuff, chewing and smoking tobacco, starch, lampblack and other painters' colors, and gunpowder. This enumeration was followed by a detailed statement of the great variety of articles embraced in the general denominations. Besides these, which he said had attained a considerable degree of maturity, there was a vast sum of household manufacturing which was made not only sufficient for the use of the families that made them but for sale also, and in some instances for exportation, and consisted of great quantities of coarse cloths, coatings, serges, and flannels, linsey-woolseys, hosiery of wool, cotton and thread, coarse fustians, jeans and muslins, checked and striped cotton and linen goods, bedticks, coverlets and counterpanes, tow linens, coarse shirtings, sheetings, toweling, and table linen, and various mixtures of wool and cotton, and of cotton and flax.

These observations were, he said, the pleasing result of the investigation into which the subject of his report had led, and were applicable to the Southern as well as to the Middle and Northern States. He also designated the principal raw materials of which these manufactures were composed, and which were, or were capable of being, raised or produced by ourselves. These were iron, copper, lead, fossil coal, wool, skins, grain, flax and hemp, cotton, wool, silk, &c., &c.

The Secretary contended that the growth and production of all the articles last named were, in common with the manufactures of which they constituted the raw material, entitled to the encouragement and specific aid of the Federal Government.

He next pointed out the various modes in which that aid might be afforded, varying its application according to circumstances; viz.:

1st. By protecting duties.

2d. By prohibition of rival articles, or duties equivalent to prohibition.

3d. By prohibition of the exportation of the materials of manufactures.

4th. By pecuniary bounties.

5th. By premiums.

6th. By exemption of the materials of manufactures from duties.

7th. By drawbacks of duties on the same materials.

8th. By encouragement of new inventions at home and the introduction of others from abroad.

9th. By judicious regulations for the inspection of manufactured commodities.

10th. By facilitating pecuniary remittances; and,

11th. By facilitating the transportation of commodities by roads and canals.

Of the power of the Federal Government to promote the objects spoken of by the means suggested, with two exceptions, he said there could be no doubt. The exceptions were the encouragement of new inventions and the facilities to transportation by roads and canals. In respect to the specific execution of these measures he confessed and regretted that there was some doubt. But to the power of giving aid, so far as that could be done by the application of money, he insisted that there was no exception: "Whatever concerns the general interest of learning, of agriculture, of manufactures, and of commerce are" he said, "within the sphere of the national concerns as far as regards an application of money;" and he proposed, first, to raise a fund out of the surplus of additional duties laid and appropriated to replace defalcations proceeding from the abolition or diminution of duty diverted for purposes of protection, which he thought would be more than adequate for the payment of all bounties which should be decreed; and, secondly, to constitute a fund for the operations of a board to be established for promoting arts, agriculture, manufactures, and commerce. To this Board he proposed to give power to apply the funds so raised to defray the expenses of the emigration of artists and manufacturers in particular branches of extraordinary importance; to induce the prosecution and introduction of useful discoveries, inventions, and improvements by proportionate rewards, judiciously held out and applied; to encourage by premiums, both honorable and lucrative, the exertions of individuals and classes in relation to the several objects they were charged with promoting; and to afford such other aids to those objects as might be generally designated by law;--adding to all this that it often happens that the capitals employed are not equal to the purposes of bringing from abroad workmen of a superior kind, and that here, in cases worthy of it, the auxiliary agency of Government would in all probability be useful. There are also valuable workmen in every branch who are prevented from emigrating solely by the want of means. Occasional aids to such persons, properly administered, might be, he suggested, the source of valuable acquisitions to the country.

The thorough and minute consideration bestowed on its numerous details, the well sustained consistency of the argument with the principles upon which it was founded, the felicity and clearness with which its author's views were expressed, and the evidence it furnished of well directed and comprehensive research, stamp this remarkable document as the ablest state paper that proceeded from his pen during the whole of his political career. But able as it was, it yet, as we shall see when we recur to the action of parties, contributed more than all that he had before done to the prostration of the political standing of its author and to the overthrow of his party. Its bold assumptions of power and the jubilant spirit in which they were expressed afforded the clearest indications, as well to his opponents as to the country, that he regarded his victory over the Constitution as complete. He spoke of the national legislature, unhesitatingly and as one having authority, as possessing, in virtue of the construction of the Constitution he had established, all the power with very limited exceptions which he insisted in the Convention ought to be given to it.

Mr. Jefferson denounced the recommendations of the report to President Washington with great warmth and earnestness. He described it as going far beyond any pretensions to power under the Constitution which had yet been set up, and as a document to which many eyes were turned as one which was to let us know whether we lived under a limited or an unlimited government.[21]

[21] 4 Jefferson's Correspondence, p. 457.

But the views of the Secretary of the Treasury in the establishment of the policy of which we have been speaking have as yet been but imperfectly described. They had a breadth and an extent of which superficial observers had no idea. The increased strength the General Government derived from turning towards itself so many and such active men as the holders and purchasers of the public debt, State and National, and the influence which the patronage attached to his financial scheme would give to the existing administration, were both important, and doubtless entered into Hamilton's designs. The views of common minds might well have been limited to such acquisitions. But these results fell far short of Hamilton's anticipations. His partiality for the English system, it is natural to presume, arose in some degree from his birth and early training; but study and reflection, I am inclined to think, had quite as much to do with bringing his mind to the conclusions it cherished with so much earnestness. Among the public men of his day there was not one who appears to have devoted a larger share of his time to examinations into and meditation upon public affairs. There was not one who wrote more or with more ease upon the subjects of government in general and public financial questions in particular. Almost every thing he said and wrote and did, in these respects, went to show that the elements of power by which the English government had been raised from a crude and in some degree impracticable condition to the seemingly palmy state at which it had arrived when his successive reports were made had been justly reviewed and thoroughly considered by him. The result of this survey was a conviction that for the favorable changes, as he regarded them, which had taken place in the condition of England she was more indebted to the operation of her bank and funding system than to any other cause. These, like his corresponding systems, had been originally formed for the accomplishment of immediate and limited objects. His were avowedly to revive and to uphold our sinking public credit; theirs, to relieve the government established by the Revolution of 1688 from its dependence upon the landed aristocracy for its revenues, and to secure the acquisition of ample means to defray the expenses of the war in which England was at the time involved. From such beginnings these principal measures, aided by kindred and affiliated establishments of which they were the parents, had with astonishing rapidity developed a great political power in the state, soon and ever since distinguished from its associates in the government of the country as the MONEY POWER,--a power destined to produce greater changes in the workings of the English system than had been accomplished by the Revolution itself.

The rival powers of the state had down to that period consisted of the crown and the landed aristocracy. The measures out of which the money power was constructed were designed, as has been stated, to render the former, restored to greater favor with the nation by the Revolution, more independent of the latter than it had hitherto been. This new power had not only performed its duty in that regard, acting in the capacity of umpire between the crown and the landed aristocracy, (the latter before so omnipotent,) but had at times found itself able to control the action of both through the influence of public opinion, to which it had given a vitality and force it never before possessed.

Mr. Bancroft, in his able history of the United States, has given a condensed and I have no doubt a very correct account of the rise and of a part of the progress of the money power in England, as they are presented by her historians. His entire remarks upon the subject are full of interest and instruction, and I regret that I am obliged to restrict myself to the following extract:--"Moreover, as the expenses of wars soon exceeded the revenue of England, the government prepared to avail itself of the largest credit which, not the accumulations of wealth only, but the floating credits of commerce, and the funding system could supply. The price of such aid was political influence. That the government should, as its paramount policy, promote commerce, domestic manufactures, and a favorable balance of trade; that the classes benefited by this policy should sustain the government with their credit and their wealth, was the reciprocal relation and compromise on which rested the fate of parties in England. The floating credits of commerce, aided by commercial accumulations, soon grew powerful enough to balance the landed interest; stock aristocracy competed with feudalism. So imposing was the spectacle of the introduction of the citizens and of commerce as the arbiter of alliances, the umpire of factions, the judge of war and peace, that it roused the attention of speculative men: that at last Bolingbroke, claiming to speak for the landed aristocracy, described his opponents, the Whigs, as the party of the banks, the commercial corporations, and 'in general, the moneyed interest;' and the gentle Addison, espousing the cause of the burghers, declares nothing to be more reasonable than that 'those who have engrossed the riches of the nation should have the management of its public treasure, and the direction of its fleets and armies.' In a word the old English aristocracy was compelled to respect the innovating element embodied in the moneyed interest."[22]

[22] 3 Bancroft's History of the United States, p. 8.

The full establishment here of a similar power, by attaching to the bank and funding systems the political influence they had acquired in England, was, beyond all doubt, the "other and still other stages of improvement" alluded to by Hamilton in his encouraging conversation with Jefferson, in which he expressed a hope, for the first time, that the inadequacy of the Constitution might yet be overcome, and the necessity of returning to the English form be at least postponed. That the leading supporters of his policy at least understood and entered into Hamilton's views will be seen in the following extract from a letter written to him by Fisher Ames, which will be found in the first volume of Randall's "Life of Jefferson," at p. 638: "All the influence of the moneyed men ought to be wrapped up in the Union (Federal Government) and in one Bank," &c.

Of the three great elements of power under the English system--the crown, the landed aristocracy, and the moneyed interest--Hamilton regarded the latter, I have no doubt, as the most salutary even in England. There was little in the pride, pomp, and circumstance of the kingly office, and still less in the feudal grandeur of a landed aristocracy, to captivate a mind like his; he advocated the monarchical form for special reasons of a very different character, and these he assigned in the Convention. Indeed, he all but expressed this preference when he said to John Adams,--"Strike out of the English system its corruptions and you make the government an impracticable machine." Corruption in some form being the means by which the money power ordinarily exerts its influence, Hamilton was not slow in foreseeing the advantages to be derived from that power in the United States. It is true that the influence it exerted in England was liberal in its character, and beneficial, at least in its political bearings, to the middle classes. We have seen that one object and a principal effect of its establishment was to reduce the overshadowing influence of the landed aristocracy which existed so long and exerted a sway so imperious over the country--an object in the accomplishment of which the members of the "stock aristocracy" were, in all probability, not a little stimulated by recollections of their past exclusions not only from all participation in the management of public affairs, but also from many social distinctions. The landed aristocracy of England is composed of a race of men superior in manly virtues and consistency of character to similar classes in other countries, but notwithstanding these undeniable and commendable traits they are, by force of their condition and by the law of their minds, in a great degree the result of that condition, unwilling to extend to their unprivileged fellow-subjects that equality in public and private rights to which we republicans consider them justly entitled. In this respect there is no difference between them, be they Whigs or Tories,--their first duty being, in the estimation of both, to "stand by their order." It is equally true that it did not comport with Hamilton's policy to promote the establishment of any power here the influence of which would enure to the increase and security of political power in the people, and that, to answer his purposes, the results of the operations of the money power here must be the reverse of what they were in England. He was too well versed in politics and parties not to know that the action of every political organization in a state takes its direction from the character and condition of its principal rival, and that all have their rivals. If one is not found to exist they will soon make one, for such is the natural operation of political parties in any degree free.

We differed greatly from England in the condition and political aspect of affairs; we had no monarchical institutions, no landed aristocracy to excite the rivalry and opposition of the money power. It was itself, on the contrary, destined, when firmly established, to become whatever of aristocracy could co-exist with our political system. Its natural antagonist would be the democratic spirit of the country,--that spirit which had been the lion in Hamilton's path from the beginning, the dread of which had destroyed his usefulness and blasted the fair prospects that were presented to the youthful patriot,--that spirit which he doubtless sincerely believed adverse to order, and destitute of due respect for the rights of property. It was to keep down this spirit that he desired the establishment of a money power here which should stand by the Government as its interested ally, and support it against popular disaffection and tumult. He well understood that, if he accomplished that desire, they would soon become the principal antagonistic influences on our political stage. He knew also, what was not less satisfactory to his feelings, that if the anticipations, not to say hopes, which he never ceased to entertain, should be realized, of the presentation of a fair opportunity for the introduction of his favorite institutions without too great a shock to public feeling; there could be no class of men who would be better disposed to second his views than those whose power in the state he had so largely contributed to establish. To be allied to power, permanent, if possible, in its character and splendid in its appendages, is one of the strongest passions which wealth inspires. The grandeur of the Crown and of the landed aristocracy affords a fair vent to that in England. Here, where it is deprived of that indulgence, it maintains a constant struggle for the establishment of a moneyed oligarchy, the most selfish and monopolizing of all depositories of political power, and is only prevented from realizing its complete designs by the democratic spirit of the country.

Hamilton succeeded for a season in all his wishes. He established the money power upon precisely the same foundations upon which it had been raised in England. He founded a political school the implied alliance between which and the Government was similar to that which was formed between the money power in England and the Revolutionary Government in 1688. A party adhering inflexibly to the leading principle of that school had survived his own overthrow, is still in existence, and will continue to exist as long as ours remains a free Government, and as long as the characters and dispositions of men remain what they are. To combat the democratic spirit of the country was the object of its original establishment, an object which it has pursued with unflagging diligence, by whatever name it may have been designated.

Having brought the general subject to this point it is due to truth and justice that I should, before I proceed farther, refer to considerations connected with Hamilton's motives which have been already but casually and partially noticed.

In all his steps he was doubtless influenced at bottom by a sincere desire to promote the good of his country, and as little by personal views as ordinarily falls to the lot of man. A riveted conviction that the masses were destitute of a sufficient love of order and respect for private rights, with an entire distrust, consequently, of their capacity for self-government, lay at the foundation of his whole course,--a course which the matured judgment of the country has definitively condemned as to both teacher and doctrine. Subsequent experience of long duration has shown, as I have remarked already, that the dispositions of our people are eminently conservative in respect to public order and the rights of property; exceptions to the general rule have been witnessed here as well as elsewhere, but they have been of very limited duration and seldom the cause of much mischief. There have been few if any countries that have been more fortunate in this regard.

I have also spoken of Hamilton's preference for monarchical institutions, upon evidence of which I have not felt myself at liberty to doubt. But it is due to the memory of that distinguished man that we should speak of his disposition in that respect with more precision than might be deemed necessary in other cases. To assume that he was a friend to monarchy as it existed in England in the times of the Stuarts and their predecessors would be doing him gross injustice. No man in the country, in his day, respected less the absurd dogma of the divine right of kings, or regarded with more contempt the reverence paid by gaping crowds to the pomp and pageantry of royalty and to the carefully guarded relics and reliquaries of the hoar institution of monarchy, than Alexander Hamilton. He was, beyond all doubt, entirely sincere when he said, in the Federal Convention, that he "was as zealous an advocate for liberty as any man whatsoever, and trusted he would be as willing a martyr to it, though he differed as to the form in which it was most eligible;" and had he been a fellow-subject and contemporary of Russell, and Sydney, and Hampden, we may believe that he would have proved himself as prompt as either to make sacrifices equal to theirs in resistance to arbitrary power. Expectations of personal advantages through the favor of royalty did not enter into the formation of his opinions. It was monarchy as modified and re-established by the Revolution of 1688 that was the object of Hamilton's preference. In the same speech from which I have just quoted he gave with manly candor his reasons for believing that the English model presented the fairest chance of any system then extant for the selection of a good executive. He contrasted the probable advantages in this regard between a chief magistrate selected, in the first instance, by Parliament and continued by descent, and one elected by the people for a limited period, and frankly argued in favor of the former. His opinion was mainly controlled by that want of confidence in the capacity of the people for self-government which he never hesitated to acknowledge, and which, as I have said, lay at the foundation of his political views. But it was not the king, as such, that he sought after, but a competent chief magistrate; and he advocated monarchical institutions only because he thought them the most likely to produce such an one. In a speech delivered by him in the New York Ratification Convention, which bears the stamp of his own revision, he said, "It is an undeniable truth that the body of the people in every country sincerely desire its prosperity, but it is equally unquestionable that they do not possess the discernment and stability necessary for systematic government." He never exhibited a preference for monarchy in the abstract; no one ever heard him express a partiality for or an attachment to this or that royal family save as their acts were more or less meritorious, and I cannot think that such considerations ever swayed his course. He treated the question not as one of personal preference, but as one involving the chances of good government. In deciding this question he may have erred, and few in our country can deny or seriously doubt that he did greatly err; but it was a question that he had a right to entertain, more especially at the formation of the Government, and one in respect to which, his opinion having been honestly formed, error could not fairly be made the subject of reproach.

CHAPTER IV.

Excitement of the Public Mind caused by Hamilton's Measures--Great Men brought thus into the Political Field--The Preponderance of leading Politicians and Commercial Classes on the side of Hamilton--Not so with the Landed Interest--Character of Farmers and Planters of the United States--Position of the Landed Interest toward the Anti-Federal Party and toward Hamilton's System--Success in maintaining its Principles greater in the Southern than in the Northern States and the Causes thereof--The Landed Interest the Fountain of the old Republican Party--Course of that Party toward Washington and his Administration--Decline of the Federal Party--Hamilton's Course in the Convention the most Brilliant and Creditable of his Political Career--His Candor and Devotion to Principle on that Occasion--His subsequent Loss of the Confidence of the Friends of Republican Government--Coincidences and Contrasts in the Public Lives of Hamilton and Madison--Their several Contributions in the First Congress to the Promotion of the Financial Branch of the Public Service--The Fate and the Fruits of each--The Country chiefly indebted to them for the Constitution--Their Treatment of it after its Adoption not the same--The Provision authorizing Amendments necessary to save the Constitution from Rejection--Memorials from New York and Virginia--Dread of a New Convention on the Part of the Federalists--Madison's Amendments-- Consequences of their Adoption--Character of Madison's Statesmanship-- Different Courses of Hamilton and Madison on Questions of Constitutional Power--Unconstitutionality of Hamilton's Measures--His Consciousness thereof--His Sense of the Obligations of Public Men--His View of the Constitution as "a Temporary Bond of Union"--Subsequent Change of Opinion, but Final Return in 1802 to his Original View--Separation between him and Madison--"Sapping and Mining Policy" of Hamilton--That Policy counteracted by the Republican Party--Discrimination between Washington and Hamilton in the Adoption of the latter's Policy--Probable Ground of Washington's Official Approval of the Bank Bill--Subsequent similar Position and Conduct of Madison--Instances of a like Transcending of Constitutional Limits under a supposed Necessity, by Jefferson and by Jackson--The Hamiltonian Rule of Construction discarded by Washington in the case of his Veto of the First Apportionment Bill--Portions of the Community liable to be attracted to Hamilton's Policy--The Principles of that Policy inaugurated in England in 1688--Extension of its Influence in this Country to almost every Class but the Landed Interest--Points of Agreement and of Difference between Hamilton and Politicians of his School in our Time--Exceptions to the General Rule--Influence of the Money Power in attracting Literary and Professional Men--Great Preponderance in Numbers of Newspapers and Periodicals supporting the Views of the Money Power over those devoted to the Advocacy of Democratic Principles--The same Fact observable in Monarchical Countries--Caucuses and Conventions not necessary to the Harmony of the Federal Party--Sagacity indicated by Hamilton's System--The Secret of its Failure in the Numerical Preponderance, often underrated, of the Agricultural Class--The Policy best adapted to succeed with our People is that of a Strict Construction of the Constitution as to the Powers of the General Government--Such the Successful Policy of Jefferson, Madison, and Jackson--Struggles of the Money Power Ineffectual till crowned with Exceptional Success in the Overthrow of Van Buren's Administration--Latitudinarianism of Hamilton's School--John Quincy Adams elected as a Convert to the Principles of the Republican Party--His early Disavowal of those Principles, and the consequent Overthrow of his Administration--Relative Power of the Landed Interest--The Safety of our Institutions depends on the Right Convictions of the great Agricultural Class--Growth of the Money Power in England--The Political Influence of that Power Beneficent in Europe but Injurious in the United States.

I have already spoken of the extent to which the public mind was excited by Hamilton's measures. Large portions of the people regarded the most prominent among them as violations of the Constitution, and most of them as servile imitations of the English system, inexpedient in themselves and contrary to the genius and spirit of our institutions. Their arraignment and vindication brought into the political field the ablest men of the country at a period when she abounded in great men. The American Revolution accomplished here that which the French Revolution, then at its commencement, and similar crises in all countries and times, have brought about, namely, the production of great men by great events, developing and calling into action upon a large scale intellects the powers of which, but for their application to great transactions, might have remained unknown alike to their possessors and to the world. Among the master minds which were thus roused to political activity were Thomas Jefferson, Alexander Hamilton, James Madison, Patrick Henry, John and Samuel Adams, John Jay, Chancellor Livingston, Gouverneur Morris, George Clinton, Robert Yates, Chancellor Lansing, John Langdon, Elbridge Gerry, Rufus King, Roger Sherman, John Dickinson, Speight and Williamson and the Rutledges, Pinckneys, and Middletons of North and South Carolina, Chace and Luther Martin of Maryland, Jackson, Few, and Baldwin, of Georgia, John Mason, Marshall, Pendleton, and Wythe of Virginia, and others; men, some of whom have under various circumstances added celebrity to the best informed communities in the world and at one of the brightest periods of the human intellect, and who, if they could now be congregated, would eclipse the great men of any country.

Hamilton's measures, of which the funding system was the pioneer, presented their first field, after the adoption of the Federal Constitution, for the display of their opinions and talents. They supported in those grave discussions, with few exceptions, relatively the same principles by which they had been influenced in respect to federal politics during the government of the Confederation, by which also they and men of their stamp had been governed under the colonial system, and to which they would have adhered, in all probability, throughout the intermediate period if they had not been driven into open rebellion by the indiscriminate and intolerable oppression of a bigoted tyrant, and by their own innate hatred of wrong and outrage, without immediate regard to the government that should result from their revolution.

Jefferson was absent from the country during a large portion of the government of the Confederation, and through the entire period of the formation and adoption of the new Constitution. He sympathized throughout with the feelings and concurred in the opinions of the Anti-Federal party, with the exceptions that he was not opposed to conferring on the Federal Government the powers to regulate commerce and to raise its own revenues; was in favor of a convention for the construction of a new constitution, and of the formation by that body of a substantive and effective federal government, composed of legislative, executive, and judicial departments; approved of the Constitution as made, with modifications which were principally provided for by amendments proposed and adopted, and was sincerely anxious for its ratification. These things have, I know, been controverted and are still disbelieved by many, but will be found fully established by references to the following documents, viz.: Jefferson's "Correspondence," Vol. I. p. 441; Vol. II. pp. 64, 162, 221, 236, 273, 303; Letter to Washington expressing his anxiety for the adoption of the Constitution; p. 310, some strong remarks in favor of it; p. 342, to Madison, congratulating him on its adoption, and p. 348, to John Jay, to the same effect.

Of Madison's character and general course I have already spoken. His position at the period now under consideration differed from that of all his contemporaries in the public service. He had supported all the commercial and financial measures advocated by the Federal party during the government of the Confederation, and had been as active, and I think as efficient, as Hamilton in his efforts to promote the call of the Federal Convention; had opposed, with ability and firmness, the Anti-Federal plan of a Constitution; had, as far as we have knowledge of Washington's opinions, acted in concert with him in the Convention, and was first selected by him at a later period to prepare his Farewell Address; had combined his labors with those of Hamilton and Jay to promote the ratification of the Constitution by the well-known papers of the "Federalist," and, upon the whole, had done more than any other man to secure that great object. Yet there had been no time, as before observed, when he could with propriety have been regarded as a member of the Federal party, in the sense in which Hamilton, Adams, and Jay were so regarded, or when he did not possess the confidence of the Anti-Federal party, in respect to all public questions other than those to which I have referred, and, what is still more remarkable, there was not, during the whole of this period, a single occasion on which his perfect probity and disinterestedness were not very generally felt and acknowledged.

Among the leading politicians of the epoch of which I speak, the preponderance in numbers, in wealth, in social position, and possibly in talent, was on the side of Hamilton; and when to these were added the commercial and numerous other classes interested in and dependent upon the money power then just rising into importance, an estimate may be formed of his ability to give tone and direction to the state and to society, and to cover with odium those who disapproved of his measures by charging them with personal hostility to Washington, who so well deserved the confidence and good will of all, and who enjoyed them to an extent that led John Adams, at a much later day, to stigmatize the deference paid to him as "impious homage." Hamilton wielded this great power with tremendous effect, for, although his judgment in the management of men was always deemed defective, he exerted, in the promotion of his particular objects, talents and industry which could not fail to produce great results. His activity and capacity for labor were not equaled by any of his contemporaries save Madison; his powers of persuasion and the effects of his eloquence were strikingly exemplified by his success in making Mr. Jefferson believe, on his first arrival at the seat of government from France, that the safety of the Union depended upon the passage of the bill for the assumption of the State debts, which had been at the moment rejected in the House of Representatives by a majority of one or two, and in inducing him to "hold the candle," as Jefferson afterwards described it, to a bargain by which Messrs. White and Lee, Southern members, were prevailed upon to vote for its reconsideration and passage on condition that Hamilton would get the requisite number of Northern members to vote for the establishment of the seat of the Federal Government on slave territory. Jefferson gives an interesting account of the earnestness of Hamilton's appeal to him on the subject, and of his own mortification and regret at having been made a party to so exceptionable a transaction in support of a measure he soon found the strongest reasons to condemn.[23]

[23] Jefferson's Correspondence, Vol. 4. p. 449.

The attention of every American community which possessed facilities for foreign commerce or manufactures, or for any of the various pursuits enumerated in his great report, and especially when they possessed also superior skill and enterprise, was at once directed to Hamilton's scheme of government for encouragement, and they certainly were not always indisposed to accept the seductive offers held out to them. But fortunately for the country and for the cause of good government there was a class, happily formidable in numbers and in great and sterling qualities, whom no wiles could win from their devotion to early principles and whom government favors could not corrupt. That class was, singularly enough, the landed interest. I say singularly, not because their fidelity to principle was at variance with their history, but with reference to the circumstance that, whilst in England it had been the principal object in building up the money power to restrict the influence of the landed interest, that power was here destined to be itself kept in check by an interest of the same name, however different in character.

Mr. Jefferson in his celebrated letter to Mazzei, in 1796, gives a description, which could not be improved, of the then political condition of the country and of its political parties: "Against us," he says, "are the executive, the judiciary, two out of three branches of the Legislature, all the officers of the Government, all who want to be officers, all timid men who prefer the calm of despotism to the boisterous sea of liberty, British merchants and Americans trading on British capital, speculators and holders in the banks and public funds,--a contrivance invented for the purpose of corruption, and for assimilating us in all things to the rotten as well as the sound parts of the British model. The whole body of our citizens, however, remain true to their republican principles; the whole landed interest is republican, and so is a great mass of talent." The term "landed interest" in its general signification, and in the sense in which it was used by Mr. Jefferson, referred to those who worked as well as owned the land,--the farmers of the North and the planters of the South,--all who made Agriculture their pursuit; a class which in the earlier periods of our colonial condition constituted almost our entire population, and have at every period in our history vastly exceeded in numbers those engaged in all other pursuits. There is no point of resemblance between them and the landed aristocracy of England, save in that they both represent the landed interest of their respective countries and that they were led in each to oppose the money power. Their difference in other respects is sufficiently manifest.

A more estimable class of men than the farmers and planters of the United States is not to be found in the world. From the landing of the Pilgrims to the present day they have exerted an effective and salutary influence, not only upon the condition of the country, in respect to its material improvement, but upon the character and strength of our political institutions. It was to their sagacity and firmness that the colonies were chiefly indebted for their success in turning away and defeating the fury of the savages, and in baffling the persevering efforts of the mother country to enslave the provinces. For the most part the descendants of ancestors who had been, to an almost unprecedented extent, exposed to the faithlessness and persecutions of power, they seldom failed to be on their guard against its approaches, however artfully disguised. Every attempt to purchase their acquiescence in measures that they regarded as encroachments upon their liberties or subversive of their rights, through governmental favors, proved abortive.

Grenville, when pressed, as prime minister, by the London merchants with the dangers that threatened the collection of their American debts from the effects of the stamp-tax, was prodigal in his offers of governmental favors to secure the submission of the colonists to the odious measure. "If one bounty," said he, "will not do, I will add two; if two will not do, I will add three." But these offers, as well as all the efforts which had been and were subsequently made by the Crown to quiet the Colonies through bounties and commercial privileges, were unavailing. The "landed interest," constituting a great majority of the colonists, was too wise to be duped, and too honest to be corrupted, by special favors of any description. Placed by the nature of their pursuits, in a great measure, beyond the reach of court and official blandishments, and less dependent on the special privileges of the Crown than those who looked to them for their support, they uniformly regarded these offers with distrust rather than desire. They had, from these and other considerations, been led to embrace the principles upon which the Revolution was founded with more earnestness, and to cherish them with a more uncalculating devotion, than many of their Revolutionary associates. The circumstance that a larger share of the defense of those principles had devolved upon them, by reason of the excess of their numbers, naturally commended more warmly to their hearts doctrines for the establishment of which they had suffered so much inquietude and encountered so many perils.

These considerations were alike applicable to, and equally influential upon, the landed interest of the North and of the South. With attachments undiminished and unchangeable to republican principles, pure and simple, subject to such limitations only as were required by convenience in their execution and necessary to deliberation in council, principles the fruition of which had been the day-dream of their ancestors through successive generations, and their own guiding-star in the gloomiest period of the Revolution, the representatives of this great interest, North and South, by large majorities, sustained the Anti-Federal party until that party was overthrown through its great error in respect to the Constitution, and were still ready to take their stand in any organization that should have for its object opposition to the heresies developed by Hamilton in his platform for the government of the administration.

The principles upon which the landed interest acted from the start, have, it must be admitted, been more successfully sustained in the Southern than in the Northern States; not because they were originally embraced with more sincerity, but from very different causes. The commercial, manufacturing, and trading classes, to whom Hamilton's policy was more particularly addressed, and upon whom it, beyond all doubt, exerted a powerful influence, were, at the beginning, far more numerous in the Northern than in the Southern States, and this disparity in their respective conditions has been constantly increasing. It was through the growing power of these classes, and of others similarly, though perhaps not equally, exposed to its influence that the Hamiltonian policy occasionally triumphed in the Northern States, and their politics thus became more unstable than those of the South.

Mr. Bancroft happily and truly describes the peculiar condition of Southern men in this regard. "An instinctive aversion," says he, "to too much government was always a trait of Southern character expressed in the solitary manner of settling in the country, in the absence of municipal governments, in the indisposition of the scattered inhabitants to engage in commerce, to collect in towns, or to associate in townships under corporate powers. As a consequence there was little commercial industry; and on the soil of Virginia there were no vast accumulations of commercial wealth. The exchanges were made almost entirely--and it continued so for more than a century--by factors of foreign merchants. Thus the influence of wealth, under the modern form of stocks and accumulations of money, was always inconsiderable; and men were so widely scattered--like hermits among the heathen--that far the smallest number were within the reach of the direct influence of the established Church or of Government."[24]

[24] Bancroft's Hist. United States, Vol. II. p. 189.

In this description of the early, which is also measurably and comparatively true of the present, state of the South, we find a solution of the circumstance that the failure of Hamilton's policy was so much more signal there than in other quarters, and that the principles upon which it was founded have there been since so perseveringly and unitedly resisted. The political principles of the landed interest, constituting an immense majority of their people, have prevailed in the administration of their State governments, save in regard to the ratification of the Federal Constitution, from the recognition of our Independence to the present day. There has also been a remarkable consistency in the political positions of their public men. In Virginia, which State has done so much to give a tone to national politics, Patrick Henry has been almost, if not quite, the only prominent man who abandoned the principles by which he had been governed during the Confederation, and embraced those of Hamilton at the coming in of the new government. Always admiring his character and conduct during the Revolutionary era, and strongly impressed by the vehemence and consistency with which he had, during the government of the Confederation, opposed every measure that savored of English origin, I pressed Mr. Jefferson, as far as was allowable, for the reasons of his sudden and great change. His explanation was, "that Henry had been smitten by Hamilton's financial policy."

The Republican party, forced into existence by Hamilton's obnoxious measures, sprang chiefly from the landed interest. The declaration of its illustrious founder, in his letter to Mazzei, that the country would yet preserve its liberties, was mainly based on the fact that "the whole landed interest was republican," and he could not have placed his reliance on a surer foundation. Farthest removed, as has been already said, from the seductive influence of the money power, abounding in strong common sense and love of country, and always greatly superior in numbers to the business men of all other classes, it constituted then, and has ever since constituted, the balance wheel of the Government. All it asks from administration is the maintenance of order, protection in the enjoyment of its civil and political rights, and the management of public affairs in a spirit of equal justice to all men. Whilst the commercial and manufacturing classes are annually approaching the National Legislature with appeals for aid and encouragement, and whilst the Congressional committees charged with their interests are from time to time convulsing the country with their measures, that which is nominally the representative and guardian of agriculture not being asked to do any thing for its support, very properly does nothing; having, indeed, no power under the Constitution to do any thing for it, the advantages of which are not common to all classes. What the farmers and planters desire more than this are "the early and the latter rain," for which they look to a source purer and more powerful than human legislation.

Thus sustained, the Republican party of 1790, headed by Thomas Jefferson, with the 'laboring oar' in the hands of James Madison, warmed into action by Jefferson's more fervent though not more deeply seated patriotism, and embracing "a great mass of talent," determined to oppose every measure of Washington's administration which they believed to be unauthorized by the Constitution, or anti-republican in its tendencies. This resolution was carried out with unflinching firmness, but, whatever has been said to the contrary, was made and designed to be performed in a manner consistent with the respect they entertained for the character and feelings of President Washington, and without even a desire to displace him from the high office with which they had contributed to invest him. It would have been strange if, in a state of party violence so excited as that which naturally sprung up, the dominant party should have refrained from aspersing the motives of their opponents by attributing to them personal hostility to a chief so justly beloved by the people as was Washington. Mr. Jefferson, in his letter to me, referring to similar charges but speaking of a subsequent period, says "General Washington, after the retirement of his first cabinet and the composition of his second, entirely Federal, and at the head of which was Mr. Pickering himself, had no opportunity of hearing both sides of any question. His measures consequently took more the hue of the party in whose hands he was. These measures were certainly not approved by the Republicans; yet they were not imputed to him, but to the counselors around him; and his prudence so far restrained their impassioned course and bias that no act of strong mark during the remainder of his administration excited much dissatisfaction. He lived too short a time after, and too much withdrawn from information to correct the views into which he had been deluded, and the continued assiduities of the party drew him into the vortex of their intemperate career, separated him still farther from his real friends, and excited him to actions and expressions of dissatisfaction which grieved them but could not loosen their affections from him."[25]

[25] See Appendix.

Such charges were freely made and with unsparing bitterness; yet I cannot but think that unprejudiced minds, if it is not too soon to expect to find many such upon this subject, would, on a careful review of facts, acquit the Republican party of them. Madcaps, and those who, looking to party for their daily bread, hope to commend themselves by extremes and by violence to those whom they sustain, are to be found in all parties and should not be allowed to make those to which they attach themselves responsible for their acts. Nothing has ever been adduced that may fairly be regarded as the act of the Republican party which proves the existence of the disposition charged against it in regard to General Washington; and the single fact that, although its opposition commenced three years before the expiration of his first term, there was not the slightest effort made to prevent his reelection, or the exhibition of any desire to prevent it, is, of itself, sufficient to refute the charge of personal unfriendliness toward him. Nor did the Republicans desire to embarrass his administration beyond what was inevitable from their opposition to measures which they regarded as unconstitutional or in the highest degree inexpedient, of which the bank and funding system were appropriate illustrations.

The Federal party, without extraordinary or difficult attention and care, might have preserved untarnished a character made respectable by illustrious names and honorable history, notwithstanding the overwhelming defeat to which it was subsequently exposed, and its principles, however erroneous, might have stood a chance of restoration to power in the course of those changes and overturns of men and things to which public affairs and political parties have ever been subject. Even error of opinion not unfrequently regains a lost ascendancy by means of the perseverance and consistency with which it is adhered to, and when the organization by which it has been upheld is maintained with the fidelity and dignity that belong to a good cause. In all these respects there was, on the part of the members of the Federal party, a complete failure. They suffered its lead to fall into less respectable hands, and its support to be lent to seceders (one after another) from the Republican ranks between whom and themselves there was no identity of political feeling, and still less of principle. The motives for this course were usually censurable, and the results generally disastrous from the beginning, and always so in the sequel. Hamilton, as has been seen, twice threw himself in the path of his party to save it from such degradation, for his intelligence and integrity appreciated the impossibility of preserving the respect of the people at large for principles, whose special advocates showed by their acts that they did not themselves respect them. His counsels were unheeded, and the banner of a once highly honored party continued to be trailed in the dust until its name was disowned by its adherents with shame and disgust.

Those who agree with me in believing that General Hamilton was sincere in the opinion he expressed that the republican system could not be made adequate to the purpose of good government here, and that the welfare of the country would be best promoted by approaching as near to the English model as public sentiment would tolerate, are well justified in holding him undeserving of censure for his introduction of the anti-republican plan which he submitted to the Federal Convention. The right of the people to "alter or abolish" existing systems, and "to institute new government, laying its foundation on such principles and organizing its powers in such form as to them shall seem most likely to effect their safety and happiness," was the corner-stone of the Revolution, in defense of which he had freely ventured his life. The Convention was not only an appropriate but the appointed place for the assertion and exercise of that right. So far from being a fit subject for censure, the submission to that body by a man in Hamilton's position, with the claims he had established upon the confidence and support of the people by his superior abilities and his Revolutionary services, of propositions which every body knew, and which he himself felt, were strongly adverse to the prevailing current of public sentiment, and the intrepidity and extraordinary talent with which he sustained them, without a single open supporter in the Convention, solely because he believed them to be right and their adoption necessary to the public good, exhibited a patriotic and self-sacrificing spirit alike honorable to himself and to his principles. His course in the Convention, for which he has been extensively reviled, was in my judgment the most brilliant and creditable portion of his political career. It presented an example of candor and devotion to principle which there was not a single one among his friends willing to follow, although there were, doubtless, a few who felt substantially as he did and sympathized with all he said, and although they all admired his gallant hearing while lamenting his indiscretion. It was, unhappily for himself, the culminating point in his political life, from which every subsequent step gradually lowered him, until he justly forfeited the confidence and countenance of every sincere friend to republican government.

Alas! how deeply is it to be lamented that this great statesman, as able as an impracticable man can be, when he knew that he was about to attempt a ladder upon the first round of which his boldest friend dared not even to place his foot, had not rather followed, in some respects at least, the example of his coadjutor and friend, James Madison. The coincidences in the occurrence of opportunities to make themselves useful to their country, and the contrasts in the ways in which these were improved and the consequences that followed, to be found in the public lives of these illustrious men, are both striking and instructive. In regard to one subject a partial reference to them has already been made. They were co-workers in a series of efforts to obtain from the Congress of the Confederation authority for the Federal head to levy and collect impost duties to enable it to perform the offices devolved upon the General Government by the Articles of Confederation, instead of trusting to the unsafe and unstable requisitions upon the States. No sooner had the first Congress of the new Government, established for that and other purposes, formed a quorum, than Mr. Madison, as we have already seen, before the executive branch had been organized, or even the President elect been informed of his election, introduced bills for the imposition and collection of duties on imported goods, which he pushed forward de die in diem until they became laws, and the duties were in the process of being collected, and the public coffers in the way of being replenished. This good work he followed up in due time by the introduction into Congress of resolutions (and the most able support of them on its floor) in favor of a commercial policy recommended by the Secretary of State, Mr. Jefferson, to improve our trade and thus increase our revenue. These were the contributions of Mr. Madison, simple, practical, and direct like their author, for promoting the financial branch of the public service under the new Government, which was committed by President Washington to the special superintendence of Alexander Hamilton as Secretary of the Treasury.

The Secretary's contributions to the same objects consisted of two very elaborate and very able reports, the first upon public credit, recommending the establishment of a funding system, and the second in favor of a national bank, embracing plans for each and, in the former, a scheme to raise funds for the payment of the interest of a debt to be funded. The eclat which he acquired by these imposing state papers was so great, and many minds are still so much dazzled by the traditional splendor of their effects upon the credit and resources of the country as to render it not a little embarrassing to discuss, in a plain, matter-of-fact way, the questions of their real influence or non-influence upon our finances.

In previous as well as in subsequent parts of this work will be found notices of the rise, progress, and effects of Hamilton's funding system, which, if they do not show that the measure, judged by its results, partook more of the character of a castle in the air than of a wise and practicable financial scheme, do not, I think, fall far short of it. But both it and the bank are now only "obsolete ideas"--to remain so probably while our Government endures. References, under such circumstances, can only be usefully made to them to show the principles and objects of men and parties.

Whilst Hamilton's measures have been, it is hoped and believed, forever abandoned--the funding system by his own political friends, and a national bank in consequence of its explicit and emphatic condemnation by the whole country--those put into immediate and successful operation by Madison not only performed at the time the useful office designed for them by the Constitution, and gradually provided for the wants of the existing Government, but have supplied it with a revenue abundantly sufficient to pay the public debt and to defray all expenses and disbursements required by the public service in war and in peace, with rare and limited additions, for nearly three quarters of a century, and will, in all likelihood, continue so to do to the end.

But the most interesting aspect of these coincidences and contrasts to which I refer is to be found in the illustrations they furnish of the use and abuse of the Constitution by those distinguished men and by their followers respectively. Co-workers again in persevering efforts to obtain from Congress or the States a call for a general convention to revise the Articles of Confederation, it would be difficult to decide which contributed most to effect that object, and it is not too much to say that it would not have been then accomplished if the efforts of either had been withheld. They were neither of them satisfied with the Constitution framed by the Convention; Madison not entirely, Hamilton scarcely at all. The former sympathized, as I have already said, with Hamilton's distrust of the State governments, made unsuccessful efforts to impose stringent restrictions upon their power, and would have been better pleased with the Constitution if it had inclined more decidedly in that direction.

They both signed the instrument notwithstanding; Hamilton under a sort of protest against its sufficiency (or rather its want of it), and Madison with apparent and, I doubt not, real cordiality. In the numbers of the "Federalist," (of which they were the principal authors,) they offered a joint and honorable testimonial to the Constitution, which became in the sequel an enduring monument to their own associated memories. Each rendered "yeoman's service" in the conventions, respectively, of New York and Virginia, to decide upon its ratification; in neither of which was the ratification probable at the beginning, and in both there is the best reason to believe that, without their powerful aid, it must have ultimately failed. In such an event the failure of the Constitution would have been next to certain.

Although Gouverneur Morris's assertion that Hamilton had comparatively nothing to do with the construction of the Federal Constitution is true, yet as Madison had a greater agency in that work than any other individual, and as the obtaining the call of the Convention and the ratification of the Constitution, in which Madison and Hamilton acted the chief parts, were also the portions of the whole transaction most exposed to the action of the States and of the public mind, and therefore the most difficult of accomplishment, it may with truth be affirmed that there were not any fifty or a hundred other men taken together to whom the country was as much indebted for the Federal Constitution as to those two gentlemen. But in their subsequent treatment of that sacred instrument, which each had done so much to bring to maturity, they, unfortunately for the country, differed very widely. The Constitution was ratified and adopted in the first instance by more than the requisite number of States, and finally by the whole thirteen. General Washington was elected President. He appointed Alexander Hamilton to be Secretary of the Treasury, and James Madison was elected a member of the first Congress. The latter, although overruled in the Convention upon points which he deemed important, acquiesced in the decisions of the majority, accepted the Constitution in good faith with a determination to do all in his power, not only to secure its ratification, but to give to the people and the States the full benefit of its provisions as those were understood by them, and to do this with the same fidelity and honor with which he would perform any private arrangement to which he had made himself a party. Satisfied from numerous exhibitions of public sentiment elsewhere as well as in the State conventions, and perhaps more particularly in that of his own State, not only that there was far greater opposition in the minds of the people at large to the Constitution as it came from the hands of the Convention than he at first supposed, but that it was, in point of fact, defective in some particulars important in themselves and well calculated to excite the solicitude of the masses, he determined to leave no means within his reach unimproved to make it, by suitable and seasonable amendments, what a brief experience convinced him that it ought to be. It might perhaps be inferred, from some general expressions used by him in the first Congress, that he felt as if something had been said or done on his part rendering his attention to this matter a special duty, although nothing of that nature is apparent; but, be that as it may, there were other considerations imperative upon a mind so circumspect and so just to prevent his losing sight of the subject.

Mr. John Quincy Adams asserts that the Constitution "was extorted from the grinding necessity of a reluctant nation." Although this may be deemed an exaggerated description no one can make himself familiar with the history of that period without becoming sensible of the truth of two positions, viz.: that vast numbers who were greatly dissatisfied with the Constitution were induced to withhold their active opposition by the embarrassed condition of the country, and that even this consideration would not have sufficed to overcome the decided Anti-Federal majority against it but for the provision authorizing amendments, and the confident anticipation that such as were proper and necessary would be speedily made. The consciousness of these truths, and a conviction that a successful operation of, and general acquiescence in, the provisions of the new Constitution were not to be expected unless proper steps were immediately taken to appease the opposition still in force among the Anti-Federalists, secured the early and unremitting attention of Mr. Madison to that point.

This view of the expectations of the country upon the subject of amendment and of the condition of the public mind in respect to it was strongly confirmed by memorials presented to the first Congress, at its first session, by the States of New York and Virginia, containing averments framed in the strongest terms, that whilst they dreaded the operation of the Constitution in its then imperfect state, they had, notwithstanding, yielded their assent to its ratification from motives of affection for their sister States, and from an invincible reluctance to separate from them, and with a full confidence that its imperfections would be speedily removed; that the existence of great and vital defects in the Constitution was the prevailing conviction of those States; that the dissatisfaction and uneasiness upon the subject amongst their people would never cease to distract the country until the causes of them were satisfactorily removed; that the matter would ill admit of postponement, and concluding with applications to Congress that they should, without delay, call a new convention with full powers to revise and amend the Constitution. Although these memorials referred to the opinions expressed by their respective State conventions that that instrument ought to undergo further revision, which, in one of them, was a unanimous expression, Congress nevertheless took no steps toward a compliance with the request they contained. But the whole subject was brought before it by Mr. Madison as soon as he had perfected his revenue measures, and he caused amendments to be carried through that body, I had almost said by his own unaided efforts, which were satisfactory to the people--certainly to that portion of them by whom the Constitution had been opposed.

A tolerably full and obviously fair account of the debates and proceedings in the House of Representatives upon this subject--those in the Senate, I fear, are lost--may be found in the first and second volumes of Lloyd's "Register of the Proceedings and Debates of the First House of Representatives of the United States," which I am sorry to find has not been transferred to Colonel Benton's "Abridgment." The subject, speaking of the ten amendments as one measure, was only second in intrinsic importance, on account of the influence its success exerted on the solidity and perpetuity of the new system, to the Constitution itself, and the debates in point of ability and earnestness, particularly on the part of Mr. Madison, not inferior to any of the discussions by which that interesting period when the foundations of the present government were laid was so greatly distinguished; one cannot read them without acknowledging the difficulty of recalling another instance in which a measure of equal gravity was so successfully carried through a public body against the obvious and decided preferences of a large majority of its members, or without admiring the extent to which that success was achieved by the exertions of one man.

Now that the dangers which environed these proceedings have passed away, they afford amusement to the curious in such matters by the picture they furnish of the twists and turns to which men in high positions and of generally fair views will sometimes resort to stave off distasteful propositions, with the hope of ultimately defeating what they do not feel it to be safe directly to oppose. The Virginia and New York applications were presented by Mr. Bland, of the former, and Mr. Lawrence, of the latter State, both friends of Hamilton; and although both were solicitous that the applications should be respectfully received, neither of them ever took a step to make them successful, nor were they in favor of the amendments proposed by Mr. Madison. That gentleman gave notice of his intention to bring the subject before the House several weeks before the day he named for that purpose. When that day arrived he moved that the House should resolve itself into a committee of the whole to receive the amendments he proposed to offer. Opposition to going into such committee came from almost all sides of the House, some urging one species of objections and some another, but generally indicative of decided unfriendliness to the views of the mover. Perceiving that his motion was neither satisfactory nor likely to succeed, Mr. Madison withdrew it, and submitted a proposition for the appointment of a select committee to report such amendments to the Constitution as they should think proper. Having done this, he, in a very able speech, went over the whole subject, stated at length the necessity that existed for some amendments, and the high expediency of proposing others, and furnished a statement of those he had intended to offer to the committee of the whole; these he trusted would now be referred to the select committee, and thus the matter would proceed there without interruption to the other business of the House.

The proposition for a select committee was not more fortunate or acceptable than its predecessor. It was opposed from the same quarters, and several who had evinced no favor toward the motion to go into committee of the whole now said that, if the subject was to be taken up at all, that would have been, but for its withdrawal, the preferable mode. Mr. Madison declared himself, as he said, "unfortunate in not satisfying gentlemen with respect to the mode of introducing the business; he had thought, from the dignity and peculiarity of the subject, that it ought to be referred to a committee of the whole; he had accordingly made that motion first, but finding himself not likely to succeed in that way, he had changed his ground. Fearing again to be discomfited on his motion for a select committee, he would change his mode, and move the propositions he had stated before directly to the House, and it might then do what it thought proper with them. He accordingly moved the propositions by way of Resolutions to be adopted by the House."

This course was also objected to on several grounds; but the majority saw that if the game of staving off the subject was not broken up by Mr. Madison's third proposition, it had at least been so far exposed as to require time to put it in some new form, and with that view Mr. Lawrence, who, as already said, was not in favor of amendments, moved that the subject be referred to a committee of the whole,--the proposition first submitted by Mr. Madison,--which was done. This occurred on the 8th of June. On the 21st of July thereafter Mr. Madison "begged the House to indulge him in the further consideration of the subject of amendments to the Constitution, and as there appeared, in some degree, a moment of leisure, he would move to go into a committee of the whole upon the subject, conformably to the order of the 8th of last month."

This proposition was met by a motion from Mr. Fisher Ames, of Massachusetts, to rescind the vote of the 8th of June, and to refer the business to a select committee. This motion gave rise to speeches professing not to be opposed to the consideration of amendments at a proper time and under proper circumstances, but showing a decided distrust of and distaste for the whole proceeding. The motion prevailed by a vote of 34 to 15, and a select committee was appointed, of which Mr. Vining, an opponent, was made chairman. The report of this committee contained substantially the amendments proposed by Mr. Madison, with some alterations and additions. These, after revision by the House, were finally passed by a vote of two thirds in both Houses, submitted to the States and ratified by them, as they now appear as the first ten of the twelve amendments that have been made to the Federal Constitution since its first adoption.

Some of Mr. Madison's colleagues occasionally expressed a desire for the success of his propositions, and similar avowals were sometimes made by two or three members from other States; but of substantial, persevering, and effective assistance, he may, with truth, be said to have had none, and two thirds of the House were at heart decidedly opposed to the amendments that were made. With all his talents, industry, and perseverance, Mr. Madison would not have been able to carry them if his exertions had not been seconded by an influence still more efficacious. The legislature of Virginia alluded to the defects of the Constitution as "involving all the great and inalienable rights of freemen," declared that its objections were not founded on speculative theory, but deduced from principles which had been established by the melancholy examples of other nations in different ages, and said, "they will never be removed until the cause shall cease to exist." It announced the "cause of amendment as a common cause," and its trust that commendable zeal would be shown by others also for obtaining those "provisions which experience had taught them were necessary to secure from danger the inalienable rights of human nature." It expressed its impatience of delay and its doubt as to the disposition of Congress; complained of the slowness of its forms, but congratulated itself on the possession of another remedy, which it was determined to pursue, under the Constitution itself--that of a convention of The States.

The New York application, signed, as Speaker, by John Lansing, Jr., who had left the Federal Convention in consequence of his dissatisfaction with its proceedings and never returned to it, though not going as much into details, employed language equally bold and uncompromising in demanding from Congress another convention, which might propose such amendments "as it might find best calculated to promote our common interests, and secure to ourselves and our latest posterity the great and inalienable rights of mankind." This memorial asserted not only that the New York Convention had ratified "in the fullest confidence of obtaining a revision of the Constitution by a general convention, as appeared on the face of its ratification," but that that body (of which Hamilton was a member) were unanimous in the opinion that such a revision was necessary to recommend that instrument to the approbation and support of a numerous body of its constituents.

These documents, and especially that of Virginia, pointed very emphatically to the source of that discontent with the Constitution which so extensively prevailed in the old Anti-Federal ranks. Even they felt that the Constitution was much better than they had expected, and the most considerate among them, those who were most capable of suspending their suspicions as to the designs of their opponents long enough to give the instrument a dispassionate consideration, were soon satisfied--and Samuel Adams, who stood at the head of the Anti-Federal party, admitted--that its general structure was free from any insuperable objection. The life-tenure given to the Federal Judges was, as it indeed might well be, regarded as inconsistent with republican principles; but it was to be remembered that those officers were expected to be, as they ought always to be, non-combatants in partisan politics by reason of their appointment to act as arbiters of the fates and fortunes of their countrymen. Upon the great point to which the attention of such men was first directed, that of the ability of the State governments to maintain their sovereignty and independence under the new system, there was no real ground for apprehension. But the Constitution was principally confined to what were more strictly public concerns, the powers and duties of the Federal and State Governments in regard to National and State affairs, with only a slight sprinkling of provisions looking particularly to the protection of the citizen against the exercise of arbitrary power; and it was accompanied by no Bill of Rights, such as those to which the people had been accustomed in respect to their State governments. In the latter cases they might more readily have been reconciled to the absence of such provisions, as those governments were carried on under their immediate observation, and they formed a part of them in much larger portions than they could expect to do of the Federal Government. The latter they were too much in the habit of regarding, at that early period, as a foreign government only remotely responsible to them. We have already spoken of the settled character of their distrust of power for which there was only a remote, if any, responsibility, and of their having been trained by experience to expect only abuses from the exercise of such authority, whether in State or Church,--an experience embracing the sorrowful and well-remembered accounts of outrage and persecution against their ancestors, and the cruel oppression of the then existing generation by the distant government of the mother country. We have seen how great had been their aversion and that of their ancestors to the establishment of a general government, and with what difficulties their consent to the call of the then recent Convention had been obtained, and what care had been taken to restrict its power. It was not therefore surprising that a large majority of them should have manifested such intense dissatisfaction when a Constitution was presented for their approval containing so few, so very few safeguards for the protection of "the great and inalienable rights of freemen," as Virginia described them--of the "great and inalienable rights of mankind," as the New York Legislature styled them--points to which the masses, especially of the Anti-Federalists, were so keenly alive.

These considerations and circumstances produced a sudden and extensive spirit of discontent which, as those States avowed, never would be appeased until its causes were removed, and with which Mr. Madison was well satisfied the new Government would not be able to contend unless some mode was devised to appease it. Although never a member of it, he had, in his long and persevering efforts to obtain the Constitution, "tasted the quality," so to speak, of the old Anti-Federal party, and understood the stuff of which it was composed. He knew very well that the call of Virginia upon her co-States to make the demand for amendments "a common cause" would not be brutum fulmen, but that the agitation for a new convention in such hands, and commenced under such favorable circumstances, with so many materials of discontent already made to their hands, would not cease until its object was gained, and what would follow no man could tell. He was not so much of a Bourbon as Hamilton; he had not pursued his thorny path through those trying scenes without learning something of the character and temper of the people, or without having his mind disabused of much that it had once entertained. No man in the country was more opposed to the call of a new convention, or more unwilling to make any amendments that would materially impair the original structure of the Constitution. The former he omitted to avow out of respect to the declared wishes of his State but the latter he repeatedly announced because it was only in harmony with his past course. But he knew that matters could not remain as they stood, and he thought a series of amendments could be made, some of which he deemed highly proper and all expedient, through which a large portion of the Anti-Federalists might be conciliated without prejudice to the system which had been adopted. This course, to be useful, must, he was satisfied, be pursued at the very commencement of the new government. He devoted himself, body and mind, to that object, and we have seen some of the difficulties with which he had to contend. Although Hamilton was not personally in Congress, he was well represented, and Madison found there, besides, many other Bourbons, in the sense in which I use that term. He prepared a plan according to the views I have described; and few exhibitions of that kind can have been more interesting than to see him stand between the Federal majority in the House and the few old Anti-Federalists who were there, and avail himself of the votes of each in turn to defeat the obnoxious efforts of the other; first to arrest by Federal aid every attempt on the part of the few Anti-Federalists to mar his project by seeking amendments which he was not himself prepared to adopt, and then to frustrate by Anti-Federal votes the efforts of a majority of the Federalists (though less than a majority of the House) to defeat his entire scheme.

That the only alternative was between a new convention and the adoption of amendments substantially like his, was the great fact which he labored to impress upon the minds of the Federal members. He introduced it in his public speeches with never-failing delicacy, but with sufficient clearness to be understood, and doubtless enforced it at private interviews as far as it was his habit to do such things. That important truth was the fulcrum on which he rested his lever, and he engineered his plan through the House and afterwards, as chairman of the Committee of Conference, through both Houses (the majorities in each alike unfriendly to it) with triumphant and under the circumstances most extraordinary success.

The dread of another Federal Convention has never failed, when the circumstances were sufficient to justify apprehension of its call, to deter the

Federalists from the adoption of projects obnoxious to the democratic spirit of the country, however anxiously desired by themselves. Pending the election of President in the House, between Jefferson and Burr, the Republicans replied to the threat of putting the Government in the hands of an officer by act of Congress, by an open, united, and firm declaration that the day such an act passed, the Middle States would arm, and that they would "call a convention to reorganize and amend the Constitution;" upon the effect of which Mr. Jefferson remarks, "the very word convention gives them the horrors, as, in the present democratical spirit of America, they fear they should lose some of the favorite morsels of the Constitution."

Mr. Madison's ten amendments consisted of provisions in favor of the free exercise of religion, of speech, and of the press; of assembling peaceably to petition the Government for a redress of grievances; of the right to keep and bear arms; against quartering soldiers in any house without the consent of the owner, except under certain qualifications; against unreasonable searches and general warrants; against being held to answer for crimes unless on presentment by a grand jury, with certain exceptions; against being twice put in jeopardy for the same offense; against being compelled to be a witness against one's self, or being deprived of life, liberty, or property without due process of law; against taking private property for public use without just compensation; in favor of a trial by an impartial jury of the district in certain cases at common law and in all criminal prosecutions, of the party charged being informed of the nature of the accusation, of being confronted with the witnesses against him, of having compulsory process for obtaining witnesses and the assistance of counsel in his defense; against excessive bail, excessive fines or cruel punishments; against the enumeration of certain rights being construed to deny or disparage others retained by the people; and, finally, that powers not delegated to the United States by the Constitution, nor prohibited by it to the States, are reserved to the States respectively or to the people.

These provisions embraced the points upon which the public mind was most susceptible, and upon which the old Anti-Federal party in particular had been, with obvious reason, most excited.

That Mr. Madison's success in this great measure saved the Constitution from the ordeal of another Federal Convention is a conclusion as certain as any that rests upon a contingency which has not actually occurred, and that it converted the residue of the Anti-Federal party which had not supported the Constitution, whose members, as well as their political predecessors in every stage of our history, constituted a majority of the people, from opponents of that instrument into its warmest friends, and that they and their successors have from that time to the present period, either as Republicans or Democrats, occupied the position of its bona fide defenders in the sense in which it was designed to be understood by those who constructed and by those who ratified it, against every attempt to undermine or subvert it, are undeniable facts.

It was by adding this great service to those he had rendered in obtaining the Convention, and in framing the Constitution in that body, that he deservedly won the noble title of "Father of the Constitution." He was neither as great a man nor as thorough a Republican, certainly not as thorough a Democrat, as Mr. Jefferson; he had less genius than Hamilton; yet it is doing him no more than justice to say that, as a civilian, he succeeded in making himself more practically useful to his country than any other man she has produced. No one would have been more ready than Mr. Jefferson to award to Mr. Madison this high distinction. He either told me at Monticello, or I heard it from him at second-hand, (I am uncertain which was the case,) that whilst he was in France, some one whom he named asked him to say whom he thought the greatest man in America, and that he replied, if the gentleman would ask him to name the greatest man in the world he would comply with the request, which addition being made, he answered "James Madison!"

This brings us to the consideration of the contrast between the conduct of Hamilton and Madison in respect to their treatment of a Constitution which they had both taken such unwearied pains to bring into existence. The course they respectively pursued upon the subjects of finance and revenue, and the measures they respectively preferred, without regard to questions of constitutional power, only indicated differences of opinion upon subjects in which such differences are apt to arise, and did not necessarily involve the political integrity of either. But we have now arrived at a point of departure in the relative course of these great men involving graver considerations, and to which it is to be regretted that the last reservation cannot be truly applied. There was no warrant in the Constitution for the establishment of a national bank, or for the assumption of the State debts, or for the unlimited claim of power by the Federal Government over the collection and disbursement of national revenue, and for its patronage of by far the largest proportion of the pursuits and interests of the country, all of which were effected by Hamilton or recommended in his Report on Manufactures, and he understood perfectly well that the Constitution conferred no such powers when he advocated successfully the first two of those measures, and asserted the power and recommended its exercise in respect to the latter.

It is not agreeable to be obliged to assume that a gentleman of General Hamilton's elevated character in private life, upon whose integrity and fidelity in his personal dealings and in the discharge of every private trust that was reposed in him no shadow rested, who was indifferent to the accumulation of wealth, who as a public man was so free from intrigues for personal advancement, and whose thoughts and acts in that character were so constantly directed to great questions and great interests, could yet prove faithless to one of the most sacred public trusts that can be placed in man--the execution of the fundamental law of the land. If Hamilton had been asked, as a private man, whether he believed it was the intention of the framers of the Constitution to confer upon Congress the power to establish a national bank, and whether he believed that the people when they ratified it supposed that it contained such a power, he would, if he answered at all, have answered "No!" He was incapable of willful deception on the subject. This discrepancy between his conduct as a statesman in the management of public affairs and his integrity and truthfulness in private life was the result of a vicious opinion as to the obligations of a public man, and in no degree attributable to any inferior sense of personal honor, nor was it ever otherwise regarded.

His position upon this point is understood to have been founded on the following opinions: That the people as a body were not capable of managing their public affairs with safety to their happiness and welfare; that it was, therefore, a proper exercise of power to give the management of them into the hands of those who were capable, and to place the latter in positions, as far as practicable under the circumstances, beyond popular control; that it was the sacred duty of those who were so intrusted to exercise their power truly and sincerely for the best interests of those for whom they acted; that if those interests could be well administered without transcending the power with which the public functionary was invested, or without the practice of deception or corruption, such would be the preferable and proper course; but if violations of the popular will, deception, or corruptions--not those of the grosser kind, like direct bribery, but such as belonged to the class he spoke of to Mr. Adams as constituting the life-giving principle of the English system--were necessary, in the best judgment of men in power, to the security or advancement of the public welfare, the employment of such means was justifiable.

Without stopping to cite authorities, I assume--on the strength of the opinion of the age in which he lived, of his writings, of his declarations, which were, beyond almost all other public men, without reserve, and of his acts--that such were his views, and content myself with the declaration that the existence of such views is the best, if not the only, excuse that can be made for his official course.

At the close of the Convention, and just before signing the Constitution, he declared that the latter might serve as a temporary bond of union, but could never suffice to secure good government. After he had succeeded in his first two interpolations, he spoke exultingly of the success of the Constitution, and hopefully of the future; this was because he knew that he had prospered in his attempt to give it a construction not dreamed of at the former period by himself, or others to his knowledge; and his hopes of the future were founded on his success also in his plan set forth in his Report on Manufactures, widening very greatly the breach he had already effected in the Constitution. In February, 1802, after his latitudinarian scheme had been arrested and was in danger of being permanently overthrown, he described the Constitution to Gouverneur Morris as a "frail and worthless fabric," the "fate" of which he had "anticipated from the very beginning." He never reproached his friends with an unwillingness to go as far as the Constitution would justify, but always attributed their failure to defects in the system, thus admitting that the measures in which he exulted and from which he hoped so much, had been established by him, not under, but outside of that instrument.

The first marked effect of Hamilton's determination to pursue the course I have described was a separation between him and his most efficient coadjutor upon many points during the government of the Confederation, and the next was the formation of the old Republican party. The motives for the separation between those distinguished associates have been made the subject, as might have been expected, of various and extensive comment. So far as I know, Hamilton never spoke of Madison, after their separation, in any other terms than those which were consistent with the knowledge he possessed of the purity and integrity of his character. Few men had such perfect control over their feelings as Mr. Madison, and few exercised more reserve in speaking of the motives of his political opponents. It has been rare indeed that he has ventured to touch upon them even when necessary to his vindication from aspersions upon his own character, a truth obvious to any one familiar with his life and writings. I however accidentally came into the possession of information upon this precise question of very great interest, which will be found in the letter below from Nicholas P. Trist, Esq. In the course of a conversation between Mr. Trist, myself, and other gentlemen, at Philadelphia, last spring,[26] upon the subject of which they had only a general bearing, the former alluded to the circumstances here given in detail, and subsequently, at my request, reduced them to the shape in which they now appear.

[26] In the spring of 1857. Eds.

Mr. Trist was a much esteemed and highly trusted friend of Mr. Jefferson, and married his favorite grand-daughter, a lady of superior intelligence, with whom I was well acquainted. He was also for many years a neighbor and confidential friend of Mr. Madison, toward the decline of the life of the latter. My knowledge of him has been derived from long and familiar intercourse with him as a confidential clerk in my department whilst I was Secretary of State, as consul of the United States at Havana, and as private secretary of President Jackson, and I do not hesitate to say that I never knew a more upright man. No one who has had opportunities to become well acquainted with his character, however politically or personally prepossessed in regard to him in other respects, will, I am very sure, fail to admit his perfect truthfulness, and the authenticity of any relation he might make upon the strength of his own knowledge.

FROM MR. TRIST.

PHILADELPHIA, May 31, 1857.

MY DEAR SIR,--My promise, however tardily performed, has never been forgotten; and now, complying with your request preferred at the time and since renewed, I give you in writing the statement made by me a month or two ago in conversation at Mr. Gilpin's; which statement you will recollect was casually elicited, as the proper commentary upon the charge mentioned by one of the company as being brought against Mr. Jefferson--the charge, namely, that he had "stolen Mr. Madison from the Federalists." This notion, by the way, involves an utterly erroneous conception of the relation which existed between the minds and characters of the two men. But I must here confine myself to doing what you asked of me.

During the latter years of Mr. Madison's life, (the exact date is recorded in a memorandum not now at hand,) the following incident occurred.

My intimate friend Mr. Davis, Law Professor in the University of Virginia, mentioned to me, as a thing which he thought Mr. Madison ought to be apprised of, that in a forthcoming Life of Colonel Hamilton, by one of his sons, the authenticity of his (Mr. M.'s) report of Colonel H.'s speech in the Federal Convention was to be denied; and furthermore he was to be represented as having "abandoned" Colonel Hamilton. This Davis had learnt from Professor George Tucker, of the same University, then recently returned from a trip to the North.

Of course, on my first visit to Mr. Madison, which occurred soon after, I told him of what Davis had said.

The effect upon his countenance was an expression of painful surprise, succeeded by a very remarkable look his face assumed sometimes, and which was deeply impressive from its concentration and solemnity. A silence of some moments was broken by his saying, in a tone corresponding to that look, "Sorry to hear it." Then a pause, followed by these words, "I abandoned Colonel Hamilton,--or Colonel Hamilton abandoned me,--in a word, we parted,--upon its plainly becoming his purpose and endeavor to adminisTRATION (administer) the government into a thing totally different from that which he and I both knew perfectly well had been understood and intended by the Convention which framed it, and by the people in adopting it."

Upon the two words which I have underscored, especially the second, and most especially its last two syllables, a marked emphasis was laid. The latter (the word administration used as a verb) is the only instance of neologism I ever observed in Mr. Madison. Its effectiveness was most striking; it hit the nail plumb on the head, and drove it home at one blow. The whole history of that business, the entire truth of the matter, was compressed into that one word. As uttered by him there was a pause at "adminis"--and then came out

"TRATION." It was followed by the word "administer," thrown in parenthetically, and in an under-tone; as much as to say, "I have been coining a word here, which, as you are aware, is not my habit; but just as I was about to say administer the government, I felt that this term is too general, too commonplace, too tame to convey the idea present to my mind; and this modification of it presented itself as exactly suited to the case."

As regards the speech, Mr. M. seemed painfully troubled at the thought of the fidelity of his report of it being disputed, and at a loss to realize the possibility of such a thing. "Why, as I once related to you, that speech was placed by me in Colonel Hamilton's own hand; and was, after deliberate perusal, returned by him with an explicit recognition of its correctness--all to a very few verbal alterations, which were made; on which occasion he placed in my hands, as the proper accompaniment of his speech in my record, and as presenting in a precise and exact shape his views as to the government which it was desirable to establish, the draft of a Constitution which he had prepared before coming to the Convention."

This substantially, if not exactly, is what Mr. M. said upon that point. He then went on to conjecture in what way Colonel H.'s biographer might have been misled into this error; not a doubt being intimated or evinced by him as to its being honestly an error. Colonel H. spoke several times in the Convention--at greater or less length, as would be seen when his (Mr. M.'s) notes were given to the world. Perhaps, among his papers notes had been found, which, in the absence of means of discriminating between remarks made on different occasions, and between notes for an intended speech and that which the speaker had actually said, might have given rise to the misconception.

To the foregoing incident you wished me to add what I was led to say, in the course of the same conversation, regarding Mr. Jefferson's habitual tone in speaking of Colonel Hamilton. This was always the very reverse of that in which he spoke of those whose characters, personal or political, were objects of his disesteem. It was invariably such as to indicate, and to infuse (certainly this effect was produced upon my mind) a high estimate of Colonel Hamilton as a man, whether considered with reference to personal matters or to political matters. He was never spoken of otherwise than as being a gentleman--a lofty-minded, high-toned man. As regards politics, their convictions, their creeds, were diametrically opposite. Colonel H. had no faith in republican government.

In his eyes the British Government was the perfection of human government, the model of all that was practically attainable in politics. His doctrine, openly avowed, was that there are but two ways of governing men, but two ways in which the business of government can be conducted: the one is through fear, the other through self-interest--that is, influencing the conduct of those upon whom the course of political affairs depends, through their desire for personal advantages, for position, for wealth, and so forth. In this country, to operate upon men through their fears was out of the question; and consequently the latter constituted the only practicable means. These political convictions on the part of Colonel H., united as they were with his splendid abilities and his lofty character as a man, both public and private, were regarded by Mr. Jefferson as having constituted the great peril to which republicanism had been exposed in our country. But for the character of Colonel H., for the man, for his honesty and sincerity and single-mindedness,--I mean considered with reference to politics,--there was never the least indication of depreciation or disrespect on the part of Mr. Jefferson; always the direct reverse.

Never, in a single instance, when Colonel H. was the subject of conversation with me, or in my presence, was it otherwise than perfectly manifest that, in Mr. J.'s habitual feeling toward him, the broadest possible line of demarcation existed between the man, the character, (the public character, I repeat, no less than the private,) and the creed by which the action and course of that character were determined; and that whilst the latter was abhorrent to his own cherished faith, and had been for him the cause of the intensest anxiety and gloomiest forebodings ever suffered by him, the former was nevertheless no less truly an object of sincere respect.

Having thus, my dear sir, at length fulfilled my promise,--though not within the limited space (far from it) which you intimated,--I tender the assurance of my respectful regard and friendly remembrance.

N. P. TRIST.

MARTIN VAN BUREN, Ex-President of the U. S.

Hamilton took the position of which the virtuous Madison, whilst standing at the brink of his grave, left behind him a description so graphic, promptly and, as was his habit, immovably. The crisis met him in his last intrenchment. He believed honestly, sincerely, and without any designs other than such as related to the public welfare, that nothing short of monarchical institutions would prove adequate to the wants of the country, but these he was well satisfied could not be obtained then, and possibly not for a long period. He had approached them in the Convention as nearly, in respect to the point of efficiency, as would afford the slightest chance of success for his plan, and he had been left without a single open supporter in that body. Regarding the Constitution, as framed by the Convention, as the only avenue to escape from anarchy, he finally promoted its passage there and its ratification by the States and people, avowedly as a temporary bond of union. Appointed to assist in carrying it into effect, and sincerely believing that, with no other powers than those only which he and Madison so well knew it was intended to authorize, it must prove a failure and the government established under it must go to pieces, he decided, unhesitatingly and absolutely, to do under it whatever he in good faith might think would promote the general welfare, without reference to the intentions of its authors. He was a man of too much good sense to do unnecessary violence to public feeling,--as he said to Jefferson "to publish it in Dan or Beersheba,"--but such was his unchangeable design. On the contrary, he entered into labored and able discussions to show that his principal measures were authorized by the Constitution, but these were in deference to the prejudices and ideas of the people, nothing more.

There is nothing in the writings, speeches, or declarations of General Hamilton inconsistent with the truth of this statement. In papers which have been referred to, and others, he submitted ingenious arguments to show that the Convention might have so intended, and that Congress had a right to hold from the words employed that it did so intend, but he was too circumspect to insist that the intention of the Convention ought not to prevail when it could be ascertained, or to make the actual intention, as a matter of fact, a point in the argument. Giving due weight to the intention of the body when that was ascertained, he adopted a course of reasoning which every body understood went to defeat it, desiring no other efficacy for the opinion he labored to establish than the vote of the majority. The better knowledge of the country overthrew his specious deductions in a short time, and its traditions will, it is to be hoped, render them forever harmless.

The principle of construction contended for by Hamilton, and for a season to some extent made successful, was not designed for the promotion of a particular measure, for which the powers of Congress under the Constitution were to be unduly extended, on account of its assumed indispensable importance to the public safety, but intended as a sweeping rule by which those powers, instead of being confined to the constitutional enumeration, were to authorize the passage of all laws which Congress might deem conducive to the general welfare and which were not expressly prohibited; a power similar to that contained in the plan he proposed in the Convention. He desired, in short, to make the Constitution a tablet of wax upon which each successive administration would be at liberty to impress its rescripts, to be promulgated as constitutional edicts.

Hamilton never well understood the distinctive character of our people, but he understood human nature too well to believe that any people could long respect or desire to uphold a Constitution the most stringent provisions of which were thus regarded or treated. Its inevitable fate is illustrated in the experience of France, after one of her unscrupulous wits had aided in consigning to general derision that litter of Constitutions which had rapidly followed one after the other, by accompanying his oath with a grimace and a jest upon the number which he had successively and with equal solemnity sworn to support. The example of France was not lost upon a mind so watchful as Hamilton's, and he did not doubt that our Constitution would be overthrown with the same certainty, if not with equal facility, after it had been long enough treated with similar disrespect, and that the door would be thus opened for the ultimate introduction, under the influence of the money power, of the only political institutions in which he placed absolute confidence. He declared it to be his opinion, in the Convention, that he regarded ours as the last chance for a republican government, and assigned that opinion as a reason for his attempt to infuse into the new system qualities as stringent as those he proposed and which he knew very well were not generally regarded as belonging to a republican system. No man better understood than he that the inviolate sanctity of a written Constitution was the life of a republican government, and that its days were numbered from the moment its people and rulers ceased thus to preserve, protect, and defend it. Mr. Jefferson spoke, in his letter, of Hamilton as "professing" that it was "the duty of its administrators to conduct the Government on the principles their constituents had elected." I did not at first, and for a long time afterwards, attach as much significance to the word I have here italicized, as I do now, when I have studied Hamilton's course more carefully. I knew the letter was written in a liberal spirit toward his memory.

As I have elsewhere said, during my visit to Mr. Jefferson we talked most of Hamilton, and the general course of Mr. J.'s remarks was substantially similar to those now related, more than thirty years after his decease, and without the slightest knowledge of what I have said upon the same subject, by his relative, Mr. Trist, who was also a member of his family. Mr. Jefferson was evidently disposed to confirm the favorable impressions I had imbibed of the personal side of Hamilton's character, and the words quoted above from his letter were designed to qualify his imputation of monarchical principles to the latter, and I can now appreciate the motive for the expression used, which did not commit him to a concession that the opinion of Hamilton in regard to the duty of administration was that upon which he acted.

With all these considerations before him, Hamilton did more than any, and I had almost said than all, his contemporaries together, to counteract the will of the people and to subvert by undermining the Constitution of their choice. If his sapping and mining policy had been finally successful, if the Republican party, mostly composed of old Anti-Federalists, led by so bold a spirit and such a root-and-branch Republican as Mr. Jefferson, had not arrested the farther progress of his principles and demolished his scheme, this glorious old Constitution of ours, of which we all seem so proud, of which it is so great an honor to have been and of which so many have been ambitious to be, regarded as the faithful expounder, under the wings of which we have risen from small beginnings to be a puissant nation,--attracting the admiration and able to command the respect of the civilized world,--would long since have sunk beneath the waters of time, an object of neglect and scorn. Our system might then have dissolved in anarchy, or crouched under despotism or under some milder type of arbitrary government,--a monarchy, an aristocracy, or, most ignoble of all, a moneyed oligarchy,--but as a Republic it would have endured no longer. In this aspect, notwithstanding his great and good qualities,--and he had many,--Hamilton's course was an outrage upon liberty and a crime against free government.

How happy would it have been for himself and for every interest if he had not parted from his friend and faithful fellow-laborer through so many and such trying scenes,--if, like Madison, not entirely satisfied with the Constitution, but knowing that many others were in the same predicament, he had applied his great talents to the business of making it as generally acceptable as possible, and in giving to the masses an administration of the

Government according not only to the form but to the spirit also in which it had been framed. The country would then at length have rested after so many storms, and his great and good friend Washington, instead of being steeped to the lips in partisan anxieties, (as his nephew, Judge Bushrod Washington, described him to me to have been within the year of his death,) would not only have had a glorious and successful administration, but would have lived in his retirement and finally passed from earth without having been ever annoyed by the canker of party spirit. His own political career would doubtless have been far more prosperous and more agreeable; no occasion would then have arisen for such reflections as he expressed to his confidential friend describing his only reward, after all his efforts and sacrifices, as "the murmurs of the friends of the Constitution and the curses of its foes," and concluding, sadly enough for one who had so greatly distinguished himself in its service, that "the American world was not made for him!"

In these views of General Hamilton's course and in the opinions expressed in respect to it, I have designed to confine myself strictly to what I consider the deliberate judgment of the country, pronounced in various ways and among others through the ballot-box--its constitutional exponent. The most prominent of his measures have been, as already said, discarded, and those who constituted the party in whose name they were first introduced have so far yielded to the current of public opinion as to abandon them forever. I have also before alluded to the gratifying circumstance that the odium attached to those measures never in any degree affected the confidence of the people in the patriotism of Washington or in his fidelity to republican institutions, or weakened their affection for him while he lived, or their respect for his memory when he was no more. These were not the results of mere personal devotion, but of an intelligent and just discrimination on the part of the people. Hamilton designed to effect a civil revolution by changing the powers of Congress from the restricted character given to them in obedience to the wishes of the people to one in effect unlimited. Washington entertained no such views. His constructions of the Constitution were designed for the cases that called them forth, and had no ulterior views.

The subject of the bank presented the principal and almost the only question upon which President Washington gave a construction to that instrument which met the disapprobation and excited the apprehensions of the old Republicans. To the assumption of the State debts Hamilton, as has been seen, succeeded in obtaining--how much to his mortification and regret his writings show--the cooperation of Mr. Jefferson, and thereby the unanimous support of the cabinet; and his Report on Manufactures, as to most of its obnoxious details, was not acted upon during Washington's administration, but in respect to its principal objects remained a dead letter. President Washington, notwithstanding the conflicting opinions of his cabinet, gave no reasons for his approval of the Bank Bill. The public were therefore left to draw their own inferences in regard to their character. Diverse opinions upon the point of course arose, and there is much reason to believe (and that belief is strengthened by his subsequent course in respect to another important matter) that he was induced to regard a bank as indispensable, in the then condition of the country, to the success of the new Government--an exigency in public affairs of that peculiar sort which men in power assume to deal with under the sanction of the great principle, Salus populi suprema lex. (See note.) Mr. Madison, who had demonstrated in Congress its unconstitutionality at its creation, who had opposed the banking system through his whole public life, and whose fame was in a very great degree founded on the ability with which he had defined the true principles of constitutional construction, in a way to exclude the idea of any power in Congress to establish such an institution, did, notwithstanding, at the close of his public career, in a condition of the country not unlike that in which President Washington acted, and viewing the subject from the same official station, arrive at the same conclusion in regard to its imperative necessity, and gave his approval to the erection of a new national bank.

NOTE.--(Feb. 16th, 1858.) Whilst reviewing the "era of good-feeling," as it was called, during the administration of Mr. Monroe, I conceived the idea of adding some account of the rise and progress of our political parties, and entered upon the task immediately, designing it to stand as an episode in my Memoirs. The subject grew upon my hands to such an extent that for the last two years it has, in necessary reading and examinations into facts, &c., occupied most of the time that could be devoted to the general object. The idea of limiting this portion to a mere digression was therefore substantially laid aside, and the dignity of a separate and distinct consideration, to which its dimensions, if nothing else, entitled it, was assigned to it. Accordingly I continued my examination of the course of parties in the United States down to the present time, including the first months of President Buchanan's administration. Whilst engaged in correcting the manuscript and arranging it to be copied, and after I had, by many pages, passed the place in the text to which this note is appended, the first volume of Mr. Randall's Life of Jefferson, recently published, came to my hands, and on reading its last two chapters first, because they have a more immediate bearing on my subject, I find the following very striking confirmation of the correctness of my inference as to the state of General Washington's mind, on the occasion spoken of:--

FROM RANDALL'S "LIFE OF JEFFERSON," VOL. 1. p. 631.

"On the subject of President Washington's feelings on the Bank Bill we find the following entry in Mr. Trist's memoranda:--

"'MONTPELIER, Friday, May 25, 1827.

* * * * *

"'Mr. Madison: "General Washington signed Jay's Treaty, but he did not at all like it. He also signed the Bank. But he was very near not doing so; and if he had refused, it would, in my opinion, have produced a crisis. I will mention to you a circumstance which I have never imparted, except in strict confidence. You know, by the Constitution, ten days are allowed for the President's veto to come in. If it does not appear within that time, the bill becomes a law. I was conversing with a distinguished member of the Federal party, who observed that according to his computation the time was running out, or indeed was run out; when just at this moment, Lear[27] came in with the President's sanction. I am satisfied that had it been his veto, there would have been an effort to nullify it, and they would have arrayed themselves in a hostile attitude. Between the two parties, General Washington had a most difficult course to steer."

* * * * *

"'The foregoing is written immediately after the conversation, which has not lasted half an hour,--Mr. Madison having stepped out, and I taking advantage of this interruption to retire to my room and commit the substance to paper. The very words I have retained, as near as I could. In many instances (where I have run a line over the words[28]) I have done this exactly.'"

This statement by Mr. Madison substantially sustains the view I have taken of General Washington's position at that period. The letters of all the leading Federalists of that day, and those that followed it for some years, show that they looked with great unanimity to Hamilton rather than to Washington for the tone and direction that was to be given to the movements of the Federal party, and leave scarcely a doubt that they would have sided with Hamilton if a difference had arisen between the two, as is here intimated by Mr. Madison.

How much is it to be regretted that the latter did not leave behind him a history of the events of his life and an account of what he knew of the views of others. No man was better informed upon all political subjects than himself. At the time he referred to, in his observations to Mr. Trist, he probably enjoyed as large a share of Washington's confidence as any other man, and was at all times most reluctant to be placed in opposition to him. Afterwards General Washington placed in his hands the papers from which to write his Farewell Address. But it was a rule of Mr. Madison's life, as I have noticed before, never to injure the feelings of any man as long as it could possibly be avoided, and he suffered long and much to avoid it. His papers will be examined in vain for imputations of faults to his contemporaries. They are even omitted in cases where they would have been the readiest and apparently the indispensable means of repelling unjust imputations upon himself. He carried this self-denial farther than any other public man. The pain and regret that he exhibited in his conversation with Mr. Trist, in respect to the parting between Hamilton and himself, were obviously genuine, but the necessity was absolute, and the danger that justice might not otherwise he done to his character imminent. He was on the eve of his departure for another world,--his well earned and well established reputation was about to lose his own personal guardianship,--and the subject was brought before him in such a way that he must either confess the forthcoming impeachments by his silence, or repel them by declaring the truth.

Some other citations which I have found occasion to make from Mr. Randall's work are incorporated in the text.

[27] President Washington's Private Secretary.

[28] We have italicized these words.

Other instances have occurred in our Government and elsewhere in which statesmen have transcended the constitutional limits of their power under a necessity sincerely believed to be controlling, trusting to that circumstance for the indulgence of their constituents; and in no case which has presented itself here has that indulgence been withheld where the motives for the assumption of responsibility were pure. Mr. Jefferson's course in the purchase of Louisiana and General Jackson's conduct at New Orleans were striking cases of that description.

But we have, fortunately, evidence the most authentic and unequivocal that President Washington never intended by his approval of the Bank Bill to express an approval of the systematic and general disregard of the intentions of the framers of the Constitution, in respect to the powers of Congress, whenever such disregard should be deemed expedient. The provisions of the first Apportionment Bill sent to him for his approval were contrary to the Constitution, and Mr. Jefferson gave an opinion to that effect and recommending a veto, whilst the opinion of General Hamilton was in favor of their constitutionality. The division by which the bill passed had been exclusively sectional, and the objection of unconstitutionality was raised by the South. The Union was, at that early period, believed to stand upon a precarious footing, and the President was seriously apprehensive that the worst consequences might result, in the then state of the public mind, if he were to throw himself on the side of his own section by a veto.

His embarrassment and concern were great, and he was sincerely desirous to avoid a resort to what was then regarded as an extreme measure. He agreed that the method prescribed by the bill "was contrary to the common understanding of that instrument (the Constitution), and to what was understood at the time by the makers of it," but thought "it would bear the construction assumed by the bill." This was the precise issue that was raised upon the passage of the bill to establish the bank, viz.: whether the actual intention, or that which was only inferential, was to prevail. That he would have withheld the veto if he had felt himself at liberty in such a case to follow the letter of the Constitution, and thereby defeat the intention of those who made it, no one, who examines the matter, will for a moment doubt. He appears to have been duly sensible of the magnitude of the question in all its bearings. On the one hand were the evils to be apprehended from a decision in favor of the South upon a disturbing question by a Southern President, in a form not only without precedent here, but very unpalatable--that of a veto; on the other was the grave objection to his committing himself in favor of the principle which had prevailed on the question of the bank in a case that did not furnish any thing like an equal excuse for departing from the honest and straightforward rule of interpreting the Constitution, like any other instrument, by the intention of those who made it. He did not fail to see that to act again, and under existing circumstances, upon the principle to which he had given his sanction in the case of the bank, would be to commit himself to Hamilton's latitudinarian doctrines in respect to the construction of the Constitution, and he vetoed the bill.[29]

[29] Jefferson's Correspondence, Vol. IV. p. 466.

It would have been well for the country if the injurious effects of Hamilton's policy and principles had been confined to his own times, but men of such rare genius, distinguished by the same eagerness, industry, and energy in pursuit of their objects, seldom fail to leave a durable mark upon the world in which they have bustled, especially when their day is contemporaneous with the commencement of a new government, and when they are intrusted with great power, as was emphatically the case with Hamilton. He and Jefferson, both answering to this description, have always been regarded by me as the bane and antidote of our political system. Every speech and every writing of Hamilton exhibited proof of deep research and laborious study. Men, governments, and political measures, were his favorite subjects of reflection and discussion. Of the former, more particularly of the mass, he had (as I have elsewhere said) formed unfavorable opinions; not that he was less desirous than others for their welfare--for few men were more philanthropic in disposition--but because of the early and ineffaceable impression upon his mind that the majority of men, in their collective capacity, were radically deficient in respect for order and for the rights of persons and of property. As he thought their fears or their private interests and passions the only alternative methods of managing them and the former inapplicable to our people, so he considered those measures of government "discreetest, wisest, best," which were most likely to enlist their personal interests and feelings on its side. Such measures he deemed indeed indispensable, and his whole scheme for the administration of the Government was founded upon this theory.

Anti-republican as these views undoubtedly were, they nevertheless pointed to principles and to a policy well calculated to make deep impressions upon large portions of the community, in which were, and will always be, found many liable to be influenced by such considerations, and ready to follow the political party organized upon them; many, if not born in the belief, certainly educated in it, that they have something to fear from the major part of their fellow-creatures, and seeing few more important objects for the establishment of governments among men than to keep these in order and to protect the well-disposed portions of society like themselves from the vices and follies of the masses. In the performance of such duties they very naturally conclude that government should look to the more intelligent and better informed classes for support, and as naturally that to enable them to render such support they should receive partial favors and extraordinary advantages from its administration. Men of this class, their associates and dependents, as was foreseen, embraced with alacrity and supported with the energy inspired by self-interest the principle of political reciprocity between government and its supporters inaugurated in England at the Revolution of 1688, and ingrafted upon our system by Hamilton in 1790. He found in the old Federal party a soil well adapted to the cultivation of that policy, and in conjunction with those who expected to share in the profits exerted all the faculties of his great mind to extend the field for its operation.

That extension soon became so great under the fostering influence of Government and the money power as to include among its supporters, either as principals or sympathizers, almost every business class in the community, saving always the landed interest, properly so called, the mechanics not manufacturers, and the working classes. When I speak of the landed interest, I allude (as I have before explained) to those only who cultivate the soil themselves directly or by the aid of employees--to the farmers and planters of the country--and do not of course include speculators in lands, who buy to sell and sell to buy, and who, of all classes, are most dependent upon the friendship and most subject to the influence of the money power.

Such a principle of political action, once fairly started in business communities, is not easily uprooted. It continued to govern the successors to the Federal party by whatever name they were called. Indeed, the discrepancy that existed between its name and its principles when it was first called Federal has obtained in all its mutations. Its principles have been the same, with a single exception, under every name, until the perturbation of party names and systems recently produced by the disturbing subject of slavery. When that influence is spent, the individuals who now constitute the so-called Republican party will in the main revert to their original positions. The exception referred to consists in the exemption on the part of his political disciples of the present day from the hallucination which Hamilton carried to his grave in regard to the possibility of the ultimate re-establishment of monarchical institutions in this country. In all other respects we have had unvarying exhibitions of his well-known sentiments upon the subjects of government and its administration; the same preference for artificial constructions of the Constitution, devised to defeat instead of to develop the intentions of those who made it; the same inclination to strengthen the money power and to increase its political influence--an object that occupied the first place in Hamilton's wishes; the same disposition to restrict the powers of the State governments, and to enlarge those of the Federal head; the same distrust of the capacity of the people to control the management of public affairs, and the same desire also for governmental interference in the private pursuits of men and for influencing them by special advantages to favored individuals and classes. A statement of the extent to which the business, as distinguished from the agricultural and other laboring classes, have been banded together in our political contests by a preference for Hamilton's principles and by the instrumentality of the money power, would be regarded as incredible if the facts were not indisputable and notorious. Such has been the case with those who hold the stock of our banks, and control their action--agencies which enter into some of the minutest as well as the most important of the business transactions of these great communities. A vast majority in number as well as in interest of these are men deeply imbued with Hamiltonian principles. The same thing may be said of our insurance companies which have been invested with special privileges of various grades, and are authorized to insure against perils by land, and perils by sea, and against perils of almost every description. The same in respect to our incorporated companies invested with like privileges, and established for the manufacture of articles made of cotton, of wool, of flax, of hemp, of silk, of iron, of steel, of lead, of clay, &c., &c. The same of companies with like privileges for the construction of railroads, of bridges, of canals, where they can be made profitable, and other constructions to which the invention and industry of man can be successfully applied. Individuals frequently go into these powerful associations with opposite political feelings, but are ultimately almost invariably induced to change them altogether, or to modify them so much as to satisfy their partners that their democratic principles are not sufficiently stringent to be troublesome. The possession of special and, in some of these cases, of exclusive privileges, is certain sooner or later to produce distrust of the less favored body of the people, and distrust grows apace to the proportions of prejudice and dislike. There are of course striking exceptions to this rule, as to every other. There are always men connected with these associations whose democratic principles are so deeply implanted in their very natures as to place them above the influence of circumstances; but they are few and far between. These changes are not the fruit of infirm purposes or characters, but are produced by influences which seem no farther traceable than is here imperfectly done, and are yet sufficiently effective to convert to Hamiltonian principles more than three fourths of the Democrats who become members of the associations of which I have spoken.

Such aggregations of wealth and influence, connected as they usually are or soon become with social distinctions, naturally come to be regarded as the fountains of patronage by those who are in search of it. The press, men of letters, artists, and professional men of every denomination, and those engaged in subordinate pursuits who live upon the luxurious indulgences of the rich, are all brought within the scope of this influence. It is perhaps in this way only that we can account for the remarkable disparity in number between the newspapers and other periodicals advocating Democratic principles and those which support the views of the money power and its adherents--a disparity the extraordinary extent of which will strike any one who visits a common reading-room, in which, amid the well-furnished shelves and full files of the publications of the latter class, it is rare that we find many of the former, often not more than a single newspaper, sometimes not one. Yet those which we do not find there represent the political principles of a large majority of the people. The same fact attracts the attention of the observer in passing through countries abroad which are under monarchical institutions.

These are among the political accretions of the money power in this country, made in a comparatively short period--these, the foreseen operations of Hamilton's policy and principles and the strata on which he designed at some time, when the prejudices of the day should have passed away, or in some crisis in the affairs of the country which might make the work easier or more agreeable to the people, to found political institutions of the same general character at least with those the realization of which had been the day-dream of his life.

To return to the point from which I started in this long and doubtless prolix review--a political party founded on such principles and looking to such sources for its support does not often stand in need of caucuses and conventions to preserve harmony in its ranks. Constructed principally of a network of special interests,--almost all of them looking to Government for encouragement of some sort,--the feelings and opinions of its members spontaneously point in the same direction, and when those interests are thought in danger, or new inducements are held out for their advancement, notice of the apprehended assault or promised encouragement is circulated through their ranks with a facility always supplied by the sharpened wit of cupidity. Their conflicts in council, when such occur, are for the same reasons less likely to be obstinate and more easily reconciled. Sensible of these facts, the policy of their leaders has been from the beginning to discountenance and explode all usages or plans designed to secure party unity, so essential to their opponents and substantially unnecessary to themselves.

Hamilton's system considered with reference to the effect it was calculated to exert upon most of the classes at whom it aimed, did great credit to his sagacity. The wonder has always been that a party which has had at its command so large a portion of the appliances generally most effective in partisan warfare should meet with such infrequent success in the elections. Strangers who visit us are especially struck with this to them unaccountable circumstance, and superficial observers at home are often scarcely less impressed by it; and yet the secret of its failure lies on the surface. Although Hamilton's policy was successful with many, it failed signally, as has been stated, with the most numerous and consequently the most powerful class of our citizens--those engaged in agriculture; a class with which the intercourse of strangers is the most limited, and the strength of which, from the seclusion and unobtrusiveness of its common life, is very apt to be underrated by other ranks even of our own people. It not only failed to attract their sympathies in his favor, but excited their dissatisfaction by its extension of governmental favors to others in which they could not participate consistently with their inherited and cherished principles, and which were not necessary to their pursuits; thus increasing that antagonism to some extent between those who live by the sweat of their brow and those who live by their wits. These adverse results of his policy continued after its execution devolved upon his disciples. Farmers and planters--the main-stay of the Democratic party--seldom allow themselves, as I have before said, to be drawn before Congress or into the audience chambers of Presidents and Cabinets, suppliants for special favors to the interest in which they are engaged. The indifference exhibited by the agriculturists of America, at the period of the Stamp Act, to the overflowing offers of bounties, is still shown by their uncorrupted successors. The promised aid to their business held out by Hamilton in his famous Report on Manufactures, both direct and consequential, therefore excited no feeling in their breasts save strong suspicions of his motives.

Our political history abounds with instances in which similar attempts to obtain the support of the many by appeals to the self-interest of the few have shared the same fate. They seldom fail to prove offensive to the taste and humiliating to the pride of our people. The wisest way to the confidence and support of the latter is to confine the action of the administration of the Federal Government to the duties specifically enjoined upon it by the Constitution, and to the able and honest discharge of them. Statesmen who act upon this rule are much more likely to close their official careers with credit to themselves and advantage to the country than by resort to experiments, however splendid or plausible. Occasions may indeed be presented on which temporary derangements in the affairs of the State and of individuals are produced of sufficient magnitude to baffle all calculations and to disappoint the best intentions and the wisest measures, but these must of necessity be of rare occurrence.

The administrations of Jefferson, Madison, and Jackson were thus conducted, and they had their reward. The success of Mr. Madison's was, it is true, greatly retarded by obstructions placed in its way by the money power, with a view to drive him to a dishonorable peace by crippling his resources; but he and his associates in the Government triumphed, notwithstanding, for that power had not then acquired the strength which it subsequently attained, and the field for the display of that which it possessed was not a safe one, while the passions of the people were excited by a state of open war and were liable to be turned with augmented fury against such as virtually aided the public enemy. It was in its palmiest state in 1832, when it demanded a re-charter of the Bank of the United States, and when, this being refused, it commenced the struggle for the expulsion of President Jackson from the chair of State. Although it lacked time to mature its measures sufficiently for the accomplishment of that particular object, it continued its assaults upon the Executive, materially weakened its influence in the National Legislature, and after a ruthless war of eight years succeeded in overthrowing the administration of his successor and in obtaining possession of the Government.

But the methods of the great men and successful Presidents whom I have named were too simple, and the tenor of their way too noiseless and even for the adventurous genius of Hamilton's school. To devise elaborate schemes for the management of that branch of the Government intrusted to his control, and of such as fell within the scope of his influence, was more to his liking. The construction and execution of these made necessary the use of powers not granted by the Constitution, and led to a perversion of its provisions, of which we have seen the consequences.

John Quincy Adams was the first President, after the civil revolution of 1800, who entered upon the duties of his office with views of the Constitution as latitudinarian as were those of Hamilton, and the only one of that stamp who possessed sufficient force of character to make his will the rule of action for his cabinet, and who lived long enough to make it to some extent effectual. Although elected as a convert to the principles of the then Republican party, he was no sooner seated in the Presidential chair than he disavowed those principles in their most important features--those of Constitutional construction--and marked out a course in that regard which he intended to pursue. He thereby united that party against his reelection to an extent sufficient to defeat it by an overwhelming majority.

Of the party which thus a second time vindicated the Constitution, by far the most effective ingredient was the landed interest. But though the most powerful, it was yet far from being its only valuable element, for, to use Mr. Jefferson's words on the former occasion, there was besides "a great mass of talent on the Republican side."

If there be any whom experience has not yet satisfied of the power of the landed interest, and of its capacity to cope successfully with the money power of the country, enormous as has been the growth of the latter, let them consider the facts disclosed by the census. By that of 1850, our population, as affecting the point under consideration, is shown to have consisted at that time of farmers, two millions three hundred and sixty thousand; of planters, twenty-seven thousand; of laborers engaged in agriculture, thirty-seven thousand; of persons engaged in commerce, trade, manufactures, mechanic arts, and mining, one million six hundred thousand; in law, medicine, and divinity, ninety-four thousand. Let them compare these with previous enumerations, and they will see how invariable and large is the disproportion in numbers between the agricultural and other classes. That disproportion must of course have been greater during our colonial existence and at the Revolutionary period, when our commerce was trifling, and we were almost if not entirely destitute of manufactures. We are hence able to form an idea of the extent to which the defense of the principles which the colonists cherished, and for the maintenance of which the Revolution was made, rested on the broad shoulders of the landed interest from the beginning to the end of that great contest.

Without the hearty and constant cooperation of that interest the impassable barrier that has been erected against the politically demoralizing and anti-republican tendency of the Hamiltonian policy could never have been maintained. I have alluded to the reasons for my belief that it is placed by its position and by the law of its nature beyond the reach of that policy, and my firm conviction that it will secure to our people the blessings of republican government as long as it remains the predominant interest in the country. It can only be when the agriculturists abandon the implements and the field of their labor and become, with those who now assist them, shopkeepers, manufacturers, carriers, and traders, that the Republic will be brought in danger of the influences of the money power. But this can never happen. Every inclination of the landed interest, however slight, in that direction has been to it a prolific source of loss, regret, and repentance. Between 1835 and 1840, when the country was stimulated to madness by the Bank of the United States and its allies, the interests of agriculture were so much neglected as to lead to large importations of breadstuffs from Europe, whilst the land was covered with luxury, soon succeeded by bankruptcy and want. But the sober second-thought of the people, in a remarkably brief period, not only brought that great branch of the industry of the country back to the point from which it had been seduced, but drove from power those who had risen to it upon the strength of a temporary popular delusion.

If any doubt the existence and agency of a political influence such as I have described under the name of the money power, or think the description exaggerated, let me ask them to ponder upon its achievements in the country from which it has been transplanted to our shores. It is but little more than a century and a half since it was first interpolated upon the English system, and we have seen the results it has in that period produced upon its rivals: every vestige of the feudal system that survived the Revolution of 1688 extinguished; the landed aristocracy, once lords paramount, depressed to an average power in the State; the Crown, still respected, and its possessor at this moment justly beloved by all, yet substantially reduced to a pageant, protected indeed by the prejudices of John Bull in favor of ancestral forms and state ceremonies, but of almost no account as an element of power when weighed against the well-ascertained opinion of the people of England. Who does not know that it holds in its hands, more often than any other power, questions of peace or war, not only in England but over Europe! How often have previous consultations with a respectable family of Jews decided the question of a declaration of war! Indeed it would have been well for humanity if so salutary a check upon the brutal passions of men and monarchs had been always equally potent--if some conservative and life-sparing Rothschilds had been able to restrain the Henries, the Louises, the Fredericks, and the Napoleons of the past.

The money power, designed from the beginning to exert a liberal influence in England as the antagonist of arbitrary power, has done much good there by the prominence and influence to which it has elevated public opinion, and this to some extent is true of other European countries. Here it was from its start, as I have said, designed to control the public will by undermining and corrupting its free and virtuous impulse and determination, and its political effects have been continually injurious.

CHAPTER V.

Slight Notice so far in this Work bestowed upon the Course of the Democratic Party, and Reasons therefor--Four great Crises in our National Affairs, viz.: The Revolution; the Confederation; the Struggle resulting in the Adoption of the Constitution, and Hamilton's Attempt to pave the way for its Overthrow--Equal Merit during the Revolution of those who afterwards formed the Federalist and Anti-Federalist Parties--Condition of the Country under the Confederation--During that Period and in the Struggle for the Constitution the Measures and Conduct of the Federalists Wiser than those of their Opponents--Culmination of the Contest of Principle between the two great Parties during the Administration of John Adams--The Object of this Work to give a general Account of the Origin and Organization of Parties, and not a History of Partisan Conflicts arising afterwards--Party Spirit, its Evils and Benefits--Randall's "Life of Jefferson"--Leadership of Hamilton and Jefferson--Their Character and Influence--Contrasts in their Careers, Principles, and Aims--John Adams's Political Principles--State of Parties in the time of Washington's Administration as described by John Q. Adams--Character of John Adams--His Services in the Revolution--Change in his Political Opinions from his Residence in England--Fidelity of Jefferson, Samuel Adams, and others to their Original Principles--Vigor and Efficiency of the Organization of the Old Republican Party--Firm Establishment of Popular Convictions against Monarchical Institutions--"Sapping and Mining Policy" of Hamilton--Growing Attachment of Republicans to the Constitution, and corresponding Dislike of that Instrument on the part of Federalists--Issue presented by Madison in the Legislature of Virginia--His Report a Synopsis of Republican Doctrines--Triumph and general Success of the Party--Lasting Effects of Hamilton's Teachings--Erroneous Theories of the Origin of Parties--Identity of the Anti-Federal, Republican, and Democratic Parties--Apparent Agreement of all Parties upon Fundamental Questions after the Ratification of the Constitution--Subsequent Controversy arose from the Efforts of the Federalists for a Latitudinarian, and of their Opponents for a Strict Construction of that Instrument.

It cannot have failed to strike the reader of these pages that a comparatively slight notice has been taken of that party which has for more than half a century, with rare and limited exceptions, administered the Government of our country. This is easily explained. During the first twelve years of the existence of this Government, the period during which the two great parties of the country received that "form and pressure" which they have never lost, the Federalists were in power, and of course principal actors in the management of public affairs. Expositions of their measures and of the circumstances under which they were brought forward, and criticisms upon those measures, naturally acquire greater prominence in a review of the period than the less salient manifestations of the opposition permit. The resistance made by the latter to those measures involved a succession of sacrifices and services which it is now difficult to appreciate at their full value, but which, when correctly estimated, reflect the highest honor upon those engaged in it and deserve the fullest notice.

The four great crises in our national affairs were, first, the Revolution; second, the government of the Confederation between the recognition of our Independence and the adoption of the present Constitution; third, the struggle for and the acquisition of that instrument; and fourth, Hamilton's attempt to make of the Government which had been established under it a delusion, and the Constitution a sham, to pave the way for its overthrow and for the final introduction of institutions more accordant with his opinions;--for, as I have remarked, no intelligent man could have expected that the people of America would long endure a Constitution subject to the treatment to which he had exposed it, and to such as he had still in store for it.

In the crisis of the Revolution, the conduct of all who subsequently composed the two great parties in the country--save the Tories, who were soon absorbed by one of them,--was equally meritorious. The difference between them in point of numbers was largely in favor of those who were afterwards called Anti-Federalists, and, still later, Republicans, and in point of talents and perhaps in social position on the side of the Federalists.

The condition of the country, during the second important juncture, may be not inaptly illustrated by the common figure of a strong man struggling in a morass. Nothing was stable, and nothing which promised substantial relief seemed for a season practicable. Of the prominent measures brought forward by both parties to extricate the country from its embarrassments, those proposed by the Federalists were the wisest, and, as the result proved, well adapted to the exigences of the occasion.

In the contest for the Constitution that party was also throughout more useful than its opponents. In this estimate the course taken by Hamilton is not regarded as the act of his party, except as to that portion of it which consisted in signing the Constitution and in aiding its adoption.

The issues involved in the fourth decisive crisis in our political fortunes were contested during the presidency of John Adams. The whole of that administration was a political campaign, occupied by bitter and uninterrupted struggles for predominance between the conflicting principles of two great parties. The most important, although perhaps not the most exciting, of the questions and measures in dispute had arisen during the administration of President Washington; but his presence and participation in the Government held the parties at bay. Political alienations had then taken place, and wounds had been inflicted which were never healed, and bitter fountains sprang up and struggled for an outlet, but they were in a great degree restrained by that consideration. The leading men among those who soon after organized the first Republican, now called the old Republican, party, made it a point to abstain from violent action, and to content themselves with protests against measures of which they disapproved, but which they could not defeat. Jefferson gave his opinion in the cabinet, and Madison made his unanswerable speech in the Congress against the bank, and the latter, with other Republicans, spoke strongly against particular features of the funding system, but both measures were nevertheless adopted by decisive majorities; and still, as far as practicable, harsh invective and reproaches against those majorities were withheld or delayed. The removal of the salient point of attack, by the withdrawal of Hamilton from the cabinet, served also to stay partisan outbreaks on the part of the Republicans, who were, throughout, not unmindful of the advantages they would give to their opponents by bringing matters to a crisis whilst Washington was at the head of the Government. On the other hand, Hamilton evidently was discouraged by the restrictions imposed upon him by the prudence of Washington. It is apparent that, although by far more confided in, on the score of his great talents, than any other member of the administration, he was yet not allowed the latitude which he thought necessary to success. No one can read his remarkable letter to Washington (to which I have referred in another connection) without perceiving that he was seriously discontented. He thought that there were men about the President who interfered with and opposed his counsels, and he avowed his suspicions to that effect in that letter to Washington, with the expression of a hope that the latter would one day understand those men better. There was, besides, as Jefferson admits, "no act of strong mark during the remainder of his" (Washington's) "administration that excited much complaint."

Discontents were, therefore, in a great degree, held in abeyance waiting the succession for more active resistance and redress. The arrival of that period-- the retirement of Washington and the election of Adams--found the field clear for the great contest for which the materials had been gathered and the hearts of the combatants prepared.

Mr. Jefferson endeavored, as far as was proper, to prevent himself from being regarded as a competitor with Mr. Adams, when the latter was elected. He wrote to Mr. Madison, requesting him to withdraw his name if there should be an equality of votes between himself and Mr. Adams, which was not an improbable result, assigning, as a reason, that the latter was greatly his senior in years, and had always stood in advance of him in public life. But notwithstanding the friendly feelings that had existed between them down to that period, their relations soon assumed a very decided character of political opposition. Then commenced that fierce partisan struggle which has never been equaled here and seldom, if ever, in any country, either in respect to the gravity and interest of the principles involved, or to the ability and firmness with which the ground of the respective parties was sustained.

A full account of the incidents of this four years' controversy would carry this work far beyond the limits of my plan and of my time. My object has been to trace the origin and first organization of our political parties. To this full notices of the early measures out of which they sprang were indispensable. Partisan conflicts upon questions that arose after their organization was completed, are to be regarded as effects rather than as causes of their existence. The spirit which controls the action of sects and parties, in church or state, is indeed selfish and perverse, becoming more and more characterized by those qualities the longer they are kept on foot. When a new measure is proposed, or doctrine announced, on either side, the problem presenting itself for deliberation eo instanti to the minds of the opposite faction, is as to the degree of strength and credit which its introduction and success may be expected to bring to its authors, and of consequent damage to their own party,--degrees, of course, dependent upon the extent of its probable advantage to the interests of religion, in one case, or of the country, in the other,--and in such deliberation the claims of religion and country are in great danger of being postponed for the interests of parties, and the new doctrine or measure of meeting with a resistance proportioned to its probable merit. It results as a general rule that it is sufficient to induce one party to oppose any given measure to know that it has been introduced by its adversary. This is an unfavorable and humiliating view of a subject which nevertheless includes great advantages in a free State, but its truth is unhappily too obvious.

The angry contests which followed each other in rapid and uninterrupted succession during the administration of the elder Adams, partook strongly of this character. They sprung out of questions which arose after the two great parties of the country--which have been substantially kept on foot ever since-- had been completely organized and had taken the field, the one to accomplish and the other to resist a great national reform which could only be constitutionally determined through the medium of a struggle for the succession. Of these I have only noticed the alien and sedition laws, and have been induced to make that discrimination partly by a conviction of their superior influence in settling the fate of parties, but principally from their relation to the report upon the question of their constitutionality prepared by Madison, under the invigorating stimulus administered by the ever active and zealous mind of Jefferson. Of this great paper I shall speak again.

For an account of those interesting partisan conflicts--which, in comparison with the men and issues of the present day, I may, without, I think, being justly reproached with overpraising the past, call a war of giants--the reader cannot, in my judgment, be referred to a source which is in the main more reliable than Randall's "Life of Jefferson." The descendants of that great and good man have contributed to the preparation of that work, apparently without reserve, a body of information of intense interest with which they have been intrusted, and which has never before been made public. With many of the members of this family it has been my good fortune to become intimately acquainted; it would be difficult to find people anywhere more unobtrusive, notwithstanding their claims upon the respect and consideration of the community, whilst in individual temperament and character they are richly endowed with those amiable, truthful, disinterested, and upright traits for which their progenitor was so greatly distinguished in the estimation of those who knew him well, and who were disposed to do him justice. Mr. Randall has faithfully embodied the valuable materials furnished by them in his work, to the execution of which he has brought, besides talent and industry, a thoroughly democratic spirit. He has entitled himself to credit for permitting Mr. Jefferson and his contemporaries, as well opponents as coadjutors, to speak for themselves in respect to public questions generally. If it should be thought in any quarter that his own commentaries betray too much warmth; and are in some instances of too partisan a character for the right tone of history, it should be remembered that they fall in those respects far short of the writers of the Federal school who have treated of Jefferson; his volumes may with truth be regarded as the first systematic defense of that statesman's entire political career, and it would not be an easy matter for any one, especially for one of Randall's years, after wading through the volumes of political and personal detraction which have been written against him, to read for the first time vindications authentic, simple, and conclusive without being sometimes betrayed into expressions which would not have been indulged at moments of less excitement.

Occasional mistakes in a work of such extent, even with the best intentions, and with what may well be regarded as the most reliable sources of information, are still unavoidable. I have elsewhere corrected a very important one in respect to Mr. Madison's vote on Giles's resolution censuring the conduct of Hamilton. I dissent also from the inferences drawn in a few instances from facts about which there is no mistake,--such as Washington's intentions respecting the rank of the major-generals for the provisional army, and the blame imputed to Jefferson and Madison,--to the latter for not accepting the office of Secretary of State when the former resigned, and to Jefferson for declining Washington's invitation to return to it; but I have not seen any statement in the whole work which I do not believe was intended to be correct, or any construction of ascertained results which does not appear to have been made in good faith.

It is conceded on all sides that Hamilton and Jefferson, during the presidency of John Adams, were the leaders of the two great parties--the substantial amalgamation of the old Anti-Federal and Republican parties leaving but two. Hamilton's position was unprecedented. Although the President and himself were, almost from the commencement of the campaign, upon very bad terms-- feeling strong personal dislike towards each other, and holding no really friendly intercourse--he notwithstanding directed the course of the administration, and controlled the entire action of the Government to a greater extent than he had done at any time during the presidency of Washington. These extraordinary results he accomplished by means of the complete ascendancy, to which I have heretofore alluded, which he possessed over the three principal members of Mr. Adams's cabinet,--Pickering, Wolcott and McHenry,--and by the peculiar influence that he was capable of exerting over the Federal members of Congress. I have referred to letters, state papers, briefs, and instructions for the action of those parties establishing the truth of this position. With very limited exceptions the control of Mr. Adams over his own administration was little more than nominal. He served the purpose, and that was his chief burden, of bearing the responsibility of unpopular measures--a fortunate circumstance for the Republicans, as he excelled most men in his capacity for adding to the odium of an obnoxious measure by the manner of executing it.

I doubt whether, in the history of the world, another occasion can be found when any two men were as successful as were Jefferson and Hamilton in impressing such great numbers of intelligent people with their own opinions and views upon the subjects of government and its proper administration.

Acts and avowed opinions speak for themselves, but to determine the motives of parties in the adoption of their measures no safer tests perhaps can be employed than the characters and dispositions of those by whom the parties themselves were founded and, in their early stages, guided. Hamilton's character, qualifications, and views have already occupied a large space in these pages. If they have been spoken of in any other than a faithful and liberal spirit, I have certainly failed to do justice to my own feelings. Of Thomas Jefferson, the founder as well as leader of the old Republican, now Democratic, party, comparatively little has been said. Opposed as they were in their opinions upon almost every public question that arose after the adoption of the Federal Constitution, there were yet occasional coincidences of sentiment which served to illustrate the elevated character of their minds, as there were also many features of their respective careers which, while broadly contrasted, furnished the strongest evidence of the sincerity and integrity of both. Not the least striking among the latter may be found in the circumstances and conditions of life in which they respectively started in the "race set before them," as connected with the ideas and opinions at which they arrived, so variant from those commonly impressed upon men by similar accidents.

Descended from a highly honored stock, it was yet Hamilton's lot to be born poor and to be left solely dependent upon his own exertions for his success in life. After a service of three years as clerk in a counting-house he was sent to this country for the completion of his education, at the expense of relatives on his mother's side. Here he made himself acquainted with the character of our dispute with the mother country, and took sides with the colonists in a manner and under circumstances highly creditable to him, and after five years' military service, in which he acquired great reputation in comparatively subordinate stations, he retired to private life, adopting the legal profession as his only resource for the support of his family.

That a man trained in such a school, and who at the same time possessed capacities to influence the public mind, when his efforts were properly directed, far superior to any of his contemporaries, would, in the condition in which he was placed, and under a government like our own, take his political position on the popular side, was an anticipation naturally entertained by the zealous friends of republican government. But we have seen, on the contrary, that there was not, throughout the wide extent of the Republic, a single man of respectable standing, more deeply (and, let me add, more sincerely) distrustful of the judgment and dispositions of the great body of the people, or more anxious to impose restraints upon the popular will, and, for the accomplishment of that object, to add to the intrinsic influence of associated wealth the facilities for its exercise afforded by the possession of political power. His case must not, however, be confounded with that of the "candied tongues" found in every community which

"Lick absurd pomp, And crook the pregnant hinges of the knee That thrift may follow fawning."

Hamilton's mind was incapable of that condescension, or, as Mr. Jefferson observed to me of him in connection with other matters, "he was far above that." He participated largely as a professional man in the favor and patronage of the commercial and manufacturing classes, but instead of his own political course being influenced by the receipt of such favors, he seldom failed to govern theirs. He was not a man to mortgage his great abilities for personal benefits of any description, and so well was his character in that respect understood that no one would have ventured to tender him any inducement which might in the estimation of the most prejudiced expose his personal independence to the slightest question or suspicion. The fact, therefore, that he pursued a course so different from what might have been naturally expected of him by people generally--a course so much less eligible for the gratification of ambitious views--affords high evidence of the integrity of his motives. It proved that he acted under the influence of opinions which had been honestly formed, and in the correctness of which he confided to the end; opinions which he doubtless hoped would in the sequel prove acceptable to the majority, but to which he felt it his duty to adhere, whatever might be the consequences to himself of his perseverance.

Mr. Jefferson, on the other hand, succeeded at the age of fourteen, in addition to other rights of primogeniture, to an inheritance which, with competent management, was sufficient to satisfy all his wants, and to a social position, when he became a man, which required no pecuniary aids to make his condition in every respect all that was desirable, and one that could scarcely be improved by any change in the government of his country. To an unusual extent devoid of the gift of oratory, personal ambition was less likely to tempt him into the paths of politics. Cherishing always a love of letters, science and the arts, blessed with a genial temper, and in every respect well qualified to adorn and to enjoy the social circle, he seemed destined for a life of elegant ease. But, happily for the cause of human rights throughout the world, and for the welfare especially of his own country, he was impressed by his Maker with an ardent love of liberty, and a zealous devotion to the generous and equalizing principles of republican government, which impelled him into the political field, and placed him from the beginning in unreserved hostility to hereditary political power in any form, to all institutions in the State which secure to particular classes or individuals a preference over others of equal merit, and to all power in government, or in individuals or associations, civil or ecclesiastical, which can be exerted to control the opinions or to coerce the consciences of men.

Moved by such impulses, and having "sworn eternal hostility against every form of tyranny over the mind of man," he entered, at an early age, upon his public career, destined to be long and eventful, and sustained throughout the character given of him on his first appearance in Congress in 1775, by John Adams,--"prompt, frank, explicit, and decisive"--"not even Samuel Adams was more so." From that time until the day of his death he gave his support, never for a moment diminished in zeal or sincerity, and varied only in its efficiency according to the positions he occupied and the influence they afforded for the purpose, to the great principle of "the equality of political rights" which Hamilton well described as "the foundation of pure Republicanism."

At the age of twenty-two--a period in Hamilton's life when his already teeming mind was meditating the establishment of institutions, and the adoption of measures to strengthen the Government, and to enable it to exercise what he deemed a salutary and necessary restraint upon the popular will, institutions and measures in the working of which, from their nature, none but moneyed men could be expected to participate--Jefferson was as actively and constantly employed in the Virginia House of Delegates, in concert with the earliest Revolutionary patriots of that State, in preparing her, as well as the hearts of the people, for the great movement then already the subject of confident anticipation with minds like theirs. There he remained until 1775, when he was appointed a delegate to the Continental Congress. Of his agency, whilst a member of that body, in preparing the Declaration of Independence, and in promoting its adoption, it is unnecessary here to speak. As soon as that noble work had been accomplished, he resigned his seat, accepted a reelection to the State Legislature as the position in which, though less exalted, he could render more useful services to the cause, and the measures to which his exertions were there directed were in harmony with the spirit of the Revolution, and designed, as avowed by himself, "to eradicate every fibre of ancient or future aristocracy, and to lay a foundation for a government truly republican." The results of the joint labors of himself and his patriotic associates were:

1st. An act to prevent the further importation of slaves, a practice which he had denounced in the Declaration of Independence as a "piratical warfare, the opprobrium of infidel powers;"

2d. An act to abolish entailments;

3d. An act to abolish primogenitureship--a right which had vested in himself;

4th. An act for religious freedom; and

5th. A bill for general education.

These were not only appropriate but indispensable steps to lay a sure foundation for republican government, State as well as National. Most, if not all of the States, followed her lead, but to Virginia belongs the high merit of having been in this respect the first in the field, and to Jefferson a large share of that merit.

Such were the men who were by common consent placed at the respective heads of the two great parties in that national struggle which resulted in what has ever since been known as "the Civil Revolution of Eighteen Hundred," a name given to it by the victors on the assumption that, although the weapons were different, the principles which were involved in it and the spirit which achieved the triumph were akin to those which distinguished the Revolution by the sword. The knowledge that Hamilton preferred monarchical institutions to every other form, that John Adams, who was at the head of the Government, sympathized very cordially with that sentiment, and the belief that most of the leaders of the Federal party partook largely of the same feeling, and were only prevented from avowing the fact by their perception of its unpopularity, caused a wide-spread and sincere alarm on the side of the Republican party for the safety of republican government in the United States. This apprehension imparted a graver character to the contest than any other considerations could have produced, and called into vigorous action much of the spirit by which the minds of the masses had been influenced in the Revolutionary War. It served to weld the members of the old Anti-Federal party and the Republicans-- between whom a concert of action had previously arisen--into a thorough union, which became permanent, because it was founded on a principle in which they heartily concurred, and which was of sufficient magnitude to absorb minor differences in their political views.

That Hamilton's settled opinion and preference were such as I have described is a point which has been, it is hoped, already too well established to admit, at this day, of an honest difference of opinion. He avowed them on the floor of the Convention in the presence of the assembled representatives, and this is equally clear, whether the sum of that declaration is tested by the copy of the speech which he himself delivered to Mr. Madison as a permanent record of his opinions, or by the notes for that speech now published by his son. He announced them to his political rival, Mr. Jefferson, in the presence of Mr. John Adams, and reaffirmed them to the former in a conversation obviously sought for the purpose of giving the form he desired to expressions of a less guarded character, and which were, under that impression, immediately reduced to writing by Mr. Jefferson, who, for the truth of his record, "attests the God that made him." He so thoroughly impressed his political coadjutor and most trusted friend--him to whom it was appointed to pronounce his eulogy at his funeral--Gouverneur Morris, with a sense of his devotion to monarchical institutions, that within six months after his death, Morris, writing to his friend Ogden, speaks of that devotion as "hobby" which Hamilton "bestrode to the great annoyance of his friends, and not without injury to himself;" also to Robert Walsh, the well-known editor of a leading Federal journal, in answer to inquiries on the subject, that "Hamilton hated republican government because he confounded it with democratical government, and he detested the latter because he believed it must end in despotism, and be in the mean time destructive to morality;" and that "he never failed on every occasion to advocate the excellence of, and his attachment to, monarchical government." It was in perfect keeping with the character of Hamilton that never, throughout his life, though constantly charged with entertaining such opinions, did he deny the imputation; he who denies it now must assume that Hamilton either did not know his own mind upon the subject, or that he had some motive for misrepresenting it, or that Mr. Jefferson deliberately falsified his repeated declarations, and that Gouverneur Morris was capable of misrepresenting his friend upon a point of so much importance when that friend had descended to his grave.

To what lengths Hamilton would have gone to subvert the existing government, and to substitute monarchical institutions, or under what circumstances he would have deemed an attempt to do so justifiable, are questions open to investigation and comment, but to discuss the fact of his constant preference for such institutions, and desire to see them established here, would be to trifle with the subject.

Mr. Adams, who was President, and in whose name the battle was fought, fell but little if any thing short of General Hamilton in his partiality for the English system. To purge the British Constitution of its corruptions, and to give to its popular branch equality of representation, were alone necessary, he thought, to make it "the most perfect Constitution ever devised by the wit of man." The alterations or amendments he suggested, sound and creditable to himself as they were, were no more than qualifications of his general preference for the English model. If Hamilton's admiration of that model was less qualified than that of Adams, it must at the same time be admitted that the former was freest from the fault of seeking to degrade and discredit republican institutions by his writings. Without undertaking to describe the specific design of Mr. Adams's "Defense of the Constitutions of Government of the United States," or of his "Discourse on Davila,"--a task, for obvious reasons, very difficult,--it may, I think, be safely assumed that such was their manifest tendency. Hamilton at least thought so at a time when the reciprocal prejudices which afterwards separated them so widely had not yet acquired a strong hold upon the feelings of either. In his interview with Mr. Jefferson on the 13th of August, 1791, before referred to, when the conversation was turned to the writings of Mr. Adams, Hamilton condemned them, and "most particularly Davila, as having a tendency to weaken the present Government;" and, after other remarks in relation to the existing Government and its chances of success, he added,--"Whoever by his writings disturbs the present order of things is really blamable, however pure his intentions might be, and he was sure Mr. Adams's were pure."

The division by Mr. Adams of governments designated as republics, into democratic republics, aristocratic republics and monarchical, or regal republics,--embracing a minute description of each, in which the Government of the "United Provinces of the Low Countries," whose powers are held by the persons intrusted with them either by hereditary title or by the selection of associates, after the manlier of close corporations, is called a "democratic Republic," and that of England a "monarchical, or regal Republic,"--was naturally displeasing to the sense and feeling of those who regarded aristocratical or monarchical or regal features as absolutely incompatible with the true idea of republican government. The voluminous and doubtless violent attacks that were made upon his writings were scarcely necessary to satisfy those who had freely undergone the sufferings and sacrifices of a long and bloody war to secure to themselves and their posterity the blessings of republican institutions, according to their acceptation of them, that the writings of Mr. Adams were designed, as was charged, to cause the term "Republican Government" to mean "any thing or nothing."

The notices taken of the general subject and of these writings in particular, by John Adams himself, by his son, John Quincy Adams, and by his grandson, Charles Francis Adams, go far to show that if not fairly liable to this construction, they were too much open to it to be persisted in. In a note attached by the author, in 1812, to the "Discourse on Davila," as published in his "Life and Works," he says: "The work, however, powerfully operated upon his (J. A.'s) popularity. It was urged as full proof that he was an advocate for monarchy, and laboring to introduce a hereditary President in the United States." His grandson, Charles F. Adams, introducing the "Discourse" in his "Life and Works of John Adams," says: "They furnished to the partisans of the day so much material for immediate political use in the contest then beginning (1790), that the author thought it best to desist, and they were left incomplete."

John Quincy Adams, in his Jubilee Address,--the occasion and character of which have been heretofore noticed,--describes the state of parties at the accession of General Washington to the Presidency in the following terms: "On the other hand no small number of the Federalists, sickened by the wretched and ignominious failure of the Articles of Confederation to fulfill the promise of the Revolution; provoked at once and discouraged by the violence and rancor of the opposition against their strenuous and toilsome endeavors to raise their country from her state of prostration; chafed and goaded by the misrepresentations of their motives, and the reproaches of their adversaries, and imputing to them in turn deliberate and settled purposes to dissolve the Union and resort to anarchy for the repair of ruined fortunes,--distrusted ever the efficacy of the Constitution itself, and with a weakened confidence in the virtue of the people were inclined to the opinion that the only practicable substitute for it would be a government of greater energy than that presented by the Convention. There were among them numerous warm admirers of the British Constitution, disposed to confide rather to the inherent strength of the Government than to the self-evident truths of the Declaration of Independence for the preservation of the rights of property and perhaps of persons."

This is language which it is easy to understand, and which covers very fairly the subject of our immediate attention. Few men enjoyed better opportunities to possess himself of correct views in regard to the opinions of his own political party than John Quincy Adams. He was by nature truthful, or if at times blinded by prejudice, never, I firmly believe, induced to swerve by sinister considerations. Accustomed from early life to indulgence in the strong expressions (both in manner and form) common to his race, he was apt to exaggerate under great excitement, but was not capable of designedly falsifying facts. In the case before us the greatest reliance may be placed upon his statements in regard to the opinions and views of a class of men of whom he thought well. The Federal party entered upon the first administration under the new Constitution, of which the election had placed it in full possession, with a weakened confidence, Mr. Adams says, in the virtue of the people,-- distrustful even of the efficacy of the Constitution itself, and inclined to the opinion that the only practical substitute for it would be a government of greater energy than that presented by the Convention, and a portion of them (how large it was difficult for manifest reasons to determine, but Mr. Adams describes it as "numerous,") warmly admiring the British Constitution, and disposed to confide to the inherent strength of such a government rather than to one founded on the principles of the Declaration of Independence. In what class or division it was the intention of Mr. Adams to place his venerable father does not appear, nor is it very clear to which he should be assigned. That he considered his opinions, which had been more impugned in all respects than those of any, save perhaps of Hamilton, as not placing him in either, is not at all probable.

John Adams's "Defense" and "Discourse" were written at different periods remote from each other, and when he himself occupied very different situations; the former before the formation of the Federal Constitution, when he represented his country as Minister to England, and the latter, which was universally regarded as the most Anti-Republican of the two, after he had been elected Vice-President. That his views were in some degree changed by time and circumstances is not improbable. Mr. Jefferson thought that he owed his support for the Vice-Presidency to the Anti-Republican tendencies of the first work, and that his election to that office and the federal sentiment that he found prevalent on his return from England, and down to the commencement of the new government, induced him to write the "Discourse," and to give to it a higher tone in the same direction. The diffusive and (if that expression is not too strong when speaking of writings of so much learning and ability) the incoherent manner in which these works were constructed, particularly the earlier one, makes it unsafe to venture to specify the precise principles they were designed to sustain. His grandson was so sensible of the deficiencies of the "Defense" in these respects that he reconstructed and improved it in his publication, but without, as he says, changing the sense, and I have no doubt that he has carried out the latter idea in good faith.

That few if any American citizens went beyond John Adams in his admiration of the British Constitution is undeniably true. In the third chapter of the "Defense,"--(see Vol. IV. p. 358, of his "Life and Works,") he pronounces an eulogium on that Constitution which goes far beyond that reported by Mr. Jefferson, (in his account of the conversation between Adams and Hamilton in April, 1791,) calling it "the most stupendous fabric of human invention," adding, that "not the formation of languages, not the whole art of navigation and ship-building, does more honor to the human understanding than this system of government." But on the very next page he commends the United States for not having followed the English model, so far as to make "their first magistrates or their senators hereditary"--differing substantially in that regard from the opinion reported by Mr. Jefferson, and showing how unsafe if not futile would be the attempt to define exactly the principles which he favored.

It may, notwithstanding, be safely assumed, first, that he was foremost among the warm admirers of the British Constitution spoken of by his son, and secondly, that he deemed our Constitution defective in omitting to provide for some depository of political power in the government, variant in principle from its general provisions, one which should be either not at all or only very remotely subject to popular control, and that he stood almost at the head of those whose confidence in the virtue of the people had been greatly weakened by occurrences following the Revolution.

The latter assumption would seem very fully warranted by the following citations from his "Defense:"[30]

"The proposition, that the people are the best keepers of their own liberties, is not true; they are the worst conceivable; they are no keepers at all; they can neither judge, act, think, or will as a political body."

"If it is meant by our author a representative assembly, they are not still the best keepers of the liberties of the people; at least the majority would invade the liberty of the minority sooner and oftener than an absolute monarchy."

"A great writer has said that a people will never oppress themselves, or invade their own rights. This compliment, if applied to any nation or people in being or memory, is more than has been merited."

"Aristides, Fabricius, and Cincinnatus, are always quoted, as if such characters were always to be found in sufficient numbers to protect liberty; and a cry and show of liberty is set up by the profligate and abandoned, such as would sell their fathers, their country, and their God for profit, place, and power. Hypocrisy, simulation, and finesse are not more practiced in the courts of princes than in popular elections, nor more encouraged by kings than people."

"The real merit of public men is rarely known and impartially considered. When men arise who to real services add political empiricism, conform to the errors of the people, comply with their prejudices, gain their hearts and excite their enthusiasm, then gratitude is a contagion--it is a whirlwind."

[30] See Randall's Life of Jefferson, Vol. I. p. 587.

The same volume (of Randall's Work) contains copious extracts from the letters of Fisher Ames and a number of other leading Federalists, derived from Hamilton's recently published papers and other sources. They breathe in general the same spirit, hankering after pre-revolutionary institutions and systems, though less boldly expressed than was done by Hamilton and Adams, and the same distrust of the sufficiency of the Constitution and above all of the capacities and dispositions of the people, the latter exhibited in assaults upon democracy and the democratic spirit of the country.

John Adams was in every sense a remarkable man. Nature seems to have employed in his construction intellectual materials sufficient to have furnished many minds respectably. It would not be easy to name men, either of his day or of any period, whose characters present a deeper or a stronger soil, one which during his long and somewhat boisterous public life was thoroughly probed by his enemies without disclosing any variation in its depths from the qualities and indications of its surface. Still more deeply was it turned up and exposed to the light by himself with the same result. His writings, which have been more extensive and more various than those of any of his contemporaries, have been given to the world apparently without reserve. These, with his diaries and autobiography, have turned his character inside out and shown us, without disguise of any sort, the kind of man he was: and the representation is invariably that of the same "always honest man" that he was three quarters of a century ago when that high praise was accorded to him by his not too partial friend, Benjamin Franklin, in a communication not designed to be over civil.

Whatever diversities may have arisen in the opinions of men in relation to the merits or demerits of his after conduct, all agree in conceding to him credit for patriotic and useful services in the times which have been happily described as those which tried men's souls. Mr. Jefferson, but two years before the death of both of them, on referring to that period, and to Mr. Adams's great services, in my presence, was warmed by the subject, and spoke of him as having been the mainmast of the ship--the orator of the Revolution, &c. It is in all probability no exaggeration of his merits to assume that there was no man in the United States, (perhaps, but not without doubt, excepting Samuel Adams,) who, before he was sent abroad in their service, did more than himself in a civil capacity to promote the cause of the Revolution. This is a high distinction--one which entitles his memory to the perpetual reverence of his countrymen. No subsequent errors of opinion, nothing short of personal dishonor and degradation, of which he was incapable, could extinguish a claim to the enduring gratitude and respect of a nation founded on such services.

He left our shores upon his foreign mission a noble specimen of a republican statesman--his heart and mind filled to overflowing with right principles, and capable of vindicating them whenever and wherever they might stand in need of support or defense. He performed his public duties with fidelity and honor, but in respect to his political opinions he returned an altered man. His "Defense of the Constitutions of Government of the United States of America," written and published in England whilst representing his country there, notwithstanding an imposing title, though agreeable to some excited painful emotions in the breasts of most of his Revolutionary associates. The dissatisfaction of the latter was not a little increased by the circumstance that sentiments and opinions, so disparaging to a form of government which had been the unceasing object of their desire, should have been ostentatiously promulgated in a country and in the presence of a government from which the right to establish it had been wrested by arms, and on the part of which the most unfriendly feelings in respect to our advancement were still entertained. It was, nevertheless, true that no circumstance contributed more toward his selection by the Federal party as their candidate for the office of Vice-President than these very avowals. His own sense of their efficacy in that respect is clearly to be inferred from the fact that he devoted the first moments of his time, whilst occupying that station, to the prosecution of the same general object, with less disguise and increased boldness, through his "Discourses on Davila."

Jefferson and Samuel Adams and others of their stamp, who had embarked in the Revolution with a spirit that could neither be appalled by danger whilst the battle raged, nor seduced by considerations of any description after it had been fought, were not slow in perceiving that Mr. Adams had not only deserted from the cause of free government, but that he regarded his first success under the new system and aspired to the still higher honor in the gift of his countrymen as fruits of his desertion. Whilst his early and best friends felt that the fabric, the erection of which had cost them so much labor and so many sacrifices, had lost one of its strongest pillars by his falling off, they were neither dismayed nor did they despair of its safety. They met his second attempt to bring free governments into disrepute with an energy that drove him, as he himself admits, stubborn and inflexible in his purposes as he always had been, to discontinue, at least in that form, assaults upon a political faith, once the object of their common devotion. This desertion on the part of one in whom they had confided so fully, and upon whose cooperation, in securing to them the full enjoyment of the political rights for the acquisition of which they had endured so many perils, they had largely depended, sank deeply into the hearts and minds of the people. The spirit of discontent was naturally much increased by the discovery that Hamilton, who had done himself so much honor, and who had raised such favorable anticipations by the chivalrous spirit and gallantry with which he had embraced and sustained the national cause was, after all, irreconcilably hostile to that system of republican government which they so highly prized, and upon the ultimate enjoyment of which they had so long meditated; that his opposition was not only open and unreserved, but that he assigned as a reason for it their incapacity and unfitness for the support and enjoyment of free institutions.

A sense of danger to the cause of republicanism in the United States was widely diffused through the public mind. There were indignities to be resented and wrongs to be redressed, besides new securities to be devised for the safety of long-cherished principles. These were considerations quite sufficient to rouse the lion of the Revolution from his lair to defend its choicest fruit from further profanation. Those classes, among the surviving patriots of that eventful day, of whom I have spoken as pervaded by a deeper hatred of kingly government than others among their Revolutionary associates, sprang to the rescue with alacrity and zeal. The descendants of the devoted spirits who first settled the ancient colony of Virginia were not unmindful of their hereditary obligations to resist the exercise of lawless power. Neither could the appeal fall unheeded on the ears of the representatives of the persecuted Huguenots, who had suffered so cruelly from the exercise of powers now sought to be revived, or of the Netherlanders of the Middle States, or on those sons of the Puritans of the East whose zeal in behalf of liberty had not been tempted to spend itself on trade and manufactures by the seductive influence of Hamilton's policy, and by the facilities they possessed for those pursuits.

Drawing its power from such sources, and sustained by a great preponderance of the landed interest in every part of the country, the old Republican party attained a degree of vigor and efficiency superior to that of any partisan organization which had before or has since appeared on the political stage. Mr. John Quincy Adams described it truly when he said that it had acquired a head which would have enabled it, if so disposed, "to have overthrown Washington's administration as it did that of his successor acting upon its principles." Jefferson's declaration to Mazzei that "we have only to awake and snap the Lilliputian cords with which they have attempted to bind us during the first slumbers that succeed our labors," was borne out by the result.

Although the audacious passion for monarchical government, which the leading Federalists had ventured to revive so soon after the Revolution, was the most exciting of the causes which inflamed the hearts and braced the nerves of the Republicans for the conflict,[31] that was not the first issue to be tried. The nature of the government to be substituted was a question that would not, in the natural order of things, arise until the fate of the existing Constitution had been settled; but as their blood was up and their hands at work, the Republicans resolved, if possible, to strangle the conspiracy against the new-born liberties of the country in both its branches by the same effort. The severity and success of the blows they directed against the restoration of the power and influence of the Crown, in any form, is strikingly illustrated by a comparison of the state in which that question was found and that in which it was left by the civil revolution of 1800. Whilst at the former period the superiority of kingly over republican government was the prevailing and absorbing sentiment among what were called the higher classes, as graphically described by Mr. Jefferson, and substantially corroborated by Gouverneur Morris's letter to Rufus King, the notion that the former would be ever practicable in this country was so thoroughly annihilated by that great struggle as never again to have been whispered in our politics. There is no exaggeration in the affirmation that there has been no day within the last forty years when a proposition for the reestablishment of monarchy in the United States, however seriously made, could have excited any other emotion than ridicule or contempt, or would not have been deemed more appropriately punished by the administration of the straight-jacket than by a trial for treason. But there has been far greater difficulty in completing the work of resistance to Hamilton's efforts to overthrow the Constitution by subverting it, through the agency of his sapping and mining policy, which was the direct issue in the election of 1800. A constitution had been established, in the construction and ratification of which the Federal party had performed a greater and more effectual part than the party opposed to it. Its general provisions were fully adequate to the support of a republican government. By a successful incorporation of the representative system with the republican form, pure and simple, its framers had happily qualified and adapted the instrument to our extensive territory, and a provision for amendments furnished a remedy against existing defects. Of the latter the omission to secure specifically and adequately the individual natural rights of men against the exercise of arbitrary power was the most important--a defect in respect to which a large majority of the Anti-Federalists were, for reasons frequently referred to, most sensitive. The Constitution was ratified by several of the States, and amongst them by Virginia and New York, with accompanying resolutions, some of them passed by the State conventions with perfect unanimity, expressing opinions that it deserved revision and required amendments. Without such resolutions the ratification could not, we are forced to believe, have been effected. We have seen with what reluctance the first Congress, Federal by a large majority, consented to make any constitutional amendments, and that nothing short of Mr. Madison's wonderful perseverance could, in all probability, have effected their adoption; but they were obtained, proved satisfactory to the Anti-Federalists, and made them fast friends of the new Constitution.

[31] See Life of Morris, Vol. III. p. 128. "But the thing which in my opinion has done more mischief to the Federal party is the ground given by some of them to believe that they wish to establish a monarchy."--Letter from Morris to King.

From that moment that instrument ceased to be an object of solicitude with the leaders of the Federal party, hardly retaining favor with any of them. This result is by no means an unusual one in the history of parties whose feelings have become to any great extent embittered. The instances are rare indeed in which any public measure or act is at the same time entirely acceptable to all sides. The "Independent Treasury" is the only clear case of the kind among us that has fallen under my observation. The letters of the leading Federalists, which have now for the first time seen the light, prove their subsequent indifference, and, in many instances, active hostility to the Constitution. Not a few who imbibed Hamilton's feelings and shared in his views upon this point had been members of the Convention, and among those to whom I have awarded so large a share of credit for their conduct in making the Constitution what it is. This was justly their due. It is not to be doubted that several of them, as I have before said, participated largely in Hamilton's objections, and would have preferred a very different instrument; but they knew that none less favorable to the supposed interests of the State governments, or less liberal in other respects, would stand the slightest chance of ratification, more especially when the circumstance of disregard to the limits and restrictions of the authority by which they had been convened was taken into consideration. They saw nothing but injury, vast and complicated, to the country from their failure, and they evinced their patriotism in yielding to this wise foresight at the sacrifice of their individual preferences. Although many of them, doubtless, did not fully share Hamilton's absorbing preference for monarchy, they very generally went to the extent pointed out by John Quincy Adams in his Jubilee Address--that was for a government of more energy than was provided for by the Constitution presented by the Convention. This they had a right to desire and to work for through amendments in the way appointed by the Constitution, but in this way they knew they could not obtain what they wanted, and they therefore yielded their ready aid to the measures he proposed by which the Constitution was to be made to mean any thing, substantially, which those who were intrusted with its execution might believe would promote the general welfare. Hamilton's course in this regard seemed to the uninitiated extremely reckless, as he appeared desirous to select objects in respect to which the excess of authority under the Constitution which he exerted was most obvious, and the subjects themselves were those in respect to which the sensibilities of his opponents were the keenest. In the whole range of measures, which, if constitutional, might appropriately proceed from his department, he could not have found a single one as to which the intention of the framers of the Constitution, adverse to the power he exercised, was better understood than a United States Bank. Mr. Jefferson brought the facts which transpired in the Convention proving such intention to his notice, and to that of the President, and they were not controverted by either.

So in regard to the Sedition Law. One of the ten amendments was especially designed to prohibit such legislation, and there were no subjects to which the Anti-Federalists and Republicans were more alive than to the liberty of speech and of the press. The same thing may be said, in respect to public sensibilities, of the Alien Act. That Act conferred a power on the President, which, though one of the prerogatives of the Crown, no prime minister dare exercise at this day in the sense in which the President was authorized to exercise it.

Yet it is now known that of these last measures the first was passed upon Hamilton's suggestion, and Mr. Charles F. Adams informs us that neither was ever made the subject of executive consultation.

But I can well conceive that these considerations, which might deter other men, were but so many recommendations with Hamilton for the course he pursued. From first to last he thought the Constitution inadequate to the purposes of what he regarded as good government, and that the sooner it was gotten rid of the better for the country. There were moments when he allowed himself to hope that he might make it answer the purpose if he were allowed to go on with it as he began. But these were only momentary impressions that soon gave way to the settled convictions of his mind, his avowals of which were uniformly the same. He declared to Jefferson in 1792, "that the Constitution was a shilly-shally thing of mere milk and water, and was only good as a step to something better,"--a declaration which the latter communicated in self-defense to Washington; and in 1802 he describes it to his friend Morris, as we have seen, as "a frail and worthless fabric," reminding him at the same time of his knowledge that such had been his (Hamilton's) opinion "from the very beginning." It was, therefore, natural that a man of his intelligence and resolution, looking with entire confidence to its failure, should think it expedient to select the most palpable as well as the most flagrant violations of the Constitution, while it was yet in its infancy and feeblest condition, and thus to prepare the public mind for the degradation he had in store for it, and to insure its speedy overthrow.

These severe measures were rendered doubly odious by the manner in which the Sedition Law was executed, and by the steps adopted to suppress outbreaks of popular discontent, but which only swelled comparative rivulets into resistless torrents and rendered the Republican cause invaluable service by giving occasion to Madison's great Report on the Constitutionality of the Alien and Sedition Laws. The judgment of the country has ever been that a more able state paper never issued from the pen of any man. It covered the entire controversy between the two parties, traced its origin to the different views they entertained of the construction and obligatory character of the Constitution, and placed the republican creed in those respects upon grounds absolutely impregnable. Hamilton was a laborious writer, but only so because his writings were so voluminous; to write was with him a labor of love, and there was no man of his day who devoted more time to political disquisitions. There was scarcely any other great public question that occupied the public mind during that period on which a publication, offensive or defensive, is not to be found in his Works. Yet if he ever attempted a reply to that Report, which attracted general attention and became the flag under which the Republicans fought, I have never seen or heard of it. I may safely assume that he never did make such attempt.

The issue was fairly presented by Mr. Madison, through the Virginia Legislature, as depending upon the answers to the following questions:--

1. What are the true principles that should be applied to the construction of the Constitution?

2. Are those who are elected by the people bound to execute it according to the intention of its framers and the understanding of those who ratified it?

3. Is it in that sense sacredly obligatory upon all who are subject to its authority?

The charge presented against the Federal party and its representatives was that they had trampled upon the sanctity of the Constitution by the application to its construction of principles known to be unsound, by setting at defiance the intentions of those who made it and for whom it was made, and by prostituting it, and claiming the right to prostitute it, to the promotion of their particular views of the public interests, regardless of such intentions, however well understood.

This Report stands as a perpetual record of that issue. The Republicans regarded its decision as involving the existence of republican government, inasmuch as no such government could be sustained for a moment longer than the Constitution was looked to as a sacred and inviolable line of duty for both rulers and ruled. They triumphed in the great contest, and they expelled from power the men who refused to recognize that principle in the administration of the government, and for that reason they placed in their stead those who would recognize it.

Madison's Report presented a faithful synopsis of the principles of the old Republicans upon fundamental questions,--those which relate to the powers of government and to the responsibilities under which they should be exercised,-- the only questions which gave rise to permanent political parties. Whilst divisions in regard to particular measures disappear with the falling off of interest in the subjects of them, those which I have described as growing out of such primordial tenets are kept alive as long as the government itself endures. So it has been in all countries where there has been any appreciable degree of freedom of opinion. England is almost, if not altogether, the only country whose institutions are sufficiently analogous to ours to admit of useful comparisons. From the time when her sovereigns traced their authority from God, and acknowledged responsibility to Him alone for the manner of its exercise, to the Revolution of 1688, by which absolutism was forever abolished and government declared to be a trust for the abuse of which the sovereign is responsible to the people, and always since, her party divisions, regarded as national, have had relation to the powers of government and to the degrees of responsibility under which they should be exercised. Whether these parties were called Cavaliers and Roundheads, Presbyterians and Jacobites, Whig and Tory, or Conservatives and Liberals, such have always been the essential dividing points. Like ourselves they have had a succession of exciting public questions not of this character which have for a time divided the community, and were earnestly contested, but which passed away without making material inroads upon ancient party divisions, and the latter resumed their sway when the temporary interruption ceased in much the same general array they would have presented if it had not occurred.

I have said that Madison's report was the flag under which the Republicans conquered. It defines the constitutional creed by which they were influenced in the administration of the government for twenty-four years successively, and under which the Democratic party, their successors, have since held the reins of the Federal Government, with infrequent exceptions--the latter never extending to two Presidential terms, and always the result of special circumstances having little bearing upon general politics.

But the political seed sown by Hamilton has not in other respects proved as perishable as have his teachings in favor of monarchical institutions. The former has never been eradicated--it seems not susceptible of eradication. I have given the reasons why this has been so with a description of the fruit it has continued to produce. These results have fostered kindred doctrines in respect to constitutions, their sanctity, their uses, and their abuses. I have also said that these doctrines have been ever cherished and enforced when circumstances were auspicious, and have constituted the chief element of our party divisions. Hence it has been that those divisions have been so uniform in their general outlines. The opposite dispositions which lead men to take different sides upon such questions have worked to the same ends from the close of the Revolution, and have been developed on all occasions of a nature to call them into action. The execution of the present Federal Constitution presented an opportunity to give them a definite and more permanent form and classification which they have maintained ever since. Individuals have changed from side to side under the influence of what they have regarded as stronger inducements, and when they have been disappointed, have generally returned to their first bias. Questions of public policy, disconnected from considerations of constitutional power, have arisen, been discussed, decided or abandoned and forgotten, whilst the political parties of the country have remained as they were.

With the authentic record before us of the issue, the contest, the result, and the efforts on the part of the defeated party to recover the ground it had lost, the supposition seems preposterous that our party divisions had their origin in the circumstances that occurred on the appointment of General Washington to be Commander-in-Chief of our Revolutionary army, as is alleged by a son of General Hamilton, in his history of the life of his father. Of the same character, though not quite so unreasonable, are the attempts which have been made by several to find their origin in the Federal Convention. That body did indeed present an occasion for the application of different opinions to the original formation of the Federal Constitution, but those opinions grew out of conflicting tenets which had divided the country into parties long before, and they were not then determined either way, but compromised upon grounds of expediency by a result which was not in point of fact satisfactory to any side, but acquiesced in by a majority obtained from the ranks of both. The proposition of President John Quincy Adams in his Inaugural Address, tracing their rise to the opposing sides taken by the people of the United States, as between England and France, and their final discontinuance to the disastrous career and termination of the French Revolution, would seem to be not less wide of the mark. The continuance of the two great parties of the country in the same state, in respect to the principles they espoused and the characters and dispositions of those who composed them, for more than half a century and for a quarter of a century before his address was delivered, is not to be denied. If it was even supposed possible that an intelligent and high spirited people like our own, with traditions and a history so eventful, and with domestic interests so important, could have been arrayed in hostile political opinions and party divisions by the influence of purely foreign questions, the continuance of those divisions in the same form and spirit for so many years after all pretense of the operation of such an influence had ceased would of itself be sufficient to refute the theory. But the objections to it are too numerous, too conclusive in their character, and too obvious to make it necessary to press them farther. The French Revolution had sufficiently developed itself to weaken, if not extinguish, the solicitude of the Republicans for its success, (who, with their leader, Thomas Jefferson, regarded its excesses with abhorrence,) before they expelled John Adams from the Presidency for the aid and sanction which he gave to Hamilton's violations of the Constitution, and his son, John Quincy Adams, was twenty-eight years afterwards driven from power for the same cause and by the same party, a party which he supposed had ceased to exist for some thirty years previous. It was by his latitudinarian avowals in respect to the constitutional powers of Congress,--when he began to talk of erecting "light-houses of the skies," and of the folly of paralyzing representatives by the will of their constituents,--that his political destiny was sealed.

That existing political divisions among the people of the United States induced the formation of preferences and prejudices in respect to England and France, was, doubtless, true, but to suppose that these constituted the foundation of their own divisions is to mistake for the cause one of its least important effects.

The Anti-Federal, Republican, and Democratic parties have been from the beginning composed of men entertaining the same general views in regard to the most desirable form of government, and to the spirit in which, and the objects for which, it should be administered. The morbid feelings of large portions of the old Anti-Federalists produced by their distrust of delegated power, founded on their knowledge of the extent to which it had been everywhere abused, led to a difference between them and the Republicans on the question of clothing the Federal Government with power to collect its own revenues, to regulate commerce, &c., and induced them to oppose the ratification of the new Constitution on that account, and on account of its deficiencies in regard to proper securities for personal rights. Their party was thereby broken down, but Jefferson and Samuel Adams, and men like them, succeeded in satisfying them of their error in respect to the outlines of the

Constitution, and Madison procured the adoption of amendments that obviated their other objections and, as I have before said, a cordial and enduring union was formed between them and the Republicans, under the latter name. Since that period the party has undergone no change, either in its organization, its principles, or the general political dispositions of the individuals of which it has been composed. Its name has been changed from Republican to Democratic, in consequence of the increasing popular development of its course and principles, and in some degree by the circumstance that its old opponent had assumed the name of Federal Republican and by a natural desire to keep the line of demarcation between them as broad and as well defined as possible.

The formation and ratification of the Federal Constitution, mainly through Federal agency, the union of the Anti-Federalists and Republicans and the cordial acceptance of the Constitution, after its amendment, by both, presented, at the commencement of Washington's administration, the fairest opportunity for a real "era of good feeling" that the country has ever known. All controversy upon fundamental questions having been removed, the doors seemed to be thrown open for an amalgamation of parties like that of which so much was said, and with so little result, during the administration of Mr. Monroe. Without any open question affecting permanently every interest, and all the people and all alike, as is the case with such as relate to and embrace the sources of power and the foundations of the government, if the Constitution had been upheld in good faith on both sides partisan contests must of necessity have been limited to local or temporary and evanescent measures and to popular excitements and opposing organizations as shifting and short-lived as the subjects which gave rise to them. But Hamilton took especial care that such halcyon days should not even dawn on the country. He had a riveted conviction--a conviction he took no pains to conceal--that the Constitution must prove a signal failure, unless it could be made to bear measures little dreamed of by those who made and had adopted it; and in his view of the welfare of the country that question could not be too soon decided. The name and influence of Washington was an element of strength toward the accomplishment of his project in that regard, upon which he had expressed a strong reliance in the letter now published by his son, without date but written between the formation and ratification of the Constitution, and he was, of course, desirous to bring all such questions to an early decision, as Washington's long continuance in office was far from probable. He, therefore, promptly seized his opportunity, and at the earliest suitable moment after the organization of the new Government, proposed the incorporation of a national bank. I have already said, and given my reasons for the assertion, that in the whole range of the affairs of the government committed to his charge, he could not have taken a single step which would have afforded such unmistakable evidence of his determination not to be controlled in his administration of the government under the new Constitution by the intentions of those who framed, or of those who ratified it; not one more likely to revive former distrusts, and to infuse new jealousies among the Anti-Federalists in respect to his hostility to republican principles, or better calculated to give new strength to their energies when the proper time arrived for the blast of the trumpet that called every man to his tent. His old friend, Madison, was one of the first to take up the gauntlet thus boldly thrown before the sincere friends of the Constitution. This was done by his masterly and unanswerable speech in Congress against the constitutionality of the bank. No one can make himself acquainted with Mr. Madison's course, and with the state of his feeling towards President Washington at that period, and fail to appreciate the regret and pain he suffered from the performance of that act of duty, not on his own account but from his extreme reluctance to be placed in the attitude of opposition to one for whom he cherished feelings of such unbounded respect and affection, and whose confidence he fully enjoyed. But for the strong and audacious movements of Hamilton, there is every reason to believe that Mr. Madison would have cooperated very cordially in the support of President Washington's administration throughout. In respect to mere questions of expediency, he would have done all in his power to give them the most desirable form and direction, and, if disappointed, would, doubtless, have been silent as to the result.

CHAPTER VI.

Glance at the General Subject as heretofore discussed in this Essay--One important Topic not yet touched upon, viz.: the Effort that has been made to secure to the Judicial Department a Superior Controlling and Dangerous Power over the Executive and Legislative Departments--The constant Aim of the leading Federalists to give undue Influence to one of the Three Great Departments--The Judicial not the Department originally preferred by Hamilton as the Depository of this Power--How that Department came to be selected for that Purpose--The Election of Jefferson the Overthrow of the

Federalists in the Executive and Legislative Departments--Efforts of the latter to retain Control of the Judicial Department--Character and Career of Chief Justice Marshall--His Efforts to control the Action of the Executive by Mandamus--Resistance by Jefferson--Account of the Proceeding by Mandamus against the Secretary of State, Madison--Opinion of the Court in Marbury v. Madison--Merits and Result of the case--Jurisdiction of the Supreme Court under the Constitution--Great Addition to its Power conferred by the Judiciary Act of 1789--Encroachment by the Federal Judiciary upon the Jurisdiction of State Courts, the Distinct Policy of the Federalists--Popular Respect for the Court and Judges favorable to the Success of that Policy--Jefferson directed the Resistance which was made to Orders of the Supreme Court, in Marbury v. Madison--His Action sustained by Congress and approved by the People--The Federalists hesitate and abandon their Attempt to carry the Encroachment they had undertaken in the Case of Marbury v. Madison--High Character of Marshall.

I have proceeded thus far in my endeavor to search out the origin, trace the progress, and define the principles of political parties in the United States. To accomplish these objects the measures they have from time to time advocated have been brought into view; opinions they have advanced partially discussed, and the means that have been employed to make them effectual considered.

The general subject, considering the interest and the importance attached to it in several aspects, has been but little canvassed, and is at best but imperfectly understood. The most important points put in issue, so far as they have arisen out of principles advanced or pretenses set up by either party prior to the election of 1800, have, it is believed, been fully, and, it is hoped, fairly presented. Here, on account of the unforeseen extent to which the subject has grown upon my hands, it would be my wish to dismiss it and to resume the thread of my Memoirs at the point at which I left it for the consideration of what I then regarded as incidental matter. To do so has been my intention through the last two hundred pages of my manuscript. But, at the stage to which I had looked as the termination of this branch of my labors, I am met by the reflection that in all I have said in respect to the doctrines, theories, and acts of parties, I have not even touched upon a great principle subsequently advanced for the action of the Federal Government, which, for reasons that will be seen and appreciated as we proceed, is of equal interest, and which, from considerations of recent application, is perhaps of more urgent importance than those upon which my attention has been bestowed.

I allude to the effort which has been made to secure to one of the three great departments of the Government--the judicial--a superior and controlling power over its departmental associates, the executive and the legislative, all of which were designed by the Constitution to be coordinate, and, in respect to their relative powers, independent of each other. This pretension, though successfully discouraged at its origin, instead of sharing the fate of other constitutional heresies which sprang from the same source, has been revived with increased earnestness at critical periods, and at this time seems to threaten to exert a dangerous influence upon our political system.

I have not noticed it before, because it was not set up until after the great struggle of 1800, and was thus separated from the questions which originated under the previous administration, most of which have been agitated to the present day, and because the period of its most imposing if not its first introduction into the political arena, unconnected with judicial proceedings,--that of President Jackson's veto against the passage of the Bank Bill,--occurred at a later period than that to which my account of political movements has been brought in my Memoirs.

It has from the beginning been the constant aim of the leading Federalists to select some department, or some nook or corner in our political system, and to make it the depository of power which public sentiment could not reach nor the people control. The judicial was not the department which Hamilton deemed the best adapted to that end, and his opinion upon such points seldom failed to become that of his party. He liked the judiciary as well on account of its being the only branch of the Government that was constituted, in regard to the tenure of office, upon the principles he preferred, and which he had proposed in the Convention for other offices also, as on account of its usefulness in protecting the rights of persons and property against vicious legislation or lawless violence. But regarding the exercise of its powers in no other light than through its judgments in cases "in law and equity" that were brought before it by parties litigant, the only sense in which they were regarded by the framers of the Constitution, he thought it too weak a department for his purpose. This was nominally to influence, but really to control, the action of the public mind--an object which, he never hesitated to declare, could only be effected by appeals to the interests or the fears of the people, and the judicial power did not possess the means to make either effectual. This opinion of the weakness of the judicial power he frequently avowed, and particularly in the 78th No. of the "Federalist." The judiciary, he there said, "was incontestibly the weakest of the three departments of power;"--that "though individual oppression might now and then proceed from the courts of justice, the general liberty of the people could never be endangered from that quarter;"--that it had "no influence over either the sword or the purse; no direction either of the strength or of the wealth of the society; and can take no active resolution whatever. It may truly be said to have neither force nor will, but merely judgment; and must ultimately depend upon the aid of the executive arm for the efficacious exercise even of this faculty." In support of these views he cited Montesquieu, who, speaking of them says: "Of the three powers above mentioned, the Judiciary is next to nothing." Thus regarding the judicial department, Hamilton selected the executive and legislative as those best adapted to his purposes. Of the means which those departments possessed he spoke in the same number of the "Federalist" in the following strain: "The executive not only dispenses the honors, but holds the sword of the community; the legislative not only commands the purse, but prescribes the rules by which the duties and rights of every citizen are to be regulated." These were the departments, through the instrumentality of which, invigorated as he designed to invigorate them by his construction of the Constitution, he hoped to make ours a practicable government. Sustained by a Congress, a majority of whom stood ready to follow his lead, and by the almost unbounded confidence of the executive, he for a season carried out his plans with great success, and enjoyed that momentary confidence which produced his jubilant remark to Mr. Jefferson.

But he soon found that, like the scriptural foolish man, he had built his house upon the sand, and the rain descended and the floods came and the winds blew, and it fell. Within the short period that he remained in the Government, some of the measures that he had brought into existence were already discredited by an offended public sentiment, and toward the close of Mr. Adams' administration--one still guided by his superintending genius--the political fabric which he had created was, by the same power, blown into atoms. It was this great overthrow that brought home to him the unwelcome conviction that other constitutional foundations than those which the Federal Convention, the people, and the States had laid, no man, without the same aid, could lay. It presented to his mind, under circumstances the most impressive, a truth which he had overlooked in the eagerness of his pursuit after power, viz., that the people were enabled by the popular provisions of the Constitution in respect to the executive and legislative departments, to break down the greater part of such structures as those which he had reared, by dismissing from their places those who had assisted in their construction, and substituting others, who, knowing their wishes, would feel it their interest to respect them; and what was passing before his eyes afforded the most reliable evidence that they would not be slow in the exercise of the rights that belonged to them. This was the handwriting on the wall that foretold the fate of all his plans, and called forth, during the brief period of his subsequent existence, his continued denunciation of the Constitution as "a frail and worthless fabric."

It was at the moment of this great disaster, when dismay prevailed in the Federal councils, whilst Hamilton was brooding over a defective Constitution which he knew the States would not alter to suit his wishes and which it was evident the people would not permit him to pervert, that the Federal party was conducted to the judicial department of the Government, as to an ark of future safety which the Constitution placed beyond the reach of public opinion. The man who planned this retreat was John Marshall--a statesman of great power, one who partook largely of Hamilton's genius, was better acquainted with the character of the people, and possessed more control over his own actions.

The period when this once powerful party was thus counseled and guided was one well calculated to cause its members to embrace the advice given to them with avidity. They had just been expelled, root and branch, from those departments of the government which the Constitution had made accessible to public opinion and subject to the voice of the people; whilst over that to which they were recommended to extend their preference and favor, the people possessed but little if any control. This difference, so acceptable to their most cherished feelings, was besides greatly increased in value by the grossly irrational apprehensions under which they labored in regard to the course of the President elect and to the dispositions of the party by which he had been elevated to power. That he participated largely in the feelings and views of the Jacobins of France, and was prepared for the introduction of their opinions and practices in this country; that religion, the rights of persons and property, and all the interests which are regarded as sacred under well regulated governments, were put in jeopardy by his election, were opinions to which there were but few dissentients in the Federal ranks. I have elsewhere referred to a letter, written during the then recent canvass by Hamilton to Washington, in which he avowed in the most solemn and deliberate manner his conviction that the Republican party desired to make our Government subservient to the policy of that of France, and would, in all probability, rally under her banner if it was unfurled in force on our shores. Similar sentiments were fulminated from pulpit and press; and there are yet, here and there, living witnesses, who will not partake of the surprise this description of the then condition of the public mind is calculated to excite on the part of the present generation because they know it to be true, and yet remember how often and with what solemnity the warning was uttered from sacred desks that Jefferson's election would be the signal for the prostration of our pulpits, the burning of our Bibles, and the substitution of some Goddess of Reason.

The promises of the mild sway of reason and justice, installed and enforced by that great statesman, with no other limitation than the removal from office of factious incumbents whose violence was calculated to obstruct the successful action of the principles he was elected to sustain, and the revocation of judicial trusts created in the last moments of a power already condemned by the people, and which were designed to counteract their will--a sway which bore upon its wings the repeal of odious taxes, the reduction of superfluous expense, the payment of the public debt, and the avoidance of all unnecessary public burdens, with a zealous concern for the rights of the States as well as for those of individuals,--made impressions upon the public mind in favor of the principles upon which it was founded, which now, after the lapse of more than half a century, are as fixed and as powerful as they were then; but at the time were scouted by Federal leaders and presses as false pretences designed to deceive the people and to clear the way for destructive changes.

Under such impressions the first object of solicitude on the part of the Federalists was to strengthen the existing organization of the judiciary by increasing the number of its tribunals and those employed in its administration, and thus to place it before the country in a more imposing attitude; and the second to enlarge its powers beyond the bounds intended to be assigned to them by the Constitution. To accomplish the first object they resorted to a stretch of power which now, when the feelings it excited have long since died away and the actors concerned in it have without exception descended to their tombs, will not, I feel confident, find a justification in the breast of a single upright man, whatever disposition he may entertain to excuse it on account of the violence of public feeling prevalent at the time.

After the fiat of the people had pronounced the absolute expulsion from office of the Federal executive within a brief and fixed period, and virtually that of the Federal party from power, they availed themselves of the remnant of authority unavoidably left to them by the forms of the Constitution to establish new courts, embracing within the jurisdiction assigned to them all the States of the Confederacy, and the district which had been set apart for the seat of the Federal Government; appointed three judges for each court, to hold their offices nominally during good behavior, virtually for life, with liberal salaries,--making in all twenty-one judges, besides clerks, etc.,--all designed to be placed beyond the power of the government that had been selected by the people to succeed them. Thus, much was done toward the accomplishment of their first object. The enlargement of the judicial power of the department was to be effected by a different process.

Among the "midnight appointments" by President Adams, (a stigma attached to them at the time, and from which they have never been rescued,) were forty-two magistrates, nominated for the District of Columbia. The list, though containing many highly respectable names, was in the main made up of opponents of the President elect, not a few of them strongly imbued with the partisan furor of the day. They were to hold their offices for a period extending beyond that for which the President himself was elected, and it was upon their cooperation Mr. Adams and his cabinet intended that his successor should be mainly dependent for the discharge of the high duty imposed upon him by the Constitution--that of causing the laws to be executed in the Federal District. The nominations were sent to the Senate on the second of March, confirmed during the night of the third, and Mr. Jefferson entered upon the duties of his office the next morning. The commissions were found on the table in the State Department with its seal attached, signed by President Adams, and if signed also by a Secretary it must have been by a locum tenens, as Mr. Marshall had some days before been transferred from the office of Secretary of State to that of Chief Justice of the Supreme Court of the United States. The commissions had not been delivered,--an act which Mr. Jefferson, as the head of the executive department of the Government, decided to be necessary to the completion of the appointment. Under such circumstances, and, doubtless, stung by the ungraciousness of the treatment he had received, he directed that the commissions should neither be recorded nor delivered, but treated as nullities. Believing the number far too large, he issued new commissions during the recess to twenty of those selected by Mr. Adams and to five others designated by himself, nominated them to the Senate at its next session, by which body they were confirmed.

This transaction furnished the desired occasion to apply the opening wedge for the enlargement of the judicial power of the Federal Government, and it was promptly and fully embraced through the proceedings that were had in the celebrated case of Marbury and Madison. The judges of the Supreme Court were to a man Federalists, and at the head of them stood, as chief justice, President Jefferson's persevering and consistent old political antagonist--John Marshall.

The Chief Justice may not have been the severest student or the most learned lawyer, but he was certainly, all things considered, the ablest judge that had ever occupied a seat upon the bench of the Supreme Court of the United States. No man was ever more rigidly just or strictly impartial in all cases of meum and tuum that were brought before him for adjudication. Under a disposition the most genial, and a childlike simplicity and frankness of manner he cherished during his whole life, as all his race have done, Federal principles and Federal prejudices of the most ultra character. These, though ordinarily kept in due check by a commendable and exemplary self-command,--a virtue he shared with, if he had not in some degree imbibed it from, his friend and neighbor, General Washington,--had nevertheless been warmed by the circumstances of the moment to a high temperature. The inducements by which he was almost forced into public life by the General, shortly before the death of the latter, have been narrated in the account I have given of my conversation with his nephew, Judge Washington, at Mount Vernon.[32] Unhappily impressed with the idea that his own as well as the interests of the country depended upon the support of Mr. Adams' administration, General Washington for once, and fortunately only for a brief season, lent himself to partisan movements and used his controlling influence to induce Mr. Marshall to offer for Congress, and in no other case has the high estimate he formed of a man's capacity been more signally verified by the result. Marshall became at once, through the influence of a single speech of extraordinary power, a leader in the House of Representatives during the most stormy period of the administration of John Adams, was subsequently appointed Secretary of War and Secretary of State by Mr. Adams, and held the latter office until his party, and the administration with it, were overthrown by the Republicans under the lead of Mr. Jefferson. He was then transferred by Mr. Adams to the place of Chief Justice. Other circumstances lent their influence to infuse ill-will into the personal relations of Jefferson and Marshall. They were natives of the same State, and although they had stood as Whigs side by side in the Revolution, the political principles maintained by Mr. Jefferson, after the establishment of our Independence, were so much more in harmony with those of Virginia as to place Marshall's views ever after under the ban of her opinion, notwithstanding the qualified sanction they received front General Washington. On the part of Mr. Jefferson, the unfriendly feelings which he believed were entertained toward him by the Chief Justice were, for him, quite earnestly reciprocated. This is shown by the following pointed extract from his letter to myself, in which, speaking of the alterations and other uses that had been made of his letter to Mazzei, he adds, "and even Judge Marshall makes history descend from its dignity and the ermine from its sanctity to exaggerate, to record, and to sanction this forgery."[33]

[32] See Note on p. 9.

[33] See Appendix.

Mr. Jefferson, apprised that steps were being taken to bring his acts in respect to the commissions under the supervision of the Supreme Court, at once penetrated the design that lay behind the particular measure, and, with that moral courage that never deserted him, prepared to defend the department committed to his charge. The head of the State Department was advised, and the clerks instructed, to make themselves parties to no act which would justly be regarded as recognizing the authority of the court to meddle in the affair, and his views were, of course, faithfully carried out by Mr. Madison, as well as by the subordinates in the department. A motion was made at the December term of the court in 1801, for a rule requiring James Madison to show cause why a mandamus should not issue commanding him to deliver those commissions to the nominees. Notice of motion was served upon Mr. Madison, but he declined to appear. He was asked by the relator whether the commissions were signed and sealed, but declined to respond to such inquiries, as did also the officers of the department. Application was also made to the Secretary of the Senate for a certificate that the nominations had been confirmed, which was also refused. A resolution was offered in the Senate directing the Secretary of the Senate to give the certificate. It was laid upon the table and no further acted upon. Upon affidavits stating these facts, except the last, a rule was obtained requiring the Secretary to show cause why the mandamus should not be issued on a day certain, of which he took no notice. The court, notwithstanding, proceeded to an ex parte hearing. "Two clerks were summoned from the department as witnesses, who objected to be sworn because they were not bound to disclose any facts relating to the business or transactions of the office. The court ordered the witnesses to be sworn, and their testimony taken in writing; but informed them that, when the questions were asked, they might state their objections to answering each particular question, if they had any. Mr. Lincoln, who had been Acting Secretary of State when the circumstances stated in the affidavits occurred, was called upon to give testimony. He objected to answering. The questions were put in writing. The Court said there was nothing confidential required to be disclosed. If there had been, he was not obliged to answer that, nor was he obliged to state any thing which would criminate himself."[34]

[34] Taken from the report of the case.

The testimony that was given is not set forth in the report of the case.

The counsel for the relator argued the questions he presented for the consideration of the court in the following order, viz.:

1st. Whether the Supreme Court can award the writ of mandamus in any case.

2d. Whether it would lie to a Secretary of State in any case whatever.

3d. Whether in the present case the court may award a mandamus to James Madison, Secretary of State.

The point involving the question of jurisdiction was, according to the invariable course of legal proceeding, the first in order of consideration, upon the plain and simple principle that if the court have no right to act definitively in the matter there is neither use nor propriety in considering even, and much less in making a decision upon, the merits of the case. That belongs to the tribunal that possesses jurisdiction. No point was clearer than the want of jurisdiction on the part of the Supreme Court, and such it will be seen was the unanimous and unhesitating opinion of the court itself. The Constitution divides the jurisdiction conferred on that high tribunal into that which may be exercised as original, and that which shall only be appellate, and separates the two in terms which leave no room for misapprehension or mistake. The language of the Constitution is--"In all cases affecting ambassadors, other public ministers and consuls, and those in which a State shall be party, the Supreme Court shall have original jurisdiction. In all the other cases before mentioned the Supreme Court shall have appellate jurisdiction" both as to the law and fact, with such exceptions and under such regulations as Congress shall make. The motion before the court was clearly an original proceeding in a matter in which it confessedly had no original jurisdiction; so the court was obliged to say, and so it ultimately said.

A pretense was set up by the relator's counsel that the court might claim the desired authority under that part of the Judiciary Act providing necessary means to enforce its appellate jurisdiction, which, after specifying the cases in which such jurisdiction may be exercised, and pointing out the way in which it may be carried into effect, adds to the authority to issue writs of prohibition to the district courts in certain cases--"and writs of mandamus, in cases warranted by the principles and usages of law, to any courts appointed or persons holding office under the authority of the United States." Now the plain intention of this clause of the sentence was to extend the right of issuing a mandamus, in the exercise of its appellate jurisdiction, to any subordinate authorities upon whom Congress might confer judicial power, whether that power was given to a court, or to a single officer not constituting a court according to the ordinary interpretation of that word. The commissioners subsequently appointed under the Fugitive Slave Act are officers of that description. To think otherwise is to suppose that the men who framed the Judiciary Act of 1789 designed by the terms they employed to give to the Supreme Court original jurisdiction in cases in which it was denied to it by the Constitution--a design too absurd and too disingenuous to have found even a momentary resting-place in the minds of those great men. The court so far countenanced this interpretation as to assume, for the sake of the argument, that the words "or persons holding office," might embrace the case before it. But it immediately proceeded to disprove the assumption by saying, "It has been stated at the bar that the appellate jurisdiction may be exercised in a variety of forms, and that if it be the will of the legislature that a mandamus should be issued for that purpose that will must be obeyed. This is true; yet the jurisdiction must be appellate not original,"--and the court goes on to show that this proceeding would in no sense be regarded as an exercise of appellate jurisdiction; adding to that demonstrative refutation the declaration, that if the act would bear the interpretation given to it by the counsel, it would be directly contrary to the Constitution and therefore void. That the court had not the slightest right to do what it was asked to do, or to take original jurisdiction of the matter in any form, was a point upon which it expressed no doubt; and if it had decided the questions in the order in which they were presented by the relator's counsel, the necessity of dismissing the motion before coming to the consideration of the merits of the case would have been too imperative to be overcome.

Under these circumstances what was the course pursued by the Chief Justice, who gave the opinion of the court, and who alone of its members appears, in the report, to have taken part in the case? He reversed the order in which the relator's counsel had presented their client's case and substituted the following:--

1st. Has the applicant a right to the commission he demanded?

2d. If he has a right and that right has been violated, do the laws of his country afford him a remedy?

3d. If they do afford him a remedy, is it a mandamus from this court?

That the question of jurisdiction is always the first in order is a proposition too plain and too well-established to be discussed. It is not only a rule in our judicial system and in that from which ours has been derived, but must of necessity be a feature in every enlightened system of jurisprudence.

This order was observed by the counsel for the relator, but was so changed in the opinion of the court as to make the consideration of the merits precede the question of jurisdiction--an arrangement for which no good reason could be given, and for which therefore none was attempted to be given. The motive lay on the face of the transaction. It was the only way in which the court could avoid the necessity of saying that they had no jurisdiction over the subject before proceeding to discuss and decide upon its merits. It was to avoid, though in appearance only, this judicial deformity that the Chief Justice reversed the order of the questions, and then in an opinion, which occupies some twenty-six pages in Cranch's Reports,[35] he attempted to prove that the withholding of the commissions was an act not warranted by law, but a violation of a vested legal right which the court pronounced it to be; yet wound up with an admission that the court had no jurisdiction of the subject, and of course no right to act upon it.

[35] See Cranch's Supreme Court Reports, Vol. I. p. 137.

If this statement is not in all respects true, then I do injustice to the Chief Justice and his associates, and the inferences I draw from it are to be turned not only from them but against myself. But if the matter, as described by the Chief Justice himself, stood in every respect as I have here narrated, then I insist--and I cannot, I am very sure, deceive myself in believing that every ingenuous mind, whatever may be its political bias, will concur with me in the position--that the course pursued by the Chief Justice and sanctioned by his associates was exceptionable in the highest degree. With the Constitution before them, it was entirely clear at the first introduction of the matter that they had no original jurisdiction of the subject, and could not, under any state of facts, comply with the application of the relator. The course should therefore have been, and doubtless under ordinary circumstances would have been, to direct the relator's counsel to confine their argument to that preliminary point and at its close, with the want of jurisdiction as apparent to the court as it proved to be, to have discharged the rule. But if the court had for any reason thought it desirable to hear the whole case, the same course should have been pursued when it came to their decision, and the merits of the case should have been left unacted upon. No end could be answered by an unauthorized decision on the merits, other than to show to the inferior tribunals what the Supreme Court would do if the case was brought before it on appeal; and that was the design attributed to the Chief Justice by Mr. Jefferson and severely reprobated. Such is not the way in which it is admissible for superior tribunals to treat such subjects; but if it could in any case be deemed excusable, it could never be so on an ex parte hearing. For myself I cannot, with equal and great respect for the principal actors, help regarding the proceedings, from the granting of the rule to show cause to the final decision, as exhibiting a culpable want of courtesy on the part of one of the three great departments of the Federal Government toward a coordinate member, at least equal in dignity and power, greatly aggravated by the political relations in which the President and the Chief Justice stood toward each other, and by the temper of the times in which they occurred.

I apply the remark to them individually, because Chief Justice Marshall was the principal, and seemingly the sole actor, in the proceedings on the part of the court, and because the retention of the commissions--the grievance those proceedings were designed to redress--was not merely an executive act, but one committed in pursuance of the specific direction of President Jefferson. This was always avowed by the latter, and the guarded manner in which the replies of Mr. Madison are stated in the report of the case is, to my mind at least, sufficient proof that the President was throughout considered and treated by the Chief Justice as the actual offender in the matter.

In respect to the soundness of the volunteer opinion of the court it would be superfluous, considering the fate that awaited it, to do more than to restate the question. This may certainly be done with more brevity and perhaps with equal distinctness.

It will not be denied that President Jefferson had the same power over the subject on the 4th March that Mr. Adams would have possessed if his term of office had not expired on the 3d. The President under our system, like the king in a monarchy, never dies. Let us then suppose that Mr. Adams, after he had signed the commission and caused the seal to be affixed to it, but before it had been recorded or delivered, had discovered that the appointee was a felon, or for any reason an obviously improper person to be made a conservator of the public peace, was he not authorized to withhold it? The appointment is made by the Constitution to consist of three acts--the nomination, the approval by the Senate, and the commissioning. The first and last devolve on the President. The signatures to them must necessarily be his own act; but Congress supplies him with a Secretary of State subject to his own directions, to do whatever else is necessary, viz.: to affix the seal to the commission; to record it; and to cause it to be delivered or transmitted to the appointee. The President is apprised of the impropriety of the appointment,--an act which the Constitution had devolved on him alone,--the commission is yet in his possession, for the office of Secretary of State is, for all such purposes, his office, and the question would not have been changed if the seal had been affixed at the President's House; can it be for a moment supposed that the Constitution intended that his power over the commission ceased the moment he attached his signature, or the Secretary the public seal, and that after that he had no right to arrest further proceedings, however strong his reasons for so doing? Can it be presumed that its framers intended to invest the President in the discharge of his responsible duty to "commission all the officers of the United States" with an authority so precise and technical? It is on all sides conceded that he is not bound to commission after the Senate has approved, but has still a right to withhold the commission at his pleasure; and it would be strange, indeed, if it was not intended to give him the power also to arrest its being put on record and delivered after he had signed it, if he saw good cause to do so. But it is not now important to weigh accurately the reasoning of the Chief Justice, which certainly partakes largely of the art and precision of special pleading; as the case was abandoned then, and no similar case has arisen for more than half a century. That the claim of Mr. Marbury and his associates, with ample facilities for its prosecution in the inferior tribunals within their reach, (Judge Cranch, the reporter of the case of Marbury v. Madison, a full believer in the judicial as well as the political infallibility of the Chief Justice, being the Federal judge in the District) should have been given up, after the determination with which it had been asserted, and the care and favor with which it had been considered and elaborated by the Chief Justice, would at the first blush seem not a little unaccountable. The fact of abandonment, in the absence of other explanation, would justify the inference that it was the result of a subsequent conviction that the proceedings were erroneous. But changes of opinion or disposition under such circumstances seldom arise, and the solution of their subsequent course is, I think, to be found in other considerations. The course pursued by the President afforded unmistakable evidence of his determination to resist at the threshold, and to the bitter end, the supervisory power of the judiciary over the other great departments of the Government, which was then for the first time sought to be introduced through the ex parte proceedings in the case of Marbury v. Madison.

With such a demonstration before them it became the Supreme Court and its supporters, before it committed itself more deeply in the attempt it had entered upon to control the action of the aroused democracy of the country represented in the executive and legislative departments of the Federal Government, to survey, with more care than had perhaps been hitherto used, the means of offense and defense with which the Constitution had invested each.

The result of such a scrutiny could not have failed to satisfy sensible men that the President elect, the new Senate, and the new House of Representatives,--

who in their respective positions had frustrated the effort of the late President to subject his successor to a dependence during his entire official term, for the performance of a highly important part of his official duties in the Federal District, upon a magistracy not of his own selection, and had thus far also defeated an attempt, springing from the same spirit and upon an enlarged scale, to saddle the country with an uncalled-for and enormous addition to the existing judicial corps, clothed with extensive authority, and to all substantial purposes irresponsible to the people,--were also invested by the Constitution with ample power not only to defeat a new effort to carry into effect before the appropriate tribunal the hostile views indicated by the proceedings in the case of Marbury v. Madison, but to reduce the power and dignity of the Supreme Court itself to a standard far inferior to those it then possessed.

The Federal Constitution declares, that "all the appellate jurisdiction conferred on the Supreme Court shall in all cases be subject to such exceptions and under such regulations as Congress shall make." Thus by the words of the Constitution the whole subject is placed under the revision of Congress and is made subject to its action. If any attempt had been made to set up anew the importance that had been constructively attached, in the case of Marbury v. Madison, to the words "or persons holding office" in the Judiciary Act, that body would instantly have relieved that act and its authors from the preposterous aspersions which had been cast upon them.

But there was matter in the background of far greater moment.

The original jurisdiction of the Supreme Court was limited to cases affecting ambassadors and those in which a State was a party. This branch of its jurisdiction has, it is well known, occupied but little of the time of the court, and has been withal very unimportant either in its character or consequences. Deprived of the influence and eclat it has derived from the exercise of its appellate jurisdiction, the court would have stood as a pageant in the federal system of but little account for good or evil. With the addition of that obtained from appeals and writs of error from the inferior tribunals of the United States, its position before the country would still have been one of little consideration.

Both branches of the jurisdiction in these respects taken collectively, their results would not have been any thing like the power and influence and dignity which the Supreme Court of the United States derived from a single clause in the Judiciary Act of 1789, extending its appellate jurisdiction to the decisions of the State courts. The assemblage of cases for its application arrayed in that pregnant section, aided by the power derived from the construction given to the provision in the Federal Constitution prohibiting the passage of State laws violating the obligation of contracts--a provision always understood to have been introduced to prevent State obstructions to the collection of British debts, but now made to override the insolvent systems of the States, etc.,--gave the Supreme Court the supervision and control of the most valuable and hitherto the most cherished portion of the legislation and jurisprudence of the State governments. To secure this control was an object always near to Hamilton's heart. He attempted it openly in the Convention by his proposition for a negative upon State laws, etc. But in the hands of the court the control of the Federal Government over State legislation was equally effective, less likely to become obnoxious, and infinitely more secure; for if it had been placed, as he proposed, in the hands of the President, or of the President and Senate, or of Congress, it would still have been deposited in places accessible to the people, and at short and stated periods liable to be overruled by their will. But here it was in the only sanctuary in a republican government he deemed safe against popular inroads, and it was this provision in the Judiciary Act which, more than all other things combined, made that department--which Montesquieu described as next to nothing in point of power, and upon the weakness of which Hamilton, before the passage of that act, descanted so freely--the most formidable and overshadowing branch of the government. The section bears the impress of his mind, and if not the work of his pen was beyond all doubt the result of his suggestions. Hamilton was not a member then, but we have seen that he made speeches in Congress through another, and I have not a doubt that, if the truth could now be known, it would appear that but few things were said or done on one side, in either branch of that body, of which he did not make a part in some form. Is it not passing strange that not a word is to be found in the Constitution to authorize Congress to confer such a jurisdiction upon the Supreme Court? Can it be for a moment supposed that such a power,--one so nearly akin to the proposition to place a veto in the hands of the Federal Government upon State legislation, one so eminently calculated to alarm the State-rights party,--would have been allowed, if it had been by anybody believed to be in the Constitution, to pass the State Conventions sub silentio? What is said in the Constitution about the appellate jurisdiction of the Supreme Court is not only satisfied by referring it to the inferior courts which Congress were authorized to "ordain and establish," but is, by the terms employed, fairly confined to them. The place in the Constitution where the authority is given to establish inferior courts to exercise those parts of the judicial power of which no original jurisdiction was given to the Supreme Court, and which were to constitute the basis for the operation of that which was to be appellate only, would have been, one would suppose, the very place in which the authority to extend that jurisdiction to the State courts would have been inserted if it was intended to be given. Again, the whole judicial power of the United States is by the Constitution vested in the Supreme Court, and in such inferior courts as the Congress may from time to time ordain and establish. That the words used embrace, and seem intended to embrace, the whole power, is apparent from the face of the Constitution, and was, besides, demonstrated by Hamilton in the first number of his "Pacificus." Madison said in the Virginia Convention, that it would be in the power of Congress to vest the inferior Federal jurisdiction in the State courts; and Pendleton and Mason intimated an expectation that this would be done; whilst Grayson said that State judges formed the principal defense of the rights of the States, and that Congress should not take from them their "only defensive armor;" and Patrick Henry, who in the days of his political orthodoxy could snuff danger to State rights in almost every breeze, apprehended that "by construction the Supreme Court would completely annihilate the State courts." Had Congress invested the inferior Federal jurisdiction in the State courts, and had they accepted the extension, the appellate jurisdiction of the Supreme Court to those courts in the cases enumerated would have been in all respects proper. But the Congress, a majority of whose members were Hamiltonian Federalists, were not, for reasons it is now unnecessary to consider, willing to admit the State courts to a participation in the administration of the judicial power reserved to the Federal Government, and proceeded at once to ordain and establish inferior courts of their own. These consisting of district courts, circuit courts and the one Supreme Court named in the Constitution, completed the organization of the Federal judiciary. Their respective jurisdictions were wisely separated and accurately defined. A small portion of that which was original was, for well-understood reasons, vested in the Supreme Court. The residue was separated and distributed among the inferior tribunals, subject to an appellate jurisdiction and supervisory power in the Supreme Court over all their proceedings. The system thus arranged was not only complete but harmonious in all its parts. The courts were clothed with the entire judicial power of the Government; were only authorized to act upon one class of subjects--those which appertained to the judicial power of the United States. The judges received their appointments from the same source, and were responsible for their conduct to one head. Looking only to judicial objects this might well be regarded as the judicial system designed by the framers of the Constitution.

If ours had been a consolidated government these provisions would have embraced the whole subject, and satisfied the wants of the whole country. But in the actual state of things in that regard they were inadequate to the accomplishment of that end. Instead of one consolidated government ours was a confederacy of sovereign States, presided over by a Federal Government which they had themselves created and clothed with such powers as they deemed necessary to its efficiency and usefulness, and as would be most likely to conduce to the freedom, prosperity, and happiness of all.

With no other bond of union during the first years of the Revolutionary contest than common danger, and obliged to struggle with a defective Federal organization, these States succeeded in constructing for themselves republican constitutions, and in several instances, before the establishment of our Independence, sustained the brunt of that struggle and came out of it with institutions fully adequate to all the purposes of good government, including systems of jurisprudence and competent tribunals for their administration. The administrators of these institutions, driven to desperation by great public and private distress,--the direct results of the oppression of the mother country,-- may in a few cases, and for a short period, have forgotten that interests liable to sequestration in war were inviolable in peace, and failed to interpose with sufficient alacrity a judicial barrier against the attempts of some of the State legislatures to throw obstructions in the way of the collection of British debts. But those were limited and temporary aberrations, which would soon have yielded to proper treatment on the part of the Federal Government. At the period of the passage of the Judiciary Act the judges who presided in most of the State courts might be compared without discredit to those who filled the benches of the Federal courts, and this relative equality has ever since been well maintained. Such has certainly been the case in the State of New York. The name of Chancellor Livingston, who was then at the head of our equity system, would lose nothing from a comparison with Chief Justice Jay, when the latter was placed at the head of the Federal courts. Our equity and common-law courts have since been graced by Chancellor Lansing, Chief Justices Lewis and Kent, and Judges Brockholst Livingston, Smith Thompson, Ambrose Spencer, Wm. W. Van Ness, and others, all men of great talents and acquirements. Nor have the courts of our sister States been wanting in this regard. The names of Theophilus Parsons of Massachusetts, Tappan Reeves of Connecticut, and Pendleton, Wythe and Roane of Virginia, with numerous others, might be added to the list. It would not be an easy matter to match these by selections from the bench of the Supreme Court of the United States, highly distinguished as its incumbents have been.

The State courts had, for nearly fifteen years before the passage of the Judiciary Act of 1789, performed, as well in peace as in war, most of the duties which the new Constitution devolved upon the Federal judiciary. The Federal Government was authorized, by the articles of Confederation, to establish inferior courts for the trial of piracies and felonies committed on the high seas, and courts for the trial of Admiralty cases, yet these powers had been carried into effect through the State judiciaries. But all at once the State courts were deemed unworthy of trust. Whence this change? Had the State courts degenerated? No such thing; they were constantly improving, the supineness of a few in respect to the interests of the mother country, blamable as it certainly was, to the contrary notwithstanding. No, the State courts had not become worse, but the implacable opponents of those whose judicial power they represented had become stronger! The old Anti-Federal party, the inflexible and powerful champion for the rights of the States, had been overthrown--forever demolished, at least in that array. The State governments were for a season helpless. Those who were always hostile to their power-- who, in the language of Hamilton after the Convention, and in the act of foreshadowing the effects of such an administration as actually succeeded, were desirous of a "triumph altogether over the State governments, and to reduce them to an entire subordination"--were all powerful in Congress. Nor was their power confined to Congress or to any particular branch of the Government. The result of the question of ratification in the different State Conventions, and the idea present to every mind that material prosperity, public and private, would be much promoted by that result, produced a great change in public sentiment adverse to the authority and influence of the State governments. It was made fashionable to deride them. The organization of the Federal judiciary was the very first opportunity that was afforded after the adoption of the Constitution to make the States feel the power which their inveterate opponents had acquired by that event, and most unsparingly was that power exercised.

The few members of that Congress who had not been entirely carried away by this current, and had the boldness to stand by the States and their tribunals-- among whom that firm and incorruptible republican, James Jackson of Georgia, was by far the most effective--were willing that a right to supervise and reverse the decisions of the State tribunals in all matters of Federal jurisdiction, should be conferred on the Supreme Court of the United States, provided only that the State courts were intrusted, as they had hitherto been, with the administration of the inferior Federal jurisdiction in lieu of the inferior Federal courts which the Bill proposed to establish. This they contended would make the system an harmonious and consistent one, and preserve the respect and consideration which was due to the State tribunals.

The proposition was literally scouted in debate and rejected by a vote of two to one in the House, and in the Senate by a still larger majority. The Bill was so constructed as to clothe the Supreme Court and the inferior courts it established with all the judicial power allowed to the Federal Government by the Constitution, with unimportant reservations which did not diminish their authority and do not require to be noticed. Ample means were thus provided for its practical extension to every party entitled to its protection, and if those who regulated the action of Congress had not been influenced by any views other than such as related to the administration of justice, its legislation would have terminated there. But that body went further. A clause was added to the Judiciary Bill professing to give to the Supreme Court appellate jurisdiction over the final judgments and decrees of the highest courts of law and equity of a State, whoever might be the parties to the suit, or whatever might have been the objects for which it had been brought, provided only that the relative powers of the Federal and State governments under the Federal Constitution in respect to several enumerated subjects had in the course of prosecution of such suit been "drawn in question," and decided against the Federal power. No matter to what extent the rights of the parties were concluded by that question, or in what form or how incidentally it had been introduced, it was sufficient that it had been raised and decided against the Federal, or in favor of the State authority, to subject the judgment or decree given by the State court to be reexamined or reversed in the Supreme Court of the United States. To confer upon that tribunal, the anomalous authority of issuing writs of error to the highest courts of other States confessedly sovereign, and which in all such matters might well be regarded as foreign States,--courts which were not established by the Federal Government, and between which and it there existed no judicial relations,--commanding those courts to send to it for reexamination, reversal, or affirmance, the record of judgments and decrees which had neither been made under Federal authority nor by judges in any sense amenable to it for the discharge of their official duties, was an idea never broached in the Federal Convention, or in the slightest degree alluded to in the Constitution it adopted.

Disputes in respect to the boundaries of power between the Federal and State governments were foreseen, and the means for acquisition and defense sought after by the special friends of each. Both looked to their respective legislatures as the theatres of encroachment, and a very serious effort was made to obtain authority for the Federal Government to confer important State appointments, and to interpose a negative upon State laws. These concessions were sternly refused by the friends of the State authorities, and if they had been granted the new Constitution would never have been ratified. No efforts have been made by Congress through direct legislation to restrain the State legislatures from encroaching on the power of the Federal Government, and it would not be an easy matter--the Constitution being silent on the subject--to establish a right on the part of the judicial power to interfere in that direction which would not also devolve on the Federal legislature, the power more particularly interested in the matter. The clause referred to in the Federal Judiciary Act looks in an especial manner to the legislative acts of each government, and seeks to establish the supremacy in the Federal system. It is possible that the framers of the Constitution intended to give Congress a right to confer such a power on the Supreme Court, but it is certainly most extraordinary if that was so that the subject should have remained unnoticed in the Convention, and have been so entirely excluded from the face of the Constitution. Be that as it may, it is well known that the authority given to the court by the statute for a long time lay in its hands a dormant power. Those who conferred it had too much their own way in the administration of the Federal Government, during the first twelve years of its existence, to require extraneous aid to push its power to the extremes they desired. It was when they had been expelled from its executive and legislative departments by the uprising of the people that their attention was more earnestly turned to that of the judiciary as one which--as well from the peculiarity of its constitution as from the views of those who were in possession of it--was best qualified for the protection of rights which they, no doubt honestly, believed in danger. Hence the movement in the case of Marbury v. Madison.

We cannot now form a complete estimate of the extent to which the character of our institutions, in view of that step and of measures of which it might have been the opening wedge, hinged upon the character and disposition of those whom the people had then just raised to power. The respect and reverence with which the minds of a vast majority of our citizens were impressed for their courts of justice, the confidence which had been reposed in their purity as indicated by the tenure of their offices, and the imposing character of those who filled them at the moment combined to deter feeble and irresolute minds from resistance to the authority of the Supreme Court of the United States, however unfavorable their estimation of the course upon which it was entering.

No unauthorized exercise of power would, for any considerable period, have passed unchecked by a people like ours, then yet fresh from a national struggle for principles better defined and defended with more steadiness and by purer means than any the world had ever witnessed in revolutionary contests. But the class of men, in any community where deference for the ermine is habitual, who will meet danger at the very threshold, and oppose resistance to judicial usurpation at the instant of its appearance, is not likely to be numerous.

Hostile to every assumption of power over the conduct or mind of man not originally authorized by man himself, however plausible the pretences upon which it might be exerted, an opposition deeply seated in his nature, matured and confirmed by study and by all the observation and experience of his eventful career, Jefferson was not the man to submit to encroachments upon institutions he had sworn to protect, and more especially upon that branch of them which a great and free people had confided to his particular care. It was no matter to a man of his knowledge of the world and approved moral courage from what quarter such encroachments proceeded, they were certain to meet with a firm and spirited opposition on his part.

The course pursued by the State department was by his express direction, and of course upon his responsibility. This he always avowed, and this would have appeared in the report of the case of Marbury and Madison, if the fact had not been designedly and for obvious reasons suppressed. It was to accomplish this object that the statement of the case which accompanies the elaborate opinion of Chief Justice Marshall was made to present an appearance so ambiguous and unlawyer-like. Mr. Madison, it is stated, refused to deliver the commission.

On what grounds? That is not stated, only that his explanations were not satisfactory to the relator. If they had been given the fact referred to would have appeared on the face of the record, and would have gone down to posterity as an answer to the reasoning of the opinion. The refusal of the witnesses--clerks in the department--to be sworn or to answer, and the decision of the court that they should be sworn and answer under certain restrictions, and that they were sworn, are all stated with much particularity, but what they said is not stated. Here, again, the fact is suppressed that the commission was retained in the executive department by the orders of the President, who, in the exercise of executive discretion, regarded it as the evidence of an appointment not completed, and which he decided not to complete.

But this was only a foretaste of the spirit with which the scheme of the Federal party to raise the judicial department of the Federal Government, not only over the States and their judicatories but over the two other departments of the General Government, was to be met. Two months had not elapsed after the delivery of the opinion of the Chief Justice in Marbury v. Madison, before the entire judicial fabric which that party had erected during the last moments of their expiring power, by which twenty-one additional federal judges were appointed, eighteen in the States and three in the District of Columbia, with large salaries and still larger power, to hold their offices virtually for life, was overthrown by the vote of a majority of Congress, a majority more confiding, more harmonious, and better disposed to second and sustain the measures of the executive than any we have ever had.

This measure--the least important effect of which was to relieve the national treasury from the payment of salaries to some twenty-seven or thirty gentlemen, whose services an experience of more than half a century has shown to have been unnecessary--was assailed with unprecedented violence. Gouverneur Morris said it had stricken down the sanctity of the judiciary, and his political associates in Congress denounced it as a gross infraction of the Constitution. He spoke of it with the same vehemence and heat with which he taunted the men who had passed it and their successors, twelve years afterwards, at the federal celebration of the restoration of the Bourbons, when he invited them, by the appellation of the "savage and wild democracy," to see, "though it should blast their eye-balls, royal princes surrounded by loyal subjects!" The attempts of Mr. Morris and his coadjutors to exasperate the public mind against the repeal of the midnight Judiciary Act recoiled upon their party. The only effects they produced were to rivet the convictions of a large majority of the people that they had acted wisely in changing their rulers, and to evoke a determination to sustain the men in power as long as they adhered to the course upon which they had entered. To the Chief Justice, his associates on the bench, and the leaders of the defeated party, this condition of public opinion presented considerations of the gravest import. The court had decided, and their decision was sustained by the latter with perfect unanimity, that the appointment of Marbury had been completed before Mr. Jefferson came into office, that the Secretary of State had therefore no right to withhold his commission, and that he could be compelled to deliver it by mandamus, provided only that the proceedings should originate in an inferior court. There was no ground for question in respect to the legality of the appointments of the midnight judges, or their clerks, if the repealing law was unconstitutional, nor of their right to their salaries. This was certainly a question for the judiciary in respect to private rights; and if the courts could compel the one Secretary by mandamus to deliver a commission wrongfully withheld, a fortiori could they compel another to pay salaries undeniably due if the repealing law was unconstitutional. The field for the writ of mandamus was thus greatly enlarged. If the withholding of a few justices' commissions constituted good ground for the institution of such proceedings as those we have referred to, the case now presented was one of much greater magnitude, and no party was ever more deeply committed before the country on a public question than they were in regard to the unconstitutionality of the Repealing Act. If they were right in that, and also in their views in respect to the powers of the Supreme Court, a mandamus would of course have been authorized to compel the treasury to pay the judges their salaries. Should they resume the Marbury and Madison case in the inferior courts, and proceed in this also, or should they abandon both and submit themselves to the stigma of having been the authors of false pretenses and unfounded clamor, was the question to be met.

The Republican party of the Union, as then constituted, was for the first time in possession of two departments of the Federal Government. Whilst in a minority they had not been regarded by their high-reaching opponents with feelings of much respect. Whatever might still have been the federal impressions of their principles or designs, there was no longer room for two opinions, in respect to their determination, their firmness and their capacity to carry out the measures they deemed necessary to the public service. Such being the circumstances in which they were placed, the Chief Justice, his associates and friends, surveyed the exposures and defenses of the only department that was left under their control, and it was natural that they should ponder upon possible consequences before they proceeded another step in a course which the other departments regarded as one of aggression.

The supervision and control of the Supreme Court of the United States over the largest portion of the legislation and jurisprudence of the State governments, designed to be secured by the twenty-fifth section of the Federal Judiciary Act and the extent to which they might be carried, were, in their political aspects, looked upon by Hamilton and his followers as constituting the only remaining sheet-anchor of the government, in the sense in which they desired to see it administered. This lay completely at the mercy of their opponents. No matter what might be their confidence in the constitutionality of the provision, the whole appellate jurisdiction of the Supreme Court is, by the express letter of the Constitution, to be exercised subject to "such exceptions and such regulations as the Congress shall make." An act of three lines repealing the clause of the Judiciary Act would except writs of error to State courts from the appellate jurisdiction of the Supreme Court, and another might abolish the use of the writ of mandamus. The members of that court had seen too much of the temper and firmness of the President and Congress to doubt the immediate adoption of such measures if the contest in regard to the boundaries of power between the departments was continued, and were too sensible of the extent to which that high tribunal was indebted for its power and dignity to that branch of their jurisdiction to push so unprofitable a collision one step farther under their present auspices. The consequence was a suspension of all movements in that direction. No more was heard of Mr. Marbury's claims to his commission, and the new judges quietly submitted to expulsions from their life-estates in offices by a law they claimed to be unconstitutional, with a court within their reach authorized to declare it such if it so believed.

Chief Justice Marshall remained at the head of the Supreme Court many years after the delivery of his opinion in the case of Marbury and Madison. During that long period he not only acquired, by the exercise of his great talent, the high distinction of which I have already spoken, but endeared himself by his personal demeanor to all who were drawn within the circle of his acquaintance. No generous mind could contemplate a man possessed of such towering intellect, placed in so elevated a position and bearing his honors with such modesty and unaffected simplicity as he habitually displayed, without being impressed with a deep interest in his character. I was not among the least cordial of his admirers, and would not for the world speak a wanton or unkind word in disparagement of his memory. But the public acts of public men are always and under all circumstances legitimate materials for history, and may be canvassed with freedom, provided they are spoken of truly, and reviewed "with good motives and for justifiable ends." To this limitation it shall be my endeavor to confine myself on this as on all other occasions.

No part of the fame which Chief Justice Marshall acquired on the bench was due to his course and conduct in the case of Marbury and Madison, which may with truth be regarded as his judicial debut. He had been snatched from the political caldron, heated to redness by human passions, almost at the moment of his first appearance on the bench. In his rapid transition from the halls of Congress and the Departments of War and State to that of the Judiciary, he had, as it were, been driven to the bench as to a place of safety before a tempest of public indignation created by the abuses of the administration of which he had been a part. Among his first acts after reaching it, and before time had been allowed for his passions to cool, before he had acquired judicial habits or had leisure to think even of the amenities that should distinguish his new position, was a severe blow at the wizard who, he believed, had raised the wind and directed the storm. But Jefferson, the "dreaming Condorcet," as Hamilton sometimes called him, proved an accomplished statesman. Wide awake, he made ample preparations for the assault, interposed effectual resistance, and the recoil and ultimate abandonment were the result. I have heretofore referred to the non-observance in these proceedings of due respect toward the acts of a coordinate department of the Government,--an obligation on the part of each from which no consideration can release them, and which in this case was rendered still more imperative by the relations, personal and political, that had existed between the President and the Chief Justice. Whatever weaknesses I may be subject to,--and doubtless they are numerous,--dogmatism, I am very sure, is not one of them. My endeavor always is to state my positions with deference to the judgments of others. But on this point I cannot refrain from insisting that no man who can divest himself of prejudice to only a reasonable extent can review these proceedings without being satisfied that the objection I have made to the course of the Chief Justice in this regard is well founded. No such omission was ever chargeable to him at a more advanced period in his judicial career; whatever exception may have been taken to the course of his decisions no one ever had reason to complain of a want of courtesy toward any branch of the government or toward individuals.

CHAPTER VII.

Renewed Attempt of the Federalists to give the Judiciary a controlling power over the other Departments on the occasion of the Bank Veto by President Jackson--Importance of the Principle of a clear Division of Powers between the several Departments, and the Independence of each--Assertion of the Principle by Jackson in his Veto Message--Unguarded expression therein--Substantial Endorsement by Webster of Jackson's Doctrine as to the Independence of the Executive--Character of the Contest waged against Jackson on behalf of the Bank--Violent and disingenuous course of Webster and Clay in the Debate--The true Doctrine declared by Senator White--Its great Importance--Merits of the Question discussed--The Judgment of the People the ultimate Test--Instances of the effectual exercise of that Judgment--Distrust of the Federalist Leaders as to the Capacity of the People.

The most imposing, and I may add the most important occasion, unconnected with judicial proceedings, on which the successors of the old Federal party, encouraged by the success of the Supreme Court in modern times, sought to avail themselves of the principle of the controlling power of the judiciary over the other departments of the Government in regard to questions of constitutional power, for which it had early and long contended, was that of the veto of President Jackson against the passage of the bill for the incorporation of the Bank of the United States.

In addition to the great and permanent importance it is to the Government and the country to keep down this heresy, we have in this case a scarcely less potent inducement for giving the matter a very thorough consideration, founded in a desire to do justice to the conduct and character of that great and good man.

The division of the powers of the Federal Government into distinct and independent departments is founded on a principle the value of which has never been lost sight of by the framers of governments designed to be free. It must at the same time be admitted that, among the principles which necessarily enter into such a system, there are not many so difficult to define with desirable certainty or to uphold in practice. The faithful and capable men who constructed ours, state as well as national, have been as successful, I believe, in this respect as any who have gone before them; and the efforts which have been so perseveringly made to counteract their patriotic designs must be attributed to an inherent spirit of encroachment which is inseparable from power in whose hands soever it may be placed.

The veto message contained the following passage:--"If the opinion of the Supreme Court covered the whole ground of this act, it ought not to control the coordinate authorities of this Government. The Congress, the executive, and the court must each for itself be guided by its own opinion of the Constitution. Each public officer, who takes an oath to support the Constitution, swears that he will support it as he understands it, and not as it is understood by others. It is as much the duty of the House of Representatives, of the Senate and of the President, to decide upon the constitutionality of any bill or resolution which may be presented to them for passage or approval, as it is of the supreme judges when it may be brought before them for judicial decision. The opinion of the judges has no more authority over Congress than the opinion of Congress has over the judges; and on that point the President is independent of both. The authority of the Supreme Court must not, therefore, be permitted to control the Congress or the executive when acting in their legislative capacities, but to have only such influence as the force of their reasoning may deserve."

To present an intelligible view of this matter, the gravity of which cannot fail to be appreciated as we proceed, it is necessary that we should in the first place ascertain and define the leading idea which its author intended to convey by the words he employed. The entire paragraph is replete with distinct avowals of his meaning, but in the midst of them are to be found a few words by which its true sense is exposed to cavil and perversion. This was a point upon which General Jackson was very liable to err, notwithstanding his natural and in other matters practiced wariness,--a qualification with which few men were more amply endowed than himself. The spirit by which alone free governments can be sustained was deeply planted in his breast by the hand of Nature; quickened into life by the blows of the enemy, whilst a prisoner and yet a stripling, it grew with his growth and strengthened with his strength. But possessed of a mind that was ever dealing with the substance of things, he was not very careful in regard to the precise terms in which his principles were defined. He was, besides, at that moment placed in a peculiar as well as difficult situation. Whilst struggling with an institution which felt itself sufficiently powerful to measure strength with the Government, and which had been itself stung to madness by his refusal to submit to its arbitrary demands, he was deprived of the assistance of the leading members of his cabinet. The Secretary of the Treasury, to whose department the subject belonged, had, in his report to Congress, placed himself on record in favor of the bank, and the Secretaries of State and of War concurred in his opinion; all three openly disapproved of, and could not cordially cooperate in, the measure the President was about to adopt--the Secretaries of the Treasury and of War, as will be seen by the letters of General Jackson to myself, which on account of the interesting matters to which they relate will be given with these memoirs,[36] pressing their opposition so far as to make it sufficient ground for proposing to retire from his cabinet--a step they were with difficulty prevented from carrying into immediate effect. That a document of such length, prepared on the spur of the occasion and under such untoward and exciting circumstances, should not have been even more vulnerable to the assaults of his astute and implacable opponents, is not a little surprising.

[36] The correspondence, including the letters of President Jackson, has received the same direction with the other MSS. of the Author. See introduction to this volume. Eds.

Few had better opportunities for knowing the state of feeling which prevailed at the Presidential mansion, whilst this matter was in progress, than myself. I arrived at New York from my brief mission to England after the Bank Bill had passed both Houses and on the day it was sent to President Jackson for his approval, and left the next morning for Washington. Arriving there at midnight, I proceeded at once to the White House, in pursuance of an invitation he had sent to New York in anticipation of my coming. I found the General in bed, supported by pillows, in miserable health, but awake and awaiting and expecting me. Before suffering me to take a seat, and whilst still holding my hand he, with characteristic eagerness when in the execution of weighty concerns, spoke to me of the bank--of the bill that had been sent for his approval, and of the satisfaction he derived from my arrival at so critical a moment; and I have not forgotten the gratification which beamed from his countenance when I expressed a hope that he would veto it, and when I declared my opinion that it was in that way only he could discharge the great duty he owed to the country and to himself. Not that he was ignorant of my views upon the subject, for in all our conversations in respect to it before I left the country,--and they had been frequent and anxious,--my voice had been decided as well against the then existing, as against any other national bank. Neither that he was himself in doubt as to the course that he ought to pursue, for he entertained none. But the satisfaction he evinced, and which he expressed in the most gratifying terms, arose solely from the relief he derived from finding himself so cordially sustained in a step he had determined to take but in respect to which he had been severely harassed, by the stand taken by the leading members of his cabinet and by the remonstrances of many timid and not a few false friends, and had as yet been encouraged only by the few about him in comparatively subordinate positions who were alike faithful to principle and to himself.

The veto message was prepared and sent in whilst I remained at Washington. The manuscript was at all times open to my inspection, although I had but little direct agency in its construction. Had it been otherwise, the few words which subsequently made that part in which they appear so conspicuous could not have escaped my notice.

The paragraph in the message which sets forth the constitutional principles which President Jackson intended to avow, contains the following declarations: 1st. That if the opinion of the Supreme Court covered the whole ground of the act under consideration, still it ought not to control the coordinate authorities of the Government. 2d. That the Congress, the Executive, and the Court must each for itself be guided by its own opinions of the Constitution. 3d. That it is as much the duty of the House of Representatives, of the Senate, and of the President, to decide upon any Bill or Resolution that may be presented to them for passage or approval, as it is for the supreme judges when brought before them for judicial decision. 4th. That the opinion of the judges has no more authority over Congress than the opinion of Congress has over the judges, and that on that point the President is independent of both. 5th. That the authority of the Supreme Court should not therefore be permitted to control the Congress or the Executive, when acting in their legislative capacities, but to have only such influence as the force of their reasoning may deserve. In none of these avowals is the principle of irresponsibility in respect to the opinion of the Supreme Court, by fair construction much less by necessary implication, carried farther than to include the President when discharging his official duties as the depository of the executive power of the Government in approving or disapproving of a Bill or Resolution sent to him by Congress for his executive action. That in all this he was perfectly right, it will be seen even Mr. Webster, latitudinarian as he was, did not venture to controvert.

But in the midst of these declarations are found these unguarded words: "Each public officer who takes an oath to support the Constitution, swears that he will support it as he understands it and not as it is understood by others." Either this declaration was applied by the President only to all such officers as those of whom he had been speaking before and of whom alone he spoke afterwards, all in the same paragraph,--to that class of officers who, singly as was his own case, or in conjunction with others as was the case with some, constituted the three great departments of the Government, whilst acting in their respective official capacities, as it was beyond all doubt intended to be applied; or he must be supposed to have held that the inferior judges of the federal courts had a right to say to the superior court, "We do not understand the Constitution as you have expounded it, and we will therefore not submit to your decision;" the same as to the judges of the State courts of every grade, and as to the officers of the custom-house and innumerable other officers of his own appointment; empowering the latter on the same ground to refuse to conform to the instructions sent to them, &c., &c. A construction, one would think, too preposterous for credulity itself to swallow.

The plain and well-understood substance of what he said was that in giving or withholding his assent to the bill for the re-charter of the bank it was his right and duty to decide the question of its constitutionality for himself, uninfluenced by any opinion or judgment which the Supreme Court had pronounced upon that point, farther than his judgment was satisfied by the reason which it had given for its decision. This covered the whole ground. It explained fully his views of the Constitution in respect to what he was doing. All beyond was both uncalled for and unnecessary. To this view of the President's power and duty under the Constitution Mr. Webster assented in the fullest manner. He said,--"It is true that each branch of the legislature has an undoubted right, in the exercise of its functions, to consider the constitutionality of a law proposed to be passed. This is naturally a part of its duty, and neither branch can be compelled to pass any law, or do any other act, which it deems to be beyond the reach of its constitutional power. The President has the same right when a bill is presented for his approval; for he is doubtless bound to consider, in all cases, whether such bill be compatible with the Constitution, and whether he can approve it consistently with his oath of office."

If the supporters of the bank had been willing to judge the President by the claim of power under the Constitution which he intended to advance in his veto message, there would have been a perfect accord of opinion between him and their great leader in the debate upon that document, and one disturbing element would have been withdrawn from the severe agitation to which the public mind was exposed. But this course neither suited the interest of the bank, nor would it have comported with the excited feelings of the implacable enemies of the President. Matters had worked to their liking. By forcing the bill through the two Houses at the eve of the struggle for the President's reelection, and thus compelling him either to sign or to encounter the responsibility of defeating it, they felt that they had involved the great opponent of the bank,--the only man whose power with the people they really dreaded--in toils from which his escape would be impossible. They were engaged in framing an issue with President Jackson and the Democratic party, looking at that time only to the defeat of his reelection but which was in 1834 so extended as to involve consequences second only in their importance to those of our struggle for independence from the mother country,--an issue, which was to decide whether the control by the people in affairs of government, the fruit of that great contest, should be continued, or be made to give place to a government controlled by the money power of the country, the trial of which continued much longer than that of the Revolution, and the ultimate results of which were the extinguishment of the bank and the first direct overthrow of the Democratic party since its accession to power in 1800. Able to count their votes in both Houses, and certain of a majority in each, the leading friends of the bank reserved their greatest efforts for the discussion of the veto, the interposition of which they understood the man they had to contend with too well to doubt.

Mr. Webster was designated by the supporters of the bank to open the discussion, and a more competent man, or one better suited for the purpose, could not have been selected. Among our public men there have doubtless been several whose mental endowments were in some particulars superior to his. Hamilton possessed more genius and eloquence. Between Clay and Webster the same disparity existed, though not in the same degree. But as a close and powerful reasoner, an adroit and wary debater,--one capable of taking comprehensive, and at the same time close views of his subject; who surveyed all the points in his case, the weak as well as the strong, and dealt with each in the way best calculated to serve his purpose, and to reduce the advantage of his antagonist to the lowest allowable point, and who was withal unscrupulous in the employment of his great powers,--he was in his day unsurpassed. Backed by a powerful moneyed institution--prepared to use its overflowing resources to any necessary extent; having Mr. Clay on his side; and knowing that what he said would, by means of the money of the bank, be brought to every mansion, and forced into every cabin, and made the subject of eulogy by a vast preponderance of the public press; it is not possible to conceive of circumstances better calculated to bring out Mr. Webster's capacities to the utmost. Those who have the curiosity to turn to the record of his vigorous effort on that occasion will see a favorable specimen of the art in which he was so great a master. His opening speech was designed to give the cue to his party, its orators and presses, in respect to the grounds upon which the election was to be contested. It contained an official programme of the campaign, showing that denunciation and intimidation were the principal weapons to be employed, and was itself the first gun fired in that direction--the signal that was to summon their political friends to the field, and to begin the attempt to fright the country from its propriety.

Mr. Webster opened his speech with statements from which the following are extracts: "Let us look at known facts. Thirty millions of the capital of the bank are now out, on loans and discounts, in the States on the Mississippi and its waters; ten of these millions on the discount of bills of exchange, foreign and domestic, and twenty millions loaned on promissory notes. The whole debt is to be paid, and within the same time the circulation withdrawn.

"The local banks, where there are such, will be able to afford little assistance, because they themselves will feel a full share of the pressure. They will not be in a condition to extend their discounts; but in all probability, obliged to curtail them.... I hesitate not to say that, as this veto travels to the West, it will depreciate the value of every man's property from the Atlantic States to the capital of Missouri. Its effects will be felt in the price of lands--the great and leading article of Western property; in the price of crops; in the products of labor; in the repression of enterprise; and in embarrassment to every kind of business and occupation. I state this opinion strongly, because I have no doubt of its truth, and am willing its correctness should be judged by the event.... To call in this loan at the rate of eight millions a year, in addition to the interest on the whole, and to take away, at the same time, that circulation which constitutes so great a portion of the medium of payment throughout that whole region, is an operation which, however wisely conducted, cannot but inflict a blow on the community of tremendous force and frightful consequences. The thing cannot be done without distress, bankruptcy, and ruin to many....

"A great majority of the people are satisfied with the bank as it is, and desirous that it should be continued. They wished no change. The strength of this public sentiment has carried the bill through Congress, against all the influence of the administration, and all the power of organized party. But the President has undertaken, on his own responsibility, to arrest the measure, by refusing his assent to the bill. He is answerable for the consequences, therefore, which necessarily follow the change which the expiration of the bank charter may produce; and if these consequences shall prove disastrous, they can fairly be ascribed to his policy only, and to the policy of his administration."

These alarming consequences were portrayed as the unavoidable result of a failure on the part of the people to effect a change in our public councils, before the expiration of the charter of the bank, which could only be done at the then next election.

No old school Federalist, who had grown to man's estate with views and opinions in regard to the character of the people which that faith seldom failed to inspire, could doubt the efficacy of such an exposition in turning the minds of all classes of the community in the desired direction. The idea of producing the catastrophe, thus held up to public view, through the direct action of the bank--a proceeding justly stigmatized as "flagitious," in his recent letter to the New York bankers, by Mr. Appleton of Boston, a distinguished and highly trusted Whig, who was in those days admitted behind the curtain and had a view of the whole ground,--had not at that time, I am satisfied, entered into the mind of Mr. Biddle, or perhaps into that of the most reckless advocate of the bank. But the sagacious leader of the Whig party understood too well the extent of General Jackson's popularity and the strength of the Democratic party to think for a moment that an attempt to carry a Presidential election against the power of both could safely be treated as a holiday affair. He knew that by far the largest portion of the classes most likely to be affected by appeals to their pecuniary interests were already on the side of the bank, and that the only chance of success in the election depended upon their ability to make impressions favorable to their views upon classes differently situated, and who in general politics were on the same side with the President. He was also well aware that among the admirers and sincere friends of General Jackson, there were in every State not a few who, confiding fully in his integrity, believing him engaged in continual struggles for the public good with a reckless opposition and sincerely wishing him success, yet distrusted his prudence, listened readily to the reports of his enemies prejudicial to his character, and were kept in constant apprehension that he would, through passion or ill advisement, commit some rash act. Virginia abounded in that class of politicians. My quondam friend Ritchie scarcely ever went to bed in those exciting times without apprehension that he would wake up to hear of some coup d'etat by the General, which he would be called on to explain or defend, and his letters to me were filled with remonstrances and cautions upon the subject. A vacancy occurring in the office of Attorney-General of the United States, I recommended the appointment of Mr. Daniel, now one of the justices of the Supreme Court of the United States, for the place. He came to Washington, was pleased with the invitation to take a seat in the Cabinet, which the General authorized me to give him, was pleased also with the office and would have been glad to accept it under other circumstances, but was, notwithstanding, induced to decline it, after a day's consultation with me, by considerations of that character exclusively. The General was not a little amused, after our friend left us, to hear me attribute his refusal to an apprehension that he might, in the discharge of his official duties be reduced to the necessity of acting against the principles of '98, or against his, the General's wishes--an alternative that he preferred not to encounter. I am free to confess that before I came to understand General Jackson as well as I subsequently did I had not a little of the same feeling. I had seen enough of him in the Senate, whilst occupying different sides in mere party politics, to satisfy me that he was incapable of acting knowingly against the public interest, but it was some time before I became thoroughly satisfied that I did not do full justice to his prudence. I will allude to a single occurrence bearing upon this point. His successful effort to remove the Indians to their Western home is well known and ought never to be forgotten, for there has scarcely been a single act of his life which has proved more beneficial to all parties than that. When the act conferring upon him the necessary powers was before Congress, which was at an early period of his administration, it was found difficult to prevail on the Pennsylvanian members of the House to support it. They were believed to be influenced by an apprehension that by supporting it they would give offense to the Quakers who, as is known, are very numerous in their State. He invited them to an interview which he asked me to attend. He remonstrated with those who came in an earnest and really eloquent manner; placed before them very forcibly the importance of the movement as well to the Indians as to the country; refuted the reasons which were given for their doubts, and as they rose to leave him, under indications not favorable to his wishes, he told them, with much emphasis, that he could not believe that the reasons they had assigned were the true motives by which they were actuated; that they were men of too much sense not to see that the measure was a proper one, but that they were afraid of their popularity; that they stood more in dread of displeasing the Quakers than they did of doing wrong; conjured them to rise superior to such motives, and to do what was right, regardless of personal consequences; told them they would find that to be the best way to make themselves popular, and concluded by saying that he should do his duty in this respect, and if the bill failed for the want of their vote it would not be his fault if their constituents were not supplied with means for forming a correct judgment between them and him. This was the substance of what was said, and said with considerable animation, I observed his eye directed toward me whilst he was speaking, and the moment the door closed on the retiring delegation he turned to me with a smile upon his countenance and said with the blandest manner, "I saw that my remarks disturbed you." I admitted the fact, and said that although they were his friends, personal as well as political, I was apprehensive that his observations, if they were made public, however true and just, might in the then feverish state of the public mind give countenance to the representations of his enemies. His reply was: "No, my friend, I have great respect for your judgment, but you do not understand these gentlemen as well as I do. They are quite honest, and wish to do what is right, but are prevented from doing it by precisely the considerations to which I alluded. They will not be offended, because they know I am their friend, and act only for the public good, and you will see that they will show a different disposition upon the subject"--and they did so. My apprehensions were more on account of what I feared he might say, from the excited manner in which he spoke, than on account of what he did actually say; and this was but one of numerous instances in which I observed a similar contradiction between his apparent undue excitement and his real coolness and self-possession in which, I may say with truth, he was seldom if ever wanting. It was to the class of

Jackson's supporters which I have described, men of Mr. Daniel's school, that Webster made his most powerful appeal; to alarm and influence them his powers were exerted to their utmost point. To do this with any chance of success a perversion of the Veto Message was indispensable. We have seen that he was obliged to admit that the President had a right, under the Constitution, to do all that he proposed by the veto. He had sworn to protect the Constitution as the chief executive officer of the government; and when an act was offered for his approval which he honestly believed was contrary to that instrument, he had the right--not the power only but the right also--to withhold his assent. This Mr. Webster admitted in so many words, and President Jackson did not by the message propose to do any thing more. And yet Webster denounced him as a ruthless tyrant, who was violating the Constitution, and uprooting the foundations of society. Look at some of his fierce denunciations: "He asserts a right of individual judgment on constitutional questions, which is totally inconsistent with any proper administration of the Government, or any regular execution of the laws. Social disorder, entire uncertainty in regard to individual rights and individual duties, the cessation of legal authority, confusion, the dissolution of free government,--all these are inevitable consequences of the principles adopted by the message, whenever they shall be carried to their full extent.... That which is now claimed for the President is, in truth, nothing less, and nothing else than the old dispensing power asserted by the Kings of England in the worst of times--the very climax, indeed, of all the preposterous pretensions of the Tudor and the Stuart races.

"According to the doctrines put forth by the President, although Congress may have passed a law, and although the Supreme Court may have pronounced it constitutional, yet it is, nevertheless, no law at all, if he in his good pleasure, sees fit to deny its effect; in other words, to repeal and annul it. Sir, no President, and no public man, ever before advanced such doctrines in the face of the nation. There never was before a moment in which any President would have been tolerated in asserting such claim to despotic power.... If these opinions of the President be maintained, there is an end of all law and all judicial authority. Statutes are but recommendations, judgments no more than opinions. Both are equally destitute of binding force. Such a universal power as is now claimed for him--a power of judging over the laws and over the decisions of the tribunal--is nothing else than pure despotism. If conceded to him, it makes him at once what Louis the Fourteenth proclaimed himself to be when he said 'I am the State.'"

Now where was his warrant for these scandalous denunciations? Was it to be found in the words "every officer," etc. to which I have referred? If so, common fairness required that he should have set them forth so that the readers of his speech might judge for themselves what the President intended by them. This he was too sagacious to do, for if he named them he was bound to give the whole paragraph. If he omitted this the President's friends would have pointed out the deception. If he gave the whole his readers would have seen that General Jackson could not have used the words in the sense attributed to them by Mr. Webster. In this dilemma he contented himself with substituting bold and reckless assumption for proof. Mr. Clay was less cautious, as it was his nature to be; he extracted the obnoxious words without the context, and founded upon them charges like these,--charges by which none who read his speech would have been misled if he had quoted the message fairly:--"There are some parts of his message that ought to excite deep alarm, and that especially in which the President announces that each public officer may interpret the Constitution as he pleases. His language is 'each public officer, who takes an oath to support the Constitution, swears that he will support it as he understands it and not as it is understood by others.' 'The opinion of the judges has no more authority over Congress than the opinion of Congress has over the judges; and on that point the President is independent of both.' Now, Mr. President, I conceive, with great deference, that the President has mistaken the purport of the oath to support the Constitution of the United States. No one swears to support it as he understands it, but to support it simply as it is in truth. All men are bound to obey the laws, of which the Constitution is the supreme; but must they obey them as they are, or as they understand them? If the obligation of obedience is limited and controlled by the measure of information, in other words if the party is bound to obey the Constitution only as he understands it, what would be the consequence?" No warrant for these broad and unfounded imputations, on the part of either of the senators, was to be found in the fact that the objections to the new Bank Bill applied equally to the old, nor for the ground thence assumed that it was the intention of President Jackson to treat that as a nullity and to embarrass its directors in winding up its concerns. There was not only nothing in the message to justify such a charge, but its whole character was directly opposite, and that too plainly to be controverted. His agency was not necessary to enable them to wind it up. The courts were sufficient for that, and they were on the side of the bank. Even if it were otherwise, there were legitimate considerations which would have justified him in allowing a charter which had received the sanction of a predecessor in office to proceed to its consummation, whatever he might think of its constitutionality. Nor had Mr. Webster or Mr. Clay a moment's doubt that it was his intention to do so. Their violent not to say savage tirades against the veteran had a different object--and that was the election. There, fortunately, they were unsuccessful, or we might yet have been in our Federal relations, as we unhappily are in those of the States, a bank-ridden people.

But I cannot allow this great constitutional question, respecting the relation which the three great departments of the Federal Government--executive, legislative, and judicial--were by the Constitution designed to occupy toward each other, to pass without farther notice. One more vitally important has not arisen nor can ever arise out of our complex and peculiar form of government, and it is also one which there is reason to apprehend has not been studied with adequate care, by many who are in other respects sufficiently astute in detecting constitutional encroachments.

General Jackson--though owing to his military employment he had not been for many years of his life much engaged in party politics--was yet, from a very early period, strongly imbued with the principles of the fathers of the republican school in regard to the objects and only legitimate purposes of Government and the true construction of the Federal Constitution. His views in these respects were sufficiently disclosed in the course of his brief services in both Houses of Congress, during the administration of Washington, and more particularly in his celebrated letter to Williamson about the year 1800.

Judge White, then his personal and political friend, followed Mr. Webster in the debate on the Veto Message and in the course of his speech laid down, in a perspicuous and satisfactory manner, the principles applicable to the question of the relative powers and duties of the several departments of the General Government which President Jackson then, as he had at all times, sustained. Deeply incensed at the gross perversions of his message, on the part of the advocates of the bank, but at all times and under all circumstances against parleying with his enemies in the midst of a battle, the President contented himself with frequent and unreserved expression of concurrence in the views which had been taken of the subject, on the floor of the Senate, by Judge

White, and although reelected under the clamor which had been raised against him upon that point, and more determined than ever to prevent, by all constitutional means, the extension of the charter of the existing bank, he was equally decided, as he had always been, not to interpose, nor did he interpose, any obstructions to the employment by it of all the means provided by the charter to conduct business to its end and to wind up its affairs after its termination.

Senator White's definition of the Constitution was expressed in the following words: "The honorable Senator argues that the Constitution has constituted the Supreme Court a tribunal to decide great constitutional questions, such as this; and that when they have done so, the question is put at rest, and every other department of the government must acquiesce. This doctrine I deny. The Constitution vests 'the judicial power in a Supreme Court, and in such inferior courts as Congress may from time to time ordain and establish.' Whenever a suit is commenced and prosecuted in the courts of the United States, of which they have jurisdiction, and such suit is decided by the Supreme Court,--as that is the court of last resort,--its decision is final and conclusive between the parties. But as an authority it does not bind either the Congress or the President of the United States. If either of these coordinate departments is afterwards called upon to perform an official act, and conscientiously believes the performance of that act will be a violation of the Constitution, they are not bound to perform it, but, on the contrary, are as much at liberty to decline acting as if no such decision had been made.... If different interpretations are put upon the Constitution by the different departments, the people is the tribunal to settle the dispute. Each of the departments is the agent of the people, doing their business according to the powers conferred; and where there is a disagreement as to the extent of these powers, the people themselves, through the ballot-boxes, must settle it."

This is the true view of the Constitution. It is that which was taken by those who framed and adopted it, and by the founders of the Democratic party. It is one which was universally acquiesced in at the formation of the Government, and for some time thereafter. It is a matter of great moment, and one which cannot be too closely scrutinized, especially at the present moment when there is abundant reason to apprehend that heresies of a marked character in respect to it are being infused into the public mind. The principle which inculcates the necessity of distributing the powers of government among several departments, and that they should be independent of each other in the performance of the duties assigned to them by the Constitution, has united in its favor the opinions of the friends of liberty everywhere from a very early period to the present time. Montesquieu said: "There can be no liberty where the legislative and executive powers are united in the same person or body of magistrates;" or "if the power of judging be not separated from the legislative and executive powers." The American Revolution provided the fairest opportunity to test the merits of this doctrine that the world had ever seen, and it was not lost sight of by the statesmen of that day. Many of the States recorded their adherence to it on the face of their constitutions, some of which were framed and adopted flagrante bello, and all paid due respect to it in the construction of their organic laws. The settlement and ratification of the Federal Constitution carried the discussion of its merit to our national councils where, and more particularly in the discussion upon the question of ratification, the matter was very closely examined and by very able hands. The opponents of the Constitution resisted it earnestly and with ability, on the ground, amongst others, that it did not provide sufficient guarantees to protect the departments from reciprocal encroachments, and to secure the required independence of each. The difficulties, inherent in the very nature of government, of carrying those securities to an extent which would silence cavil in respect to them, obtained for this objection advantages which, in view of the well understood reverence of the people for the main principle, caused no small degree of inquietude to those able defenders of the Constitution--Madison, Hamilton, and Jay. The numbers of the "Federalist" which touch upon this point are full of interest and will well repay re-perusal. They afford the strongest evidence of an earnest adherence, on the part of those great men, to the general principle, and will, if I do not deceive myself, be found quite inconsistent with several positions which have since been taken upon the subject. In the 47th number of the "Federalist," Mr. Madison thus expresses his own views, and of course those of his associates, Hamilton and Jay, as they acted in concert: "One of the principal objections inculcated by the more respectable adversaries to the Constitution, is its supposed violation of the political maxim that the legislative, executive and judiciary departments ought to be separate and distinct. In the structure of the Federal Government no regard, it is said, seems to have been paid to this essential precaution in favor of liberty. The several departments of power are distributed and blended in such a manner as at once to destroy all symmetry and beauty of form, and to expose some of the essential parts of the edifice to the danger of being crushed by the disproportionate weight of other parts.

"No political truth is certainly of greater intrinsic value, or is stamped with the authority of more enlightened patrons of liberty, than that on which the objection is founded. The accumulation of all powers, legislative, executive, and judiciary in the same hands, whether of one, a few, or many, and whether hereditary, self-appointed, or elective, may justly be pronounced the very definition of tyranny. Were the Federal Constitution, therefore, really chargeable with this accumulation of power, or with a mixture of powers having a dangerous tendency to such an accumulation, no further arguments would be necessary to inspire a universal reprobation of the system".... In No. 48, speaking of the three great departments, he says: "It is equally evident that neither of them ought to possess, directly or indirectly, an overruling influence over the others in the administration of their respective powers." ... In No. 49, he notices a proposition of Mr. Jefferson to authorize a Convention upon a call of two of the three departments, for "altering the Constitution or correcting breaches of it," and says,--"The several departments being perfectly coordinate by the terms of their common commission, neither of them, it is evident, can pretend to an exclusive or superior right of settling the boundaries between their respective powers." He then goes on to urge objections to too frequent appeals to the people in that form, and sustains the opinion that it would be better to rely on other safeguards against encroachments which he details. In Nos. 78 and 81, General Hamilton, admitting that "there is no liberty where the power of judging be not separated from the legislative and executive powers," shows at great length the comparative weakness of the judicial power, and the very slight probability that "the general liberty of the people can ever be endangered from that quarter."

The provisions of the Constitution will be searched in vain for any which indicate a design on the part of its framers to give to one of the departments power to control the action of another in respect to its departmental duties under that instrument. All legislative power granted by the Constitution was vested in a Congress, to be composed of two Houses. The executive power of the Government was vested in a President. Specific powers to be exercised in conjunction with the Senate, as well as some in respect to which a question might arise whether they would otherwise have passed to the executive, were added, but the Constitution in respect to the legislative power, contained no limitations or restrictions. All executive authority to be exercised under it was granted to the President, and he was hence spoken of by the writers of the "Federalist" as the sole depositary of executive power. By the third article of the Constitution the same expression is used in respect to the Supreme Court, &c.: "The judicial power of the United States shall be vested in one Supreme Court and certain inferior tribunals." But as these terms would, standing by themselves, have conveyed all the judicial power of the United States to the Supreme Court, and as no such grant could be properly made because a large share of it had, in a previous part of the Constitution, been granted to a court of impeachment, of which the Supreme Court only supplied the presiding officer on a single occasion,--the trial of a President,--and was designed to be still farther restricted, the Constitution immediately proceeds to say, that "The judicial power shall extend to all cases in law and equity arising under this Constitution, the laws of the United States, and treaties made, or which shall be made, under their authority; to all cases affecting, ambassadors, other public ministers, and consuls; to all cases of admiralty and maritime jurisdiction, etc." No oath to support the Constitution is prescribed by it, in regard to the incumbents of the legislative or judicial branches of the Government, other than the general provision that all officers of a certain description, (which included them,) whether belonging to the Federal or State governments, should swear to support the Federal Constitution.

In regard to the executive department the case is very different. The Constitution requires from the President, and from him only, that he should, in addition to the oath of office, before he enter upon its duties, swear "that he will, to the best of his ability, preserve, protect, and defend the Constitution of the United States."

Is it not surprising that under a Constitution so constructed, exhibiting on its face such features, the idea should ever have been advanced that it was to the judicial power of the Government that its framers looked for the preservation of that sacred instrument? So far as it concerns the private rights of citizens and foreigners in questions of meum and tuum, growing out of the laws and Constitution of the United States, or controversies regarding the separate and special interests of contending States, or of the United States, and in respect to the rights of foreign ministers and consuls, it was intended to be supreme and so made, nor has its supremacy in all these respects ever been questioned. But it seems very absurd to suppose that it was intended to oblige the President of the United States,--the officer clothed with the whole executive power of the

Government; the only officer, except the Vice-President, who is chosen by the whole people of the United States; the champion, designated by the Constitution itself to "preserve, protect, and defend" it in the performance of the executive duties committed to his charge,--duties affecting what Hamilton happily describes as "the general liberty of the people," to distinguish it from affairs of meum and tuum,--to keep his eye upon the Supreme Court calendar, and to gather from its decisions in respect to the private rights of parties litigant the measure of his constitutional powers, and to stop or go on in the execution of the important national offices assigned to his department as its judgments may be deemed to authorize or forbid his further proceeding. I can easily understand why a class of men, born with certain dispositions and trained to corresponding opinions, should desire such a construction of the Federal Constitution; but in the face of facts and considerations like these, I can find no explanation of the boldness with which so groundless a pretension has been advanced, other than in the recklessness by which the spirit of political encroachment is and will be characterized as long as it finds facilities for its gratification in the weakness or the passions of mankind. The deeper the subject is looked into, the more apparent to all bona fide searchers for truth will become the fallacy of the principle which claims for the Supreme Court a controlling power over the other departments in respect to constitutional questions. Inquirers of this description cannot fail to appreciate the difficulty, nay the impossibility of reconciling Mr. Webster's unreserved admission of the President's "undoubted right in the exercise of his functions, when a bill is presented for his approval, to consider in all cases whether such a bill be compatible with the Constitution, and whether he can approve it, consistently with his oath of office," and to approve, or refuse to approve according to the result, with his severe denunciation of him for regarding an act as unconstitutional, which had been approved by one of his predecessors, but which he, notwithstanding, conscientiously believed to be unconstitutional, and for withholding the power of the executive from the execution of any such act. Everybody knows that an act which is contrary to the Constitution is a nullity, although it may have passed according to the forms of the Constitution. That instrument creates several departments, whose duty it may become to act upon such a bill, in the performance of their respective functions. The theory of the Constitution is that these departments are coordinate and independent of each other, and that when they act in their appropriate spheres they each have a right, and it is the duty of each to judge for themselves in respect to the authority and requirements of the Constitution, without being controlled or interfered with by their co-departments, and are each responsible to the people alone who made them for the manner in which they discharge their respective duties in that regard. It is not therefore to be presumed that that instrument, after making it the President's especial duty to take an oath to preserve and uphold the Constitution and prevent its violation, intended to deny to him the right to withhold his assent from a measure which he might conscientiously believe would have that effect, and to impose upon him the necessity of outraging his conscience, by making himself a party to such a violation. The Constitution, which was framed by great men, the form of which has been so much and so justly admired, is not so imperfect nor subject to such a reproach. The matter does not necessarily end with a refusal on the part of the executive to do an act which he believes Congress had no right, under the Constitution, to require his department to perform. Although the President, representing one of the three great departments of the Government, possesses in this respect a right which neither the citizen nor any other officer or officers of the Government, not having the control of such a department, can exercise, yet if he allows himself to be governed by unworthy motives he is liable to impeachment and expulsion from office. It is in this way, or by his removal by the people, that the wrong he does to the public is redressed. But this is not all. If the act has been passed according to the forms of the Constitution, and is judged to be constitutional by the judicial department of the Federal Government, it is obligatory upon the citizens, binds and controls their private rights and personal interests, and can be carried into effect in respect to those by the judiciary, which also judges for itself regarding the constitutionality of such law. It is the department by which laws, affecting as well the private rights of the citizen as those of the States, which can be made the subjects of litigation, are carried into effect. It has ample power conferred upon it to cause its judgments and decrees to be executed. Officers are appointed whose duty it is made by law to obey its orders, and these officers have the right given to call out the civil power of their respective districts to enable them to execute judicial decrees. Nor do the rights secured to it by the Constitution stop here. If resistance is offered to the execution of a judgment or decree--made by the proper court to which jurisdiction of the matter which such judgment or decree seeks to enforce is given by the Constitution--too great to be overcome by the civil power, it is the duty of the President, upon the request of the officers of the court, to order out the military power to sustain that of the judiciary. It would be no answer on his part to such a call to say that the right which the decree or judgment seeks to enforce arises under a law which he deems unconstitutional. That is, under the circumstances, a matter that he has no right to inquire into. The decision of that question has been delegated to a different department, and has by that department been decided differently. The Constitution requires that the judgments of that department, upon subjects committed to it, should be enforced. It makes that enforcement, in extreme cases, the duty of the military. The President is intrusted with the command of that force and, in such a case, his power in regard to it is ministerial only. It is his duty, in such a case, to sustain the judicial power by the aid of the military, and if he failed in its performance he would subject himself to impeachment and removal from office. Not only is the entire power of the government thus pledged to the maintenance of judicial authority, whilst acting in the line of its duties, but there lies no appeal from its judgments or decrees. They are final and obligatory upon the rights and interests of the parties. They can neither be reversed by any other tribunal, nor is it in the power of the remaining departments of the Government united to set them aside or to treat them as a nullity, however contrary to the Constitution they may be.

We are not without experience upon this point. Our history bears indelible record of the abuse of power in that form during the administration of the elder Adams. The unconstitutionality of the Sedition Law will now be scarcely controverted by any ingenuous mind. The Supreme Court, nevertheless, decided it to be constitutional, tried citizens for having violated its provisions, and caused fines and imprisonment to be inflicted upon them. When a majority of the Senate of the United States, friends of the bank, placed upon its journal an unconstitutional act of condemnation against President Jackson, for the steps he had taken to relieve the country from that institution, the same body, after its political complexion had been sufficiently changed through the influence of an offended public sentiment, not only reversed the sentence but expunged it from the record. This it had a right to do, because both acts were committed by the same branch of the same department. But the executive and legislative departments had no such power over the unconstitutional sentences that were pronounced under the Sedition Law, because they had no right to interfere with the acts of a coordinate department. The President had an express right to pardon such offenses, and the national legislature had a constitutional right to return the money collected from those who committed them, and they did so. But the judgments of the court remained, and will forever remain, unreversed. In England, judicial convictions, attainders, judgments of forfeitures of franchises, etc., may be reversed by act of

Parliament, but no such interference by one department of the government with the authorized proceedings of a coordinate department are permitted by our Constitution, simply because the great departments of our Government are by the Constitution made coordinate and independent of each other. Can any reflecting mind, in view of these facts, doubt the sufficiency of the protection which that instrument provides for the personal rights of the citizen and for private interests of every description, or for a moment apprehend the disorganization of society described by Mr. Webster as a consequence of carrying into effect the principles avowed by President Jackson?

The judicial power of the Federal Government, according to the description here given of the binding force, the finality and efficiency of its decisions upon the parties and their rights in all cases which may be brought before it, answers all the purposes of its institution. Was it the intention of the framers of the Constitution that it should be clothed with other powers, and if so, what are they? The duties imposed on the executive and legislative departments are of higher importance than those of the judiciary, in proportion as the interests of the nation are of more consequence than the separate interests of individuals and minor associations. They include the question of peace or of war, and the maintenance of the latter, international obligations in the forms of treaties, their construction and execution, the regulation of foreign commerce and commerce among the States, the regulation of the currency, the establishment of a mint, the assessment and collection of the national revenue, the raising, regulating, and command of an army and navy, the establishment of a general and of particular post-offices, the regulation and protection of the Indian tribes, and many other duties which it is unnecessary to specify. In none of these is it contemplated by the Constitution that the judicial power shall take a part. The powers and duties of the other departments upon these subjects are to some extent specified in the Constitution, and the residue are left to the direction of the legislature which acts, in respect to them, through the Executive as the department especially charged with the execution of the laws. In the performance of their high duties these departments are, at almost every step, met by constitutional questions. The Houses of the legislature, in every law or resolution that they pass, have to consider whether it is authorized by the Constitution to which they have sworn to conform, and the President and Senate, when they make a treaty, are bound to consider and decide the same question. The President, as the sole depositary of the executive power, is under a similar obligation. His first inquiry is, whether the Constitution authorizes him to apply the power of his department to the execution of the business before him, or, if it is one of the numerous functions which the legislature is in the constant habit of calling upon him to perform, has the legislature power under the Constitution to direct the thing to be done, and can he do it consistently with his oath to preserve and uphold that instrument?

How are they to act in the decision of these questions? By what considerations are they to be controlled? They know that they are responsible to the people, under whose commission they act, for all they do. The Constitution does not give to one department the right to decide such questions for another, either in terms or by necessary implication, nor subject them to any other responsibility, nor place before them any guide for the government of their decisions other than their own discretion and their own consciences, and has caused to be placed upon their consciences an oath that they will, in no event, act contrary to that instrument. Under such circumstances, I ask, what are they to do? What can they do, consistently with the duty they owe to God, to their country, and to themselves, other than to decide such questions for themselves, following the dictates of their own judgment? Can it be believed that those who framed and adopted the Constitution intended to place these high functionaries,--the only representatives of the people, in the great departments of the government, over whose continuance in office the people possess control--to place them, in respect to their official acts, about which a constitutional question can be raised, under the guidance of a department over which the people possess no such control, to be regulated by its decisions in private actions, to which such functionaries are not parties, and of which decisions they are, notwithstanding, to take notice at their peril. If a system so anti-republican could have been designed by those who made the Constitution, is it to be supposed that they would have omitted to declare, on the face of the instrument, that such was their intention, leaving those functionaries to grope their way to its discovery. Such a question--one in which the character of our political institutions is so much involved, and upon a right understanding of which their ultimate safety may depend--should be stripped of every uncertainty. The claim set up for the Supreme Court must be good throughout, or it is not good at all. The principle, that the final decision of constitutional questions belongs exclusively to the supreme judicial tribunal, set up in Mr. Webster's speech, must be true throughout, or it cannot be true to any extent. It amounts to this: the incumbents of the legislative and executive departments, in respect to questions of constitutional power, are ministerial officers only.

Constitutional questions are points in respect to which they have no right to exercise their own discretion, but are bound, at every important step, to look to the judiciary for guidance, and if they omit to adopt its decisions, if it has made any, they do so at their peril:--the former department at the hazard of having its laws, if the Supreme Court regard them as unconstitutional, treated as a nullity, not only when they are relied upon "in cases in law and equity," but in all cases, and everywhere. From the nature of their action, members of Congress do not subject themselves to personal responsibility, except when they act corruptly. But the situation of the incumbent of the executive department is less favorable. Deprived of all discretion, and bound to thus understand his position, he encounters personal responsibility, in certain cases, whichever way he may act. If he find a law upon the statute book, approved by one of his predecessors--and to relieve the country from which has perhaps been one of the reasons for the removal of the latter from office--a law which he deems unauthorized by the Constitution, but which the Supreme Court holds to be constitutional, he must either violate his oath of office and execute it, or refuse to do so and expose himself to impeachment for a failure in the discharge of his official duties. If he persists in the observance of a law which the Supreme Court has, in a private suit, held to be unconstitutional, he incurs a similar responsibility; and if he omits its observance, he does violence to his own conscience by failing to perform his official duties according to his oath. Let me illustrate this view of the subject by particular and possible cases. Take that referred to by General Hamilton in his papers written in defense of President Washington's proclamation of neutrality, over the signature of "Pacificus."

The President has power, by and with the advice of the Senate, to make treaties with foreign governments. Private rights, subject to judicial investigation, often grow out of public treaties. The interpretation and enforcement of these rights belong exclusively to the judiciary, and in the execution of its power it may hold the treaty, under which the claim arises, unconstitutional for any of the reasons for which laws may be so regarded. Its decision is binding and final upon the parties and their interests.

Then comes the execution of that treaty between the governments that are parties to it. This, on our part, belongs exclusively to the legislative and executive departments. The duty of the former is to pass the laws necessary to its execution, and that of the latter to see to their enforcement, and to do such other acts as he may do, under the Constitution, without a law.

A foreign government calls for the interference of these departments to redeem the national faith, pledged through executive instrumentality, and for the redemption of which the executive, and the legislature, where necessary, are the agents designated by the Constitution. They see and feel their duty, but have been rendered powerless. The Supreme Court has decided the treaty to be unconstitutional. No matter how obscure the parties by whom its interference was asked, no matter how unimportant the interest in respect to which the decision was made, from the moment it is promulgated, it becomes a rule of action for every department of the government, and every public functionary as well as every citizen. If the national legislature passes a law to carry into effect the void treaty its law becomes a nullity. If the executive issues an order for its execution, or toward the performance of the treaty in any way to his subordinates, they are not bound to obey it, and the Supreme Court will sustain them in their contumacy. If he take measures to enforce his authority, he makes himself amenable to that tribunal. Acting in such a matter as a ministerial officer only, without a right to employ his own discretion, he subjects himself to impeachment if he persists.

Alexander Hamilton--who, if he was not the one who suggested the latitudinarian doctrine of "implied powers," was certainly its most effective supporter, and through life its watchful guardian--in No. 1 of Pacificus, has said that though the judiciary department is charged with the interpretation of treaties, "it exercises this function only where contending parties bring before it a specific controversy;" that "it has no concern with pronouncing upon the external political relation of treaties between government and government;" that "this proposition is too plain to need being insisted upon;" that "it belongs to the executive department to exercise the function in question, when a proper case for it occurs," "as the interpreter of the national treaties, in those cases in which the judiciary is not competent,--that is, between government and government; as the power which is charged with the execution of the laws, of which treaties form a part; as that which is charged with the command and disposition of the public force."

James Madison, in conjunction with Hamilton and Jay, in the numbers of the "Federalist," avows doctrines at war with this assumption of power in the Supreme Court. Thomas Jefferson, whose anxious patriotism was always alive to such subjects, and the political thoughts and studies of whose life were exclusively directed toward the protection of human rights through the instrumentality of free governments, opposed the doctrine vehemently, from first to last, and long after his retirement from public life, its passions and excitements, expressed himself in regard to it, on different occasions, in terms which follow. In 1815, in answer to the direct question put to him by a citizen of Georgia, he says:--"The second question, whether the judges are invested with exclusive authority to decide on the constitutionality of a law, has been heretofore a subject of consideration with me in the exercise of official duties. Certainly there is not a word in the Constitution which has given that power to them more than to the executive or legislative branches. Questions of property, of character, and of crime, being ascribed to the judges, through a definite course of legal proceeding,--laws, involving such questions, belong, of course, to them, and as they decide on them ultimately and without appeal, they, of course, decide for themselves. The constitutional validity of the law, or laws, again prescribing executive action, and to be administered by that branch ultimately and without appeal, the executive must decide for themselves, also, whether, under the Constitution, they are valid or not. So, also, as to laws governing the proceedings of the legislature; that body must judge for itself the constitutionality of the law, and, equally, without appeal or control from its coordinate branches. And, in general, that branch which is to act ultimately, and without appeal, on any law, is the rightful expositor of the validity of the law, uncontrolled by the opinions of the other coordinate authorities." Again, so late as 1819, in a very interesting letter to Judge Spencer Roane, he says:--"My construction of the Constitution is very different from that you quote. It is that each department is truly independent of the others, and has an equal right to decide for itself what is the meaning of the Constitution in the cases submitted to its action; and especially, where it is to act ultimately and without appeal.... But you intimate a wish that my opinion should be known on this subject. No, dear Sir, I withdraw from all contests of opinion and resign every thing cheerfully to the generation now in place. They are wiser than we were, and their successors will be wiser than they, from the progressive advance of science. Tranquillity is the summum bonum of age. I wish, therefore, to offend no man's opinion, nor to draw disquieting animadversions on my own. While duty required it, I met opposition with a firm and fearless step. But loving mankind in my individual relations with them, I pray to be permitted to depart in their peace, and, like the superannuated soldier, 'quadragenis stipendiis emeritis,' to hang my arms on the post."

Mr. Jefferson, in these letters, speaks of his uniform opposition to the opposite doctrine, and refers to the inconvenience that may at times arise from conflicting decisions. But that, he thought, might be safely dealt with through the prudence of public functionaries, and he names instances when they were so treated: one in England, where an instance of difference occurred, in the time of Lord Holt, between the judges of England and the House of Commons; and another in this country, when a difference of opinion was found to exist between the Federal Judiciary and the House of Representatives. The Supreme Court decided, in a case of meum and tuum, that William Duane was not a citizen, and the House of Representatives, upon a question of membership, decided that William Smith, whose character of citizenship stood on precisely the same ground, was a citizen. These decisions were made in high party times, whilst the Federalists were in power. Duane was an Irishman, who had married into the family of Dr. Franklin, and was editor of the "Aurora," the most prominent Republican newspaper. Smith was an ardent Federalist from South Carolina, a man of good talents himself, but who delivered speeches in the House prepared by Hamilton in his closet, as was charged by Jefferson at the time, and has now been fully proved by the publication of Hamilton's private papers.

But the establishment of the constitutional rule sustained by Jefferson would not have saved the country from practical inconveniences, which he did not notice because he knew them to be unavoidable. A concession to the other great departments of the right to decide for themselves constitutional questions applicable to, and that necessarily arise in the discharge of, their official functions, still leaves them, to a serious extent, dependent upon the judicial power. Whilst it would exempt the incumbents from the penalty of impeachment when they act in good faith, they and their subordinates remain liable whenever their acts may be construed into an injurious interference with the property or personal rights of individuals, to be called before the judicial tribunal, to be there subjected to a different interpretation of the Constitution from that which they, or their superiors in authority, have placed upon it, and to be melted in damages for their public acts, however pure their motives may have been.

In a government, constructed like ours in some degree of conflicting parts, it is ever difficult, if not at times impossible, to prevent such a discrepancy, and those who framed ours, upon the whole, were wise in not attempting to do so. As a tribute to the personal rights of man and the security of private property, existing provisions go far to atone for whatever of individual injustice they may occasion. The legislative department has the power to indemnify those who suffer in this way and invariably does so when they have acted in good faith. The losses thus incurred by individuals, in the first instance, are in the end transferred to the whole community, which is abundantly remunerated by the benefits it derives from the system as a whole. Should a federal organization ever obtain which shall attempt, through an abuse of its power, to exert a dangerous influence over the Government, to an extent and in a way to arrest the attention of the people, they will neither be at a loss for a remedy nor fail in its adoption.

But to extend the control of the judiciary, through their decisions "in cases in law and equity," over the action of the other departments in the discharge of the duties assigned to them, for the extent and gravity of which we have only to look to the Constitution, and which, for the most part, steer entirely clear of private and separate interests, would be a measure of a very different character. It was upon these public functionaries that the entire political power of the Federal Government was intended to be conferred, and to the limited tenure by which they held their offices and to their direct responsibility to the people that the latter have always looked for the means to control their action. It is upon this swift and certain responsibility they have hitherto relied for their ability to bring the government back, without great delay, to the republican track designed for it by the Constitution, whenever it might be made to depart from it through, the infidelity of their representatives. Truly says Mr. Jefferson, in one of his letters last referred to, "when the legislative or executive functionaries act unconstitutionally, they are responsible to the people in their elective capacity. The exemption of the judges from that is quite dangerous enough. I know no safe depository of the ultimate powers of the society but the people themselves; and if we think them not enlightened enough to exercise their control with a wholesome discretion, the remedy is not to take it from them, but to inform their discretion by education. This is the true corrective of abuses of constitutional power."

Nor have the people been slow to exert their powers to reform abuses which they honestly, whether erroneously or not, believed to exist, by displacing representatives whom they considered unfaithful, whenever the occasion has seemed to them of sufficient magnitude to call for its exercise. The commencement of the nineteenth century was made forever memorable in our political annals by a display of this power, and it was again exerted in 1828, in 1840, in 1844, and in 1852. The result of the election of 1848 was altogether occasioned by divisions in the Democratic party, and I feel that I venture nothing in attributing that of 1840 mainly to a mistake in the public mind, which it has since magnanimously acknowledged, and with that atonement I am more than satisfied.

But if the incumbents of the legislative and executive departments have no right to decide for themselves constitutional questions that arise in the performance of their official functions; if it be indeed true that the National Legislature, in discharging the important duties of laying and collecting taxes, duties, imposts, and excises; in borrowing money on the credit of the United States; in regulating commerce with foreign nations, and among the several States, and with the Indian tribes; in establishing uniform rules of naturalization and on the subject of bankruptcies; in coining money and regulating the value thereof, and of foreign coins, and fixing the standard of weights and measures; in providing punishment for counterfeiting the securities and current coin of the United States; in establishing post-offices and post-roads; in promoting science and useful arts; in constituting tribunals inferior to the Supreme Court; in defining and punishing piracies and felonies committed on the high seas and offences against the law of nations; in declaring war; granting letters of marque and reprisal, and making rules concerning captures on land and water; in raising and supporting armies; in providing and maintaining a navy; in making rules for the government and regulation of the land and naval forces; in providing for calling forth the militia to execute the laws of the Union, suppress insurrection and repel invasion; in providing for organizing armies and disciplining the militia, and for governing such parts of them as may be employed in the service of the United States; in the exercise of exclusive jurisdiction in all cases whatsoever in the ten-mile-square and in the forts of the United States; and in making necessary and proper laws for carrying into execution the foregoing powers and all other powers vested by the Constitution in the Government of the United States, or in any department or officer thereof: and that the President, in assuming command of the army or navy of the United States and of the militia of the several States, when called into their service; in making treaties by and with the advice of the Senate; and in the appointment of all the officers of the United States, with limited and specific exceptions, and in filling up all vacancies that may arise during the recess of the Senate; in receiving ambassadors and other public ministers; and in taking care that the laws be faithfully executed,--are both bound to look to the decisions, of the Supreme Court, "in cases of law and equity" that are brought before them, for the character and extent of their powers under the Constitution, and to be governed by them, what becomes of the distinguishing feature of Republican Government--the responsibility of the representative to the people for the faithful performance of his duties? A people so intelligent, and withal so just as ours, would surely never think of dismissing one branch of their public servants for acts in respect to which they had placed them under the absolute guidance of another branch. To single out one department from the rest by placing its incumbent under a special oath to protect and preserve the Constitution, and then to make it his duty to obey the directions of another in that very function, absolutely and unconditionally, would, I cannot but think, be going quite as far in that direction as the character of any people for justice and wisdom could bear.

To whom are the members of the Federal Judiciary responsible for the truthfulness of their constitutional expositions and for the wisdom of the steps they take to make them effectual? To no human being. They can only be displaced by impeachment and criminal conviction. That mere error of judgment, without positive proof of corruption, can never be made the basis of such a proceeding, is known to all. Is it not, then, most apparent that to place the fidelity to the Federal Constitution of the representatives of the people and of the States and of most of the effective officers employed in the conduct of public affairs, save only those that are of a judicial character, under the supervision of that department, is nothing less than to divest the Government of its republican features and to substitute in its place the control of an irresponsible judicial oligarchy--to make the Constitution a lie, and turn to mockery its most formal provisions, designed to secure to the people a control over the action of the Government under its authority? Is it not remarkable that a doctrine, so clearly anti-republican in its character and tendencies, should have been so long kept on foot under a system so truly republican as ours, and may we not trace its origin to the same inexhaustible fountain from whence have proceeded the most tenacious of our party divisions--an inextinguishable distrust, on the part of numerous and powerful classes, of the capacities and dispositions of the great body of their fellow-citizens?

The want of a proper respect for the people, as has been often said, was Hamilton's great misfortune. If he could have felt otherwise, he would have been a Republican. This distrust of the capacity and disposition of the masses, which had been the bane of his life, retained its hold upon his strong mind and ardent feelings when he bequeathed it to his political disciples, and it has been the shibboleth of their tribe ever since. In a large degree wealthy and proud of their social position, their fear of the popular will, and desire to escape from popular control, instead of being lessened, is increased by the advance of the people in education and knowledge. Under no authority do they feel their interests to be safer than under that which is subject to the judicial power, and in no way could their policy be more effectually promoted than by taking power from those departments of the Government over which the people have full control, and accumulating it in that over which they may fairly be said to have none.

CHAPTER VIII.

Exceptional Countenance given by the Democratic Party to the Federalist Doctrine of the Supremacy of the Judicial over the other Departments on the Occasion of the Dred Scott Decision--Former Acquiescence of the Country as to the Power of Congress over Slavery in the Territories--That Power brought in question by General Cass, in 1848--The Result a Rupture in the Democratic Party and Defeat of Cass--The subsequent Election of Pierce--Repeal of the Missouri Compromise--Dangers of that Step--The Kansas-Nebraska Act-- Opinions of the Judges in the Dred Scott Case how far extra-Judicial-- Probable Motives of the Chief Justice and his Brethren--The Author's Recollections of Taney--The Motives of the Judges Good, but their obiter dicta a Mistake--The Course of President Buchanan, with respect to the Dred Scott Decision, an Abandonment of the Democratic Principle of the Independence of each of the three great Departments in deciding Constitutional Questions-- Subsequent Action of the Democratic Party on this Subject--Importance of returning to original Doctrines of the Party.

If this essay shall be ever published, the censures I have bestowed upon the old Federal party and its successors for their persevering efforts to destroy the balances of the Constitution, in this respect of the relative powers of the departments, will doubtless be met by those who still sympathize with its opinions, by a reference to the proceedings in the case of Dred Scott. Of this no one will have a right to complain, so long as those who so refer confine themselves to facts; for truth is truth, whatever may be the circumstances under which it is applied, and wrong is wrong, by whomsoever it may be committed and by whatever party it may be sustained. It will be alleged that the Supreme Court, now composed of gentlemen who are acknowledged members of the Democratic party, has in that case set up the right to guide the official action of the executive and legislative departments of the Government upon a great constitutional question,--that the Executive has recognized that right, and has promised to conform his own course to it when exercised, and that these proceedings have received the approbation and support of the Democratic party.

In the notice I propose to take of that case, it is not my intention to discuss the correctness or incorrectness of the decision that was made in respect to the power of Congress to legislate upon the subject of slavery in the Territories. I will however state in advance and in few words the view I now take of the general subject.

The acquiescence of the country in the power of Congress referred to, from the Presidency of Washington to that of Polk inclusive, is well known. Every President signed bills for carrying it into effect, when any such became necessary and were presented for their approval, and the other great departments of the Government not only complied with the rule but, in innumerable instances, recognized its validity. This continued until the year 1848, when a point, which had so long been considered settled, was brought in question by an opinion expressed by General Cass, then being a candidate for the Presidency, in a letter to Mr. Nicholson, of Tennessee, adverse to the powers of Congress. The Democratic party, whose candidate he was, adopted his opinions, and the consequences were a rupture in that party, the elevation of an old-school Federalist to the Presidency, and an administration of the Federal Government upon the long exploded principles of Federalism. In 1852 the Democracy of the Union, instructed by experience in regard to the destructive tendency of slavery agitations, resolved to avoid them in future, united on General Pierce as their candidate, supported him on their old and time-honored principles, and elected him by a triumphant majority.

This result, so auspicious to the country, was unhappily followed by the repeal of the Missouri Compromise, and a consequent reopening of the agitation upon the subject of slavery, in a form and under influences more portentous of evil than any which had before attended it.

I received information of that event whilst I was abroad, a sojourner in a country which was under the dominion of an absolute monarch,-- circumstances which never fail to increase the attachment of a true-hearted American, however orthodox he may have been before in his devotion, to home and its inestimable institutions. Although forever withdrawn from public life, I could not be indifferent to a measure promising such startling consequences. Having had full opportunities to become acquainted with the evil which the infusion of slavery agitation into the partisan feelings of the country was capable of producing, I felt, in all their force, the dangers to which our political fabric would be exposed by that act, and mourned over its adoption. Whatever may be thought or said of it in other respects, in regard to its influence in exciting sectional animosities to a far more perilous height than they had ever reached before there is not now room for two opinions.

Under the feelings of the moment, I naturally extended to the substitute Congress had provided, the odium which, in my view, belonged to the act of repeal, and could see no adequate relief save in a restoration of the Compromise. But as passion subsided I became convinced of the impracticability of that step, and turned my attention to a more careful consideration of the Kansas-Nebraska Act, and I became satisfied that, if honestly executed, it was all that could, under existing circumstances, be done, or, perhaps, desired. Having been a second time invited by my old political friends of Tammany Hall, before the Presidential election of 1856, to submit my views upon the then state of the question, I gave them in a letter which presented the whole subject in a form and was written in a spirit which many thought well calculated to make favorable impressions on well-intentioned and sober-minded men. It contained a simple and truthful description of the position I had before occupied upon the slavery subject, an exposition of the reasons by which I was yet satisfied that it had been well taken, and of the ground of my expectation that Mr. Buchanan would do all in his power to cause the Kansas-Nebraska Act to be carried into full and fair effect.

I have read all the opinions given by the judges in the Dred Scott case with care, and will state the impressions which they have made upon my mind. I had never examined the question, and learned, with serious misgivings as to its correctness, that the court had decided that a man of African birth, though free and, in the State in which he resided, entitled to all the rights of a citizen, was not also a citizen of the United States. My mind remained in this state, with partial alleviations of my anxiety, derived from newspaper sketches of the subject referring to instances in which the principle had been acted upon in the administration of public affairs, until I read very deliberately the voluminous opinions of the judges. The able, judgelike, and I may add, statesmanlike, views taken by Chief Justice Taney and by Justice Daniel, of that branch of the subject, have satisfied me that the judgment of the court upon it was right. I am now convinced that the sense in which the word "citizen" was used by those who framed and ratified the Federal Constitution was not intended to embrace the African race, whose ancestors were brought to this country and sold in slavery. I shall content myself with stating the result of my reflections, without going into details, as that would be to re-argue the question, which would be foreign to my present object. I do not say that the subject is free from difficulties. No adverse opinion could pass through the ordeal of so subtle and masterly an argument as that of Justice Curtis, who bestowed more attention upon the point than his dissenting brother, and escape unscathed.

The weight of facts and argument is, notwithstanding, in my judgment, on the side of the decision of the court.

A decision in favor of a free black man's right to institute a suit in the Federal court, on the grounds of citizenship and his residence in a different State from the defendant, would undoubtedly establish his right under the Constitution to the enjoyment in a slave State of all the privileges allowed to its own citizens. The extent to which such a construction and the practical operation of the rights which might be claimed under it would increase the difficulties, already so great, of maintaining the unity and harmonious action of the Federal system, will be more and more apparent the deeper the matter is considered. I think it is quite certain that if the Constitution had been supposed to contain a provision legitimately authorizing such consequences, it would not have been agreed to by the slaveholding States, nor, in view of the liberal spirit evinced even by the latter at the time of the formation of the Constitution in regard to the extension of slavery, would such a provision have been insisted upon by their brethren of the States which had the happiness to be comparatively free from the institution. The decision must, therefore, be regarded as fortunate, as

I cannot but hold it to be correct. For though the personal rights of individuals, however humble their position in society, are not the less important and their protection no less the duty of government, yet the great community may felicitate itself that claims like these,--the practical enjoyment of which, while of little value, relatively, to the few who assert them, may endanger the peace and welfare of millions,--are extinguished through the agency of the organ of the Government constituted for their adjustment. It is in such cases, when confined to its necessary and legitimate duties, that the salutary influence of that high tribunal is felt by all.

The plaintiff, Dred Scott, alleged in his declaration--as he was bound to allege to give the Circuit Court jurisdiction of the cause--that he was a citizen of Missouri. Sandford, the defendant, plead to the jurisdiction and alleged for cause of abatement that Scott was not a citizen of Missouri as averred in his declaration, "because he is a negro of African descent; his ancestors were of pure African blood and were brought into this country and sold as negro slaves." To this plea there was a demurrer by which the facts set forth in the plea were admitted, and upon the issue in law thus joined the Circuit Court gave judgment that the demurrer be sustained. The plea, it will be perceived, did not aver that Scott was a slave, or state any fact from which the inference that he was such unavoidably resulted. The plaintiff was, therefore, to be regarded in the decision upon the demurrer as a free man, and was so regarded by the Circuit Court and by the Supreme Court.[37] The effect of the final decision, assuming it to have been the opinion of the court, was that the judgment of the Circuit Court upon the demurrer be reversed, and a mandate issued directing the suit to be dismissed from that court for want of jurisdiction. This disposed of every question in the case that entered into, or could exert the slightest influence upon the personal rights of the parties or the ultimate judgment of the Supreme Court. Judge Daniel in his opinion--inferior to none that were delivered--admitted this in so many words: "According to the view taken of the case as applicable to the demurrer to the plea in abatement in this cause," (said he,) "the question subsequently raised upon the several pleas in bar might be passed by, as requiring neither a particular examination nor an adjudication directly upon them." This was, beyond all doubt, the true condition of the case. Every other question bore upon one point only, and that was, whether Scott had become a free man,--a question not put in issue by the plea in abatement, and according to the opinion of the court of no real consequence in the decision of the cause.

[37] The opinion of the Supreme Court is thus summed up by the Chief Justice: "And upon a full and careful consideration of the subject the court is of opinion that upon the facts stated in the plea in abatement Dred Scott was not a citizen of Missouri within the meaning of the Constitution of the United States, and not entitled as such to sue in its courts; and consequently that the Circuit Court had no jurisdiction of the cause and that the judgment on the plea in abatement is erroneous."

The result would, therefore, seem to be that every thing subsequently said and done by the court was extrajudicial--obiter dicta decisions, which, not affecting the merits of the case, are of no authority. But the court, anticipating such an objection, made very considerable efforts, in advance, to repel and disprove it. Both the Chief Justice and Judge Wayne insisted earnestly on the circumstance that this was a writ of error to the Circuit Court and not to a State court; that the question did not relate to the jurisdiction of the Supreme Court, but of its own inferior court, and that in such cases it was the practice and the duty of the Supreme Bench to take a wider range in the correction of errors than when the case came up from the State courts, and the question was whether the Supreme Court had a right to act in the matter. In the latter case they admitted that the judges ought to stop the moment they found that none existed, and if they did not, all beyond was extrajudicial. They urged that the general judgment in favor of the defendant, in a case in which the Circuit Court had no jurisdiction, was an error apparent on the record which it was proper in the Supreme Court to correct by a reversal of that judgment, and that for this purpose it became necessary to decide the issue presented by the special plea which involved the constitutionality of the Missouri Compromise Act; and, finally, that the case was one which the court had not sought, but which had been brought before it in the regular course of judicial proceedings; that the issues it involved were those which the parties had presented for the decision of the court, and that it was its duty to dispose of them.

That the court had neither sought the case nor exerted any agency in framing the issues it presented was undeniably true, and the reasons assigned in justification of its course are certainly entitled to great respect. How far their strength is impaired by the following considerations, those who have sufficient curiosity to study the case will judge for themselves. That the parties, at the commencement of the proceedings in the Supreme Court, were both desirous to have the issue joined upon the merits examined and decided upon by that court, is very evident, but it is questionable whether the wishes and interests of both were not superseded by its action. The plaintiff secure, as he supposed, by the stand he had acquired in the Circuit Court through the decision of that tribunal upon the demurrer in his favor, was of course solicitous to reverse the judgment which had been given by that court in favor of the defendant upon the merits. The defendant had two objects in view,--the first of which was to reverse the judgment upon the demurrer, and, if he failed in that, to sustain the judgment in his favor upon the merits. On the argument of the cause it was made a grave question whether the point raised by the plea to the jurisdiction was legally before the Supreme Court,--a question of no small difficulty and one in regard to which there was a diversity of opinion to the last, even among the judges who were in favor of the decision of the court. It was contended by the plaintiff in error that the defendant had conceded the jurisdiction of the Circuit Court by pleading over, and that he had not brought his writ of error to reverse his own judgment. But the Supreme Court overruled these objections, reversed the judgment in his favor, and directed the suit to be dismissed from the Circuit Court for the want of jurisdiction. By this decision, which the plaintiff could not foresee, and was not bound to anticipate, all his interest in a decision upon the merits was of course superseded. The defendant having succeeded in driving the plaintiff out of the court below, could have no possible desire that the judgment rendered in his own favor should be reversed; affirmed it could not be on account of the want of jurisdiction in the Circuit Court. His application to the Supreme Court to have that point of the case acted upon was therefore superseded by its own act. Such anomalous proceedings, as an elaborate opinion in favor of all the claims set up by a party terminating with the reversal of a judgment in his favor, are happily of rare occurrence in judicial tribunals so able and elevated as ours. It is perhaps questionable whether the judgments for the defendant in the court below did not fall with the dismissal of the cause from before the Circuit Court for want of jurisdiction, without farther interference on the part of the Supreme Court. Still in a case involving so many and such extraordinary complications, the latter might well feel itself at liberty to decide also the questions that were raised and had been very fully discussed before it upon the merits of the cause. But on what grounds it could regard such a course as obligatory and necessary to the complete administration of justice between the parties litigant before it, I cannot see, and I find it difficult to believe that the members of the court would have given themselves the trouble to prepare such elaborate opinions upon questions the decision of which was not necessary to the judgment of the court, if their solution could have had no other bearing than upon the personal rights of Dred Scott. I think it more likely that the judges who united in the opinion that the Missouri Compromise Act was unconstitutional, seeing the extraordinary revolution which its repeal had produced in the political and fraternal feelings of the people of the United States, and sincerely believing the safety of the Union endangered by continued agitation upon so disturbing a subject, hoped to arrest it by the judgment of the Supreme Court upon the point in question,--a step which, if not actually called for, they yet believed fully justified by the case before them.

Chief Justice Taney, who, by his superior intellect and elevation of character, was enabled to give to such a movement its greatest impulse, was not exempt from an original bias in favor of the doctrine advanced by Mr. Webster in the discussions upon the Bank Veto, when the latter declared,--"Hitherto it has been thought that the final decision of constitutional questions belonged to the supreme judicial tribunal. The very nature of free government, it has been supposed, enjoins this; and our Constitution, moreover, has been understood so to provide clearly and expressly."[38] The peculiarity of these expressions challenges our attention in passing. The guarded and sly manner in which they put forth the doctrines of the old Federal party, without assuming the responsibility of affirming them, is in their author's best manner.

[38] The italics are mine.

Nor did the Chief Justice stand alone in that position among his judicial brethren. He had occupied a distinguished place in the Federal ranks to an advanced period in his professional life; he had acquired an enviable fame at the Bar, and had left it, as most old lawyers do, with feelings of admiration and respect not only for his professional brethren but for the Bench, in the influence and power of which they seldom fail to take the deepest interest. It was hardly to be expected that he should, on taking his seat, have proved insensible to the esprit du corps which had long prevailed in and around that high tribunal, and which, directed by the plastic hand of John Marshall, had charmed minds as strong as his own, even although professing opposite political principles. Story and Thompson, who had been stars of considerable magnitude in the old Republican party, were in succession subdued by Marshall's magnetic influence to conditions in this regard favorable to the acceptance of almost any extension of the doctrine of the supremacy of the Supreme Court.

Although the master-mind which gave it life and by which it was installed has departed, the proceedings now the subject of our review give us abundant reason to apprehend that the spirit has retained its place and power. In respect to many hardly contested issues brought before the Court, occurring vacancies and new appointments have doubtless worked important changes in its opinions; but on that of the supremacy of the judicial over the other departments of the Government in constitutional questions, there are yet, it is to be feared, few dissentients on the Bench, and least of all on the question from which opposition to the decision in the Dred Scott case proceeded. That decision was therefore pronounced under the full persuasion that, in addition to its quieting effect upon the public mind, it, of right, ought to have a controlling influence over the action of the other departments of the Government; that it ought to influence the action of Congress in particular, and that, if an attempt should be made to revive the condemned act, it would guide the course of the Executive. Judge Daniel, in the modest, hesitating terms in which he expressed his concurrence in the farther proceedings, which he admitted to be unnecessary, seems to have thought it due to the political school in which he had been reared to put some qualification upon the power of the court to settle the conflicting views upon the subject that prevailed out of doors and might find place in the other departments of the Government. But my worthy friend, Judge Wayne, had no such reserve. He thought that the case, in addition to private rights of great value, involved "constitutional principles of the highest importance, about which there had become such a difference of opinion that the peace and harmony of the country required the settlement of them by judicial decision."

The Chief Justice was too circumspect not to content himself with action, and not to avoid expressions open to unfavorable criticism. I cannot suffer the allusions I have made to circumstances in the previous career of this excellent man to pass without a disclaimer of the slightest intention to impeach his motives in any thing. I have known him long and well. We stood shoulder to shoulder by the side of General Jackson at the most eventful period of his second term of office, and did all we could do to sustain him by our cooperation and advice. I do not know that we differed on any point; and I do know that there could not have been a more upright and vigilant public officer than he was; nor could any man have had a more faithful or a more efficient friend than he proved to that noble old man. I witnessed from beginning to end the virulent and violent persecutions he experienced at the hands of his old Federal and Whig friends, and was deeply affected by the steady, self-possessed and manly spirit with which he endured them. This impressed me with a respect for his character and a personal attachment which no after-occurrence has weakened. He was my choice as the candidate of the Democratic party for the Presidency in 1852, and there has been no time since at which I would not have rejoiced to see him at the head of the Government. I would have expected to find in him some defects, which being bred in the bone would come out in the flesh, but that never was with me, as was known to my familiar associates in political life, an objection to the elevation to office of gentlemen whose political status was similar to his own. I took them cum onere, and sometimes, though certainly not always, gained by the experiment. He was a man of innate as well as cultivated integrity in sentiment and action, and the longer we live the higher value we learn to place on this quality in a public man. Conscious of the importance of sincerity and truthfulness in all the movements of Government, whose office it is to enforce the observance of moral obligation, men of this character can never be induced to countenance public measures unless they are not only pure in themselves, but supported by pure means. Such a man was Roger B. Taney, and such men I never suspect of unworthy motives in any thing they say or do. Neither have I the slightest doubt of the good intentions by which his associates on the bench were influenced in the proceedings of which I am speaking. Yet I cannot but think that in going beyond the necessities of the case they made a grievous mistake. The question, which the court undertook to settle, was political, and had assumed a partisan character of great virulence. There are two classes in every community whose interference in politics is always and very naturally distasteful to sincere republicans, and those are judges and clergymen. Their want of sympathy, as a general rule, for popular rights, is known throughout the world, and in this country that repugnance received an enduring impulse from the unanimity with which a vast majority of both classes banded themselves on the side of power, in the stormy time of the first Adams, and from the bitterness with which they railed from the bench and the pulpit at the public-spirited and patriotic men, who sought to relieve the country from misrule. Both were again called to the political field, though on different sides, during our recent troubles; yet the circumstance that the judges took part with a majority of those who constituted the Democratic party of the United States was not sufficient to neutralize the dislike to their interference in politics which was seated in the Democratic mind. To add a deeper shade to this trespass upon the time-honored creed of the Democratic party, the anti-Democratic doctrine was conveyed to the public in a form professing to be a necessary adjudication in the regular course of the administration of justice, whilst it is, to a considerable extent at least, exposed to the imputation of having in truth been an extrajudicial opinion, voluntarily and not necessarily delivered,--a mode of bringing before the country the opinions of the supreme bench, formerly much in use, but which, since the case of Marbury and Madison, has been peculiarly repulsive to Democrats, and which Mr. Jefferson spent much time in holding up to odium.

To do full justice to Mr. Buchanan in respect to the extent to which this action of the Supreme Court received his sanction, it becomes necessary to state with more precision than might otherwise be deemed requisite, in connection with admitted facts, his avowals on the subject, which are contained in his inaugural address.

The Kansas-Nebraska Act was designed to settle, as far as an act of Congress could do so, two points, viz.--1st, that Congress possessed no power to legislate upon the subject of slavery in the Territories, and therefore it repealed the Missouri Compromise Act; and 2d, that it belongs to the majority of the people of the Territory to decide whether slavery shall or shall not exist within its bounds.

President Buchanan treated every point which the Kansas Act professed to settle as removed from the scope of partisan warfare, and congratulated the country on the happy conception through which the Congress had accomplished results so desirable.

That body recognized in the fullest manner the power and the right of a majority of the people of Kansas to decide upon their domestic institutions, including the subject of slavery, but was silent as to the period when that right should be exercised. That was, therefore, left an open question, and the President expressed his views in regard to it in the following words: "A difference of opinion has arisen in regard to the time when the people of a Territory shall decide this question for themselves. This is happily a matter of little practical importance, and besides it is a judicial question, which legitimately belongs to the Supreme Court of the United States, before whom it is now pending, and will, it is understood, be speedily and finally settled. To their decision, in common with all good citizens, I shall cheerfully submit, whatever this may be, though it has been my individual opinion," etc.

It is not necessary for the purpose of this reference to inquire either how far that question was decided by the Supreme Court, in the case referred to, or whether the President does justice to its importance. In respect to the latter point it is well known that a contrary opinion is extensively entertained. It will not be denied that the case he speaks of was that of Dred Scott, and that the questions to be decided in it related only to the personal rights and interests of the parties to the suit. It is in the settlement of such only that the Supreme Court could exercise jurisdiction upon such a subject, and all will admit that if it belongs to a Territory to determine the question of the toleration of slavery there, the occasion of the formation of its State constitution will be a proper time for the settlement of that question, if a majority consent that the decision shall be so long deferred. The question in regard to the true time can, therefore, only arise, when a majority wish to act upon the subject at an earlier period. If such an attempt be made, the most extreme advocates for judicial supremacy would not pretend that it would be competent for the Supreme Court to arrest the proceedings by injunction or writ of prohibition, or any other process. It could, therefore, only be in cases involving individual interests, which might be supposed to be affected by such a proceeding on the part of the Territory, that the judicial tribunals could interfere, and it was to such a case that the President was understood to refer. It was of an expected decision of the court in a case in law, brought for the settlement of private rights, that the President spoke, when he said that, though he had an opinion of his own, he would, notwithstanding, submit to the decision of the court upon the point, whatever that might be. By this declaration he announced to his constituents that in the exercise of the executive power upon the subject, whenever that might become necessary, he would take notice of the decision of the Supreme Court in the case he referred to as then pending, and would feel it to be his duty to maintain the rule it should lay down in respect to the particular question of which he spoke, and a fortiori in respect to the main question, the right of the Territory to act upon the matter, and that he would do so because the court had so decided without reference to his individual opinion in the premises--the consequence of which would be, that if his official sanction or cooperation should become necessary to a settlement of the question of slavery by the people of the Territory, he would give it if the people had acted conformably to the rule prescribed by the court, or withhold it if they had acted contrary thereto; and that if Congress should undertake to legislate upon any part of the subject against the decision of the Supreme Court, in respect to its constitutional powers, he would withhold his assent from any bill of that character which the two houses might pass.

It is our duty, and must be our aim, to interpret the language employed by the President according to what we, in good faith, believe to have been his intention. Attempts to pervert the sense of what is said by a man placed in his situation and acting under his grave responsibilities, would not injure him, and could not fail to recoil upon their author. If, dealing with his avowals in that spirit, we are yet bound to believe that the declaration which I have described is the legitimate interpretation and effect of his language, it is not only our right but our duty to speak of it as we conscientiously think it deserves. It can be scarcely necessary to say that those who regard the Republican principles of government applicable to the question before us, as they have been set forth in this work, as the true and only principles of the Constitution, must either abandon the tenets of their predecessors and their own convictions, or treat the declaration of Mr. Buchanan as a voluntary and seemingly a ready sacrifice of a most cherished principle of the Democratic faith--the reciprocal independence of the great departments of government; a principle the importance of which was apparent to and insisted on by the friends of liberty long before the establishment of our independence, and for the practical enforcement of which the American Revolution was regarded as presenting the best opportunity ever offered. For the security of this principle the fathers of our political school made the greatest efforts, and the invasion of it was met by Mr. Jefferson, at the commencement of his administration, with characteristic firmness, and was the subject of his anxious watchfulness during the closing scenes of his life.

The recent action of the Democratic party upon this subject must be considered with many grains of allowance. The long-continued support of a majority of the people,--the only test of political merit in a Republic,--has secured a preference for its principles of which it may well be proud; and the general fidelity of its members to the faith they profess is creditably illustrated by the fact that after all the changes to which its organization has been exposed, its ranks, whatever may be the case as to some of its leaders, are mainly composed of men with like dispositions with those by whom that organization was effected; yet its best friends set up in its behalf no claim to infallibility, nor do they pretend that its members have never failed in their duty to the cause. They know that men do not escape from their liability to err by uniting with a political association. Circumstances of the gravest character have besides put the adherence of its members to the principles of their party, in the matter under consideration, to a severer test than any to which they have hitherto been exposed. For the first time since its ascent to power in the Federal Government, two of the three great departments, the Executive and the Judicial, are presided over by gentlemen who, though raised to their places by its favor, had not been bred in its ranks but joined them at comparatively advanced periods in their lives, with opinions formed and matured in an antagonist school. The motives by which these gentlemen were led to enlist under the Democratic banner were, beyond question, of the purest character, and the high position to which they have been raised by their new friends shows that they were appreciated as they deserved. Most of the principles and opinions they formed in the ranks of the adversary have doubtless been changed, and ours adopted in their stead, but, unfortunately, that which is the subject of our present remark appears not to have been among the number.

Several of the members of the President's cabinet and of the bench of the Supreme Court, perhaps a majority of each, stand in the same category. In Congress the state of things is not materially different; when we look at the gentlemen who have been most prominent in the Kansas embroilment, on the side of the administration, we find an unprecedented number of the same class. It is most proper to avoid referring unnecessarily to names in a work of this character, especially when such reference is not for particular commendation, but the innocence of the motive in this case will excuse a slight departure from the rule. Among the most prominent of those who have taken the lead on the Democratic side in the two houses of Congress in respect to the affairs of Kansas, will be found the names of Toombs, of the Senate, and Stephens, of the House--both from Georgia, and both, for aught I know or have ever known, honorable men, doubtless actuated by good motives. I know neither personally, and never heard of either particularly, save as extreme partisans in the ranks of our opponents. I will not vouch for precise accuracy as to dates, but I am persuaded I will not err materially in saying that neither professed to belong to the Democratic party until after their appointment and election to their present posts. All of these gentlemen not merely believe, as it is very natural that they should, in this supremacy of the judicial power in such matters,--an idea always heretofore scouted by the Democracy of the land,--but they maintain it before the country, under circumstances rendered very imposing by their high official positions, as a test of party fidelity. The Executive, whose elevation to power cost the Democracy so fearful a struggle, and from whose success so much was and still is expected, has done this clearly and undisguisedly in respect to the support of Lecompton, and virtually in respect to the question of judicial supremacy. Mr. Stephens offered a resolution declaring the support of the Lecompton Act, a measure closely interwoven with the principle of which we are speaking, as a test question in the Democratic caucus over which presided Mr. Cochran,--a promising young man from New York, descended from a family as thoroughly imbued with Hamiltonian Federalism as any this State has produced (one of them Hamilton's brother-in-law), brought up till he arrived at man's estate among the straightest of the sect, and on that account entitled to greater credit for throwing himself with becoming zeal into the Democratic ranks, but for the same reason less likely to embrace their creed in its full extent, and less qualified to instruct them in the principles of their faith.

But there is an obstacle to an adherence on the part of the Democratic party to their ancient faith, in respect to these proceedings of the court, far more potent than those to which I have referred. This arises from the circumstance that those proceedings had their origin mainly in a sincere belief that they were necessary to protect a paramount and absorbing interest in nearly half the States of the Confederacy, with the security and quiet of which the citizens of those States believe their happiness and welfare to be inseparably involved. These are also the States in which the Democratic party possesses comparatively its greatest influence, and in some of which the true principles of the Constitution have in general, and especially at earlier periods in our history, been sought after with great avidity, and in which that under consideration found its earliest, ablest, and most persevering supporters. I need not speak of the control which this belief is capable of exerting over most of those who are by their position brought within the range of its practical operation. Minds thus excited find no insuperable difficulty in placing the object of their solicitude upon the footing of the salus populi, or in looking upon any measure that tends to its security as justifiable, because it is in execution of the suprema lex. Before such a feeling, so widely diffused, constitutional objections and all the principles which on ordinary occasions bind the consciences and influence the actions of men, are seldom, if ever, of much avail.

Neither will full justice have been done to the subject, notwithstanding this formidable array of hindrances in the path of duty, if I omit to refer to the inducement, always so strong with political parties, to avail themselves of every opportunity that presents or seems to present itself to "commend the poisoned chalice" to the lips of their opponents--a temptation they find it hard to resist, however much their own hands or consciences may have to be soiled in the operation. Few of the present generation who have made themselves at all conversant with the course of public affairs, need to be told how constant and openly professed has been the faith of the old Federalists and their political successors in the infallibility and omnipotence of the decisions of the Supreme Court of the United States upon constitutional questions. The complaints of the old Republicans and their successors upon that head have been both loud and long continued. When they made the country ring with them in respect to the unconstitutionality and tyrannical character of the Alien and Sedition Laws, the ready and only reply of their opponents was, that it belonged to the judicial power to decide upon their constitutionality, and that their expediency was a matter to be solved in the breast of Congress. In more modern times, when its unconstitutionality was objected to the second Bank of the United States, the decision of the Supreme Court in favor of the power of Congress to establish it was the equally ready and confident answer to all complaints on that ground. Other and similar instances might be referred to, but it is unnecessary. For the first time since the formation of the present Government the supreme bench, considerably changed in the political complexion of its members and tempted, doubtless more or less under the pressure of an all-absorbing popular influence at the South, to borrow a leaf from the book of our political opponents, has undertaken to control, adversely to the views of those opponents, a great political question by an extrajudicial decision of the court. As one of the consequences, a hue and cry has been raised against that august tribunal, hitherto revered by them as the only political sanctuary; trusted as the ark of safety;--a clamor reaching to a demand for the reorganization of the court itself;--a point never even approached by the Democracy when their displeasure has been raised to the greatest height by its unauthorized assumptions of political power. It is not then surprising that portions of the Democratic party should have been led to give the qualified assent which they have given to the Federal principle under consideration. I say qualified, for the guarded manner in which those who so assent have urged the influence which the decision of the court ought to have upon the question, must have been apparent to all; and this has been very much to their credit, especially in the slaveholding States. The references which have been made to the doings of the judiciary, in most instances, have savored more of what is known in the law as a plea of estoppel than of a claim of right,--a plea by which the truth or falsity of any matter brought forward by one party is waived, and its admission resisted on the ground that the party relying upon it has precluded himself from introducing it by some act or concession appearing upon the record, or established aliunde. If the doctrine of estoppel could be applied to politicians, it would certainly not be difficult to show that the Federal party and its successors are very clearly estopped from objecting to the action of the Supreme Court of which we have been speaking.

It may, under such circumstances, be safely assumed that the Democratic party has not committed itself to a departure from its professed principles upon this subject to an extent which it cannot be relieved from without a sacrifice of self-respect on the part of its members, or without serious prejudice to its well-earned title to the confidence of the country. That it will so relieve itself its past good sense and active patriotism forbid us to doubt. Let us hope that the protecting care of a kind Providence, which has hitherto carried our country in safety through so many perils, will in His own good time afford us a breathing spell at least, from the baleful excitements attendant upon slavery agitation. When that happy period arrives ... besides the incalculable advantage it will bring to the highest interests of all parties and all sections of our country, the Democrats in the slaveholding States will not fail to see the folly of asking their political coadjutors in the free States to cooperate in the support of measures and principles in sustaining which they cannot be sustained at home. The hair-breadth escape of their common party from destruction at the last Presidential election, and the deplorable condition to which the Democratic party has been reduced in the non-slaveholding States, by a past disregard of that consideration, will then be allowed their proper admonitory effect. All will then acknowledge that in the steps which have recently been taken, having their origin in the same bitter and deplorable source, the Democratic party, always before the able and zealous defender of the Constitution against similar inroads, had entered upon a path which leads directly and inevitably to a revolution of the Government in the most important of its functions--a revolution which would in time substitute for the present healthful and beneficial action of public opinion the selfish and contracted rule of a judicial oligarchy, which, sympathizing in feeling and acting in concert with the money power, would assuredly subvert the best features of a political system that needs only to be honestly administered to enable it to realize those anticipations of our country's greatness which now warm the hearts and animate the patriotism and nerve the arms of her faithful sons.

CHAPTER IX.

Effects of our Leading Party Conflicts in the Light of Seventy Years' Experience--Contest as to the Relative Powers of the State and General Governments--Merits and Faults of the Parties to that Contest--The Credit of settling the Struggle upon right Grounds due to Jefferson's Administration--Attempt of the Federalists to give undue Supremacy to the Judicial Department and Failure of that Attempt--Hamilton's Funding System--History of its Establishment, Continuance, and Overthrow--The National Bank Struggle--The Protective System--Clay's American System--Internal Improvements by the General Government--Overthrow of these Measures the beneficent Work of the Democratic Party--No such Contributions to the Public Welfare made by the Opponents of that Party--The Debt of Gratitude due from the Country to Madison, to Jackson, and especially to Jefferson.

It will not be deemed inappropriate to close this review of the rise and progress of our political parties, and of the principles upon which they have acted, with a fuller notice of the advantages and disadvantages which have resulted to the country from their conflicting acts and pretensions during an experience of more than seventy years. In deciding the character of parties by their works we will but follow the dictates of unerring wisdom, by which we are taught to judge the tree by its fruit.

A great question, and naturally the first that arose in the formation of our political system, related to the power that should be reserved to, and the treatment that should be extended towards, the State governments. Rivalries between them and the Federal head could not be prevented. To mitigate the evil by dealing justly and wisely with the State authorities, was all that could be done. Each of the great parties which have divided the country had, from the beginning, its own, and they were conflicting opinions, in respect to the spirit in which this important subject should be dealt with. These, and the acts and sayings they gave rise to, have been herein freely spoken of, and what has been said need not be repeated. The facts and circumstances brought into view, consisting in a considerable degree of the reiterated declarations of the parties themselves, with a mass of others supplied by contemporaneous history, fully justify the belief that if Hamilton and Morris, and the influential men of the party of which the former was through life the almost absolute leader, could have had their way, the State governments would have been reduced to conditions in regard to power and dignity which would not only have destroyed their usefulness, but from which they must have sunk into insignificance and contempt; to which state it was the avowed wish of those leaders to depress them. This desire was frustrated in the Federal Convention, not so much through favorable feeling towards the State authorities as by a conviction on the part of a majority--a conviction which could neither be disguised nor suppressed--that the old Anti-Federal party would be sufficiently strengthened by a plan of the Constitution, against which a design clearly hostile to the State governments could be fairly charged, to enable that party to prevent its ratification. John Quincy Adams, to his declaration that the "Constitution was extorted from the grinding necessity of a reluctant nation," might have added, with equal truth, that the Constitution, in the form it bore on this point, was extorted from the Convention by a necessity not less effectual. Hamilton's design to attain the object he had failed to accomplish in the Convention, by "administrating" the Constitution, in the language of Madison, into a thing very different from what they both knew it was intended to be, was defeated by the old Republican party.

The lowest point to which the State governments would have been reduced, if the influence that was exerted to lessen their power had not been defeated in the way I have described, must of necessity be matter of speculation only. Hamilton, as we have seen, declared candidly that he knew of no reason why he did not advocate their total overthrow other than the manifest strong desire of the people for their retention; whilst Morris, with equal openness, said that if they could not abolish them altogether, it was nevertheless desirable to pull the teeth of the serpents.

There can be but little doubt that a complete triumph of the Federal policy would have resulted in a decline of the State governments, if they escaped extinguishment, from the condition which they occupied at the period of the recognition of our Independence to mere municipal authorities, without sufficient power to render them extensively useful--fit theatres only for the exercise and enjoyment of the patronage of the Federal government.

The Anti-Federalists, like their opponents, could only look with favor on one side of this great question. I do not complain of their partiality for the State governments, for it was in them a natural and inherited feeling, one which had been cherished with equal ardor from a remote period in our history by men whose places they filled and whom they most resembled. Their fault was the exclusiveness of their preference. They could not and did not deny that a general government of some sort was indispensable, and they should therefore have stood ready to confer upon it such powers as were necessary to enable it to sustain itself and to qualify it for the successful performance of the duties to be assigned to it. This they would not do. They, on the contrary, allowed their local prejudices and their suspicious, in some instances well founded but unwisely indulged, to lead them to persistent refusals to concede to the Federal head means which a sufficient experience had shown to be absolutely necessary to good government. Public and private interests suffered from that cause, and they were justly held responsible for the consequences. Their conduct was as unjustifiable and as suicidal as was the unmitigated warfare waged by leading Federalists against the State governments; and no political course adopted by public men or political parties, of which it could be said that it was intentionally wrong, has hitherto, to their honor be it spoken, long escaped rebuke from the American people.

The Anti-Federal party by their pertinacious, nay morbid perseverance in a wrong course, exposed themselves to the same penalty which was at a later period inflicted upon their old opponents--as a party they were overthrown and ruined.

The merit of discouraging and finally extinguishing this unnatural, unprofitable, and unnecessary struggle between the friends of the General and State governments, and of vindicating the Federal Constitution, by placing the peculiar principle it sought to establish for the government to be constituted under its authority, that of an imperium in imperio, upon a practicable and safe footing, was reserved for the administration of Thomas Jefferson. For the evils arising from the pernicious rivalry between agencies, upon the harmonious cooperation of which the framers of the Constitution relied for the success of that instrument, the remedy recommended by Mr. Jefferson in his inaugural address, as expressed in his own inimitable language, was "the support of the

State governments in all their rights, as the most competent administrations for our domestic concerns, and the surest bulwark against anti-republican tendencies: the preservation of the General Government in its whole constitutional vigor, as the sheet-anchor of our peace at home and safety abroad." These propositions, so simple, so natural, and so plainly in accord with the spirit of the Constitution, though, in common with other suggestions from the same source designed by their author to give repose to an over-agitated community, received at the time with indifference by incensed partisans, met with a cordial welcome from the great body of the people. Their fitness and probable efficacy could not be successfully controverted, and although they did not escape factious opposition, a majority of the people, tired of the unavailing agitation which the subject had undergone, and more and more satisfied of Mr. Jefferson's sincere desire to advance the general interest, embraced them with constantly increasing earnestness, and sustained them until they became the successful as well as settled policy of the Government. Angry passions, having their origin in this prolific source of partisan strife, which swept over and convulsed the country during the Government of the Confederation, and for at least twenty years after the adoption of the new Constitution, have been subdued. The State governments, increased in number from thirteen to more than thirty, with no other powers than those reserved to them by the undisputed provisions of the Constitution, have advanced to a degree of dignity and usefulness which has enabled them to extend to their citizens seven eighths of the aid and protection for which they look to government, either State or national, and has also removed from their representatives all fear of the encroachments of the Federal Government; whilst the latter, having proven itself able to sustain itself without the aid of constructive powers, and to perform with promptitude and success all the duties assigned to it, is no longer disturbed by apprehensions of the factious spirit and grasping designs once so freely charged upon the State authorities.

For this auspicious state of things we are beyond all doubt indebted, more than to any other cause, to the conservative character of Democratic principles and the unwavering fidelity of the party that sustains them.

To understand truly the advantages which the country has derived from the success of this policy, and the defeat of that to which it was opposed, we have only to picture to ourselves what the condition of the State governments must have been if the latter had triumphed, and to compare it with the actual state of things. Assuming that the desire to divest them of the authority which they had gradually acquired, as occasions for its exercise were developed by the necessities of the public service, at one time so strong with leading Federalists and as we have seen so openly avowed, had been limited to what was actually proposed, viz., to give to the General Government the power to appoint their governors, and through them the most important of their minor officers, including those of the militia, with an absolute veto upon all State laws,--what, judging according to the experience we have had, would now have been the character and condition of those governments? Without the authority required to make themselves useful, or respectability sufficient to excite the ambition of individuals to be honorably employed in their service, and thus to divide their attention and regard between the Federal and State governments, they would have sunk gradually into feeble, unimportant, characterless establishments-- mere places for the sinecure appointments of the former. Contrast institutions like these--and only such could have been possible under the policy advocated by the leading Federalists--with the galaxy of independent governments of which we now boast, such as no confederation, ancient or modern, possessed, vested with authority and dignity, and filling the States respectively with monuments of their wisdom, enterprise, usefulness, and philanthropy; and contrast the Federal Government, resting as it now does on these tried and ample foundations, with one based on establishments like those to which it was proposed to degrade the States, and we will have some idea of the dangers that the people of the United States have escaped, and the advantages they have secured by the wisdom of their course and the patriotism of those who advised it. If the Democratic party of Jefferson's time, and under his lead, had effected nothing else for the country, they would have done enough in this to deserve the perpetual respect and gratitude of the whole people.

Yet this was but the beginning of their usefulness, subsequent to the adoption of the present Constitution.

No sooner had the efforts of the leaders of the Federal party to break down the power and influence of the State governments been arrested through the triumph of the Democratic party in the great contest of 1800, which was to a great extent carried on in their defense, than an attempt was set on foot to rescue a portion of the political power lost by the former, by raising the judicial power--the dispensers of which were to a man on their side--above the executive and legislative departments of the Federal Government. Of this enterprise, its origin, progress, and present condition, I have taken the notice which I thought was demanded by its importance. That it was unsuccessful, and that the balance of power between those departments, so necessary to the security of liberty and to the preservation of the Government, has not been destroyed, is altogether due to the persevering opposition of the Democratic party under the same bold and capable leader.

Where the points in issue between political parties have been of so grave a character as those in the United States, it is not an easy matter to decide on their relative importance, or in which the right and the wrong was most apparent. Whilst some have resolved themselves mainly into questions of expediency, in respect to which errors may be committed without incurable injury to our institutions, there have been others striking at their roots, which would, if differently decided, have ended in their inevitable destruction. The two to which I have referred were emphatically of the latter character, and hence the inestimable value of the successful resistance that was made on the Democratic side.

Hamilton's funding system, though involving in respect to the assumption of the State debts a grave constitutional question, was in its principal features one of expediency. Yet it was an important one, by reason of the serious consequences that were apprehended from its assumed tendency, and produced impressions upon the public scarcely less marked than were made by any public question which had before or has since arisen in this country. The character of that system, and the injuries that were anticipated from its establishment, have been spoken of in a previous part of this essay. Only a slight consideration of the operations of a similar system elsewhere will be sufficient to show how greatly the welfare of nations has been affected by their course in respect to it.

Of these, England, from her present condition in regard to her public debt, compared with that in which it is believed she might have stood if her course in that respect had been guided by wiser counsels, presents the most instructive example. Ours derives interest scarcely less impressive from the evils we have avoided by abandoning, whilst that was yet in our power, the further imitation of her example after we had fully begun to imitate it. That the system was established here with much eclat, and under explanations and circumstances indicative of a determination on the part of the men in power to adhere to it as long as and whenever a public debt existed, all know. It is also known that the practice of funding the public debt, for which it furnished the plan, has long been discontinued. Through what agency and upon what inducements that discontinuance has been brought about, and who is entitled to the credit of protecting the country from the evils flowing from the practice elsewhere, can only be ascertained by an impartial examination of its further history. To bestow that attention upon the subject is perhaps not necessary for instruction or example, as a national bank has not become more completely an "obsolete idea" amongst us, or more thoroughly condemned in public opinion than a funding system. Still there are many considerations which render such an examination an object of curiosity certainly, and one not destitute of higher interest. If the change which was effected in the policy and action of the Government in this regard has been as advantageous as with the light which experience has thrown upon the subject cannot be longer doubted, it is highly proper that those who brought about the reform should have the credit of it.

No important transaction upon which patriotism of such an order and intellects of such caliber as distinguished the public men of that day were earnestly employed, can be without interest to inquiring minds of this. It is so long since the whole affair has passed from public attention as to make it an unfamiliar subject to most of us. I confess it was so to me, and those who read these sheets will not complain if the interest I have taken in following it to its termination shall at least save them from some of the trouble that would otherwise have been necessary to master its details.

Strongly excited by the first appearance of the project at the head of Hamilton's programme, as well described by Madison in his interesting statement to Mr. Trist, the old Republicans in and out of Congress, with Jefferson as their adviser and at their head, rallied promptly in earnest and unyielding opposition to its consummation. Overborne by a large majority in the first Congress, devoted as it was to Hamilton and his measures, they could not defeat the bill for its establishment, and were obliged to content themselves in the first instance with efforts to expose its objectionable features to the people, in the hope of rendering it too odious to be persisted in. They also resorted, as they often afterwards did on similar occasions, to the State legislatures for advice and cooperation. That of Virginia, the President's native State, as well as the place of his residence, denounced the scheme very soon after its introduction, in resolutions of much power, touching the subject upon the points in respect to which it was most exceptionable. Its opponents in Congress also kept a watchful eye upon the steps taken by the Secretary towards its execution, and followed every important movement by calls for information and by pertinent resolutions. These calls were generally upon the Secretary, occasionally on the President himself. As early as 1792, the Republicans caused the introduction of, and gave efficient support to, a resolution that "measures ought to be taken for the redemption of so much of the public debt as by the act making provision for the debts of the United States, they have the right to redeem." In this resolution, which was adopted by the House, a provision was inserted, against the votes of the old Republicans, to direct the Secretary of the Treasury to prepare the plan for the contemplated redemption. Those who were opposed to its preparation by that officer desired to have it done by a committee, and apprehended obstacles on his part to an efficient prosecution of the reform they supported.

The resolution, though not expressly such in its terms, was obviously designed as a side-blow at the funding system. That the Secretary so regarded it was sufficiently apparent from the graceful notice, in his report, of the circumstance that "the House had predetermined the question in regard to the expediency of the proposed redemption, and only submitted to his consideration the best mode of carrying it into effect." He then proceeded to state the different ways in which the object in view might be accomplished, designated that which he thought most expedient, pointed out the increased burdens on the people it would require, and specified the taxes the imposition of which he thought would be necessary. His report was drawn up with his accustomed skill and ability, but the measure was no further prosecuted at that time.

The President was subsequently called upon, at the instance of the Republicans, for copies of the commissions and instructions under which Hamilton had borrowed some twelve millions of dollars in Europe in virtue of a provision of the act establishing the funding system, and a call was at the same time made upon Hamilton for an account of the manner in which the money had been applied. These calls brought from the President copies of the commission and instructions, the latter of which were very precise and in strict conformity, in every respect, to the law, and from Hamilton an elaborate report, drawn with a degree of care and power unusual even with him. He appears to have anticipated a storm, and to have prepared himself for every contingency, as far as his conduct could be sustained by the facts. Those who derive pleasure from the intellectual efforts of great minds, however remote the occasion that called them forth, will not begrudge the time spent in reading his report.

A series of resolutions introduced into the House by Giles of Virginia, charged the Secretary with having violated both the law and the President's instructions, by the manner in which he had executed the authority confided to him. These resolutions, after a long and animated debate, were thrown out by strong votes, of the composition of which Mr. Jefferson undertakes to give an account in his annals. But no unprejudiced mind can read Madison's unanswerable speech, which will be found in the first volume of "Benton's Abridgment of the Debates of Congress," p. 431, without being convinced that the truth of both charges was established. He proves by the Secretary's own letters that on the very day of the receipt of the President's instructions he commenced arrangements, which he, notwithstanding, carried into effect, for an application of the funds diametrically opposite to that which the President had directed him to make.

Mr. Randall, in his "Life of Thomas Jefferson,"[39] has accidentally fallen into a singular mistake in saying that "Mr. Madison voted with the majority on every division" on that occasion, and on that assumption proceeds to show "that Jefferson put a less charitable construction on the motives of the majority," by giving the following entry in his "Ana": "March the 2d, 1793. See, in the papers of this date, Mr. Giles's Resolutions. He and one or two others were sanguine enough to believe that the palpableness of these resolutions rendered it impossible the House could reject them. Those who knew the composition of the House,--1. Of bank directors; 2. Holders of bank stock; 3. Stock-jobbers; 4. Blind devotees; 5. Ignorant persons who did not comprehend them; 6. Lazy and good-humored persons, who comprehended and acknowledged them, yet were too lazy to examine or unwilling to pronounce censure,--the persons who knew these characters foresaw that the three first descriptions making one third of the House, the three latter would make one half of the residue; and of course that they would be rejected by a majority of two to one. But they thought that even this rejection would do good, by showing the public the desperate and abandoned dispositions with which their affairs were conducted. The resolutions were proposed, and nothing spared to present them in the fullness of demonstration. There were not more than three or four who voted otherwise than had been expected."

[39] Vol. II. p. 119.

Mr. Madison voted with the minority on every division, and so far was he from acting otherwise that William Smith, of South Carolina, the devoted friend of Hamilton, charged him with saying after the vote that "the opinion of the House on the preceding resolutions would not change the truth of facts, and that the public would ultimately decide whether the Secretary's conduct was criminal or not."

The character of this debate and the open disregard of the President's instructions by the Secretary, which it established, were not likely to pass unheeded or even lightly regarded through the proud and sensitive mind of Washington.

Other circumstances may be referred to which show quite clearly that the latter was not at ease upon the subject of the finances. Among these is one of a very striking character, not known at the time, and only recently disclosed through the publication of the "Hamilton Papers" by order of Congress. I allude to the correspondence between him and Washington, to which I have before referred for another purpose, and which will be found in the fourth volume of "Hamilton's Works," commencing at page 510. The committee appointed by Congress to examine the state of the treasury preparatory to Hamilton's resignation, then expected but postponed for a season, were charged by that body to "inquire into the authorities, from the President to the Secretary of the Treasury, respecting the making and disbursing of the loans" which were the subject of the debate and proceedings above referred to. Hamilton thought the inquiry beyond the province of the committee, but wishing to be prepared, if they should decide otherwise, furnished the President with a statement of the facts, as he understood them to be, with a view to his approval. Washington indorsed on it a certificate which was very unsatisfactory to Hamilton, who thereupon addressed to him a long and earnest letter, in which he complained vehemently, and with the frankness and boldness natural to him, of not having been sustained by the President in a delicate and responsible part of his official duties in respect to the public debt. It does not appear that Washington made any reply to this extraordinary letter, or that he did anything further upon the subject which had called it forth.

Whilst the proceedings which led to the debate of which I have spoken were going on, a bill was introduced on the recommendation of the Secretary, for a second assumption of State debts, and authorizing a loan to be opened for that purpose. Notwithstanding strenuous efforts on the part of the Republican members to prevent its passage, the bill passed the House, but only by the casting vote of Mr. Speaker Trumbull. These circumstances were brought to the notice of the President by Jefferson, before the bill was acted upon by the Senate, and it was rejected by that body. He speaks in his "Ana" of the prevalent impression that the bill had been defeated by the interference of the President, through Lear, with Langdon, who till that time had gone steadily for the funding system but now opposed its extension. Jefferson says, "Beckley knows this."

But whatever may have been the state of feeling between these great men, arising out of the condition of the finances, or the course of the Secretary in respect to them, we have the best reasons for believing that there was a growing sentiment in the Federal party adverse to the expediency of keeping on foot the funding system. It soon began to lose the brilliant hues in which it had been clothed, at its first introduction, by the very imposing report of the Secretary. Our foreign creditors showed an unwillingness to subject their debts to its operation, and the means taken to find subjects to be embraced by its provisions could not fail to excite odium against the measure. The people were not a little predisposed to listen favorably to the charges that were made against it on the part of the Republicans, by the circumstances heretofore noticed that it was so close an imitation of the English system, and adopted upon the heel of the Revolution. The growing jealousy of the people, and consequent increase of public clamor against it, caused a wide-spread conviction through the Federal ranks that the entire success of the Republican party could only be prevented by its abandonment,--a conviction greatly strengthened and stimulated to action by the startling fact that, although the President had just been reelected by the unanimous vote of the people, the country was convulsed by partisan rancors, for which there was no other apology than the measures of his administration, and the Confederacy which he came into power to cement was in imminent peril of disruption by their violence. Neither was this the worst nor the most humiliating view of the case. For the first time during our existence as an independent nation, even including the period of the proverbially weak government of the Confederation, our free institutions suffered the discredit of an open rebellion against the authority of the Federal Government springing up in the Quaker State, one of the oldest and best settled in the Confederacy and in which was established the seat of that Government, against the imposition of a tax always and everywhere odious, an "infernal tax," as Jefferson called it;--an insurrection of so much importance as to induce Washington to call into the field a force numerically larger than was ever concentrated at one place during the War of the Revolution, or ever organized in one body in the course of two wars through which the country has since passed, and nearly if not quite double that with which Scott fought his way through a hostile nation of eight millions, and entered the City of Mexico in triumph. No feature in the character of Washington has ever been disclosed which will allow us to believe for a moment that those scenes could have failed to disturb and agitate deeply his lofty and sensitive spirit. We have a fact, now for the first time, as far as I know or believe, revealed in Randall's "Life of Jefferson," which gives us some clue to the current of Washington's thoughts at that very critical period of his life. Hamilton, whose resignation was about to take effect, applied to have the time prolonged until after the impending insurrection had been suppressed, on the ground that as it was menaced in consequence of a measure of his Department, it would not be proper for him to leave his post until the crisis had terminated, and he had also asked for leave to attend the troops to the scene of the outbreak. Both of these applications had been readily agreed to by the President. In the midst of these movements, between the first Proclamation offering pardon to the rebels upon their return to duty and the second calling the troops into the field and announcing the intended application of military force, an express was sent to Mr. Jefferson with an invitation to him to resume his former place in Washington's cabinet. This fact is indisputable, for Jefferson's answer declining the invitation is published by Randall.

What was the nature and what the extent of Washington's design in this application? The assumption is justified by the lapse of time and by other circumstances, that as no record of his intentions has come to light none exists, and it is therefore a question on which we are only able to speculate; but there is another question, the answer to which, though not quite certain, may be made so, and which, when ascertained, would throw much light upon the subject of our speculations.

Was Hamilton advised of the application to Jefferson, and was it made with his approbation? The thorough examinations and publications which have been made of the papers of both Washington and Hamilton, without the disclosure of a single reference to the main fact, authorize the belief that Hamilton never was a party to the movement in any shape. In respect to Hamilton's papers, this inference is particularly strong, as, from the quasi-rivalry which has recently been set on foot by his descendants between his own fame and that of Washington, it may well be presumed that if they could have furnished evidence of such an act of disloyalty to Federalism on the part of Washington as his invitation to Jefferson, who had, after his retirement, openly charged Congress with the most flagrant corruption, and traced its origin to the measures of the Secretary of the Treasury, the information would certainly not have been withheld from publication. The same considerations lead with still greater confidence to the conclusion that no movement had been made towards any other than a temporary change of purpose in regard to his resignation on the part of Hamilton. Washington's letter giving his consent to the postponement, is published among the "Hamilton Papers," and from all that was said or done upon the subject it is quite clear that no attempt was made by him to dissuade Hamilton from carrying his resolution into effect, and that such resolution was final on the part of the latter from the beginning.

Incidents occurring at an early period of their relations were well calculated to induce circumspection in such a matter on both sides. The uncertainty in regard to Washington's ulterior intentions in the step he had just taken will become more apparent the more the question is considered. Mr. Randall seems to infer from it a desire on his part to return to the system of a balanced government with which he commenced his administration. But to the consummation of such a design the assent of Hamilton was absolutely indispensable, and that, with the lights before us, we may safely assume was neither asked nor given. I find it, besides, difficult to resist the conclusion that Washington's preference for that sort of government must by that time have been greatly weakened if not entirely extinguished. He had tried it under circumstances far more eligible than those then existing or than he could reasonably anticipate, and had found it disastrous. Jefferson had in the most positive terms declined an attempt to coalesce with Hamilton, as made impossible by the radical differences in their political principles. The same differences continued, and their personal relations had now become much more embittered. For these and other reasons that could be given, it is extremely difficult to reconcile with his well-known prudence the design hypothetically attributed to Washington by Randall.

If there is the force in these suggestions that they appear to me to possess, we would seem to be driven to the conclusion that Washington contemplated, in military language, a change of front dependent upon Jefferson's acceptance; that he meant not only to place Jefferson at the head of his cabinet, but to give an increased effect to his principles in the future administration of the Government. I confess that this is a startling supposition, even to my own mind, and one in respect to which I feel that I cannot go much beyond surmise. A step of so decided and so pregnant a character, taken under the pressure of a situation for many reasons so critical, could not have been thought of by such a man as Washington without ulterior, well-considered designs. What were they, if not of the character I have suggested? I can conceive of no other answer to this question which is not more inconsistent with well-known facts.

Considerations were not wanting to persuade him that his second term, under an administration thus directed, would be more agreeable as well as more auspicious for the country than the first had been. I have before referred to the contrast between Jefferson and Madison on one side, and Hamilton on the other, presented by the fact that whilst the former entered upon the discharge of public offices with feelings and views similar to those with which they accepted private trusts, considered themselves under equal obligations to respect the rights and to carry into full and fair effect the intentions of the parties chiefly concerned, and would have regarded a failure to do either as much a violation of the principles of probity and honor in one case as in the other, the latter neither entertained nor professed to act upon such opinions; he had on the contrary a conviction, which he never changed, that there were deficiencies in the popular mind which made it impracticable on the part of men in power to deal safely with the people by appeals to their good sense and honesty, and that they could only be successfully governed through their fears or their interests. Hence his justification of measures addressed to their passions and particular interests, and hence his indifference to the faithful observance of the Constitution as a moral or honorable obligation and his utter recklessness of constitutional restraints in his public career, notwithstanding the perfect uprightness of his dealings in private life.

Washington's personal character has been never correctly appreciated, if the former of these systems or ideas was not more congenial with his taste and with the suggestions of his heart than the latter. In giving his assent to the bill for the establishment of the bank, he could not shut his eyes to the fact that he was sanctioning a measure which he had conclusive reason to believe was never intended to be authorized by the Constitution, framed by a convention over which he had presided. Reasons of supposed state necessity we are warranted in believing reconciled his conscience to the step, but it cannot be doubted, without injustice to his character, that it was a hard service and altogether repugnant to his feelings. His inquietude under these restraints upon his natural inclinations was exhibited on more than one occasion. His letter to the venerable Edmund Pendleton, (one of the purest of men,) published by Randall, was one of them. That rumors were rife in respect to the measures decided upon by Federal cabals if Washington had refused to sign the Bank Bill we learn from several sources, and no one who knew Mr. Madison can doubt that he spoke with full knowledge when he said to Trist as already quoted, that if the President had vetoed the Bill "there would have been an effort to nullify it" (the veto), "and they" (the leading Federalists) "would have arrayed themselves in a hostile attitude." It is, besides, against nature to suppose that Washington's consciousness of the past condition of things in this regard and recollection of the scenes referred to by Madison, had not been painfully revived by the offensive letter he had received from Hamilton only four months before the period of which we are speaking.

The probable correctness of the inference under consideration ought not to be tested by the character of the subsequent relations between Washington and Hamilton. Jefferson declined the President's invitation to resume his former seat in his cabinet promptly but respectfully and kindly. Mr. Randall says that he has read a declaration by President Washington to the effect that he would have offered the place to Madison, upon Jefferson's declension, if he had not ascertained that he would not accept it. These successive and marked steps by the most prominent leaders of the Republican party, taken in connection with the results of the preceding Congressional elections, and the avowed principles upon which they had been conducted, show clearly that the lines had been distinctly and finally drawn between the Republicans who had hitherto sustained the administration in general and the Federal party; the opinion at which Jefferson and the Republicans had arrived being that the differences which had arisen, founded as they chiefly were on the interpretation of the Constitution and the degree of sanctity attaching to that instrument, could not be satisfactorily settled by any divided counsels, or by any the most liberal and friendly dispositions of the President; that the season for obtaining present redress and future security upon those points through such means had passed away, and that their proper course, whilst continuing their respect for and their confidence in Washington to the end, was to support the measures of his administration as far as they could consistently with their avowed principles, and to place the Government in the hands of men of their own school at the earliest practicable moment after his voluntary retirement.

The President, having greatly against his inclination consented to stand by the helm for another term, and having been reelected by the unanimous vote of the country, had no other course to pursue than to carry on the Government under its existing organization, relying for his support upon the Federal party, with such cooperation as his measures might draw from its opponents. Hamilton resigned at the end of the quarter, his resignation was accepted in the way I have described, and as the actual and acknowledged leader of the Federal party, though out of office, he kept up his relations with Washington's administration as well as with that of his successor, Mr. Adams, as has been already set forth. The administration having been virtually, and, in the English sense, actually overthrown by being reduced to a minority in the popular branch of the national legislature, the President, having signally failed in his disinterested and patriotic attempt to arrest the adverse current by a reconstruction of his cabinet so as to place at its head the known and acknowledged leader of the opposition to the principal measures of the Government, and obliged by his reelection to remain at his post till the expiration of his second term or to retire with discredit, turned his attention to an earnest survey of the policy to which so disastrous a state of things might be attributed. That it had not originated in any objections personal to himself was shown by the fact that the same election which exhibited the evidence of dissatisfaction, on the part of a majority of the people, with the measures of Government, demonstrated also by his unanimous reelection their continued confidence in him. Those measures to which the deprecated result was attributed were the bank and the funding system. Jay's treaty had no agency in producing it, that disturbing question not having then arisen, and its only effect, in this respect, was during the last year of Washington's administration to increase the majority against the Government to so great an extent as to enable the Republicans to carry Kitchel's resolution condemnatory of the President's own act in refusing to lay before Congress the instructions and papers connected with the negotiation of the treaty, by a vote, including absentees whose sentiments were known, of very nearly two to one.

The bank, to the operations of which Jefferson, whilst in retirement, openly and unreservedly attributed the corruption of Congress, had passed beyond reach, but the funding system was yet open to the action of the Government. It was in respect to this ill-omened and ill-fated measure that the tocsin had been first sounded of that alarm which now extensively pervaded the public mind, and it was beyond all doubt that no other act of the Government had proven a more prolific source of popular discontent. It was not the existence of the debt of which the people complained; they gladly accepted that burden, on the contrary, as the price of their liberties; but it was the system devised by Hamilton for its management and for the treatment of their fiscal affairs generally that excited their severe displeasure. They believed that the politico-fiscal agencies congenial with, and cherished features of, monarchical institutions had been adopted in servile emulation of the English system, and as they were acknowledged sources of corruption in that system, that they had been introduced for similar effect here. Hamilton's oft-avowed preference for the English model gave much color to the first part of this conclusion, and the exasperated feelings of our people toward that government predisposed the public mind against the whole policy. Nor were these resentments without adequate cause. No independent nation was ever worse treated by another than was ours by Great Britain from the recognition of our Independence until after the war of 1812. So arrogant and outrageous was her conduct at this very period that Washington, as appears by his published letters to Hamilton in August 1796, found it difficult to keep the expressions of his dissatisfaction within the bounds demanded by his official position, and Hamilton was driven to admit in his reply that "we were subject to inconveniences too nearly approaching a state of war" to be submitted to. But these were not the only nor even the principal objections of the people against the funding system. They were satisfied by reason and observation that there could never be a proper economy in public expenditures, or a check to the increase of public debt so long as Government was not only under no obligation to pay the principal of such debts but had no right so to do or the right only in respect to a mere pittance, as was the case with our funded debt. The power to convert the credit of the nation into revenue by such a policy, of which Hamilton boasted, was a power in which they thought no government could be safely indulged. If the argument in favor of that opinion, which need not be repeated here, was not sufficient to establish its soundness, the experience of the mother country, which was constantly before their eyes, afforded conclusive demonstration of it. I have elsewhere stated the extent to which the debt of England had then already increased, and the force with which her ablest writer on political economy and finance had traced that alarming growth, by the lights of experience and reason, to those features in her funding system.

Hamilton had been throughout and still remained devoted to what we may call English principles in the management of our finances, and constantly desirous to extend them to every species of our public debt, foreign and domestic. General Washington was wedded to no such views. The subject belonging peculiarly to Hamilton's department, and having full confidence in him, he acquiesced in the course he recommended, but he was always open to conviction, and only wished to leave the question of its continuance to be decided by its results. In the course of a conversation with Mr. Jefferson, designed to prevail on him to remain in the cabinet, the latter says that Washington touched upon the merits of the funding system, to which he knew that Mr. Jefferson was earnestly opposed, and expressed himself thus: "There is a difference of opinion about it, some thinking it very bad, and others very good; experience was the only criterion of right which he knew, and this alone would decide which opinion was right." The disappointment generally experienced by the original friends of the system cannot have failed to reach Washington, and it is impossible that the discredit which the measure had brought upon his administration could have escaped the notice of so sagacious and generally dispassionate an observer of the course of events. Hamilton was to leave him in a month or two, and he was destined to pass through an ordeal becoming every day more and more severe. To relieve his Government as far as practicable from odium from any source, was therefore a suggestion of duty and interest to which he could not but give heed. The measure of which we are speaking challenged his attention. The power of the Government over it, without the consent of its creditors, was, it is true, very limited, but it could relieve the system to some extent of a portion of its unpopularity by lessening its character of irredeemability. The annual eight per cent. for interest and principal (only two per cent. towards the principal, which was all the Government had a right to pay, but was never obliged to pay), it could make itself liable to redeem punctually, and could give to the creditors securities which would put it out of its power to evade its undertaking.

This was all that could be done, and it was not to be doubted that the accomplishment of this through the interference of Washington, with a return to the old mode of raising money, would go far to allay honest apprehensions, and to remove prejudices against his administration without disadvantage to the public service certainly, and, I may add, without the slightest departure from the course which it became him to pursue. He determined to pursue it. That the resolution in regard to the policy finally adopted upon this point originated with Washington alone, without consultation with, or advice from, Hamilton, is rendered certain to my mind from contemporaneous circumstances, some of which will be referred to. He, of course, communicated his intention to Hamilton, who proposed to take charge of all the preliminary steps that could be adopted during the short period of his remaining in office to prepare the way for the contemplated change. This was proper in itself and assented to by the President, who thus, as was his way on most occasions, enabled Hamilton to give to the whole affair the shape he thought best. The funding system was emphatically his measure, and if it was to be discontinued, it was proper that he should be permitted to make its exit as graceful as was practicable.

The intended movement was preceded by the President's speech to Congress in November, 1794, from which I extract this passage: "The time which has elapsed since the commencement of our fiscal measures has developed our pecuniary resources so as to open a way for a definitive plan for the redemption of the public debt. It is believed that the result is such as to encourage Congress to consummate this work without delay. Nothing can more promote the permanent welfare of the nation, and nothing would be more grateful to our constituents. Indeed, whatsoever is unfinished of our system of public credit cannot be benefited by procrastination; and, as far as may be practicable, we ought to place that credit on grounds which cannot be disturbed, and to prevent that progressive accumulation of debt which must ultimately endanger all governments."

This was substantially the only part of the speech which related to any other matter than the Pennsylvanian insurrection, and no one familiar with Hamilton's writings can doubt that the entire paragraph was prepared by him,-- a proceeding common and in this instance particularly proper. It presented in general terms a gratifying assurance of the improvement in the revenues of the Government, and the promised advantages to the national finances. No reference is made to the character of the measures by which those advantages were to be secured; these might be provisions for the immediate reduction of the debt, or at the least for an earlier reduction than that which was authorized by law.

On the 25th of January, eleven days before he left the department, Hamilton tendered to the Senate an elaborate "plan for the further support of public credit on the basis of the actual revenue." It was not his annual report, nor had it been called for by the Senate, but had been prepared, he said, as a part of his duties, according to the Act by which they were prescribed, and in conformity with the suggestions of the President. It fills twenty-seven pages, small print, in the large folio edition of the American State Papers, and, being his last, was of course prepared with great care and, as much of course, with great ability. Jefferson thought, at times, that Hamilton did not himself understand his own complicated and elaborate reports on the finances, but in this I am persuaded he was entirely mistaken. Hamilton evidently held the thousand threads which traversed these voluminous works with a firm and instructed hand, and perfectly understood their several and manifold connections with the body of the documents and the results to which the whole and every part tended. That he meant that others should understand them as well as he did is perhaps not so certain.

His plan did not even look to a present reduction of the debt, which would seem to be the natural consequence of a revenue so prosperous as that he had described in the speech; that would have been an impossibility. At the date of his report the debt had increased four millions from what it was when the funding system was established, independent of the assumption of those of the States, and at the end of Mr. Adams's administration, the increase stood at eight millions. I have not examined the result for each year, but am confident that I hazard little in affirming that there was not a single year, from the first period to the last, during which the public debt was not increased. Mr. Jefferson, in a letter to Mr. Madison, written in 1796, expressed the opinion that, from the commencement of the new government till the time when he ceased to attend to it, the debt had augmented a million a year. The preceding statement shows the correctness of his calculation.

Neither did Hamilton propose any measures by which the payment of the debt might be accelerated, but the reverse. The whole debt then stood as follows: foreign debt, between thirteen and fourteen millions; domestic debt funded, including those of the States, between sixty and sixty-one millions, and domestic debt unsubscribed, between one and two millions. The foreign debt was payable by installments, ending at the expiration of fifteen years. His plan was to offer the foreign creditors one half of one per cent. interest, annually, more than it then drew, if they would consent to make it a domestic debt, and postpone the redemption of the principal till 1818, which would defer it between eight and nine years; or, if they refused that, it might remain redeemable at any time they proposed, so that the redemption of the principal was not accelerated by making it less than the fifteen years. A law authorizing such a change was passed, the offer made and declined. The debt was suffered to stand as it did, and the last payment was made during the administration of Mr. Madison. In respect to the funded debt, all that the report proposed (and that proposition was carried into effect by law shortly after Hamilton retired) was to add materially to the existing provisions for the payment of the public debt, and to provide effectually that the funds set apart for that should be regularly and inviolably applied, first, to the payment of as much of the funded debt as the Government had a right to pay annually, which was two per cent. of the principal besides the interest, and after that to the then existing public debt generally; that is to say, in regard to the funded debt, it changed the option of the Government to pay the two per cent. into a positive obligation, and provided adequate funds for that purpose. It was calculated that these provisions would redeem the funded debt bearing an immediate interest in 1818, and the deferred funded debt in 1824; they did so, and thus the funded debt was extinguished. All succeeding loans, as well under the administrations of Washington and Adams as subsequently, were made redeemable at or after a certain period, save in rare and very limited instances controlled by special circumstances and not constituting modifications of the general rule of the Government.

By this step Congress carried into effect an object for which the Republicans had striven since soon after the establishment of the funding system, and upon the resolution to accomplish which Hamilton had interposed a temporary obstruction by his report in December, 1792. The funded debt was changed into a simple debt payable by regular though small installments, at stated and certain periods. Its ultimate redemption was made certain, and the further practice of funding successfully discountenanced. That was done which Washington desired to have done; not indeed in the plain, straightforward way in which he would have done it, for that would have shown that the Government, in deference to public sentiment, had, to borrow a common phrase, taken the back track; an exhibition which Hamilton's course was designed to avoid. What the latter undertook to do he did effectually and in good faith, but a careful perusal of his last expose will show how little the whole proceeding was in harmony with his individual feelings.

The following are extracts from that extraordinary paper:--

"To extinguish a debt which exists and to avoid the contracting more are always ideas favored by public feeling; but to pay taxes for the one or the other purpose, which are the only means of preventing the evil, is always more or less unpopular. These contradictions are in human nature; and happy indeed would be the country that should ever want men to turn them to the account of their own popularity or to some other sinister account.

"Hence it is no uncommon spectacle to see the same men clamoring for occasions of expense when they happen to be in unison with the present humor of the community, whether well or ill directed, declaiming against a public debt and for the reduction of idirected, declaiming against a public debt and for the reduction of it as an abstract thesis, yet vehement against every plan of taxation which is proposed to discharge old debts or to avoid new by the defraying of exigencies as they emerge. These unhandsome acts throw artificial embarrassments in the way of the administration of a government."

These observations afford evidence of the wounded spirit under which he was acting, and also of the strong sense he entertained of the influence which a necessity for taxation is calculated to exert upon the minds of a legislature anxious for the redemption of a public debt. Do they not further explain the motive for the array of taxes that would be required to carry into effect the Resolution of 1792, in favor of making provision for the redemption of the funded debt, contained in his report upon that resolution?

When speaking of now resorting to the old practice of anticipating revenues, that is, by making provision for the payment of both principal and interest, in the departure from which practice the English Funding System had its birth, he says:--

"This would be at the same time an antidote against what may be pronounced the most plausible objections to the system of funding public debts; which are, that, by facilitating the means of supporting expense they encourage to enterprises which produce it, and by furnishing in credit a substitute for revenue, likely to be too freely used to avoid the odium of laying new taxes, they occasion a tendency to run in debt. Though these objections to funding systems--which, giving the greatest possible energy to public credit, are a great source of national security, strength, and prosperity--are very similar to those which speculative men urge against national and individual opulence, drawn from its abuses; and though perhaps, upon a careful analysis of facts, they would be found to have much less support in them than is imagined, attributing to those systems effects which are to be ascribed, more truly, to the passions of men and perhaps to the genius of particular governments; yet, as they are not wholly unfounded, it is desirable to guard, as far as possible, against the dangers which they suppose, without renouncing the advantages which these systems undoubtedly afford."

When we find him thus dallying with a pet system on the eve of its abandonment, thus filling a paper designed to prepare the way for that result with his reasons for deprecating it, who can suppose that its impending fate was of his own suggestion, or doubt that he looked to its restoration under more favorable auspices?

The Secretary very naturally endeavors in this paper to place the provisions now recommended in respect to the Sinking Fund upon the same footing with those contained in his first Report upon public credit, conformably to which his funding system was established. Without the slightest desire to assail or to weaken any of his attempts to rest his acts on the most favorable ground consistent with truth, it is yet due to the memories of the patriotic men who by their fearless and persevering efforts succeeded in discrediting that dangerous system, and finally in causing it to be discontinued from the operations of our Government, that the circumstances under which they acted should not be misrepresented. The difference between the provisions of the Sinking Fund first and now adopted was great indeed. The grant of the funds to the first, to say nothing of their insufficiency, lacked the essential quality of being irrevocable, but was left subject to the action of Congress. There was therefore no reason to think that more might be expected from the Sinking Fund here than had been realized in England, where it had not only been found entirely ineffectual even in time of peace, but the funds vested in the Commissioners had on more than one occasion been used as a basis for new loans. But now, when the business of redemption was entered upon in earnest, that matter was placed upon a very different footing. The funds were not only more ample, but they were vested in the Commissioners as an irrevocable trust, and the faith of the Government was pledged that its execution should not be interfered with. As widely different were the dispositions of the Government and the sentiments of its principal supporters. On the former occasion the proposals submitted to Congress by the head of the Treasury Department, and most trusted officer of the Government, were to fund the entire debt of the United States upon the following terms, viz: 1st. That the whole principal should be forever irredeemable at the option of the United States; 2d. That they should not even reserve to themselves a right to pay more than two dollars upon a hundred of the principal, however full their coffers, and however great their convenience to pay; and, that no obstacle might be wanting to the redemption of that pittance, he proposed further to assume and fund in the same way twenty-five millions of the debts of the States which the Federal Government was under no obligations to pay and was not asked to assume. This policy was entered upon in the face of the fact that the debt of England, under a similar system, had, in eighty years, increased from some five millions to two hundred and seventy-six millions of pounds sterling, and was still increasing.

After these propositions had been substantially adopted by Congress and sustained by the Government, Hamilton, having the entire direction of its affairs, and knowing the spirit and firmness with which those who disapproved of his schemes always maintained their views of the public interest, had no right to complain of, and ought not to have been surprised at, the opposition he encountered from them, under the weight of which his Funding System, in respect to the future action of the Government in the management of its finances, soon became a dead letter, no further thought of than to get rid of the debts that had been contracted under it, with the intent to return to the old mode of anticipating revenue, that of direct loans payable at or after specific periods, principal as well as interest; the only way by which, as Adam Smith had demonstrated, a nation could avoid a permanent and ruinous public debt,-- a view of the subject which came too late for England, but was, happily, in season for us. Though the Government had, by the Act of March 3d, 1795, passed to carry into effect the improved views of Washington, placed the management of our finances upon a better footing, no progress was made in the reduction of the public debt; but the act doubtless accomplished much in restraining its increase. It was not an easy thing to keep down the public debt under an administration which, like that of Mr. Adams, in pursuance of the express advice of Hamilton to Wolcott, paid upon its loans an annual interest of eight per cent., the highest that had then ever been paid except by England to her bank upon the loan obtained from it on its first establishment.

Upon Jefferson's accession to power he denounced a public debt, in his message to Congress, as a "moral canker," and invoked the aid of the legislature for its extinction at the earliest practicable period. The Committee of Ways and Means, with John Randolph at its head (his brightest period of public usefulness), entered upon the subject "con amore." They called upon the Secretary of the Treasury for a thorough exposition of the state of the public debt, and for his opinion in regard to the best mode of dealing with it. Mr. Gallatin's reply, which may be found in the publication of American State Papers,--title "FINANCE," Vol. I.,--gave a full statement of the then condition of the debt, and pointed out the defects through which the Act of March 3, 1795, had been rendered inadequate to the accomplishment of all the objects for which it was designed. I will refer to but one of them, which consisted in its limiting the appropriation for the redemption of the public debt, beyond that which had been funded, to "surpluses which shall remain at the end of every calendar year, and which, during the session of Congress next thereafter, shall not be otherwise specially appropriated or reserved by law." Our experience of the action of Congress has been too full to make it necessary to speak of the extreme improbability of any considerable surpluses being left by that body acting under no more specific restraint than that which is here provided, and upon examination of the books of the treasury it was found that so far from there having been any such surpluses from the establishment of the present Government in 1789 till the close of the year 1799, the appropriations charged upon the revenue by Congress had exceeded, by nearly a million of dollars, the whole amount of such revenue, whether collected or outstanding.

To remedy results so unfavorable to the accomplishment of the object in view, the Secretary advised specific appropriations of such sums as, upon a fair estimate of the wants and resources of the country, ought in the opinion of Congress to be applied to the payment of the public debt, and to make such appropriations irrevocable and their application mandatory on the Commissioners of the Sinking Fund. The committee adopted the suggestion with alacrity as one which, in addition to securing the early performance of a sacred duty, could not in their opinion fail to induce economy on the part of Congress in its disposition of the public funds. They therefore reported a bill, which became a law, appropriating annually to the Sinking Fund seven millions three hundred thousand dollars for the payment of the public debt. This sum was increased to eight millions in consequence of the purchase of Louisiana. During the administration of Mr. Madison the annual appropriation was increased to ten millions, besides an additional appropriation of nine millions, and one of four millions if the Secretary of the Treasury should deem it expedient; and all of these appropriations were made irrevocable and compulsory as respected the action of the Commissioners of the Sinking Fund.

The consequences of this change in the action of the Government upon the subject of the public debt and of this liberality of appropriations under Democratic administrations, were the discharge of thirty-three millions of the principal of the debt, besides the payment of interest on the whole, during the Presidency of Mr. Jefferson, and its final extinguishment under President Jackson, notwithstanding the intervention of a war with England commenced at a period of the greatest financial embarrassment.

I have been induced to take so extended a notice of this matter as well by the circumstance, to which I have before referred, that it presented a leading subject of party divisions in this country, as because of the influence which it and its adjuncts the Bank of the United States and the Protective System have exerted upon our politics. It has been seen that the Funding System, however, preceded the bank in its establishment, and it became also an "obsolete idea" many years before the latter was declared to be such by its most devoted advocate and reckless supporter, Daniel Webster. That the bank did not share that fate at a much earlier period was because Henry Clay and John C. Calhoun, both disciples of the old Republican school,--the former one of the ablest among the opponents of the revival of the bank in 1811,--tempted by the political allurements of the day in 1815, advocated the establishment of a new bank, and because that pure man and patriot, James Madison, under mistaken impressions in respect to the absolute necessity of such an institution, gave his assent to its incorporation.

No public question was ever longer or more severely agitated in any country than that of the existence of a national bank has been in this. Madison acquired enduring honor by his unanswerable speech against its constitutionality. It divided the cabinet of President Washington, and contributed with other causes to give birth to a political party which kept his administration at bay, overthrew that of his successor, has sustained itself in power ever since (with brief and easily explained interruptions), and is now, after the lapse of nearly seventy years, in full possession of the Federal Government. It gave position in 1811 to Henry Clay as one of the strong minds of the country, derived from his speech against rechartering the bank, by far the best speech he ever made and nearly equal to that of Madison in 1790, and it enabled that venerable revolutionary patriot, George Clinton, to add new laurels to his already great fame by his casting vote against the passage of the bill for its re-incorporation. Whilst in 1815 it marred forever the political fortunes of Clay and Calhoun, then standing at the head of the rising Republican statesmen of the country, in 1830 it made memorable and glorious the civil career of Andrew Jackson through his celebrated veto--a noble step in that fearful issue between the respective powers of the Government and the Bank, on the trial of which that institution justified and confirmed Jefferson's gloomy forebodings at its first establishment by spreading recklessly and wantonly (as is now well understood) panic in the public mind and convulsions in the business affairs of the people, through which incalculable injury was inflicted upon the country, and by wasting its entire capital of thirty millions in wild speculation and in corrupt squandering upon parasites and political backers. It did not however prove too strong for the Government, as Mr. Jefferson apprehended, but was itself overwhelmed in utter defeat and disgrace. So thorough has been its annihilation that its books and papers were a few months since sold by auction, in Philadelphia, by the ton, as waste paper!

Who can call to mind without amazement the extent to which the impression was fastened on the public judgment that a national bank was of vital necessity to the healthful action of the Federal Government, indispensable to the collection of its revenues, to the management of its finances, to the transfer of its funds from point to point, and, above all, to the execution and support of domestic exchanges, without which the most important business of the country would be unavoidably suspended, and now see that all this was sheer delusion; or who can reflect upon the bold and profligate action taken by the bank to force a compliance with its application, without acknowledging and admiring the wisdom of the Federal Convention in refusing, as it did almost in terms, to confer upon Congress the power to establish such an institution, so inefficient for good and so potent for mischief, or without applauding the true conservatism and patriotic spirit of the Democratic party during a forty years' struggle to expel from our system so dangerous an abuse, or without rejoicing that that great object was finally achieved and blessing the memory of the brave old man to whom the achievement is mainly to be credited.

The Protective System was another of the important measures brought forward at the commencement of the Government, and had its origin in the prolific mind of Hamilton. Efforts have been made to trace its commencement to the legislation of the first Congress, but they have not been successful. The idea of protection, beyond that which is incidental to a tariff for revenue and could be effected without losing sight of the revenue point, was not, at that time, broached in Congress or inferable from the character of the duties imposed. It was in Hamilton's masterpiece--his elaborate report, nominally upon manufactures, but embracing in its range every pursuit of human industry susceptible of encouragement under an unlimited government--that the subject was first brought to the notice and recommended to the favorable consideration of Congress.

I have already described, more fully, perhaps, than might on first impression be thought necessary, the length and breadth of that famous document, the boldness and extravagance of its ultra-latitudinarian pretensions to power in the Federal Government, including unlimited authority to raise money by taxes and an equally unlimited power to spend it in any way which Congress might think would be conducive to the general welfare. The vehement denunciation of its character by Mr. Jefferson and his friends, with continually increasing indications of popular discontent, prevented Hamilton from attempting any measures worthy of notice to carry into effect his recommendations--and no assumptions, beyond the revenue standard, were acted upon by the administrations of either Washington or Adams.

The enforcement of Hamilton's recommendations was reserved for the close of the War of 1812, a period of which I have already spoken as one which brought on the political stage a new class of Presidential aspirants, members of a succeeding generation and unknown to revolutionary fame. Among the most prominent of these stood Crawford, Clay, Calhoun, Adams, Webster, and Lowndes,--the latter, perhaps, the most likely to have succeeded, if his useful life had not been brought to a premature close.

In the same year, 1815, was revived the idea of a national bank, and no fitter associate could have been devised for it than the Protective System. They had a common origin, even in their political aspects, were designed for a common effect, and were moreover alike adapted to the immediate policy of two of the Presidential aspirants of the Republican stamp, Clay and Calhoun,--that of conciliating the good-will of those who still clung to the wreck of the Federal party, which having been shattered and disabled by its course in the war, was at the moment drifting upon the political seas. Henry Clay, with better qualifications for success than his not less ambitious rival, seized the prize in view, and after long competition from the latter, and against perpetual, though sometimes concealed opposition from Webster, attached the mass of the Federal party to his fortunes, and held them there to the close of his remarkable life. Shouldering a large share of responsibility for the reintroduction of a national bank, he added to his programme the Protective System, stopping in the first instance at a protective tariff, but willing, as was clearly seen, to embrace Hamilton's entire scheme, and superadding to these a system of internal improvements by the Federal Government, in respect to which he went, on the point of constitutional power, beyond his great prototype. These were the elements out of which he constructed his famous "American System." A convert to theories and measures hostile to the earliest and most cherished principles of the old Republican party, he of course soon lost his position in its ranks, and was in due season installed as the leader of that with which all its wars have been waged. Possessing certain qualities eminently adapted to attract the popular admiration, and which could not have failed to elevate him to the Presidency if he had remained in the Democratic party and had adhered to its principles, he infused into the torpid body of the Federal party elements of strength, of which it had always stood in need; besides bringing to it a leader of fascinating manners and brilliant talents, he gave a new and more captivating form to the platform of principles and policy in support of which its original members and their descendants had been trained, excepting only the Funding System, which had not only been tabooed by the good sense of our people, but as to which England was yet uttering warnings to other nations of too fearful import to allow its revival here to be for a moment contemplated even by a politician so bold and too often reckless as Clay. Thus reinvigorated and backed by the money-power of the country, during a quarter of a century, and with never quailing spirit, he conducted that party, under various names but striving always under the banner of the same

"American System," through a succession of political campaigns which left their injurious traces upon the country.

The fruits of this warfare against the Democratic party and its principles are familiar to politicians and observers of our times. The Bank of the United States, after filling the country with distress and ruin, itself perished; the proposed system of internal improvements by the Federal Government was happily broken down by his opponents before it involved the country in inextricable embarrassments, and the Protective System, after being finally overthrown in England, from which country we had copied it, was abandoned here also, and consigned by the judgment of the people to the same oblivion with its kindred delusions.

The promotion of internal improvements by the General Government was an assumption of power by Congress, against which, from its first inception till its substantial overthrow, the Democratic party interposed a steady, persevering, and inflexible resistance. The general character of the abuse, its origin, progress, and extirpation through Democratic agencies, are fully presented in another part of this work.[40] Here the probable effect upon the national treasury of arresting the practice will alone be noticed.

[40] Referring to the Memoirs of the writer. See Introduction. Eds.

In his annual message to Congress, December, 1834, President Jackson says:-
-

"When the bill authorizing a subscription on the part of the United States for stock in the Maysville and Lexington Turnpike Companies passed the two Houses, there had been reported, by the committees of internal improvements, bills containing appropriations for such objects, exclusive of those for the Cumberland Road and for harbors and light-houses, to the amount of about one hundred and six millions of dollars. In this amount was included authority to the Secretary of the Treasury to subscribe to the stock of different companies to a great extent, and the residue was principally for the direct construction of roads by this Government. In addition to those projects, which had been presented to the two Houses, under the sanction and recommendation of their respective committees on internal improvements, there were then still pending before the committees, and in memorials to Congress, presented but not referred, different projects for works of a similar character, the expense of which cannot be estimated with certainty but must have exceeded one hundred millions of dollars."

The same message contained also the following suggestions:--

"From attempts to appropriate the national funds to objects which are confessedly of a local character, we cannot I trust have any thing further to apprehend. My views in regard to the expediency of making appropriations for works which are claimed to be of a national character, and prosecuted under State authority, assuming that Congress have the right to do so, were stated in my annual message to Congress in 1830, and also in that containing my objections to the Maysville Road Bill.

"So thoroughly convinced am I that no such appropriations ought to be made by Congress, until a suitable constitutional provision is made upon the subject, and so essential do I regard the point to the highest interests of our country, that I could not consider myself as discharging my duty to my constituents in giving the executive sanction to any bill containing such an appropriation. If the people of the United States desire that the public treasury shall be resorted to for the means to prosecute such works, they will concur in an amendment of the Constitution prescribing a rule by which the national character of the works is to be tested, and by which the greatest practicable equality of benefits may be secured to each member of the Confederacy. The effects of such a regulation would be most salutary in preventing unprofitable expenditures, in securing our legislation from the pernicious consequences of a scramble for the favors of Government, and in repressing the spirit of discontent which must inevitably arise from an unequal distribution of treasures which belong alike to all."

These declarations of President Jackson that he would approve no bill containing appropriations even for objects of a national character, until an amendment of the Constitution was adopted placing such expenditures upon an equal footing towards all the States, were reiterated in his Maysville veto. My election to the Presidency, and the knowledge that I cordially approved, and was determined to sustain, the ground taken in those two state papers upon the subject of internal improvements, with the large Democratic vote in Congress, always opposed upon principle to such grants, effectually closed the doors of the national treasury against them for seven years.

All similar applications, save for harbor and river appropriations, were thus driven, as was anticipated, to the State legislatures. The money expended for such improvements, when authorized by the States, were chargeable upon the treasuries of the States, to be collected by direct taxation. When made by incorporated companies under authority derived from the States they were at the expense of their stockholders. All must be sensible of the salutary check which these circumstances are calculated to exert by increasing the circumspection and prudence with which such expenses are incurred; and yet what immense amounts of money have been irrecoverably sunk upon such works, and what widespread embarrassments have they at times created in the financial affairs of the country, through the headlong enterprise and adventurous spirit of our people!

We have only to imagine a transfer of the seat of these operations to the halls of Congress to estimate the sums that would have been drawn out of the National Treasury and carried to the States to be, for the most part, expended upon local objects,--the scenes of log-rolling and intrigue to which such scrambles would have given rise, and the utter unscrupulousness of the applications that would thus have been produced. What millions upon millions of the public funds would have been worse than uselessly expended during the twenty-seven years that have elapsed since the Democratic party, through their venerable and fearless President, took the first effectual step to break up the practice! The one hundred millions for which bills had been reported, and the other hundred millions of applications pending before Congress when the Maysville veto was interposed, according to the President's message, furnish ample data upon which to found our calculations. No sum would seem to be too large at which to place the probable amount of our national debt if the plans of their political opponents had in this regard been crowned with complete success. In view of such an event who will be bold enough, with the subsequent experience of the country before him, to place even a conjectural estimate upon that amount or upon the extent to which valuable improvements, through individual enterprise or under State authority, would have been postponed or arrested forever by a further prosecution of the policy into which such persevering efforts were made to lead the Federal Government. For preservation from such prodigality and debt, and from the corruptions that would have followed in their train, we are plainly and undeniably indebted to the successful enforcement of the principles of the Democratic party.

[A space was here reserved in the original Manuscript for an intended notice of the advantages derived to the country from the establishment of the Independent Treasury; a measure proposed by Mr. Van Buren in the first year of his Presidency and in his first communication to Congress, and supported by the Democratic party.

In consequence, however, of the interruptions to which this work was subjected (and which are referred to in the Introduction), the contemplated addition to it was never supplied.--EDITORS.]

The measures of which I have spoken as the cherished policy of the old Federal party and its successors taken as a whole were justly described by Jefferson, in his much-abused letter to Mazzei, as "a contrivance invented for the purpose of corruption and for assimilating us in all respects to the rotten as well as the sound parts of the British Constitution." A persuasion of their practical useful usefulness in some respects entered more or less into the motives of the leaders on the occasions both of their creation and of their attempted resuscitation; but that they were by both regarded principally as elements of political strength, and adopted as means by which to build up and sustain an overshadowing money power in the country, through which the Democratic spirit of the people might be kept in check, is at least equally certain. Doubtless both of those political leaders honestly believed such a check to be necessary to the public good. With Hamilton this faith had from the beginning constituted an integral part of his political system. Clay had been, in his youth, too much a man of the people to avow such a belief, but that he became a convert to it in after-life I have no doubt. But the Democratic spirit of the country did not stand in need of any such restraint as that which they designed to place upon its course.

I have thus adverted to some of the advantages the country has derived from the action of the Democratic party, to which must be added the benefits conferred on the States by an extension of kindred principles to the administration of the local governments. If its opponents are asked for a statement of their contributions to the public welfare when in power and by their efforts to defeat the measures of the Democratic party, or to name a great measure of which they were the authors and which has stood the test of experience, or one in the establishment of which they have been prevented by factious or partisan opposition, but which would now be received with favor by the people, or a principle advocated by them for the administration of the Government, in which they have been defeated but which would now be so received, or an unsound one set up by their opponents which they have successfully resisted,--what must be the replies to questions so simple yet so comprehensive and important! Can it, on the other hand, be now denied that notwithstanding the conceded capacities of their leaders, and their possession of superior facilities for the acquisition and favorable exercise of political power, their time and their resources have been mainly employed in efforts to establish principles and build up systems which have been to all appearance irrevocably condemned by the people, and in unavailing efforts to defeat measures and principles which, after a full experience, have proved acceptable to them, and through the influence and operation of which the country has been gradually raised to great power and unexampled prosperity.

The course of events to which I have referred has had the effect of breaking up as a national organization the party so long opposed to the Democratic party, leaving the latter the only political association co-extensive in its power and influence with the Union,--and the sole survivor of all its national competitors. Of the eleven Presidents elected since its accession to power in the Federal Government, including the one in whose election it achieved its first national triumph, nine were avowed supporters of the cause it sustained, and eight its exclusive candidates. During the sixty years which will, at the end of the present Presidential term, have passed away since the occurrence of that great event, the chief magistracy of this country has been in the hands of professed supporters of its principles, with the exception only of four years and one month.

Born of the spirit which impelled our early colonists to forsake the abodes of civilization to establish among savages and in the wilderness the sacred right of opinion, which encouraged and sustained them in all their wanderings and sufferings and perils, and which finally conducted the survivors through a long and bloody war to liberty and independence, and representing the feelings and opinions of a majority of the people, it has labored zealously and, in the main, successfully, to give effect to those by which that momentous struggle was produced, to realize its promises, to maintain the sanctity of the Constitution, and to uphold "that equality of political rights" which Hamilton, though he could not find it in his judgment to favor, yet truly described as "the foundation of pure Republicanism."

For the signal success of its beneficent and glorious mission the country is indebted to the virtue and intelligence of the men of whom this great party has from time to time been composed,--much to the ability, industry, and devoted patriotism of James Madison; largely to the iron will, fearlessness, and uprightness of Andrew Jackson; and more conspicuously still to the genius, the honest and firm heart, and spirit-stirring pen of its founder, Thomas Jefferson, who stands, in my estimation, as a faithful republican, pure patriot, and wise and accomplished statesman, unequaled in the history of man. His opinions deliberately formed on important public questions, do not appear to have undergone material change or modification, except perhaps in the case of the issue raised in respect to the necessity of an amendment of the Constitution to justify the admission of Louisiana into the Union. Certain it is that he never entertained one which he could justly be accused of having concealed or recanted to propitiate power or to promote his own popularity, or which he was not on all suitable occasions prompt to avow and to defend. The presence of this noble spirit, and a readiness to encounter any sacrifice necessary to its free indulgence, were manifest in every crisis of his eventful life; nor were his last moments on earth without an impressive exhibition of its continued ascendency, even when reason and sense were passing away.

APPENDIX.

FROM THOMAS JEFFERSON,

TO MARTIN VAN BUREN.

MONTICELLO, June 29, 1824.

DEAR SIR,--I have to thank you for Mr. Pickering's elaborate Philippic against Mr. Adams, Gerry, Smith, and myself; and I have delayed the acknowledgment until I could read it and make some observations on it.

I could not have believed that, for so many years, and to such a period of advanced age, he could have nourished passions so vehement and viperous. It appears, that for thirty years past, he has been industriously collecting materials for vituperating the characters he had marked for his hatred; some of whom, certainly, if enmities towards him had ever existed, had forgotten them all, or buried them in the grave with themselves. As to myself, there never had been any thing personal between us, nothing but the general opposition of party sentiment; and our personal intercourse had been that of urbanity, as himself says. But it seems he has been all this time brooding over an enmity which I had never felt, and yet that with respect to myself as well as others, he has been writing far and near, and in every direction, to get hold of original letters, where he could, copies, where he could not, certificates and journals, catching at every gossiping story he could hear of in any quarter, supplying by suspicions what he could find nowhere else, and then arguing on this motley farrago, as if established on gospel evidence. And while expressing his wonder that "at the age of eighty-eight, the strong passions of Mr. Adams should not have cooled;" that on the contrary "they had acquired the mastery of his soul" (p. 100); that "where these were enlisted, no reliance could be placed on his statements" (p. 104); "the facility and little truth with which he could represent facts and occurrences, concerning persons who were the objects of his hatred" (p. 3); that "he is capable of making the grossest misrepresentations, and, from detached facts, and often from bare suspicions, of drawing unwarrantable inferences, if suited to his purpose at the instant" (p. 174); while making such charges, I say, on Mr. Adams, instead of his "ecce homo" (p. 100), how justly might we say to him, "mutato nomine, de te fabula narratur." For the assiduity and industry he has employed in his benevolent researches after matter of crimination against us, I refer to his pages 13, 14, 34, 36, 46, 71, 79, 90, bis. 92, 93, bis. 101, ter. 104, 116, 118, 141, 143, 146, 150, 151, 153, 168, 171, 172. That Mr. Adams' strictures on him, written and printed, should have excited some notice on his part, was not perhaps to be wondered at. But the sufficiency of his motive for the large attack on me may be more questionable. He says (p. 4), "of Mr. Jefferson I should have said nothing, but for his letter to Mr. Adams, of October 12th, 1823." Now the object of that letter was to soothe the feelings of a friend, wounded by a publication which I thought an "outrage on private confidence." Not a word or allusion in it respected Mr. Pickering, nor was it suspected that it would draw forth his pen in justification of this infidelity, which he has, however, undertaken in the course of his pamphlet, but more particularly in its conclusion.

He arraigns me on two grounds, my actions and my motives. The very actions, however, which he arraigns, have been such as the great majority of my fellow citizens have approved. The approbation of Mr. Pickering, and of those who thought with him, I had no right to expect. My motives he chuses to ascribe to hypocrisy, to ambition, and a passion for popularity. Of these the world must judge between us. It is no office of his or mine. To that tribunal I have ever submitted my actions and motives, without ransacking the Union for certificates, letters, journals, and gossiping tales, to justify myself and weary them. Nor shall I do this on the present occasion, but leave still to them these antiquated party diatribes, now newly revamped and paraded as if they had not been already a thousand times repeated, refuted, and adjudged against him, by the nation itself. If no action is to be deemed virtuous for which malice can imagine a sinister motive, then there never was a virtuous action; no, not even in the life of our Saviour himself. But he has taught us to judge the tree by its fruit, and to leave motives to him who can alone see into them.

But whilst I leave to its fate the libel of Mr. Pickering, with the thousands of others like it, to which I have given no other answer than a steady course of similar action, there are two facts or fancies of his which I must set to rights. The one respects Mr. Adams, the other myself. He observes that my letter of October 12th, 1823, acknowledges the receipt of one from Mr. Adams, of September 18th, which, having been written a few days after Cunningham's publication, he says was no doubt written to apologize to me for the pointed reproaches he had uttered against me in his confidential letters to Cunningham. And thus having "no doubt" of his conjecture, he considers it as proven, goes on to suppose the contents of the letter (19, 22), makes it place Mr. Adams at my feet suing for pardon, and continues to rant upon it, as an undoubted fact. Now, I do most solemnly declare, that so far from being a letter of apology, as Mr. Pickering so undoubtingly assumes, there was not a word nor allusion in it respecting Cunningham's publication.

The other allegation, respecting myself, is equally false. In page 34, he quotes Doctor Stuart as having, twenty years ago, informed him that General Washington, "when he became a private citizen," called me to account for expressions in a letter to Mazzei, requiring, in a tone of unusual severity, an explanation of that letter. He adds of himself, "in what manner the latter humbled himself and appeased the just resentment of Washington, will never be known, as some time after his death the correspondence was not to be found, and a diary for an important period of his Presidency was also missing." The diary being of transactions during his Presidency, the letter to Mazzei not known here until some time after he became a private citizen, and the pretended correspondence of course after that, I know not why this lost diary and supposed correspondence are brought together here, unless for insinuations worthy of the letter itself. The correspondence could not be found, indeed, because it had never existed. I do affirm that there never passed a word, written or verbal, directly or indirectly, between General Washington and myself on the subject of that letter. He would never have degraded himself so far as to take to himself the imputation in that letter on the "Samsons in combat." The whole story is a fabrication, and I defy the framers of it, and all mankind, to produce a scrip of a pen between General Washington and myself on the subject, or any other evidence more worthy of credit than the suspicions, suppositions and presumptions of the two persons here quoting and quoted for it. With Doctor Stuart I had not much acquaintance. I supposed him to be an honest man, knew him to be a very weak one, and, like Mr. Pickering, very prone to antipathies, boiling with party passions, and under the dominion of these readily welcoming fancies for facts. But come the story from whomsoever it might, it is an unqualified falsehood.

This letter to Mazzei has been a precious theme of crimination for Federal malice. It was a long letter of business, in which was inserted a single paragraph only of political information as to the state of our country. In this information there was not one word which would not then have been, or would not now be approved by every Republican in the United States, looking back to those times; as you will see by a faithful copy now enclosed of the whole of what that letter said on the subject of the United States, or of its government. This paragraph, extracted and translated, got into a Paris paper at a time when the persons in power there were laboring under very general disfavor, and their friends were eager to catch even at straws to buoy them up. To them, therefore, I have always imputed the interpolation of an entire paragraph additional to mine, which makes me charge my own country with ingratitude and injustice to France. There was not a word in my letter respecting France, or any of the proceedings or relations between this country and that. Yet this interpolated paragraph has been the burthen of Federal calumny, has been constantly quoted by them, made the subject of unceasing and virulent abuse, and is still quoted, as you see, by Mr. Pickering, page 33, as if it were genuine, and really written by me. And even Judge Marshall makes history descend from its dignity, and the ermine from its sanctity, to exaggerate, to record, and to sanction this forgery. In the very last note of his book, he says, "a letter from

Mr. Jefferson to Mr. Mazzei, an Italian, was published in Florence, and republished in the 'Moniteur,' with very severe strictures on the conduct of the United States." And instead of the letter itself, he copies what he says are the remarks of the editor, which are an exaggerated commentary on the fabricated paragraph itself, and silently leaves to his reader to make the ready inference that these were the sentiments of the letter. Proof is the duty of the affirmative side. A negative cannot be positively proved. But, in defect of impossible proof of what was not in the original letter, I have its press-copy still in my possession. It has been shown to several, and is open to any one who wishes to see it. I have presumed only, that the interpolation was done in Paris. But I never saw the letter in either its Italian or French dress, and it may have been done here, with the commentary handed down to posterity by the Judge. The genuine paragraph, retranslated through Italian and French into English, as it appeared here in a Federal paper, besides the mutilated hue which these translations and retranslations of it produced generally, gave a mistranslation of a single word, which entirely perverted its meaning, and made it a pliant and fertile text of misrepresentation of my political principles. The original, speaking of an Anglican, monarchical, and aristocratical party, which had sprung up since he had left us, states their object to be "to draw over us the substance, as they had already done the forms of the British Government." Now the forms here meant, were the levees, birthdays, the pompous cavalcade to the state house on the meeting of Congress, the formal speech from the throne, the procession of Congress in a body to reecho the speech in an answer, &c., &c. But the translator here, by substituting form in the singular number, for forms in the plural, made it mean the frame or organization of our government, or its form of legislative, executive, and judiciary authorities coordinate and independent; to which form it was to be inferred that I was an enemy. In this sense they always quoted it, and in this sense Mr. Pickering still quotes it, pages 34, 35, 38, and countenances the inference. Now General Washington perfectly understood what I meant by these forms, as they were frequent subjects of conversation between us. When, on my return from Europe, I joined the government in March, 1790, at New York, I was much astonished, indeed, at the mimicry I found established of royal forms and ceremonies, and more alarmed at the unexpected phenomenon, by the monarchical sentiments I heard expressed and openly maintained in every company, and among others by the high members of the government, executive and judiciary, (General Washington alone excepted,) and by a great part of the legislature, save only some members who had been of the old

Congress, and a very few of recent introduction. I took occasion, at various times, of expressing to General Washington my disappointment at these symptoms of a change of principle, and that I thought them encouraged by the forms and ceremonies which I found prevailing, not at all in character with the simplicity of Republican government, and looking as if wishfully to those of European courts. His general explanations to me were that when he arrived at New York, to enter on the executive administration of the new government, he observed to those who were to assist him, that, placed as he was in an office entirely new to him, unacquainted with the forms and ceremonies of other governments, still less apprized of those which might be properly established here, and himself perfectly indifferent to all forms, he wished them to consider and prescribe what they should be; and the task was assigned particularly to General Knox, a man of parade, and to Colonel Humphreys, who had resided some time at a foreign court. They, he said, were the authors of the present regulations, and that others were proposed so highly strained that he absolutely rejected them. Attentive to the difference of opinion prevailing on this subject, when the term of his second election arrived he called the heads of departments together, observed to them the situation in which he had been at the commencement of the government, the advice he had taken and the course he had observed in compliance with it; that a proper occasion had now arrived of revising that course, of correcting in it any particulars not approved in experience, and he desired us to consult together, agree on any changes we should think for the better, and that he should willingly conform to what we should advise. We met at my office. Hamilton and myself agreed at once that there was too much ceremony for the character of our government, and particularly, that the parade of the installation at New York ought not to be copied on the present occasion; that the President should desire the Chief Justice to attend him at his chambers, that he should administer the oath of office to him in the presence of the higher officers of the government, and that the certificate of the fact should be delivered to the Secretary of State to be recorded. Randolph and Knox differed from us, the latter vehemently; they thought it not advisable to change any of the established forms, and we authorized Randolph to report our opinions to the President. As these opinions were divided, and no positive advice given as to any change, no change was made. Thus the forms which I had censured in my letter to Mazzei were perfectly understood by General Washington, and were those which he himself but barely tolerated. He had furnished me a proper occasion for proposing their reformation, and, my opinion not prevailing, he knew I could not have meant any part of the censure for him.

Mr. Pickering quotes, too (page 34), the expression in the letter of "the men who were Samsons in the field, and Solomons in the council, but who had had their heads shorn by the harlot England;" or, as expressed in their re-translation, "the men who were Solomons in council, and Samsons in combat, but whose hair had been cut off by the whore England." Now this expression also was perfectly understood by General Washington. He knew that I meant it for the Cincinnati generally, and that, from what had passed between us at the commencement of that institution, I could not mean to include him. When the first meeting was called for its establishment, I was a member of the Congress then sitting at Annapolis. General Washington wrote to me, asking my opinion on that proposition, and the course, if any, which I thought Congress would observe respecting it. I wrote him frankly my own disapprobation of it; that I found the members of Congress generally in the same sentiment; that I thought they would take no express notice of it, but that in all appointments of trust, honor, or profit, they would silently pass by all candidates of that order, and give an uniform preference to others. On his way to the first meeting in Philadelphia, which I think was in the spring of 1784, he called on me at Annapolis. It was a little after candle-light, and he sat with me till after midnight, conversing, almost exclusively, on that subject. While he was feelingly indulgent to the motives which might induce the officers to promote it, he concurred with me entirely in condemning it; and when I expressed an idea that if the hereditary quality were suppressed, the institution might perhaps be indulged during the lives of the officers now living, and who had actually served, "no," he said, "not a fibre of it ought to be left, to be an eye-sore to the public, a ground of dissatisfaction, and a line of separation between them and their country;" and he left me with a determination to use all his influence for its entire suppression. On his return from the meeting he called on me again, and related to me the course the thing had taken. He said that from the beginning, he had used every endeavor to prevail on the officers to renounce the project altogether, urging the many considerations which would render it odious to their fellow citizens, and disreputable and injurious to themselves; that he had at length prevailed on most of the old officers to reject it, although with great and warm opposition from others, and especially the younger ones, among whom he named Colonel W. S. Smith as particularly intemperate. But that, in this state of things, when he thought the question safe, and the meeting drawing to a close, Major L'Enfant arrived from France, with a bundle of eagles, for which he had been sent there, with letters from the French officers who had served in America, praying for admission into the order, and a solemn act of their king permitting them to wear its ensign. This, he said, changed the face of matters at once, produced an entire revulsion of sentiment, and turned the torrent so strongly in an opposite direction that it could be no longer withstood; all he could then obtain was a suppression of the hereditary quality. He added that it was the French applications, and respect for the approbation of the king, which saved the establishment in its modified and temporary form. Disapproving thus of the institution as much as I did, and conscious that I knew him to do so, he could never suppose I meant to include him among the Samsons in the field, whose object was to draw over us the form, as they made the letter say, of the British Government, and especially its aristocratic member, an hereditary house of lords. Add to this, that the letter saying that "two out of the three branches of legislature were against us" was an obvious exception of him; it being well known that the majorities in the two branches, of Senate and Representatives, were the very instruments which carried, in opposition to the old and real Republicans, the measures which were the subjects of condemnation in this letter. General Washington then, understanding perfectly what and whom I meant to designate, in both phrases, and that they could not have any application or view to himself, could find, in neither, any cause of offence to himself; and therefore neither needed, nor ever asked any explanation of them from me. Had it even been otherwise, they must know very little of General Washington, who should believe to be within the laws of his character what Doctor Stuart is said to have imputed to him. Be this, however, as it may, the story is infamously false in every article of it. My last parting with General Washington was at the inauguration of Mr. Adams, in March, 1797, and was warmly affectionate; and I never had any reason to believe any change on his part, as there certainly was none on mine. But one session of Congress intervened between that and his death, the year following, in my passage to and from which as it happened to be not convenient to call on him, I never had another opportunity; and as to the cessation of correspondence observed during that short interval, no particular circumstance occurred for epistolary communication, and both of us were too much oppressed with letter-writing, to trouble, either the other, with a letter about nothing.

The truth is that the Federalists, pretending to be the exclusive friends of General Washington, have ever done what they could to sink his character, by hanging theirs on it, and by representing as the enemy of Republicans him who, of all men, is best entitled to the appellation of the father of that republic which they were endeavoring to subvert, and the Republicans to maintain. They cannot deny, because the elections proclaimed the truth, that the great body of the nation approved the republican measures. General Washington was himself sincerely a friend to the republican principles of our constitution. His faith, perhaps, in its duration, might not have been as confident as mine; but he repeatedly declared to me that he was determined it should have a fair chance for success; and that he would lose the last drop of his blood in its support, against any attempt which might be made to change it from its republican form. He made these declarations the oftener because he knew my suspicions that Hamilton had other views, and he wished to quiet my jealousies on this subject. For Hamilton frankly avowed that he considered the British Constitution, with all the corruptions of its administration, as the most perfect model of government which had ever been devised by the wit of man; professing however, at the same time, that the spirit of this country was so fundamentally republican, that it would be visionary to think of introducing monarchy here, and that, therefore, it was the duty of its administrators to conduct it on the principles their constituents had elected.

General Washington, after the retirement of his first cabinet, and the composition of his second, entirely Federal, and at the head of which was Mr. Pickering himself, had no opportunity of hearing both sides of any question. His measures, consequently, took more the hue of the party in whose hands he was. These measures were certainly not approved by the Republicans; yet were they not imputed to him, but to the counsellors around him; and his prudence so far restrained their impassioned course and bias, that no act of strong mark, during the remainder of his administration, excited much dissatisfaction. He lived too short a time after, and too much withdrawn from information, to correct the views into which he had been deluded; and the continued assiduities of the party drew him into the vortex of their intemperate career, separated him still farther from his real friends, and excited him to actions and expressions of dissatisfaction, which grieved them, but could not loosen their affections from him. They would not suffer this temporary aberration to weigh against the immeasurable merits of his life; and although they tumbled his seducers from their places, they preserved his memory embalmed in their hearts, with undiminished love and devotion; and there it forever will remain embalmed, in entire oblivion of every temporary thing which might cloud the glories of his splendid life. It is vain, then, for Mr. Pickering and his friends to endeavor to falsify his character, by representing him as an enemy to Republicans and republican principles, and as exclusively the friend of those who were so; and had he lived longer, he would have returned to his ancient and unbiased opinions, would have replaced his confidence in those whom the people approved and supported, and would have seen that they were only restoring and acting on the principles of his own first administration.

I find, my dear Sir, that I have written you a very long letter, or rather a history. The civility of having sent me a copy of Mr. Pickering's diatribe, would scarcely justify its address to you. I do not publish these things, because my rule of life has been never to harass the public with feedings and provings of personal slanders; and least of all would I descend into the arena of slander with such a champion as Mr. Pickering. I have ever trusted to the justice and consideration of my fellow citizens, and have no reason to repent it, or to change my course. At this time of life too, tranquillity is the summum bonum. But although I decline all newspaper controversy, yet, when falsehoods have been advanced, within the knowledge of no one so much as myself, I have sometimes deposited a contradiction in the hands of a friend, which, if worth preservation, may, when I am no more, nor these whom it might offend, throw light on history, and recall that into the path of truth. And, if of no other value, the present communication may amuse you with anecdotes not known to every one.

I had meant to have added some views on the amalgamation of parties, to which your favor of the 8th has some allusion; an amalgamation of name, but not of principle. Tories are tories still, by whatever name they may be called. But my letter is already too unmercifully long, and I close it here with assurances of my great esteem and respectful consideration.

TH. JEFFERSON.

[Enclosed in the above.]

EXTRACT OF A LETTER FROM TH. JEFFERSON, TO PHILIP MAZZEI,

April 24, 1796.

"The aspect of our politics has wonderfully changed since you left us. In place of that noble love of liberty and republican Government which carried us triumphantly through the war, an Anglican, Monarchical and Aristocratical party has sprung up, whose avowed object is to draw over us the substance as they have already done the forms of the British government. The main body of our citizens, however, remain true to their republican principles. The whole landed interest is republican, and so is a great mass of talent. Against us are the Executive, the Judiciary, two out of three branches of the legislature, all the officers of the government, all who want to be officers, all timid men who prefer the calm of despotism to the boisterous sea of liberty, British merchants, and Americans trading on British capitals, speculators, and holders in the banks and public funds,--contrivance invented for the purpose of corruption, and for assimilating us in all things to the rotten as well as the sound parts of the British model. It would give you a fever were I to name to you the apostates who have gone over to these heresies; men who were Samsons in the field, and Solomons in the council, but who have had their heads shorn by the harlot England. In short, we are likely to preserve the liberty we have obtained only by unremitting labors and perils. But we shall preserve them; and our mass of weight and wealth on the good side is so great as to leave no danger that force will ever be attempted against us. We have only to awake and snap the Liliputian cords with which they have been entangling us during the first sleep which succeeded our labors."

###

Made in the USA
Middletown, DE
03 April 2023

28154354R00179